Japanese Foodways, Past and Present

D1566004

JAPANESE FOODWAYS, PAST AND PRESENT

*Edited by Eric C. Rath
and Stephanie Assmann*

UNIVERSITY OF ILLINOIS PRESS
URBANA, CHICAGO, AND SPRINGFIELD

Publication of this book was
supported by a grant from the
L.J. and Mary C. Skaggs Folklore Fund.

Library of Congress Cataloging-in-Publication Data
Assmann, Stephanie, 1970–
Japanese foodways, past, and present / edited by Eric C. Rath
and Stephanie Assmann.
p.   cm.
Includes bibliographical references and index.
ISBN 978-0-252-03563-0 (cloth : alk. paper)
ISBN 978-0-252-07752-4 (pbk. : alk. paper)
1. Cookery, Japanese.
I. Rath, Eric C., 1967– II. Title.
TX724.5.J3J39   2010
641.5952—dc22   2010016576

Contents

LIST OF ILLUSTRATIONS   vii

ACKNOWLEDGMENTS   ix

INTRODUCTION   1
Eric C. Rath and Stephanie Assmann

Part I   Early Modern Japan

1   *Honzen* Dining: The Poetry of Formal
Meals in Late Medieval and Early
Modern Japan   19
ERIC C. RATH

2   "How to Eat the Ten Thousand Things":
Table Manners in the Edo Period   42
MICHAEL KINSKI

3   "Stones for the Belly": *Kaiseki* Cuisine
for Tea during the Early Edo Period   68
GARY SŌKA CADWALLADER AND
JOSEPH R. JUSTICE

4   Meat-eating in the Kōjimachi District
of Edo   92
AKIRA SHIMIZU

5   Wine-drinking Culture in
Seventeenth-century Japan: The Role
of Dutch Merchants   108
JOJI NOZAWA

Part II Modern Japan

6   The History of Domestic Cookbooks
    in Modern Japan   129
    SHOKO HIGASHIYOTSUYANAGI

7   Imperial Cuisines in Taishō Foodways   145
    BARAK KUSHNER

8   Beyond Hunger: Grocery Shopping,
    Cooking, and Eating in 1940s Japan   166
    KATARZYNA CWIERTKA AND
    MIHO YASUHARA

9   Rāmen and U.S. Occupation Policy   186
    GEORGE SOLT

10 Bentō: Boxed Love, Eaten by the Eye   201
    TOMOKO ONABE

Part III Contemporary Japan

11 Mountain Vegetables and the Politics
    of Local Flavor in Japan   221
    BRIDGET LOVE

12 Reinventing Culinary Heritage in
    Northern Japan: Slow Food and
    Traditional Vegetables   243
    STEPHANIE ASSMANN

13 Rāmen Connoisseurs: Class, Gender,
    and the Internet   257
    SATOMI FUKUTOMI

14 Irretrievably in Love with Japanese
    Cuisine   275
    DAVID E. WELLS

    CONTRIBUTORS   285

    INDEX   289

List of Illustrations

1   A three-tray *honzen*
    meal from *Ryōri kondateshū*   22

2   Snipe in (eggplant) jars from
    Shichi no zen jūkyū kon no maki   32

3   A supervisory housewife and a
    servant from *Shirōto ryōri nenjū sōzai
    no shikata zen*   135

4   An old housewife and two servants
    from *Sōzai ryōri no okeiko*   137

5   A young housewife in a kitchen from
    Katei yōshoku ryōrihō   139

6   A housewife and maid discussing
    kitchen tasks from *Renovating Kitchens*   151

7   Members of a neighborhood farm group
    preparing steamed buns   222

8   Local female farmers work part-time
    at company headquarters   230

9   A female farmers' group from
    Yuda's Makino district   232

10 The three basic types of Japanese knives   276

11 Cutting a carrot into a plum blossom   277

12 Peeling daikon   278

13 Tempura   283

Acknowledgments

THE IDEA FOR THIS BOOK originated during a panel on the topic of "(Non) Consumption of Food in Japan: Past and Present" that the editors prepared for the annual meeting of the Association for Asian Studies (AAS) in March 2007. The organization of this panel made us realize the sheer number of fascinating and novel research topics centered on Japanese food, which is why we decided to give these different perspectives a collective voice in an edited volume. During the following two years, we were very fortunate to work with contributors who not only represent a variety of scholarly disciplines and perspectives on the study of food but also come from different countries.

The publication of this volume would not have been possible without the support of four people who, during various stages, helped to bring this project to a fruitful outcome. We are deeply grateful to Professor Theodore Bestor, Harvard University, who served as a discussant at our panel and provided valuable and insightful comments on our work that we incorporated in this volume. We also sincerely thank Kendra Boileau, senior editor for Asian Studies and Food Studies at the University of Illinois Press who was very enthusiastic about our project from the start and supportive in taking our book through the different stages of the publication process. Also, we would like to express our sincere thanks to two reviewers, Professor Samuel Yamashita at Pomona College and an anonymous reviewer, for their helpful and encouraging comments on the entire volume. We further wish to thank Hans Martin Kramer and David Henry for their involvement in two panels on food that the editors organized for the annual meeting of the Association for Asian Studies in 2007 and 2008. Their insightful ideas on the topic of meat-eating in Japan have inspired the currently evolving discourse on the topic of meat consumption in premodern Japan and to which we hope this volume will make a contribution.

With this publication we hope to provide new scholarship in the area of Japanese Studies and Food Studies and to inspire further research on the fascinating topic of food in Japan.

Eric C. Rath and Stephanie Assmann
Japanese Foodways, Past and Present

Japanese Foodways, Past and Present

Introduction

ERIC C. RATH AND
STEPHANIE ASSMANN

WITH SUSHI NOW AVAILABLE in many European and American supermarkets, more people outside of Japan have become aware of Japanese foods—or at least some interpretations of them, like the "California (sushi) roll." At the same time in Japan, more Japanese have greater access than ever before to foreign cuisines such as Chinese, Korean, French, and Italian, and to domesticated versions like the "curry doughnut" to the point that "multiculturalism is the defining feature of the culinary scene in contemporary Japan," as one of our contributors to this volume, Katarzyna Cwiertka, noted in her recent book, *Modern Japanese Cuisine* (2006, 7). Japanese food demonstrates an incredible diversity, from the blue-collar worker's steaming bowl of rāmen noodles to the multicourse *kaiseki* meals served at elite restaurants, from lovingly crafted *bentō* box lunches that use heirloom vegetables to dishes like crane soup found in centuries-old cookbooks to delicate modern confectionery. Both the commonplace and the unfamiliar parts of Japanese food have compelling stories to tell that shed light on life in Japan, past and present.

Globalization has brought increasing familiarity with foreign foods in both Japan and abroad, but the term *foodways* in the title of our book deserves some explanation. Foodways can be defined in terms of the eating habits of a people, of a historical time period, or of a region.[1] But the term also serves as an indication that there is something more to food than just food. Food is essential to so many facets of human life that it is hard to list all the "ways." We can consider production, consumption, and circulation of foods in the concept of foodways as well as political, economic, cultural, social, and religious dimensions to these. If we consider the subject chronologically, we can add disjunctures and continuities in practices, beliefs, and habits surrounding foods. Our contributors demonstrate that food in these systems and contexts casts light on a range of larger issues—from foreign policy to traditional medicine to perceptions of other countries to understandings of the past. Accordingly, rather than delimit *foodways* by disclaimers and jargon, in this book we have chosen to examine food from the broadest possible perspective, leaving the individual authors—who include a tea master and a chef as well as scholars from the disciplines of history, anthropology, and sociology—the opportunity to define their own terms in their discussions of specific moments and corners in past and present Japan.[2]

Despite this interdisciplinary approach, we address two reoccurring themes in this book that can best be described as food in relation to status and place. Postwar Japan has long been perceived as the only non-Western industrialized nation whose society shows minor status differences: Some 90 percent of Japanese consider themselves to be middle class! However, sociologists point out that status differences do exist in the forms of income discrepancies and social mobility, and these are also pertinent issues in Western industrialized nations. Regarding the current sociological discourse on the so-called gap society (*kakusa shakai*), two recent works written by Japanese sociologists that discuss status discrepancies from the perspectives of income and inter-generational mobility are noteworthy. In his book *Economic Discrepancies in Japan from the Perspective of Income and Property* (*Nihon no keizai kakusa: Shotoku to shisan kara kangaeru*, 1998), the sociologist Tachibanaki Toshiaki has argued that based on analysis of the Gini coefficient, which measures the degree of income inequality in a nation, income discrepancies are increasing in Japan. Sociologist Satō Toshiki has described the "pedigree society" (*gakureki shakai*) in his book *Unequal Society Japan: Goodbye Middle Class* (*Fubyōdō shakai Nihon: Sayōnara sōchūryū*, 2000) and found that there is a strong correlation between the professional occupation of the father and the professional occupation of the son, suggesting that social intergenerational mobility is less pronounced in Japan than had been assumed. Both works analyze the decay of the Japanese "middle class" and argue that social inequality is increasing in Japan.

Despite this fear of growing social inequality in Japanese society, consumption practices of middle-class Japanese remain powerful tools for analyzing subtle status differences. Using Pierre Bourdieu's concept of cultural capital and applying this concept to the Japanese "middle class," the sociologist John Clammer writes in *Contemporary Urban Japan: A Sociology of Consumption* that consumers who are part of the same economic position construct their "class consciousness" around consumption habits, which allows them to accumulate cultural capital and to engage in a symbolic competition (Clammer 1997, 103–5). In other words, Japanese are increasingly defining themselves by their habits of consumption: shaping their personas and designating their personal status and group affiliation by what they buy.

The complicated relationship between the globalization of foodways and the integrity of national identity through maintaining eating habits is the second theme in our volume. Globalization has led to the increasing popularity of Japanese culinary specialties abroad and to the embrace of foreign cuisines in Japan; but globalization has also evoked consciousness of the erosion of national identity, of which foodways are an essential part. For example, our contributors identify foreign foodways that have been domesticated and native foodways that are currently being "rediscovered" as a means to counteract Japan's low food self-sufficiency rate and to assuage fears of food safety. By using food as a tool to analyze status differences on the one hand and the relationship between globalization and national identity on the other, we hope to provide insights to these crucial issues for an audience beyond Japan specialists.

Chronologically, this book is divided into three sections. The first section covers the mid-fifteenth through the late nineteenth centuries, corresponding to the late medieval (1450–1600) and early modern periods (1600–1868). This historical span overlaps with the traditional periodization of the Muromachi (1336–1573), Momoyama (1573–1600), and Edo or Tokugawa period (1600–1868). The second part focuses on modern Japan from the Meiji period (1868–1912) through the mid-1950s. The third and last section investigates food issues in contemporary Japan in the period since the 1950s.

The writers hope that this volume will contribute to illuminating the long history of Japanese foodways and spur additional English-language research on food in Japan, particularly for the premodern era. While a growing number of scholars—especially in anthropology (see Ashkenazi and Jacob 2000; Bestor 2004; and Cwiertka 2005, 2006) but also in Japanese literature (for instance, Aoyama 2008)—have taken up the topic of food in modern and contemporary Japan, studies of Japanese foodways in English focusing on the period before the twentieth century lag, notwithstanding a few seminal works such as the historical survey of Naomichi Ishige (2001) and anthropologist Emiko Ohnuki-Tierney's (1993) meditation on rice and identity over the course of Japanese civilization. Agriculture has been an enduring interest for historians of all periods, but our impression from these studies is that primary attention is given to the political welfare of the peasants and secondarily to farming methods. In other words, food as the object of production often takes a back seat to the monetary value of the harvest itself, which is an important dimension given that rice and other grains were used as currency and to pay tribute in premodern Japan, but it is only one aspect of food production to the point that we only rarely glimpse what and how people ate and how they thought about food. Most of the previous research on dining in premodern

Japan has focused on the elite *kaiseki* cuisine of the tea ceremony (for example, Kumakura 1989, 55–59). Susan Hanley's (1997) survey of the physical well-being of people in the early modern period includes important data about diet. And a translation of the research of the historian of Japanese culture Nishiyama Matsunosuke's work (1997) describes some of the pleasures of dining as well as the pains of famine in the same era. However, all of these topics await further exploration for the premodern period, and we hope to point out some directions for future studies with this book.

LATE MEDIEVAL AND EARLY MODERN JAPAN

Japan enjoys a long culinary history, and the chapters in this section survey prominent styles of cooking in late medieval and early modern Japan, including *honzen ryōri* used for formal banquets, meals served for tea events (*chakai*) called *kaiseki,* and Iberian foods and methods of cooking them called "Southern Barbarian cuisine" *(nanban ryōri).* One chapter describes the earliest history of Japan's love of European wine, and another sheds light on one of the most contentious issues in the history of the Japanese diet: the extent to which Japanese ate beef and other meats before the opening to the West in the late nineteenth century when meat-eating became more widely accepted and popularized.

In chapter 1, Eric Rath describes the formula used for laying out dishes on trays that comprise the structure of a *honzen* meal—a style of dining that began with elite samurai in the 1400s and spread to wealthier commoners in the early modern period. He compares the creation of a *honzen* meal to the art of writing poetry since both relied on structure and literary imagery for effect. Rath shows how food could be used for artistic and intellectual stimulation, two parameters apart from modern nationalism that can be used to distinguish a cuisine from ordinary modes of eating. Yet, in contrast to modern Japanese cuisine, *honzen ryōri* was a banquet cuisine that found its highest expression in meals reserved for the military and aristocratic elites. Therefore, it remained an elite practice in its more elaborate form but one whose rules could be applied, adapted, and aspired to by different status groups.

The diffusion of elite customs to a wider audience extended to table manners for *honzen* meals as well other rules of etiquette as described by Michael Kinski in chapter 2. Kinski indicates that in contrast to medieval collections of rules of behavior and custom written for high-ranking samurai, early modern books of etiquette and table manners transcended status boundaries, at least for the people who were educated enough to read about them, in that they spoke to a general readership. Manners are one of the elements in "culinary culture," but in Kinski's analysis we see also that food and dining were viewed in the early modern period as important to perceptions of self in terms of gender, body consciousness, and maintenance of relationships with other people. The history of food-etiquette books indicates the evolution of written, "nonjuridical norms for social intercourse." This development is all the more remarkable for the fact that its stimulus was from wealthier and more educated sections of the commoner population rather than being imposed from above.

Kaiseki ryōri, foods served to accompany tea gatherings, is the subject of chapter 3 by Gary S. Cadwallader and Joseph R. Justice. Their translations of a range of *kaiseki* menus from the period remind us that this refined style of food preparation and eating once had many variant approaches. On the one hand, practitioners of the "rustic tea" (*wabicha*) of Sen no Rikyū (1522–91) favored simple and small servings of food befitting the way of writing *kaiseki* (懐石) with the Chinese characters that refer to the monk's warm rock tucked inside the robe on a cold night to stave off hunger. On the other hand, regional lord (*daimyō*) devotees of tea masters Furuta Oribe (1544–1615) and Kobori Enshū (1579–1647) preferred more lavish meals, reflecting an older way of writing *kaiseki* (会席)—literally "meeting and sitting" together, which can be loosely translated as "banquet." Connections with other styles of eating are evident in both forms of *kaiseki*. Like *honzen ryōri*, both forms of *kaiseki* meals are served on trays and require the observance of elaborate rules to eat. Tea masters were earlier exponents of Iberian (*nanban*) sweets, which appear occasionally in the translated menus in this chapter. Though not completely vegetarian since they make use of fowl and fish, tea menus—especially the simplified ones of one soup and three side dishes (*ichijū sansai*) of the *wabicha* masters—excluded beef, revealing the influence of vegetarian (*shōjin*) cooking (Harada 1989, 17). The simplified "stones for the belly" version of *kaiseki* has come to dominate tea practice since the Meiji period (1868–1912), but Cadwallader and Justice's chapter indicates that was not an automatic or uncontested decision in the early modern period (Kumakura 2002, 17).

Both the *honzen* and *kaiseki* serving styles eschewed the use of beef and other meat. Yet samurai hunted boar and deer as part of their military training, occasionally chasing and killing these animals on shrine and temple grounds (Ishikawa 1988, 43). However, when it came time to plan formal banquets for samurai, their chefs and tea masters preferred the use of game fowl and fish, judging by the contents of medieval culinary texts (*ryōrisho*) written beginning in the mid-fifteenth century. More widely in society, it seems that beef and other meats were eaten up to the dawn of the early modern period, although the extent to which this occurred is still a subject of scholarly debate (Kumakura 2002, 173).[3]

The reasons for meat consumption and avoidance were complicated and are the subject of chapter 4 by Akira Shimizu. Some gourmands in the early modern period believed that eating meat was poisonous: it literally "turned one's mouth around" (*kuchi ga magaru*) (Harada 2003, x); but meat, Shimizu explains, was also one of the earliest health foods "eaten for medicinal reasons" (*kusuri gui*). Shimizu challenges notions of Japanese scholars, including Harada Nobuo, who find the avoidance of meat to be central to the definition of foodways in the early modern period (Harada 2004, 13), arguing that the debate over meat consumption was more ambivalent. Food scholars such as Matsushita Sachiko have recognized that despite new prohibitions, consumption of domesticated and wild animals continued in that period, and the meat of these animals was sold openly in city "beast markets" (*momonjiya*) (Matsushita 1998, 139–40). Shimizu presents a portrait of one such market to examine the place of meat-eating in the foodways of early modern cities. He explores the writings of supporters and detractors of the beast market, revealing how views regarding meat consumption changed over the course of the early modern period.

Western and Chinese visitors to Japan consumed beef, pork, and other meats, and meat's association with foreign culture was one of the reasons many Japanese avoided it, but it was also one of its attractions; and this was also true for Western alcoholic beverages like wine. Iberian missionaries, who by some estimates converted approximately 300,000 Japanese to Christianity before being banned from Japan in the first decades of the seventeenth century, consumed beef and chicken, as did many of their converts. Warlord Hosokawa Tadaoki (1563–1645), whose wife Gracia (1563–1600) was a famous convert, ate beef and showed a fascination for Iberian foods until later in his career when he began to persecute Christians enforcing government edicts against them (Ego 2004, 17–19). Despite the banishment of the Portuguese in 1639 and the earlier withdrawal of the Spanish from Japan in 1624, Iberian sweets like Castilian cake (*kasutera*) and sugar candies (*konpeitō, aruheitō*) became favorites in Japanese confectionery. By their foreign associations, meat, wine, and Iberian confectionery can be lumped into the category of the Southern Barbarian style of foods (*nanban ryōri*), which became a catchall in the early modern era—though a loosely defined one—for foreign-sounding foods or methods of preparation.

Less well documented than Japan's demand for foreign-inspired sweets and the imported sugar to create them is the influence of Western alcohol on foodways in early modern Japan, but in chapter 5 Joji Nozawa demonstrates the keen desire among elite Japanese for wines from Dutch merchants forced to live and trade at the Kyūshū ports of Hirado (1609–41) and later Nagasaki (from 1641). In a period when Christianity was ruthlessly suppressed in Japan, the religious associations of wine and the communion could be conveniently forgotten in the enjoyment of this beverage. Having adapted the formalities that accompanied the drinking of sake, which often used elaborate ceremonies to confirm differences in social status, wine became a luxurious beverage to enjoy in forging lateral relations between Japanese officials, merchants, and scholars of Dutch learning (*rangaku*) and their Dutch counterparts. Drawing upon the daily records and the bookkeeping of Dutch merchants, Nozawa documents how Japanese in the seventeenth century transformed from passive recipients of wine culture to active participants, indicating that the contemporary wine boom in Japan has long historical roots.

MODERN JAPAN

The Meiji and Taishō (1912–26) periods brought significant changes to Japanese foodways, including the introductions of new foods to the diet and new attitudes toward food preparation and consumption. In the Edo period, the warrior government used sumptuary legislation to differentiate the foodways of status groups: Peasants could not eat tofu, commoners could not eat certain game fowl like cranes, and many shoguns considered tempura too common a dish.[4] In the Meiji period with the abolition of these status categories, Japanese began to think of their food identities in national terms, marked by the appearance of new words like Japanese cuisine (*washoku*, *Nihon ryōri*) and Japanese sweets (*wagashi*), created to identify natives foods against their foreign counterparts. The Japanese cuisine that emerged was not xenophobic; rather, it was indicative of the spirit of the times in that it sought to preserve and develop key elements of the past while incorporating foreign foods and modern cooking methods. Several of the essays reflect on Japanese imperialism and the effects of war on the Japanese diet. The period Barak Kushner covers witnessed Japan's emergence as an imperialist power in the wake of victories over Russia in the Russo–Japanese War (1904–5) and the annexation of Korea in 1910, to name a few steps in a process that led ultimately to World War II. Katarzyna Cwiertka and Miho Yasuhara examine foodways during the war years and the 1940s, while George Solt's essay covers the immediate postwar era.

One familiar example of this culinary appropriation is rāmen, a food some now called a national dish (*kokumin shoku*), with movies and museums dedicated to it, bespeaking its cultlike status today. Yet rāmen's history reveals the Chinese influence on Japanese foodways and of the impact of U.S. foreign policy after World War II, as revealed in chapters by Barak Kushner and George Solt in this section.[5]

While Kushner and Solt focus on foreign food, which was mostly consumed outside the home in modest eateries, the first and last essays by Shoko Higashiyotsuyanagi and Tomoko Onabe respectively examine the changing role of women in food production inside the home in modern Japan.

Shoko Higashiyotsuyanagi provides us with a sense of the changes in Japanese cooking in her chapter on domestic cookbooks of the Meiji period. Culinary books have a long history in Japan, with the first for a popular audience, *Tales of Cookery*, appearing in print in 1643. Yet few of the hundreds of cookbooks published in the early modern period were directed toward the preparation of ordinary meals and focused instead on the dishes and rules for formal *honzen* banquets or the tea ceremony. Hence the Meiji-era cookbooks Higashiyotsuyanagi surveys, which provide recipes for everyday meals, represent an important development in the history of Japanese cookery. They also reveal an important moment in the history of women. Heeding the charge of the Meiji government for women to be "good wives and wise mothers" (*ryōsai kenbo*), authors and publishers of Meiji-era cookbooks valorized the role of women's domestic labor in the formation of a strong nation (*fukoku kyōhei*), and they targeted an ever-increasing audience of female readers. This audience began with the "supervisory housewives," who did not cook themselves but instructed servants in their culinary duties, and gradually expanded to the middle-class "practical housewife," who performed these tasks herself. Higashiyotsuyanagi's research indicates the cooperation of cookbook authors and publishers in disseminating government policy and new gender roles.

Higashiyotsuyanagi also shows in her research that foods such as pork and potatoes became part of the Japanese diet and were represented in cookbooks for the "practical housewife." While Western consumption practices like eating beef were on the one hand admired as "progressive" and emulated during the Meiji period, Taishō-era foodways adapted from Chinese, Korean, and Taiwanese culinary practices were despised as "backwards" in the eyes of the colonial Japanese power on the other hand, as Barak Kushner describes in his survey. Yet, at the same time, East Asian dishes like rāmen were being incorporated into Japanese foodways, and foodstuffs grown in colonial areas, such as Taiwanese sugar, were becoming increasingly important in the Japanese diet. Based on Chinese and Japanese cookbooks, travel literature from the time, essays by prominent Japanese in the 1920s, and secondary sources, Kushner shows how the late Meiji and early Taishō eras formed the roots of what can be considered the "Japanese taste"—his rendering for the word *washoku*—that set the stage for a modern diet that finally embraced Chinese cuisine on equal terms after World War II.

Katarzyna Cwiertka and Miho Yasuhara challenge the assumption that life in wartime Japan in the 1940s was dominated by bleakness and hunger, revealing that mundane activities such as cooking, eating family meals, and even occasional dining out did in fact continue with necessary modifications during wartime. Based on diaries, menus from the famous department store Mitsukoshi, and excerpts from the women's magazine *The Housewife's Companion* (*Shufu no tomo*), which missed no edition even during these difficult times, the authors show how Japanese people found creative and innovative ways to maintain a reasonably balanced diet despite the rationing of food and the lack of availability of certain foods such as rice and sugar. In this context, the authors underscore the importance of the black market that operated from 1938 onwards and functioned both as an essential means for survival and for maintaining an underground restaurant business. Similar to the importance of food and color that Tomoko Onabe describes in her chapter about box lunches, color combinations of foods were used to evoke a sense of patriotism during wartime, as exemplified by the National Flag Bentō (*hinomaru bentō*) that places a red pickled apricot (*umeboshi*) in the center of white boiled rice to represent the Japanese flag.

Militaristic food disappeared quickly in the postwar era, but foodstuffs retained their political use and associations with place. George Solt looks at the importance of rāmen in the historical context of the U.S. food aid program set up to combat communism during the occupation period following World War II. His contribution examines the import of wheat that led to a considerable shift in people's diet from rice to wheat and other substitute staples such as sweet potatoes and soybeans. The dependence on these substitute foods led to long-term changes in the eating habits of Japanese people. For example, the U.S. food aid program introduced school lunches (*kyūshoku*) that were based on bread and milk, with the effect that younger Japanese grew accustomed to these school lunches and adapted to a more wheat-based nutrition in their adult lives (Cwiertka 2006, 157–58). While Kushner's chapter stressed the unwilling inclusion of Chinese food during the Taishō era, Solt shows that

Chinese foods such as rāmen and dumplings (*gyōza*) became increasingly popular in the immediate postwar period due to the nutritional value of these foods and their taste. This change of perception of Chinese food is symbolized by the rising popularity of rāmen and led to the invention of an instant version of this originally Chinese noodle-soup in 1958 and the inclusion of rāmen into wider Japanese food culture. Despite the greater acceptance of these foods, Solt points out that negative perceptions of Chinese and Koreans endured.

Rāmen is a likely option for a working man's lunch, but children, especially those in kindergartens that do not have lunch programs, turn to the elaborate box lunch made by their mothers when it is time for the same meal (Allison 1991). In the final chapter in this section, Tomoko Onabe traces the historical development of the *bentō*, the Japanese lunch box, from the Meiji period until contemporary times. She describes how color combinations and elaborate crafting of food components have placed greater emphasis on appearance in the *bentō* than on nutritional content. She further reveals how "boxed love" expressed in a *bentō* has gradually come to be seen as a marker of maternal and spousal affection. Whether modern cookbooks that describe how to make *bentō* still depict women as servants of the state as they did for their Meiji-period counterparts is a subject for debate, but women unquestionably remain servants in having to spend enormous time and energy in creating ephemeral culinary beauty for their children and husbands.

CONTEMPORARY JAPAN

The past few decades have seen reactions in Japan to perceived problems associated with modernity, including the effects of globalization, increased levels of obesity due to the consumption of processed and fast foods, scandals involving tainted food products and expired foods, and the overuse of pesticides and fertilizers in agriculture. One response to these problems has been to reevaluate developments in Japan's recent culinary history to return to perceptions of how things were or should become. Thus, in the chapters in this section, we find attempts to identify and revive heirloom foods and the communities that produced them, as Bridget Love and Stephanie Assmann describe; to make consumption of certain foods more inclusive, as Satomi Fukutomi documents; and to valorize attention to detail, seasonality, and quality, as is evident from David Wells's essay of his experiences studying the art of restaurant *kaiseki* cuisine.

In the past decades, rural Japan, the subject of Bridget Love's essay, is facing several dire problems, most notably a migration in its population as young people leave for better economic opportunities in the city. Love documents an effort of one rural area in Northern Japan to revive its local economy and community through food, specifically *sansai*—mountain herbs and vegetables that are gathered in the wild and used in prepared dishes like pickles. Based on two years of ethnographic research in Nishiwaga, a small town in Iwate prefecture in the Tōhoku area in Northern Japan, Love delineates the role of local government, agricultural groups, and women in Nishiwaga to market *sansai* to people outside the community. She reveals that defining a local or traditional food is relatively easy in comparison to solving the lasting problems of depopulation, cutbacks in government subsidies, and an aging farm population.

Apart from the critical issue of the revitalization of rural areas through the revival of regional cuisine, the topic of food safety has attracted attention as Japan has been shaken by a number of food scandals that partially involved imported food. One scandal in 2008 involved Chinese dumplings (*gyōza*) tainted with pesticides. As a response to these food scandals, a return to nationally produced food (*kokusan*) is currently perceived as a way to increase food safety. Taking Miyagi prefecture in Northern Japan as an example, Stephanie Assmann investigates "slow food," "traditional vegetables," and the potential of other initiatives. She argues that initiatives such as Slow Food Japan promote a return to local and supposedly safer foodways, but the accessibility and availability of these local foods is quite restricted and confined to the small audience that can afford luxurious food items. She concludes that despite the fact that local foodways are currently not fully integrated into Japanese daily food practices, the future significance of local food products lies in their potential linkage with tourism and in their use in conventional and even fast-food restaurants.

Rāmen, the Chinese noodle dish, is a reoccurring topic in this volume. While Kushner and Solt analyze rāmen as a foreign food, Satomi Fukutomi looks at the noodle soup in contemporary Japan from the angles of class, gender, and the Internet. Fukutomi shows that rāmen is considered a national food (*kokumin shoku*), especially popular among male blue-collar workers, which has been gentrified and made more appealing to women in contemporary Japan. Based on interviews, ethnography at a rāmen shop (*rāmen'ya*), and the observance of online communities, Satomi Fukutomi examines how the popular noodle dish rāmen has evolved into a connoisseurial object. Fukutomi argues that practices of rāmen consumption demonstrate that connoisseurship is not confined to rare gourmet foods or to elite groups of people. Rāmen consumers, who come from all walks of life, have developed a highly refined connoisseurship for rāmen as demonstrated in online communities dedicated to rāmen eateries and the appearance of stylish "new wave" rāmen shops. While Tomoko Onabe focuses on the gendered dimension of food *preparation* in her essay about *bentō*, Satomi Fukutomi's study illustrates that gendered issues exist in food *consumption* by looking at the phenomenon of women claiming a place at the table in eateries that were perceived as being reserved for men.

This volume concludes with a personal account of a chef who gained experience studying in cooking schools and restaurants in Japan. In their contribution, Cadwallader and Justice focused on the *kaiseki* cuisine that accompanies the tea ceremony; David Wells, a professional chef living and working in Tokyo, describes his years of study in Japanese culinary schools and work in Japanese restaurants trying to master the more elaborate form of banquet *kaiseki* served in Japan's finest restaurants. This autobiographical account offers an insider's view of a chef who is "irretrievably in love with Japanese cuisine" despite the many obstacles to success for a foreigner in Japan's conservative culinary scene.

JAPANESE FOODWAYS: ADAPTING, EXPANDING, AND VARIED

Across the span of six centuries, despite myriad changes, food in Japan is closely associated with place and status, as the chapters in this volume reveal. In contemporary Japan, wine continues its association with European culture and remains a refined beverage just as the *kaiseki* cuisine of both the tea ceremony and of elite restaurants has a select (i.e., wealthy) audience. Conversely, the more popular rāmen, once closely tied with Chinese food, has now become largely divested of its foreign roots to become not only a national dish, but also one with local variations such as Hokkaidō and Kyūshū rāmen—the former includes corn while the latter uses a stock made from pork bones. Adding to these local differences are modern rāmen chefs and connoisseurs who seek to remake the humble bowl of noodles into a gourmet food. We can see a similar status transformation and articulation of place in discussions of local vegetables and gathered mountain herbs. Reidentified as "local"—both from a national perspective and a more discrete regional one—these heirloom foods, which once fell out of cultivation or fashion in the modern period, have in the process of their strategic rediscovery become expensive gourmet delicacies. The history of meat-eating likewise reveals changing affiliations of place and status. Once disguised with euphemisms like "mountain whale" when eaten supposedly for medicinal purposes (*kusuri gui*), meat consumption had a complex relationship with domestic and foreign foodways in the early modern period. This relationship may have reached a crescendo in the Meiji period with the wider adoption of "Western habits" of meat-eating, but the interplay between meat and nationality continues to find resonance in more recent discussions of the safety of imported beef and reactions to the global spread of American fast-food hamburger chains like McDonald's. Modernity has made certain foods more available, and we detect a democratizing of Japanese cuisine over the centuries as measured by the fact that cookbooks and other writings about food are now published for an almost universal audience compared to their predecessors of the early modern period. Nevertheless, important differences—expressed by individual purchasing power and preference for things like expensive sweets or handmade box lunches—remain within Japanese foodways. As much as any similarities, the variety found within Japan's food culture, past and present, deserves the attention of future research.

NOTES

1. An interesting parallel to the word *foodways* is the Japanese term *shoku seikatsu*—literally, "food lifestyle." Like foodways, *shoku seikatsu* joins together two different words. Culinary historian Harada Nobuo, a leading scholar in the field, has defined *shoku seikatsu* broadly to include eating for subsistence at one end and haute cuisine at the other. Harada offers narrower terms like food culture (*shoku bunka*) and culinary culture (*ryōri bunka*), though he admits that the meanings of these words are hard to pin down (Harada 1992, 1–2).

2. One example of the problems in applying standard definitions to culinary terms is offered by the Japanese word *ryōri*, which shifts in meaning depending on the context. *Ryōri* can also be translated into English as cookery, a style of cooking, a dish, or a kind of food (Hosking 1996, 120). Sometimes it is also appropriate to translate *ryōri* as cuisine, as in the expression *Japanese cuisine* (*Nihon ryōri*), which has been defined by one of our contributors as representing national identity and cultural homogeneity, the product of industrialization and modernity (Cwiertka 2006). Rendering the same term *ryōri* as cuisine in the premodern era—that is, before the rise of a modern state in the late nineteenth century—is problematic. In premodern Japan, sometimes *ryōri* best refers to a style of food preparation and other times to a style of dining. It could also refer to a particular dish.

3. In that regard, it is interesting to note the absence of discussion about meat-eating for the Buddhist clergy until the beginning of the early modern period when priests from the True Pure Land school (*Jōdo shinshū*) argued for it and for the legitimacy of clerical marriage (Jaffe 2005, 256–57).

4. For a discussion of how the foodways of samurai contrasted with other status groups in the Edo period, see Rath (2008).

5. The Shin Yokohama Rāmen Museum that opened in 1996 offers an educational and entertaining tour of both the history of rāmen and the regional variations of the noodle dish. Rāmen has also been featured prominently in popular movies such as *Tampopo* (1985), the story of a young female rāmen shop owner who challenges the association of rāmen as a "male food."

WORKS CITED

Allison, Anne. 1991. "Japanese mothers and obentōs: The lunch box as ideological state apparatus." *Anthological Quarterly* 64, no. 4: 195–208.

Aoyama, Tomoko. 2008. *Reading Food in Modern Japanese Literature*. Honolulu: University of Hawai'i Press.

Ashkenazi, Michael, and Jeanne Jacob. 2000. *The Essence of Japanese Cuisine: An Essay on Food and Culture*. Philadelphia: University of Pennsylvania Press.

Bestor, Theodore. 2004. *Tsukiji: The Fish Market at the Center of the World*. Berkeley: University of California Press.

Clammer, John R. 1997. *Contemporary Urban Japan: A Sociology of Consumption*. Oxford: Blackwell.

Cwiertka, Katarzyna J. 2005. "Culinary culture and the making of a national cuisine." In *A Companion to the Anthropology of Japan*. Ed. Jennifer Robertson, 415–28. Malden, Mass.: Blackwell.

———. 2006. *Modern Japanese Cuisine: Food, Power and National Identity*. London: Reaktion Books.

Ego Michiko. 2004. *Nanban kara kita shoku bunka*. Fukuoka: Tsuru Shobō.

Hanley, Susan B. 1997. *Everyday Things in Premodern Japan: The Hidden Legacy of Material Culture*. Berkeley: University of California Press.

Harada Nobuo. 1989. *Edo no ryōrishi: Ryōribon to ryōri bunka*. Tokyo: Chūō Kōronsha.

———. 1992. "Edo no shoku seikatsu to ryōri bunka." In *Edo no shoku bunka*. Ed. Edo Iseki Kenkyūkai, 1–18. Tokyo: Yoshikawa Kōbunkan.

———. 2003. *Edo no shoku seikatsu*. Tokyo: Iwanami Shoten.

———. 2004. *Edo no ryōri to shoku seikatsu*. Tokyo: Shōgakukan.

Hosking, Richard. 1996. *A Dictionary of Japanese Food: Ingredients and Culture*. Rutland, Vt.: Tuttle.

Ishige, Naomichi. 2001. *The History and Culture of Japanese Food*. London: Kegan Paul.

Ishikawa Hiroko, ed. 1988. *Shoku seikatsu to bunka: Shoku no ayumi*. Tokyo: Kōgaku Shuppan.

Jaffe, Richard, M. 2005. "The debate over meat eating in Japanese Buddhism." In *Going Forth: Visions of Buddhist Vinaya*. Ed. William M. Bodiford, 255–75. Honolulu: University of Hawai'i Press.

Kumakura, Isao. 1989. "Sen no Rikyū: Inquiries into his life and tea," trans. Paul Varley. In *Tea in Japan: Essays on the History of Chanoyu*. Ed. Paul Varley and Kumakura Isao, 33–69. Honolulu: University of Hawai'i Press.

———. 2002. *Nihon ryōri bunkashi: Kaiseki o chūshin ni*. Kyoto: Jinbun Shoin.

Matsushita Sachiko. 1998. "Edo jidai no ryōri no shuzai to chōrihō." In *Nihon ryōri no tenkai*. Vol. 7 of *Zenshū Nihon no shoku bunka*, 133–55. Tokyo: Yūzankaku Shuppan.

Nishiyama, Matsunosuke. 1997. *Edo Culture*. Honolulu: University of Hawai'i Press.

Ohnuki-Tierney, Emiko. 1993. *Rice as Self*. Princeton, N.J.: Princeton University Press.

Rath, Eric. 2008. "Banquets against boredom: Towards understanding (samurai) cuisine in early modern Japan." *Early Modern Japan: An Interdisciplinary Journal* 16:43–55.

Satō Toshiki. 2000. *Fubyōdō shakai Nihon: Sayonara sōchūryū*. Tokyo: Chūō Kōron Shinsha (Chūō Shinsho).

Tachibanaki Toshiaki. 1998. *Nihon no keizai kakusa: Shotoku to shisan kara kangaeru*. Tokyo: Iwanami Shinsho.

PART I *Early Modern Japan*

1 *Honzen* Dining
The Poetry of Formal Meals in Late Medieval and Early Modern Japan

ERIC C. RATH

"BEEF—IT'S WHAT'S FOR DINNER"—according to highway billboards in rural Kansas, at least. These signs picture an enormous steak dwarfing smaller white and green lumps that remain hard to identify for a driver at 70 mph. The clearer message presented is the necessity of beef for the evening meal; but these signs hardly offer a universal definition of dinner or any other meal. In Japan, beef was not widely consumed until the late nineteenth century. We might instead imagine a version of such a sign from premodern Japan proclaiming that "Rice is what's for dinner!" because the Japanese word for meal, *gohan*, literally means rice. Yet that statement also needs qualification because only the social and economic elite in premodern Japan could dine on white rice.[1] The rest of society made do with brown rice mixed with other grains and beans. White rice did not become a central staple for most of the population until the 1960s (Harada 2003, x).

However, there is more to a meal than just a single dish. In an attempt to describe the many factors that define a meal, Mary Douglas offered that meals are composed according to an accepted structure following rules similar to those used for writing poetry (1997, 36–54). Douglas's analogy resonates well for premodern Japan, where the dominant structure for the most formal meals shared several similarities with poetic conventions. These meals, called *honzen ryōri*, which translates literally as "main tray cuisine," constituted the dominant style of banqueting for the elite from the Muromachi (1336–1573) through the Edo periods (1600–1868). In the Edo period, wealthy commoners learned about the style through printed culinary books (*ryōribon*) and adopted it for weddings and other festive occasions; *honzen* dining also inspired the earliest full meals served in the first restaurants, which opened during the late seventeenth century in cities. And *honzen* dining remained the most formal style of eating until the twentieth century, one still used in parts of Japan and on some special occasions such as for traditional weddings. Additionally, the components of the *honzen* meals, consisting of rice, soup, and side dishes, formed the basic elements of a Japanese meal until after World War II when eating habits became more varied (Kumakura 2002, 168–70).

Like Japanese poetry, which joins phrases of five or seven syllables to create long or short poems, the number of trays and the dishes on them determined the complexity of *honzen* meals. Adding more trays and dishes to a *honzen* meal made it akin to the more formal *waka* poems of five lines of 5, 7, 5, 7, 7 syllables, while meals of a single tray with a few dishes run parallel to a simple *haiku* of just three lines of 5, 7, 5 syllables. Interestingly, *honzen* meals were often described in similar shorthand that indicated the number of trays and dishes, providing a measurement of the complexity and formality of the meal. Important both to Japanese poetry and cuisine were seasonal imagery and wordplay. The aim of this chapter is to explore further the rules for *honzen* meals in late medieval and early modern Japan (1400–1868) by first examining their structure and then briefly sampling their aesthetic imagery. Though not an exclusive list of all of the elements of a formal meal in premodern Japan, a common structure and aesthetic language were what chiefly typified *honzen* dining.[2]

THE STRUCTURE OF *HONZEN* CUISINE

Sitting on the floor rather than on a chair at a table, Japanese since ancient times ate their meals from trays to keep their food off of the ground. Commoners in the Nara period (710–84) used wooden boards as rests for their simple meals of brown rice and vegetables. Picture scrolls such as *Story Book of Hungry Ghosts* (*Gaki sōshi*), dating from the early Kamakura period (1185–1333), depict aristocrats dining from individual trays that were raised farther off of the floor on a narrow supporting stand, which brought the meal closer to the guest, making it easier to eat. In the subsequent Muromachi period (1336–1573), chefs in the employ of elite samurai served multiple trays of food around a "main tray" called a *honzen*, creating Japan's first cuisine in the process. These chefs drew upon earlier forms of ceremonial banqueting (*shikishō ryōri*) employed by the imperial court for dining on formal occasions, which were imbued with formal rules of behavior following established courtly precedents (*yūsoku kojitsu*).

According to the rules for creating these banquets, the main tray always contained rice, a soup, side dishes, and pickles as well as utensils, namely chopsticks and sometimes a toothpick to clean the teeth. The *honzen* might also have salt and vinegar to use as condiments, especially in the Muromachi period when many dishes were served without seasoning and it was expected that diners would flavor their own dishes to taste. Each additional tray had at least one soup and various side dishes that were prepared grilled, raw, or simmered. Besides the quality and rarity of the ingredients, what differentiated one *honzen* meal from another was the number of soups and side dishes; indeed, the word for *number* (*okazu*) became synonymous with these side dishes.

Like different types of Japanese poetry that are differentiated by their lines of syllables, *honzen* banquets came to be described by a shorthand that referenced the number of trays and dishes on them. Five-five-three or seven-five-three were typical formations that indicated banquet menus of three trays, each with a soup, and a corresponding number of side dishes on them, totaling thirteen side dishes for the former and fifteen for the latter.[3] Seven-five-three (*shichi, go, san*) was thought to be an especially auspicious combination, one found in other areas of Japanese culture such as the visit of children to a shrine at three, five, and seven years of age; and it was also called *shime*, which means "total sum," and was an alternate way of reading the same Chinese characters.[4] These trays were positioned in front of the diner next to the main tray, and the trays were served simultaneously. From the diner's perspective seated at the main tray, the second tray was to the right and the third tray was to the left of the main tray. Since the number four (*shi*) was a homonym for the word for death, the fourth tray was called the "additional tray" (*yo no zen*). It was placed behind the second tray. A fifth tray could be added behind the third tray (Ogura, Komatsuzaki, and Hatae 2003, vol. 1, 162). Other trays bearing additional foods could be brought out later for guests to enjoy, but these would not be considered as part of the initial calculation of trays and dishes.

Banquets featuring three, five, or seven trays for each diner were standard, although the preferred number of trays varied by historical period and according to the occasion (Ogura et al. 2003, vol. 2, 161).

In the Edo period, the central and domainal military governments (*bakufu* and *han*) set limits on the number of trays of food that different ranks of samurai could be served at banquets. For example, top advisors to the shogun on the council of elders (*rōjū*) were allowed three trays with ten side dishes, while regional lords in charge of their own provinces (*kuni mochi daimyō*) could only have two trays, each with a soup, and a total of seven side dishes between them. Lesser samurai had to make do with one soup and five side dishes (Harada 1989, 7). In the same period, sumptuary legislation restricted

A three tray *honzen* meal with one additional tray (*mukōzume*)
from *Collection of Menus* (*Ryōri kondateshū*) published in 1671.
Note that the perspective is of someone facing the guest who
would be seated behind the main tray bearing the chopsticks.
(Courtesy of Iwase Bunko)

commoners to a maximum of two trays of food and placed additional restrictions on the types of foods they could serve (Maruyama 1999, 186).[5]

As Michael Kinski explains more fully in his chapter in this book (chapter
2), there were clear rules of etiquette for *honzen* meals that stipulated how
to eat from the various trays. In that regard, Ise Sadatake (d. 1784), a noted
expert on warrior custom who came from a lineage that specialized in that
topic, offered a few pithy warnings about bad table manners. He called the
first mistake, "soup to soup [meaning] sipping the soup on the main tray
and immediately sipping the soup on the second and third trays." The next,
called "side dish to side dish [meant] eating a side dish and then immediately
eating from another side dish." In other words, diners should eat something
else, probably rice, to cleanse their palate between drinking a soup and
consuming the side dishes. Other faux pas on his list included:

> "Beyond the tray"—passing over the main tray to take something resting on
> the far part of another tray. "Corrupt chopsticks"—being lazy and constantly
> eating one dish or forever holding a rice bowl. "Two-handed beginning"—
> taking up a rice bowl and chopsticks at once when they should be taken
> up one at a time. This occurs at the beginning of the meal. [Only] a moron

(*moroto*) uses both of his hands at once. . . . "Side chopsticks"—turning a chopstick on its side and licking off a grain of rice or a piece of food stuck on it. . . . Chopsticks are something that should be dampened [only] a little. (Ise 1985, 301)

The final comment indicates that diners should not shove chopsticks deeply into their food or their mouths but use just the tips for eating. That the preceding mistakes had names indicates that they were common ones, still considered bad manners today.

The *honzen* meal constituted only one portion of a lengthier session of eating and drinking. Smaller trays of snacks to accompany sake and rounds of formal toasts might precede the *honzen* meal. So much sake might be consumed before the banquet—at a typical proceeding, participants consumed at least nine shallow cups (*sakazuki*) of sake—that during the banquet sake was usually not served. Drinking resumed afterwards, accompanied by more trays of food: soups called *atsumono* to differentiate them from the soups known as *shiru* served at the *honzen* along with additional snacks, thick and thin green tea with sweets, and sometimes an additional meal later in the day called the "after meal" (*godan*).[6]

Conversely, the abbreviated form of *honzen* meals, consisting of just one tray with one soup and three side dishes (*ichijū sansai*), became the simple meals favored by some practitioners of the tea ceremony as described in Gary Cadwallader and Joseph Justice's essay in this book (chapter 3). Accordingly, from a structural standpoint, one can consider tea cuisine to be an abbreviation of *honzen* dining since it uses the same components of rice, soup, and side dishes. This mode of categorization is evident in the culinary book *Collected Writings on Cuisine and an Outline on Seasonings* (*Ryōri mōmoku chōmishō*) published in 1730, a work that was one of nearly a thousand different culinary books published in the Edo period. Rather than document what people actually ate, culinary texts suggested what they could eat and how, providing models for cooking and dining. Hence they are a useful source for understanding ideal meal structure. Culinary historian Kawakami Kōzo identified several subcategories of culinary books and noted that those featuring recipes (*chōri hō*) and menus (*kondate*) were the most typical, especially by the eighteenth century when *Collected Writings on Cuisine and an Outline on Seasonings* (hereafter *Collected Writings*) appeared (Kawakami 1998, 112). *Collected Writings* can be considered a representative work since it combined the two genres of recipe collections and information about cooking. It further included advice about planning *honzen* meals of different complexity.

Under the heading "Menus," the author of *Collected Writings*, Shōsekiken Sōken (n.d.), offered four *honzen* menus, placing them in order of complexity by season, with spring being the most complicated and winter the simplest.[7] The reasons for this method of organization are uncertain and not specified, although it was a structure found in other genres of writings, including poetry. For example, each of the first chapters in the tenth-century *Collection of Poems Ancient and Modern* (*Kokinshū*) is dedicated to a season, beginning with spring and ending with winter. Just as the poems in these sections could be composed and appreciated year-round, in *Collected Writings* all four meals could be served year-round with changes in the ingredients so they were not limited to a particular month of the year. This structuring at first appears odd given the importance of preserving seasonality to modern Japanese cuisine. But, Edo-period culinary writings freely violated modern rules of seasonality by including foods in menus not available in a given month.[8] Appreciating seasonality, in other words, was not restricted to specific months of the calendar; hence, Shōsekiken could organize his discussion of menus according to this four-part structure. He prefaced his remarks by noting that he would restrict his comments to the arrangement of the dishes (*ryōri toriawase*), noting that there were other rules that needed to be followed in creating a menu but that he would omit these. Thus, rather than explore all of the components of a meal, Shōsekiken concentrated only on their structure.

> Spring: three soups, ten side dishes. This is a meal for aristocrats. [It includes] snacks for the ceremony of the three rites [i.e., *shikisankon*, see below] and the rites themselves, banquet tables, sweets for tea, the after meal, and an afternoon meal.

> Summer: two soups and five side dishes. The plan for an ordinary banquet. Celebrations, weddings, and other ceremonies are included in this [category] but I have not set these down.

> Autumn: one soup and five side dishes. A typical meal.

> Winter: one soup and three side dishes. The meal for a tea ceremony. The details of that are omitted. (Shōsekiken 1985, 232)

Examining this list from the bottom, the winter menu for the tea ceremony is an abbreviated version of the autumn menu, which the author presents as "typical." Two soups and five side dishes were the maximum number allowed for commoners according to *bakufu* sumptuary legislation promulgated in 1668 (Maruyama 1999, 186). The summer "banquet" adds another soup, necessitating another tray, but preserves the same number of side dishes as the autumn meal. Accordingly, there is a considerable gap between the commoner's summer banquet and the spring banquet "for aristocrats." This status distinction is heightened by Shōsekiken's abstruse word choices to describe the components of the aristocratic banquet. The snacks served for the formal rounds of drinking preceding the banquet (*shikisankon*), usually called *sakana*, are idiosyncratically called "hors d'oeuvres" (*onkuchitori*), a word usually used in reference to sweets served with tea after the banquet. The *shikisankon* itself is referenced as the "the arrival" (*gozachaku*), which is another odd turn of phrase, distancing the courtly version of a custom practiced by commoners at weddings and other festive occasions.[9]

Turning to the three model menus that he presented later in his book, we begin with the one for spring to be served to aristocrats.

Shikisankon (*onkuchitori*) snacks
    Tray with dried chestnuts, flattened abalone, konbu seaweed
Shikisankon
Simmered dish of various things (*zōni*) "something with something"
Sake
Soup of something
Snacks of something

The *shikisankon*, or ceremony of the three rounds of drinks, was a formal ritual derived from warrior custom in which participants toasted each other using three cups of sake for each of the three rounds of drinks. Snacks were served to accompany the sake, but these had largely symbolic value and they were not consumed. They were instead considered to be lucky talismans. Flattened abalone (*uchi awabi*) signified smiting (*utsu*) one's enemy, dried chestnuts (*kachiguri*) denoted victory (*katsu*), and another word for *konbu* seaweed was *kobu*, which could be taken as an abbreviation of the word "rejoicing" (*yorokobu*). The sixteenth-century culinary text *Transcript of Lord Ōkusa's Oral Instructions* (*Ōkusadono yori sōden no kikigaki*) includes the pithy statement about the symbolism of these three foods: "On departing for battle: smiting (*utte*), winning (*katte*), and rejoicing (*yorokobu*) are brought together." The same text notes later: "On returning from battle, winning, smiting (*utte*), and rejoicing are brought together" (*Ōkusadono yori sōden no kikigaki* 1985, 102, 104). This passage suggests the order in which these snacks were to be handled during the *shikisankon* to ensure their felicitous properties either before departing for a battle or returning from one. Shōsekiken noted the basic structure of the ritual service of sake and snacks before the meal, but he omitted the particulars of the dishes that followed. The soup, snacks, and *zōni* (a rice cake in broth with other ingredients) for the formal rounds of drinks are all listed as "something" (*nani*) or "something with something," indicating the structure but omitting the specifics.

However, he did list the dishes for the menu that followed.

MAIN TRAY—SERVED WITH [PAPER?] WRAPPED CHOPSTICKS
Fish Salad (*namasu*)—mixture of halfbeak (*sayori*), cockle *(akagai)*,
    thinly sliced squid, chestnuts, ginger shoots (*hajikami*), and kumquat
    as garnish
Salt, Japanese pepper
Pickles
Soup: dark miso, crane, burdock root, daikon, and "bridal [chrysanthe-
    mum] leaves" (*yomena*)
Rice

Fish salad (*namasu*) was both a typical dish for the main tray and the predecessor to sashimi, differentiated from the latter in that it included fruit, vegetables, and other ingredients, and it was served with dressings other than soy sauce, like vinegar. The example here is an elaborate one, combining a fish prized in the spring for its elegant qualities, seafood, and other ingredients. Crane soup was a delicacy restricted to the court and the samurai elite in the Edo period (Matsushita 1998, 141). One late seventeenth-century tea master who was also an expert on warrior custom, Endō Genkan (n.d.), explained in his guide to serving banquets to elite warriors that it was a good idea to include leg muscle from the crane in the soup so that guests would be sure not to mistake it for another fowl and recognize the rarity of the dish (Endō 1985, 95–97). This suggests that crane soup lacking a conspicuous leg bone may have looked and tasted like duck, chicken, or even a less noble fowl.

Raw fish appears again on the second tray.

SECOND TRAY
Sashimi—carp in long thin slices with roe, spiced sake, wasabi
Soup—clear broth, sea bream, and citron

Marinated fish are prominent in this menu for they appear on all three trays. The second tray contains sashimi, and the third includes a marinated fish dish and a marinade of abalone in soy sauce with a lichen called *iwatake*. The last ingredient was especially rare since it only grows wild on mountain cliffs, making it difficult to harvest (Hosking 1996, 63).

Were it not for the rarity and status of the dishes, one might mistake the first two trays of food as coming from a commoner banquet since the number of side dishes on the first two trays—three and one respectively—was well within the bounds of the sumptuary laws applying to commoners. It seems too that the salt and pepper on the first tray are meant to be one of the ten side dishes served, which would appear to lend an air of modesty to the banquet.[10] Yet the presence of the third and fourth trays indicates that this is clearly a banquet for nobles. Only the upper reaches of warrior society, such as the members of the shogun's senior council mentioned earlier, could legally sit down to a third tray of food at a banquet. Additional trays were the preserve of people of even higher status, namely the shogun and members of the imperial court.

THIRD TRAY

Plate of sake-marinated fish: salted salmon with flakes of preserved bonito

Soup of rice bran miso (*nuka miso*), leafy greens, and freshwater clams (*shijimi*)

Plate of dark soy sauce marinade: marinated abalone, kumquats, and *iwatake* lichen

The diners were also served a fourth tray of food called the "added in back" (*mukō musubi*). This tray was more commonly called the "included in back" (*mukōzume*) and it was located behind the main table, as in the illustration on page 22. It was not counted as a fourth tray because it lacked a soup. Instead, it usually contained grilled foods, as in the case here.

GRILLED ITEMS ON A TRAY "ADDED IN BACK" (*MUKŌ MUSUBI*)

Grilled dish: small sea bream simmered in soy sauce with ginger

Plate of simmered duck with dropwort and *enoki* mushrooms

Assortment of grilled dishes: Skylark (*hibari*), fish cake, dried cod

Pickles: "pears" [salted and fermented fish intestines] and arrowhead in spicy miso[11]

After the *honzen* banquet, plans for feasting continued with sake served along with six snacks and two soups followed by tea with sweets. Shōsekiken then added an "after meal" (*godan*), an additional, less formal meal of light snacks that occurred after a banquet later in the day. He further appended an additional meal of two trays and three side dishes to be followed by more snacks, including three inedible culinary displays on presentation trays (*shimadai*).

These inedible displays are mentioned only in passing in Shōsekiken's menu, but they are well known from other culinary writings. The first he listed was a spiny lobster whose feelers and body had been bent to resemble the shape of a boat (*ise ebi no funamori*). The second was cooked snipe displayed with its feathered wings attached and posed so that the bird looked like it might take flight (*shigi no hamori*). The third dish (*awabi no kaimori*) featured aba-lone served on its shell with other decorative elements like paper streamers (Shōsekiken 1985, 245–48). All three dishes were specialties of chefs called *hōchōnin* in the employ of the aristocratic and military elite, and the dishes incorporated decorative items like colorful paper. The anonymous *Culinary Text* (*Ryōri no sho*), composed in 1573, provides a description of the lobster dish: "The shell is opened and the meat is served upon it. Raise the feelers up like a ship's mast, and stand the legs off to the sides. . . . It is best served with painted decorations on it in silver and gold" (*Ryōri no sho* 1985, 157). These decorative dishes served after the banquet were usually not meant to be consumed (Ōtsubo and Akiyama 1998, 99). Yet, *Transcript of Lord Ōkusa's Oral Instructions* provides an elaborate description of how guests carefully had to admire game fowl served *hamori* fashion before eating them. The text advises readers to bow to the dish several times, to pay particular attention to the flowers decorating it, and to offer sufficient praise about the dish before digging into the meat (*Ōkusadono yori sōden no kikigaki* 1985, 105–6). The inclusion of these dishes confirms that this *honzen* banquet would have been quite grand, almost rivaling an actual one presented to Emperor Gomizuno'o in 1626 described later in this chapter.

The stages set forth in the banquet for aristocrats indicate the rhythm of a full banquet. Like a long poem, the banquet linked together different seg-ments, each with its own meter: the *shikisankon* consisting of three rounds of drinks, the *honzen* meal of three (or more) trays of food, followed by an ad-ditional numbers of snacks to accompany sake. As Shōsekiken demonstrated in his examples, a banquet could be lengthened further with the supplement of the after meal (*godan*) and even an additional two-tray meal as well. Given the constraints of sumptuary law and financial means, the long form of the banquet presented here was something commoners and most samurai could only appreciate by reading about it. They had to content themselves with shorter forms when they created their own meals for special occasions.

The other menus presented in *Collected Writings* would have been more feasible for commoners to create, including even the most fancy of the three: the summer banquet menu that featured two soups and five side dishes. This meal included an additional soup to be served with sake and snacks.

MENU FOR SUMMER
Main Tray—two soups and five side dishes
Fish salad: sweetfish with water pepper vinegar (*tadesu*)[12]
Slices of daikon radish, gingered chestnuts, and chopped *udo*[13]
Soup—blue heron, garnish (*torizukushi*),[14] broth with miso
Rice

SECOND TRAY
Chilled simmered dish (*nizamashi*): bamboo shoots, wheat gluten in the
     brocade style,[15] and pickled apricot (*umeboshi*)
Soup—greens with *enoki* mushrooms
Grilled dish: "shore-grilled" sea bass covered in soy sauce[16]
Salad—"pear" [preserved fish entrails] and dried abalone[17]
Grilled assortment: quail and flounder grilled with salt
Soup to be served with sake and snacks: large spiral shellfish with
     mioga buds[18]
Snack—grilled "fly" fish (*hae*) with vinegar and miso[19]

Without the previous aristocratic menu to compare it to, this one could be considered quite lavish for its blending of fowl (heron and quail) with fresh-water and ocean fish.

In an age when most people usually ate brown rice or other cooked grains and a few side dishes for daily meals, the one-tray *honzen* meal for autumn in *Collected Writings* might suggest a much closer approximation to average meals in its simplicity of one soup.[20] Yet the choice of ingredients in this menu and the number of side dishes reveal that it too represented an ideal to be enjoyed on special occasions for most diners.

MAIN TRAY—ONE SOUP FIVE SIDE DISHES
Fish and vegetable salad: horse mackerel, gingered chestnuts, and diced
     vegetable garnishes
Soup of red miso, daikon with its leaves, *shimeji* mushrooms,[21] and
     small clams
Rice
Pickles

Grilled over cedar: sea bream, onions, cracked Japanese pepper
Simmered dish: *matsutake* mushrooms with citron[22]
Grilled dishes: quail and sardines
[Snack]
Soup for the snack—razor clam (*mategai*)
[Unnamed] snack

Though simple, the dishes betray a wide variety of ingredients, some of which—like the *matsutake* mushrooms and the sea bream grilled over cedar wood—were considered delicacies, making the meal extravagant when compared to ordinary meals that might not even include one fish or fowl dish but have instead just one or two servings of vegetables or pickles to accompany rice and soup. It is also interesting to note how this meal expands beyond its one soup and five dishes to add one more couplet: a soup and an unnamed snack to accompany sake, a further indication that it is meant for a special occasion and not intended for daily fare. In that light, Shōsekiken's remarks that this was a "typical meal" need to be interpreted as indicating that this was a banquet meal suitable for wealthy commoners who could afford it and not an everyday event for most people.

By grouping complex aristocratic banquets together with less sophisticated versions, Shōsekiken Sōken, author of *Collected Writings*, illustrated that *honzen* meals shared a basic structure, a fact that resonates with Mary Douglas's more general observations about meals. "Each meal carries something of the meaning of the other meals," Douglas writes, "each meal is a structured social event which structures others in its own image" (Douglas 1997, 44). It did not matter whether or not Shōsekiken's readers could actually prepare the aristocratic banquet (or the others) since they could still read about that meal and appreciate its complexity, and perhaps even gain some inspiration to bring to the creation of an actual meal and judge the outcome. Shōsekiken's menus are closer to an ideal than a reality, something they share with menus written in other contexts. Writing about the historical context of medieval England, Anne Wilson has identified what she terms "ideal meals," ones that were never meant to be made but were instead intended to serve as models for chefs and their patrons to plan banquets (1991, 98). For late medieval and early modern Japan, such an ideal was the *honzen* meal for its structure of rice, soup, and side dishes that could be modified for a variety of occasions and to suit a range of audiences.

Banquets preserved the *honzen* structure even when the enormous amount of dishes presented threatened to violate it, as the example of one of the most famous banquets in the Edo period illustrates. In the ninth month of 1626, Shogun Tokugawa Iemitsu (d. 1651) and his father, Hidetada (d. 1632), entertained Emperor Gomizuno'o (d. 1680) at a lavish series of meals at Nijō Castle in Kyoto. One record of the banquet is some forty meters in length, testifying to the number of dishes served, which amounted to over nineteen trays of food that took some twenty chefs to prepare (Murai 1979, 17; 1991, 311). There is also an illustrated version of highlights of some of the banquet dishes entitled *Scroll of Seven Trays and Nineteen Rounds of Drinks* (*Shichi no zen jūkyū kon no maki*), which dates to the Edo period and is in the private collection of Mankamerō restaurant in Kyoto. One of the dishes featured in this picture scroll is snipe cooked in eggplant, called "snipe in [eggplant] jars" (*shigi tsubo*). This was a well-known ceremonial dish that, like bird served with its wings (*hamori*) and the lobster in the shape of a boat (*ebi no funamori*) dishes, was meant to be admired, not eaten.

The full course of several days of banqueting is too lengthy to consider here, but one of these meals can provide an example of *honzen* cuisine in its most extravagant form. The evening meal on the sixth day of the ninth month consisted of three trays of food with seven side dishes. This meal was actually less elaborate than the one earlier in the day that followed a structure of seven-five-three (i.e., three trays each with a soup and bearing seven, five, and three side dishes respectively). Nevertheless, what distinguished the evening meal was the large number of dishes that came after the *honzen* meal proper to accompany the drinking of sake. It seems that the chefs and their Tokugawa patrons chose to preserve a rather simple *honzen* structure but followed this with an opulent display of several additional dishes (*hikimono*) and snacks.[23]

MAIN TRAY
Fish salad: sea bream, sea cucumber on a stick, ginger, and wasabi
Soup: fresh crane, *matsutake* mushrooms
Pickles
Boiled duck
Rice

Snipe in [Eggplant] Jars (*shigi tsubo*) from *Scroll of Seven Trays and Nineteen Rounds of Drinks* (*Shichi no zen jūkyū kon no maki*), Edo period. (Courtesy of Mankamerō)

SECOND TRAY
Grilled fresh bonito
Taro stem salad
Soup of sea bass simmered in salt
Sea bream grilled over cypress wood with cockle
    and the meat of small bird[24]

THIRD TRAY
Cypress wood serving board on a stand made of fan paper:
    octopus, periwinkle clam, tiger prawn, fish cake[25]
Soup of potatoes (*sokuimo*)[26]

Accompanying foods (*hikimono*)
   Grilled snipe
   Sea urchin sushi
   Steamed abalone
   Soup of freshwater clams (*shijimi*)

Snacks (*sakana*) to accompany sake
   Octopus "cherry" simmer [octopus simmered with soybeans]
   Dried citron (*yubeshi*)[27]
   "Cherry label" (*sakura noshi*)[28]
   Dried cockle on small skewers
   Freshwater nori from the Fuji River

Soup of small shrimp and mushrooms (*kinoko*)

Side Dishes
   Arrowhead
   Dried salted mullet roe (*karasumi*)
   "Hard" nori (*kata nori*)[29]
   Sun-dried anchovies (*tatami iwashi*)
   Boiled abalone
   Peeled chestnuts (*mizuguri*)

Soup of fish cake and *matsutake* mushrooms

Side Dishes
   "Hawk's wing" (sea bream) fishcake
   Grilled wheat gluten
   Small birds on short skewers
   "Ant fruit" [i.e., pears]
   [Grilled eel] *kabayaki* style[30]
   Peeled (*takuru*) [fruit][31]
   Fan shell (*tairagai*)
   Tangerines
   Dried tilefish from Okitsu

A Wealth of Seven Varieties of Sweets[32]
   Artificial flowers to be used for eating the sweets (*kisoku*)
   [Decorative] twisted flowers (*musubi bana*)
   Yōkan[33]
   Yōhi[34]
   Kasutera

Snow rice cakes (*yukimochi*)[35]
Persimmons
Aruheitō
Konbu twists

If the banquet can be compared to a poem, then the first part conformed to the rules for *honzen* dining, but the snacks accompanying the sake and a more relaxed atmosphere at the end were like free verse, allowing the chefs and the shoguns to express their talents and largesse and to show off some exotic foods. For example, the tilefish was imported all the way from Okitsu in modern Shizuoka prefecture, an area long famous for these fish. The fact that the freshwater nori came from the Fuji River, which is also in Shizuoka, suggests an attempt to make a connection with this province, known as Suruga in the Edo period, which was the site of the first shogun Tokugawa Ieyasu's residence from 1607 until his death in 1616. Chefs in the employ of the Tokugawa may have brought or imported these foods to Kyoto to evoke Ieyasu's memory. Of special interest are the sweets served, which included Iberian confectionery: the soft sugar candy *aruheitō* and the sponge cake *kasutera*, both rarities in 1626, but ones that would become popular later in the Edo period.[36]

POETIC DISHES

As we have seen, part of the elegance of a *honzen* meal was its adherence to a set structure; yet as this section explores, some of the most artistic aspects of a meal were those that brought focus to specific parts within the structure, the same way that literary devices like alliteration, metonymy, and wordplay call attention to specific words within a poem. Flavor, color, and aroma as well as the rarity of the dishes, the quality of the preparation, and flair of presentation could draw attention to any dish, but a literary comparison is especially apt in the Edo period when there developed a fondness for foods with poetic names such as the sweets called "autumn field," "misty moonlit-night rice-cake," and "card game cake," among others.[37] Poetic food names evoked references to noted places, famous people, and natural phenomena.

Notwithstanding a few named display dishes like lobster in the shape of a boat crafted by medieval chefs, the custom of applying poetic names to foods has existed since the turn of the seventeenth century and it is found first in Japanese confectionery. The last two decades of the seventeenth century witnessed a profusion of these artistic names that coincided with the rise of the confectionery business (Harada 1989, 88). Sweet makers used a greater number of names in this period to create a wider variety of products from the same basic ingredients of refined sugar, rice flour, and adzuki bean paste (Akai 2005, 127). Size, shape, design motifs, and coloration could be used to create different sweets, but what set them apart were their names (*mei*). Confectioners turned to their chief customers—tea masters and aristocrats—for these names. Kyoto sweet maker Toraya has served as a purveyor to the court since the reign of Emperor Goyōsei (1586–1617) and claims today that more than fifty of its sweet names came from emperors or members of the aristocracy (Shashi Hensan Ininkai 2003, 11, 41).

Poetic names for dishes are found scattered in several culinary books, but two works that take these as their primary focus are by an author named Hakubōshi (n.d.), *Delicacies from the Mountains and Seas* (*Ryōri sankai kyō*) and *Anthology of Special Delicacies* (*Ryōri chinmishū*), published in 1750 and 1764 respectively. Like most cookbook authors, the biographical information we know about Hakubōshi comes from his texts, and in the preface of the second book he identifies himself as living in the eastern part of Kyoto and "proficient in the ways" of cooking (Hakubōshi 1985a, 73; 1985b).[38] Both books are organized into five volumes and contain 230 recipes each in no apparent order. The recipes themselves are easy to make, amounting to no more than a few sentences each. Their charm is their imaginative names.

One section can serve as a sampling of both works and of the ways in which poetic names could transform even simple dishes into something artistic. The third volume of *Anthology of Special Delicacies* begins as the other volumes do with a table of contents (Hakubōshi 1985a, 99–100, 101–110). Of the forty-six dishes in this section, approximately half have poetic names descriptive of more than their principle ingredient or cooking technique. These poetically named dishes include:

Teika's Rice (*Teika meshi*)
Blue Sea Tofu (*seigai tofu*)
Chrysanthemum Leaf Setting (*kiku no ha kaishiki*)
Pine Cone Tofu (*matsukasa tofu*)
Mt. Fuji Salad (*Fuji ae*)
Kimono Sleeves (*koromode*)
Imitation Truffles (*shouro modoki*)
Day and Night Yams (*chūya imo*)
Three-Cup Pickling (*sanbai zuke*)
Genji Persimmons (*Genji kaki*)

Twisted Sea Bream (*nejidai*)
Ise Tofu (*Ise dōfu*)
Blinded Rice Cakes (*mekuri mochi*)
Uji River (*Ujigawa*)
Foreign *Yuba* (*ikoku yuba*)[39]
Buddha's Name Soup (*nenbutsu jiru*)
Grilled Akita Pinks (*Akita fusube sennō*)
Moss-Simmer (*koke mushi*)
Japan Salad (*Wakoku ae*)
Hailstone Tofu (*arare dōfu*)

The dishes listed here take their names from a variety of sources. Teika's Rice is a homage to the Kamakura-period poet Fujiwara no Teika (1162–1241), editor of the *New Collection of Ancient and Modern Poems* (*Shin kokinshū*) and a noted commentator on the Heian-period classics *Tosa Diary* and *Tale of Genji*. Genji Persimmons is a tempura recipe named after the Minamoto (Genji) warrior's white battle flag, which resembled the color of the fried persimmons in the recipe. The Blue Sea of the tofu dish is actually taken from the name of a dance form popular in the early modern period in which the performers wore clothes decorated with wave patterns. Mt. Fuji Salad, Ise Tofu, Uji River, Foreign Yuba, Grilled Akita Pinks, and Japan Salad reference locations. Other dishes are visual puns: Neither Pine Cone Tofu nor Moss Simmer uses its featured ingredients. Instead they rely on other foods to give the appearance of these, similar to the recipes for Imitation Truffles, Hailstone Tofu, and, of course, the dish Uji River, which consisted of dumplings made from rice and yams. Comparable visual puns include the dish Kimono Sleeves, which consists of a covering of scrambled egg over simmered tofu, suggesting a yellow robe over white skin. Buddha's Name Soup is a pun on the main ingredient, a fish called *kanagashira*, which is a type of gurnard, a name that is a play on words for the word *bell* (*kane*) rung in time to the chanting of the Amida Buddha's name. Dishes such as these add punctuation to a *honzen* meal, particularly for commoners who could not afford to have multiple trays of exotic foods. Accordingly, Hakubōshi's text resembles a poetic catalogue of vivid imagery—mixed with a bit of doggerel—that awaits a poet-chef to incorporate it into a larger structure.

Poems may qualify as *waka* or haiku if they have the requisite number of syllables, but they still will fail as art without a sensitive use of words. Similar rules underlay the creation of the formal style of dining called *honzen* cuisine in late medieval and early modern Japan. These meals required an adherence both to structure and to a sensitive use of ingredients and careful creation of dishes, similar to the mindful selection of words for a poem. Knowing these rules might not have completely answered the question of what was for dinner, since *honzen* meals were served only on formal occasions, yet those who learned these rules would know what to expect and what to take delight in when they sat down to their banquet trays. Culinary rules, like those governing the creation of poetry, were initially restricted to the elite in the medieval period, but through the growth of the publishing industry they became more widely known in the early modern period. Though more people were able to read about elaborate meals, few actually had the necessary social status and economic means to be able to partake of the most elaborate ones. Yet that did not stop readers from the vicarious enjoyment of reading about food, and it would not prevent humble chefs and diners from drawing connections between their modest meals and the more elaborate culinary masterpieces of higher status groups.

NOTES

1. The extent to which commoners ate white rice in premodern Japan varied by historical period and is a subject of scholarly debate. Harada Nobuo contends that commoners living in cities began to eat more white rice by the Edo period (Harada 1992, 4). However, approximately 85 percent of the population lived in rural areas at that time, and the peasants there subsisted on brown rice and other grains such as millet.

2. For a broader discussion of *honzen* dining and the meaning of cuisine in premodern Japan, see Rath (2010), chapters 3 and 6 especially.

3. Pickles, which appeared on the first tray, were counted as a side dish only if more than two soups and five side dishes were served for the entire meal, but not for meals of one soup and three side dishes (Harada 2003, 118).

4. Personal correspondence with Konishi Shigeyoshi, owner of Mankamerō restaurant and twenty-ninth head of the Ikama school of cuisine.

5. The classic study of Edo-period sumptuary laws remains Shively (1964).

6. Sometimes premodern authors switched these terms, but generally the *shiru* accompanied the rice with the main meal and the *atsumono* was paired with the sake and snacks after the meal. This was also true in tea ceremony cuisine (Kumakura 2002, 82).

7. Like most of the authors of culinary books, we know little about Shōsekiken Sōken beyond his name. A portion of this discussion of Shōsekiken Sōken's *Collected Writings* appears in chapter 6 of Rath (2010).

8. Kumakura Isao has noted a similar disregard for seasonality in tea ceremony writings before the nineteenth century (2002, 116).

9. On commoner's use of the *shikisankon* for weddings and other purposes, see Lindsey (2007, 83, 94).

10. Without counting the salt and pepper, the dishes on all the trays add up only to nine side dishes, one short of the ten indicated by Shōsekiken in his guidelines for the winter menu cited earlier.

11. Despite the fact that the first dish is written with the Chinese characters for pear (*nashi*), it is more likely to be *nashimono*, salted and fermented fish intestines. Arrowhead (*kuwai*) is a small bulb that grows in water. It needs to be peeled and boiled to be eaten.

12. "*Tadesu* is a dip served with [sweetfish] *ayu* and is made by steeping the pounded leaves or leaf buds of the varieties of [water pepper] called *aotade* or *sasatade* in vinegar or [vinegar mixed with soy sauce] *nihaizu*" (Hosking 1996, 151).

13. *Udo* is a stalk like celery except both the leaves and the stalk can be eaten.

14. The modern editors cannot identify *torizukushi*, although the term bears a similarity to a matching game played with painted shells called *kaizukushi* (Shōsekiken 1985, 248–49). Since it is also glossed as "garnish for fowl" (*toritsuma*), I have translated it that way here.

15. Wheat gluten in the brocade style (*nishikifu*) appears in other culinary texts and tea writings, but what this dish actually was remains uncertain (Shōsekiken 1985, 249).

16. "Shore-grilled" (*hamayaki*) refers to several ways to cook fish: either grilling with salt or by baking in a *shiogama*, the pot used for making sea salt (Matsutshita 1996, 172).

17. Regarding pears, see note 11.

18. *Mioga* (*myōga*) are fragrant buds with a taste reminiscent of mild ginger, used frequently for pickles and as a garnish.

19. *Hae* is more commonly called *haya*, and it is a type of carp.

20. Daily meals in the Edo period, even for some high-ranking warriors and the shogun, could accurately be called monotonous in their limited variety of side dishes to accompany rice and soup (Rath 2008, 52–55).

21. These small golden mushrooms grow in clusters.

22. *Matsutake* are one of the most coveted mushrooms in Japan. They are gathered in the fall.

23. My translation is from *Gomizuno'oinsama Nijōjō gyōkō onkondate* (1958, 10–12). I referred to notes in Ebara (1991, 157–60).

24. *Kotori heso* literally means bird's bellybutton; the meaning is unclear according to Ebara (1991, 158), but it is probably some type of bird meat.

25. Ebara indicates that the periwinkle clam (*kisago*) was decorative and not meant for eating (1991, 159).

26. The meaning of *sokuimo* is unclear and the dish is omitted from Ebara's text. Potatoes (*imo*) is my guess. It could also be *taro*.

27. Ebara identifies *yubeshi* with a recipe for a sauce made from citron (*yuzu*),

miso, ginger, and sesame by the same name in the 1623 publication *Tales of Cookery* (*Ryōri monogatari*) (Ebara 1991, 158–59).

28. Ebara admits the meaning of "cherry label" is unclear (Ebara 1991, 159).

29. Ebara surmises that the nori was not eaten (Ebara 1991, 160). Presumably it was too hard to eat.

30. Ebara identifies "ant fruit" as pear, and the *kabayaki* dish in which the fish is deboned and skewered then grilled with a sweet sauce *was* a cooking method commonly used for eel (Ebara 1991, 160).

31. Peeled fruit is my guess; Ebara offers no notes about *takuru*.

32. The menu found in *Ryōri taisei* omits the contents of the "wealth of sweets." The ones listed here are from the morning of the eighth day of the ninth month (*Gomizunoʾoinsama Nijōjō gyōkō onkondate* 1958, 18).

33. *Yōkan* is a firm gelatinous sweet made from pureed adzuki beans, sugar, and kudzu (*kuzu*) starch in this period. Today it is usually made with agar (*kanten*) instead of kudzu starch (Nakayama 2006, 146).

34. This sweet may be a variation on the popular soft sweet made from rice flour called *gyūhi*, sometimes written as "cow hide." If so, the *yōhi*, which is written here phonetically, might translate as "sheep's hide," and it would presumably resemble the other confectionery.

35. In *Southern Barbarians' Cookbook* (*Nanban ryōrisho*), which dates from around this period, this sweet appears as a variation on *uirō*, a gelatinous cake made from glutinous rice (*Nanban ryōrisho* 2003, 39–40). Recipes for *kasutera*, *aruheitō*, and *yōkan* are also found in this text.

36. The reference to *kasutera* here is one of the earliest found in Japanese sources (Akesaka 2001, 23).

37. These sweets and the names of 247 others appear in *Records of Precious Treasures for Men* (*Otoko chōhō ki*), a guide to common knowledge first published in 1693 by Namura Jōhaku (1993, 326–42).

38. Some scholars take the reference to mean that he might be a chef working in a restaurant in that part of the city. Others view him as a professional writer and not a chef (Kawakami 1998, 124).

39. The delicacy *yuba* is the skin that forms on heated soybean milk.

WORKS CITED

Akai Tatsurō. 2005. *Kashi no bunkashi*. Kyoto: Kawara Shoten.

Akesaka Eiji. 2001. "Tobu kasutera nabe: Kasutera to kasutera nabe no bunkashi." *Wagashi* 8:21–32.

Douglas, Mary. 1997. "Decyphering a meal." In *Food and Culture: A Reader*. Ed. Carole Counihan and Penny Van Esterik, 36–54. New York: Routledge.

Ebara Kei. 1991. *Ryōri monogatari ko: Edo no aji kokon*. Tokyo: San'ichi Shobō.

Endō Genkan. 1985. "*Cha no yu kondate shinan*." In *Nihon ryōri hidden shūsei: Genten gendaigoyaku*. Vol. 11. Ed. Issunsha, 5–208. Kyoto: Dōhōsha.

"*Gomizunoŏinsama Nijōjō gyōkō onkondate.*" 1958. In *Ryōri taikan.* Vol. 2. Ed. Hasegawa Seihō, 7–21. Tokyo: Ryōri Koten Kenkyūkai.

Hakubōshi. 1985a. "*Ryōri chinmishū.*" In *Nihon ryōri hidden shūsei: Genten gendaigoyaku.* Vol. 14. Ed. Issunsha, 71–133. Kyoto: Dōhōsha.

———. 1985b. "*Ryōri sankaikyō.*" In *Nihon ryōri hidden shūsei: Genten gendaigoyaku.* Vol. 14. Ed. Issunsha, 7–70. Kyoto: Dōhōsha.

Harada Nobuo. 1989. *Edo no ryōrishi: Ryōribon to ryōri bunka.* Tokyo: Chūō Kōronsha.

———. 1992. "*Edo no shoku seikatsu to ryōri bunka.*" In *Edo no shoku bunka.* Ed. Edo Iseki Kenkyūkai, 1–18. Tokyo: Yoshikawa Kōbunkan.

———. 2003. *Edo no shoku seikatsu.* Tokyo: Iwanami Shoten.

Hosking, Richard. 1996. *A Dictionary of Japanese Food: Ingredients and Culture.* Rutland, Vt.: Charles E. Tuttle.

Ise Sadatake. 1985. "*Teijō zakki.*" In *Nihon ryōri hidden shūsei: Genten gendaigoyaku.* Vol. 18. Ed. Issunsha, 255–306. Kyoto: Dōhōsha.

Kawakami Kōzo. 1998. "*Edo jidai no ryōrisho ni kan suru kenkyū (dai 2 hō): Tokugawa jidai ni okeru ryōrisho no shippitsusha ni tsuite.*" In *Nihon ryōri no hatten.* Vol. 7 of *Zenshū Nihon no shoku bunka,* 109–26. Tokyo: Yūzankaku Shuppan.

Kumakura Isao. 2002. *Nihon ryōri bunkashi: Kaiseki o chūshin ni.* Kyoto: Jinbun Shoin.

Lindsey, William. 2007. *Fertility and Pleasure: Ritual and Sexual Values in Tokugawa Japan.* Honolulu: University of Hawai'i Press.

Maruyama Yasunari. 1999. "*Kinsei ni okeru daimyō, shōmin no shoku seikatsu: Sono ryōri kondate o chūshin to shite.*" In *Shoku seikatsu to shokumotsu shi.* Vol. 2 of *Zenshū Nihon no shoku bunka.* Ed. Haga Noboru and Ishikawa Hiroko, 173–98. Tokyo: Yūzankaku Shuppan.

Matsushita Sachiko. 1996. *Zusesetsu Edo ryōri jiten.* Tokyo: Kashiwa Shobō.

———. 1998. "*Edo jidai no ryōri no shuzai to chōrihō.*" In *Nihon ryōri no hatten.* Vol. 7 of *Zenshū Nihon no shoku bunka,* 133–55. Tokyo: Yūzankaku Shuppan.

Murai Yasuhiko, ed. 1979. *Kyō ryōri no rekishi.* Tokyo: Shibata Shoten.

———. 1991. *Buke bunka to dōbōshū.* Tokyo: San'ichi Shobō.

Nakayama Keiko. 2006. *Jiten: Wagashi no sekai.* Tokyo: Iwanami Shoten.

Namura Jōhaku. 1993. *Onna chōhō ki, otoko chōhō ki.* Ed. Nagatomo Chiyoji. Tokyo: Shakai Shisōsha.

"*Nanban ryōrisho.*" 2003. In *Kinsei kashi seihōsho shūsei.* Vol. 2. Ed. Suzuki Shin'ichi and Matsumoto Nakako, 7–62. Tokyo: Heibonsha.

Ogura Kumeo, Komatsuzaki Takeshi, and Hatae Keiko, eds. 2003. *Nihon ryōri gyōji, shikitari daijiten,* 2. vols. Tokyo: Purosatā.

"*Ōkusadono yori sōden no kikigaki.*" 1985. In *Nihon ryōri hidden shūsei: Genten gendaigoyaku.* Vol. 18. Ed. Issunsha, 97–143. Kyoto: Dōhōsha.

Ōtsubo Fujiyo and Akiyama Teruko. 1998. "*Chōsen tsūshinshi kyōō shoku (dai 2 hō): Shichi go san honzen ryōri to hikae.*" In *Nihon ryōri no hatten.* Vol. 7 of *Zenshū Nihon no shoku bunka,* 89–105. Tokyo: Yūzankaku Shuppan.

Rath, Eric, C. 2008. "Banquets against boredom: Towards understanding (samurai) cuisine in early modern Japan." *Early Modern Japan: An Interdisciplinary Journal* 16:43–55.

———. 2010. *Food and Fantasy in Early Modern Japan*. Berkeley: University of California Press.

"*Ryōri no sho.*" 1985. In *Nihon ryōri hidden shūsei: Genten gendaigoyaku*. Vol. 18. Ed. Issunsha, 145–64. Kyoto: Dōhōsha.

Shashi Hensan Ininkai, ed. 2003. *Toraya no goseiki: Dentō to kakushin no kei'ei*, 2 vols. Tokyo: Kabushiki Gaisha Toraya.

Shively, Donald. 1964. "Sumptuary regulation and status in early Tokugawa Japan." *Harvard Journal of Asian Studies* 25:123–64.

Shōsekiken Sōken. 1985. "*Ryōri mōmoku chōmishō.*" In *Nihon ryōri hidden shūsei: Genten gendaigoyaku*. Vol. 1. Ed. Issunsha, 219–323. Kyoto: Dōhōsha.

Wilson, C. Anne. 1991. "Ideal meals and their menus from the Middle Ages to the Georgian era." In *Appetite and the Eye: Visual Aspects of Food and Its Presentation within Their Historic Context*. Ed. C. Anne Wilson, 98–122. Edinburgh: Edinburgh University Press.

2 "How to Eat the Ten Thousand Things"

Table Manners in the Edo Period

MICHAEL KINSKI

EATING IS AN INDIVIDUAL ACT. What one person has eaten, no other can ingest again. Yet due to an elaborate corpus of rules—that is, table manners— this egoistic activity is transformed into a social event and the solidarity of those joined in a meal is promoted (Simmel 1957, 243–50). Besides the communal character of dining, the aesthetic dimension has to be stressed. Etiquette prescripts negate the animalistic nature and basic needs: With the combination of a stylized form of behavior and the embellishment of the meal through the utensils and service ware used, a social ceremony replaces the gross materialistic reality of eating and drinking (Bourdieu 1979).

It certainly cannot be claimed that the eating culture as it developed during the Edo period (1600–1868) resulted in the total emphasis of form and mannerism on the one hand, and the negation of carefree delight in eating on the other.[1] Elements of this culture—cooking manuals and the growing number of restaurants, for example—indicate otherwise. However, this culture was embedded in a tradition of etiquette that placed great emphasis on the aestheticization of the outward aspects of the meal as well as the formalized behavior of the participants.[2]

The function of etiquette rules as a lubricant of social interaction has been acknowledged throughout the ages. Nevertheless, at least with the advent of the enlightenment in Europe, they have been regarded as being an accommodation of behavior to convention while lacking a truly ethical dimension.[3] Since the Meiji period (1868–1912), a similar attitude spread gradually in Japan.[4] Until then, the Japanese understanding of etiquette owed its foundation to the Chinese tradition. In the *Records of Rites* (Chin. *Liji* / Jap. *Raiki*), compiled between 206 BCE and 220 CE, the rules for eating are conceived of as the foundation of the system of etiquette and are particularly valued. Etiquette or, holistically, "rites" (*li* / *rei*) lie at the heart of all human activities and provide a basis for those virtues that support human interactions. As a result, people acquire a sense of modesty, which guarantees social stability. "Rites" guide human emotions and prevent friction. For this purpose, they appear as concrete manner-rules, and in consequence norms for eating undergird the complex web of social relations.

Aware of Chinese classics like the *Record of Rites* and influenced by them, an indigenous tradition of etiquette developed in Japan. Before the Edo period, this took the form of *yūsoku* or "[courtly] knowledge" and *kojitsu* or "cases of precedent from former times." However, both of these were restricted to behavior on formal occasions either at the imperial palace or at the court of the shogun or regional lords (*daimyō*). They did not contain, at least with regards to food consumption, much detail when it came to the questions of how to eat a certain dish or how to handle the diverse utensils used in a meal. Such information can be found, but it retreats behind much more elaborate details about the foods to be served or the description of the utensils required for serving them (Kinski 2002).

In contrast, during the Edo period, collections of etiquette rules increasingly focused on concrete acts and bodily movements, almost completely eclipsing information on dishes and the utensils as was the case in the preceding age (Kinski 2002, 115–24). Apart (and different) from the experts of "methods of rites" *reihō* in shogunal employ, an increasing number of books that introduced rules of etiquette for almost all situations circulated in society. Manuals of etiquette in a strict sense, as well as works of encyclopedic dimensions such as "[time- and trouble]-saving collections" (*setsuyō shū*), "things [= letters] going hither and thither" (*ōrai mono*), or "records of precious treasures" (*chōhō ki*),[5] included chapters on "methods of discipline" (*shitsukekata*) or *reihō* (Kinski 2001). These appear to establish etiquette rules for a warrior society, but a closer examination reveals that these instructions were not related to a specific social group in society but rather point to an orientation toward standardization and generalization. The rule collections provide a guide to all situations of social life—in many cases following the same choice of subjects, often making use of the same wording and heightening their applicability by eclipsing reference to the concrete setting in which actions took place (Kinski 2001).

Etiquette books still took the context of warrior society for granted, but it was not the court of the shogun that was highlighted; instead, rules were gradually set in the context of middle- or even lower-class warriors entertaining one another. Moreover, with the exception of some rules, such as the method to examine a sword (*koshi no mono o miru ni wa . . .*), these could be applied in the context of merchant society as well. And, to be sure, the Edo period witnessed a popularization of certain rules that were presented in concise form in a variety of media, not only addressing warriors but also other segments of society. However, there are few clues that allow the modern observer to determine the degree to which such manuals spread throughout society and found practical application.[6]

Historian Matsumura Kōji focuses on one subgenre of advice book literature, namely dietetic writings such as Kaibara Ekiken's (1630–1714) *Admonitions for Nourishing Life* (*Yōjō kun*, 1713). It is Matsumura's conclusion that the recipients of such were male city-dwellers who were the heads of a household—probably a warrior household—who were in possession of a comparably high degree of income and education (Matsumura 1997, 99). In addition, members of the leading strata of rural society, too, were consumers of dietetic works and a much broader spectrum of advice books (Yokota 1995, 315–53; 1996, 48–67; 2002). Female readers targeted by numerous etiquette rule collections probably came from similar social milieus. This view is supported by the observation that already during the Edo period, works by scholars such as Ekiken were regarded as endeavoring to offer advice for the everyday activities of the common populace.[7]

Only a minute historical analysis of those who bought and read advice books can lead to a comprehensive picture of the actual readers of such works. Some light already has been shed on this matter. Yokota Fuyuhiko examined the book inventories and the reading habits, as they can be reconstructed from diary entries, of merchants living in countryside communities surrounding Osaka during the late seventeenth and early eighteenth centuries.[8] Among these private book collections are representatives of the advice book literature, such as Ekiken's *Secrets of the Three Rites* (*Sanrei kuketsu*, 1699) (1910/1973) and two writings by Namura Jōhaku (died after 1694), namely, *Records of Precious Treasures for Women* (*Onna chōhō ki*, 1692) (Kinsei 1981) and *Records of Precious Treasures for Men* (*Otoko chōhō ki*, 1693) (Yokota 1995, 337; 2002, 325).

On the other hand, Yokoyama Toshio's research offers insights into the spread of just one single work over all segments of society. As far as this could be ascertained, the sixty-four known examples of the *Inexhaustible Storehouse of [Time- and Trouble]-Saving Use for Innumerable Generations* (*Eitai setsuyō mujin zō*, 1831)[9] were in possession of widely different members of society, including court nobles, higher and lower warrior families from various parts of the country, merchant houses in and around Kyoto, doctors, village headmen, scholars, and musicians. One owner even seems to have been an express courier from the city of Kanazawa (with the rank of a lower warrior) (Yokoyama, Kojima, and Sugita 1999, 197–222).[10] The following words in the *Collection of Enlightening Illustrations on Human*

Relationships (*Jinrin kunmō zui,* 1690) provide recognition early in the Edo period of the wide dissemination of etiquette rule collections: "The records of House Ogasawara, as the form of rites (*reishiki*) of the warrior houses they are the method of rites that reach as far as the common people" (Tanigawa Kenichi 1982, vol. 30, 381).

It is not the place here to analyze the Edo period "methods of rites" or the "manner for disciplining" in their entirety, but with regards to the "rites of eating" the following features can be pointed out. Etiquette literature shows a concern with normatizing bodily movements. This includes not only the technical aspects (e.g., handling chopsticks properly or following the expected sequence of eating from dishes) but also the natural results of eating, such as producing noises while chewing. A second concern is the relationship between the participants of a meal according to their relative social status (*mibun*). Implicit in this is respect on the part of the inferior, and, at least in some cases, consideration on the part of the superior. Thus, the culture of etiquette or *rei* in Japan can be analyzed within the scope of personal cultivation central to Confucian thought in the context of social interdependency. The early modern rule collections differ from the writings on *rites* or "cases of precedent from former times" (*kojitsu*) of the preceding Muromachi period (1333–1573) in that they aim at a general applicability, regardless of differences in status or age.[11] The provision for exceptions in the earlier writings of the *kojitsu* tradition disappear during the Edo period and etiquette gains a more comprehensive character of universal appeal.

These observations are revealed by a look at a concrete example. Although more than one hundred rule collections can be ascertained in the context of household encyclopedias and guidance books alone, these have never become the focus of scholarly attention. Even the number of texts that have been transcribed and published in modern script is small.[12] However, these etiquette manuals provide a more vivid picture of the rules for eating properly, the context in which this takes place, and the organization of such rule collections than any secondary account can hope to achieve. For this purpose, a rather short and concise specimen based on the author's transcription will be introduced in translation here. Especially the first paragraph—much longer than the others—is of interest, as it introduces the most central information concerning participating in a dinner: the correct order of eating and general questions of behavior (e.g., eating noises); by contrast, the subsequent paragraphs touch on how to deal with a number of selected dishes.

"How Women Should Eat the Ten Thousand Things" is part of the *Chastity Bookstore House for Teaching Women Loyalty* (女忠教操文庫、*Onna chūkyō misao bunko*, published in 1801).[13] The latter is an exhortatory work that, like so many others in this age, shows a main text covering about two thirds of each page, while the top third is taken up by a column of different content. While the main text holds forth on the moral education of women (with a focus on "loyalty" and "filial piety" in the first half, and the "seven [reasons for] divorce" in the second), the column on the top touches on subjects of a more practical nature starting with "Good and Bad in the Compatibility of Men and Women" (*nannyo aishō no zenaku*). This is followed by "How Women Should Eat the Ten Thousand Things." Like other Edo-period guidance books (or chapters), this is not an original composition.[14] It closely follows a chapter of the same title in the *Record of Precious Treasures for Women* (*Onna chōhō ki*, 1692). This work by Namura Jōhaku is well known as one of the most representative advice books of the Edo period. The exemplary role of this text for collections of table manner rules can be gleaned from the fact that it was not only republished several times but that a considerable number of such chapters included in encyclopedic works were also modeled on it. One of these was the chapter under consideration here. For its transcription, translation, and reproduction, a facsimile edition of the original printed in 1801 was used.

THE CHASTITY BOOKSTORE HOUSE
FOR TEACHING WOMEN LOYALTY
　　How Women Should Eat the Ten Thousand Things
　　[1] Item.[15] In case of a [normal] meal/eating table (*zenbu*)[16] one should eat rice (*meshi*)[17] first.[18] [2] In case of a festive meal/eating table (*iwai no zen*)[19] and other [meals] rice is piled up high.[20] [3] At such times, the serving woman (*kaizoe kayoi no onna*) ladles [the rice] into the [rice bowl's] cover and serves it. [4] One should eat about two or three mouthfuls (*nihashi sanbashi*) of rice, and then eat of the ingredients of the soup (*shiru no mi*) only.[21] [5] One should not drink (*suu*)[22] from it. [6] Next, one should eat from the side dish (*sai*) in the left corner [of the eating table]. [7] As for the side dishes, in any case one should first eat the vegetarian [dishes] (*shōjin mono*). [8] Now one should again eat [some] rice, eat from the contents of the second soup (*ni no shiru*), and [then] eat [from] the second side dish. [9] As for the side dishes, in any case one should eat from one kind up to two or perhaps three kinds.[23] [10] Especially, it is not allowed to reach over the eating table for something that is in a far place and eat from it.[24] [11] One should not eat at the same time from two side dishes one after another. [12] This is called "wandering chopsticks" (*utsuribashi*) and is

wrong.[25] [13] In any case, it is not distressing to eat up to two mouthfuls from one sort [of side dish at a time]. [14] Be it rice or a side dish, one should only again eat from them after one has finished eating what one [already] has in one's mouth. [15] One should not eat again while one has still [something] in the mouth. [16] One should eat in such a way as not to make any loud noises with the mouth. [17] To turn over something grilled (*yakimono*)[26] and [continue] to eat it: this should not happen with either men or women.[27] [18] Moreover, one should not pour soup over the rice and eat it. [19] If, [however], it is in a reception room where one can relax (*kokoroyasuki zashiki*),[28] one should pour the soup [over the rice] before the hot water (*yu*) is served. [20] One should place the chopsticks down [on the eating table] and [then] pour the soup with the right hand.[29]

[21] Item. About eating rice gruel (*kayu*). [22] One should not pour soup over it. [23] One should not leave anything [of it].[30]

[24] Item. About eating rice-cake soup (*zōni*).[31] [25] Women, when drinking soup, should put the chopsticks down [on the eating table], take the bowl up, and drink two or three mouthfuls.[32]

[26] Item. About eating hard rice (*kowaii*).[33] [27] It should be served on a split-wood tray (*hegi*) or a small square [tray] (*kokaku*).[34] [28] [Even] if there are chopsticks, it is something that is not eaten with chopsticks. [29] One should take with the hand [directly from the hard rice] and eat it.[35]

[30] Item. Rice cakes (*mochi*)[36] should be eaten by picking them with a toothpick (*yōji*). [31] One can also eat them by taking from them with the hand.

[32] Item. About eating steamed cakes (*manjū*).[37] [33] One should take them with the left hand, tear a piece off them with thumb and index finger, and eat. [34] If they are served together with a soup one should eat them with chopsticks. [35] But [in that case], the steamed cakes are served after cutting them into four parts.

[36] Item. About eating [rice in] a leaf wrap (*chimaki*).[38] [37] Whether [wrapped in] plant or bamboo grass [leaves], one should position the leaf point on the right side, take up the chopsticks and hold them ready,[39] turn the spot with the end of the leaf to the top, hold the [leaf wrap] with the left [hand], unfasten the knot with the right, and [then] eat. [38] [Rice in a] leaf wrap is also offered by putting in two slanted incisions and cutting it into three [parts].

[39] Item. About eating fine noodles (*sōmen*).[40] [40] While leaving the soup [in its place on the eating table] one should take one or two chopstick's full of fine noodles out of the bowl, put them into [the soup], then take up

the soup and eat. [41] Thereafter it is safe to hold the soup [bowl] in the hand, take up the [noodles], put them [in the soup] and eat. [42] [Every time] when one changes [i.e., fills up] the soup, one should at first place the soup [on the table], take up [the noodles], put them into [the soup], [then] take up [the soup bowl] and eat.

[43] Item. As for the eating of warm noodles (*udon*) it is the same.[41] [44] In case of buckwheat noodles (*sobakiri*) it should not happen that in an unfamiliar place (*kyakushin naru tokoro*) one eats them by pouring soup over them like men. [45] One should eat them like fine noodles. [46] One should not put pungent or bad smelling [things] into the soup.

[47] Item. If one eats ginger (*shōga*)[42] or [Japanese] horseradish (wasabi)[43] [one's] complexion will become bad. [48] If one eats red peppers,[44] boils (*dekimono*) will appear on [one's] face. [49] If one eats roasted chestnuts (*yakiguri*)[45] or baked potatoes (*yakiimo*),[46] [one's] breath will turn bad. [50] Aside from these, in all cases one should not eat things that are pungent.

[51] About eating a Makuwa melon (*Makuwa uri*).[47] [52] One should cut it along its length into four parts, place toothpicks with it, place it on a plate, and [then] serve it. [53] One should take a pick, detach and throw away its seeds, pick it with the toothpick, and eat it.

[54] Item. About drinking tea.[48] [55] [Tea that] is served on a tray one should take with the right [hand], drink, pass it to the left [hand], and put it down. [56] The serving woman takes [the tea bowl], puts it on the tray, takes it up, and refills it. [57] If the tea is [too] hot, one should not drink it by slurping it or [after] swirling around the tea bowl [to cool it].

[58] Item. About drinking [rice] wine during a formal wine cup [event] (*sakazuki*).[49] [59] One should place one's left knee [on the floor], place the right knee over it and move it to the left [knee as well],[50] place the left hand [on the floor], take the wine cup with the right hand, raise it lightly up to the apex,[51] hold it forth, bend one's head and drink. [59] Delicacies (*sakana*)[52] one should receive with the hands,[53] and take them while folding a nose [blowing] paper, put [the delicacies] inside [the paper], place [the latter on the floor] at one's side, and take it along at the time one stands up.[54] [60] One should not place the wine cup from which one has drunk back on the tray. [61] [Instead] one should place it to the right side of the tray on the tatami floor. [62] The wine-pouring person (*shakunin*) should take it, place it on the tray, and take it back to the front (*saki*). [63] Even in the case that one forces wine [on another guest], one should turn to the group of women attendants (*jorō shū*) who are present, and say to them: "Please be so kind to pour [more wine]." [64] [However], for a guest with whom

they have an intimate understanding (*kokoro yasuki*), women (*jochū*)[55] might also do [the pouring] directly [by themselves]. [65] When taking up (*hasami*)[56] a delicacy [in order to serve it to a guest], one should in any case take up a little bit of something that does not dirty the hand, offer it, and put down the chopsticks by rearranging them [with their ends] pointing to the opposite direction [toward the guest]. [66] They [the chopsticks] should not be put down by rearranging them so that [their ends] point to one's own direction.

THE ORDER OF THE MEAL AND THE GENERAL CHARACTERISTICS OF ETIQUETTE RULES

The previous text conveys the richness of Japanese culinary tradition as it appears in other works of the same era—especially cookery books—only in a sketchy manner. That is true for the number of dishes as well as for their combination and presentation. Whereas the text's model in the *Precious Treasures for Women* mentioned different types of meals like the "Seven-Five-Three" and the "Five-Five-Three" that had their place in the highest echelons of society on formal occasions, here the reader is confronted with the "[normal] meal from the outset." The "festive/congratulatory meal" is less elitist than the "Seven-Five-Three" and the "Five-Five-Three" but likewise is bound to a far-from-everyday event—a marriage, for example—as described in the second sentence.[57] This is an indication that this rule collection and similar ones did not focus on one variety of a meal but were intended to introduce general rules for eating that claim validity on any occasion. Accordingly, the dishes do not represent an entire repertory nor do they trace in a structurally accurate manner the succession of foods in a standardized form of a meal. Rather, the kinds of food—like "rice" and "soup"—were chosen that had a place in most possible arrangements, foods for which the rules belonged to the most elementary knowledge of table manners. Additionally, one finds dishes that are difficult to eat (noodles or "steamed cakes") or dishes that easily come into conflict with thresholds of shame and repugnance.[58]

Generally, all dishes mentioned in this chapter represent stages in the course of a formal meal. "Rice," "soup," and "side dishes" are constitutive elements of every eating event. The allusion to a "second soup" and a "second eating table" hints at a meal with a "main eating table" and at least one other table as, for example, served when entertaining guests. In addition to ordinary "rice" as the most basic component, the text also has "rice gruel" (*kayu*) and "hard rice" (*kowaii*) that were sometimes part of the same meal.

Some of the dishes mentioned besides "rice" and "soup"—namely, grilled fish—could find a place on one of the first two "eating tables." Others in the second half of the text functioned as "sweets accompanying tea" (*ocha gashi*) or they belonged to an "after meal," the "later [meal] stage" (*godan*) that might have followed the banquet. The first group counts "rice cakes," "steamed cakes," "[rice in] a leaf wrap," "roasted chestnuts," "baked [sweet] potatoes," and "Makuwa melon"; the second included noodles like *sōmen*, *udon*, and *sobakiri*. The end of the main meal is set by a round of tea, but tea can again be served following an "after meal." Also, an exchange of wine cups is part of a formal meal, especially between the main stages, such as between the main meal and the "after" meal.

The thirteen mostly short paragraphs outline a number of basic norms for eating. As these lack broader explication, one may surmise that this rule collection and similar ones did not address a specific readership. The absence of any contextual specifications should rather be taken as a sign that they addressed a broad "general" audience; at least, the dishes that are mentioned point to a formal meal. The context of these rule collections, therefore, is not the everyday meal eaten at home, but an event that includes social interaction with outsiders and therefore transcends the private sphere.

Thus, these rules concern the behavior in a place of social exchange and do not allow any inference with regard to the eating act in private everyday situations; in other words, they do not say anything about the internalization of norms that—surpassing the sphere of public life—mold one's personality to a degree where behavior in the domestic area (screened from the controlling eye of the public) is normatized as well.[59] However, an analysis of these rules brings into relief a number of characteristics of etiquette rules in general that allow speculation on their scope of applicability.

SYSTEMATIC OF RULES FOR BEHAVIOR

Below, a number of categories will be used to classify the unsystematic presentation of etiquette rules in Edo-period advice books and identify the value orientations that lie at their heart: ritualization, general rules for behavior, views regarding shame and repugnance, prohibitions, social rank, respect (politeness), and consideration for others. It is possible to further differentiate between these categories and arrange them in subgroups according to the various areas in which they try to shape the eater's behavior. The first distinction is that between technical rules of behavior and norms of human relationships: In the first group, value-free and value-laden rules are found, and in the second group horizontal and vertical rules can be distinguished.[60] In this way, for the technical prescriptions, one arrives at a subgroup of value-free norms that are either general in nature (general rules for behavior) or that have a disciplinary effect on the body and its operations (ritualization). The value-laden subgroup refers to actions that for unspecified reasons are forbidden because they trespass thresholds of shame and repugnance. For those rules that concern norms of human relationships, an additional bipartition is possible as well. "Vertical" prescriptions focus on differences of rank between the participants of an interaction or call for a mode of behavior relative to the status of the partner and include provisions for those forms of interaction that demonstrate respect for social rank. "Horizontal" rules, on the other hand, emphasize consideration for the feelings of the other person.

The application of these categories shows that "How Women Should Eat the Ten Thousand Things" advances only such rules that may be classified as technical. The absence of prescriptions concerning rank as well as the exclusion of status gradations and their reflection in behavior indicates an effort to list only rules of a general character that can claim validity in any place and in any group. The only difference conceded on the level of the persons involved is that between men and women. The latter should not eat "buckwheat noodles" by pouring "soup" over them like men are allowed to do—at least, women should refrain from doing so in "unfamiliar places" [44].[61]

RITUALIZATION

In this context, ritualization means a choreography of bodily movements. Its result is a fixed "form" that leads to uniform behavior, thus contributing to the propagation of a certain social standard with stability of the encounter as its aim. In an exemplary manner, the ritualization of eating is evinced in Kaibara Ekiken's *Secrets of the Rites for Eating* (*Shokurei kuketsu*). The explanation of the sequence of movements at the beginning of the eating act gives a good impression:

> If one takes up the chopsticks, first one should take them up in reverse manner [from above], clamp them in between the ring finger and the small finger of the right hand, take off the cover of the rice bowl with the thumb, index finger, and middle finger and pass it over to the left hand. One should put down [both] on the right side [of the eating table]. Moreover, in the case that the side dish bowl, too, has a cover one should open it with the left hand. . . .

At first, one takes up the rice bowl with the left hand, takes the chopsticks properly in correct order, eats once or twice of the rice and puts it down. [Next] one takes up the soup bowl with the left hand and eats of the contents. Then, one should eat again of the rice, drink of the soup . . . and eat of the side dish on the main eating table. If there are two side dishes on it, one should [first] eat of the one standing on the left. If pickles are standing on the left, one should eat [at first] of the right hand side dish. One should not eat of side dishes [on other eating tables] before having eaten of the side dishes on the main eating table first.

One should eat in the order rice, soup, side dish, rice, soup, side dish several times. It is wrong to change from rice to a side dish, or from one side dish to another, or from the soup to a side dish. It is also wrong to change [directly] from the main soup to the second soup.[62]

These prescriptions structure the course of the eating act in a ceremonial manner and embed the bodily movements in an accurately choreographed frame. To be able to perform the minutely spaced eating acts in a natural manner that does not betray uncertainty or artificiality, the eaters must have mastered the necessary motion sequences and disciplined themselves accordingly. To recognize these table manners as relevant and to follow them simultaneously means to undergo a disciplining of the body—and the entire personality—that does not allow for the natural spontaneity of eating and the drives that motivate it.

The exposition of norms for eating in "How Women Should Eat the Ten Thousand Things" does not attain the elaborateness of Ekiken's *Secrets of the Rites for Eating*. Nevertheless, a similar tendency toward ritualization or normatization of acts as well as the sequences of movements is evident. In the first ten sentences, discipline and the mastering of the prescribed sequence of motions that determines the order in which "rice," "soup," and "side dishes" should be eaten, is expected. However, what is the most striking about the *Secrets of the Rites for Eating* are the detailed specifications for the motion sequences: taking up the chopsticks, uncovering the bowl, passing the cover to the other hand, putting it down in a specified place, and so forth. That "How Women Should Eat the Ten Thousand Things" had a similar script of behavior in mind, can be inferred from a later passage where receiving a "soup bowl" is described: "If, [however], it is in a reception room where one can relax, one should pour the soup [over the rice] before hot water is served. One should place the chopsticks down [on the eating table] and [then] pour the soup with the right hand" (19–20). Further examples of this are the descriptions about opening a "leaf wrap" (37) and eating "noodles" (40–42). All these cases convey an eating technique according to an accepted standard; they provide technical support to eschew uncertainty and loss of face through offensive behavior. At the same time, however, the sequences of movement constitute forms of acting that—as socially accepted standards—possess independence of the concrete persons applying them and demand a control of their bodily movements irrespective of their personal feelings.

GENERAL RULES FOR BEHAVIOR

Adherence to ritualized forms distinguishes the above group of rules from a number of other rules of a technical kind that do not mold corporeal motor functions. That is to say, the latter do not dissect movements into strings of acts following a minute choreography but focus instead on a single technical detail. Sentence 7, for example, states: "As for the side dishes, in any case one should first eat the vegetarian [dishes]." And number 13 reassures the reader that "it is not distressing to eat up to two mouthfuls from one sort [of side dish at a time]." "Hard rice" should be eaten with the fingers and not with chopsticks (28–29). These and similar sentences transmit a basic but neutral knowledge about the consumption of a number of dishes. They offer the reader a sense of security and self-assurance but do not stigmatize misconduct as disgraceful, shameful, or embarrassing. This, however, occurs in another group of prescriptions that condemn or censure explicitly improper ways of behavior.

VIEWS OF SHAME AND REPUGNANCE

Etiquette rules represent cultural values, and this is especially true for the ones that proscribe behavior viewed as shameful and repugnant. Although the text does not consistently use words that express shame or embarrassment, what could be considered distasteful can be inferred.[63] Two types of behavior are stigmatized: bodily expressions and deficiencies in eating technique.

As an example of prohibitions of bodily expressions, sentence 16 admonishes readers not to produce noises in the mouth when eating. This rule expresses a concern to be found in a large number of writings. However, clarification is necessary: There is a marked contrast between "How Women Should Eat the Ten Thousand Things" and other writings addressing women, on the one hand, and etiquette collections for the general reader on the other. The control to be exerted over bodily expressions is more severe with women. Of the ninety etiquette collections from the Edo period that I have investigated, about a third addresses women only. Among these, seventeen collections contain a prohibition of eating noises as an offensive bodily expression. Of these seventeen collections, twelve speak of "mouth noises" (*kuchioto*) or "tooth noises" (*haoto*) in general. Another five warn against noises while eating certain dishes, such as noodles. Of the remaining sixty works directed at men or the general reader, only thirteen address eating noises in some way, and only two of these works contain a comprehensive prohibition. All the others warn against noises when eating one dish or the other (noodles, grilled fowl, rice gruel, or bones among them) (Kinski 2005, 211–22).

That eating or drinking noises were considered as repugnant can also be gleaned from sentence 57, which rules against slurping tea that is too hot to be drunk comfortably. Olfactory exudations/emissions of the body, too, are disavowed. Sentence 50 calls upon the reader not to eat anything causing bad breath as, for example, roasted chestnuts or potatoes. And number 48 warns against "red peppers" causing "boils" on the face.[64] All of these instances aim at exerting a control over natural expressions of the human body that could annoy the sensory perceptions of other diners.

The second group of precepts, however, focuses on reactions of shame and repugnance that have no grounds in any kind of bodily signal and that do not offer any means to understand the reasons behind them than the conjecture that they represent socially proscribed acts somehow intruding upon the sense of shame. The most representative example is the category of taboos concerning chopstick usage. In this text, only one example is mentioned: It is distasteful to eat from one "side dish" and immediately take from another without eating "rice" in between (11). The *Secrets of the Rites for Eating* mention six chopstick taboos, and Ise Sadatake, too, has a list of six prohibitions.[65] Also, it is a matter of distress to turn a grilled fish upside down in order to eat the bottom side. Therefore, one eats only the upper side and then leaves the rest untouched (17).[66] As a matter of social discountenance, one can also consider a mode of behavior that transgresses the threshold between the sexes: Sentence 44 expects that men and women in certain situations will handle the eating utensils in a different manner.

PROHIBITIONS

In addition to these stigmatizations, the text gives a number of actions that are disqualified on grounds of being technically wrong. Generally, here as well as in similar texts, no reasons or explanations are given. As to sentence

14, it is possible to speculate that an impression of avarice might occur if the eater fills his mouth again without having chewed and swallowed the preceding mouthful.[67] In many other cases, however, the reader is confronted with what seems to be nothing else but arbitrary interdictions, conventions without social validation. This is shown distinctly in sentence 11: "One should not eat at the same time from two side dishes in a row."

ETIQUETTE AS A PRINCIPLE
OF SOCIAL ORGANIZATION

Etiquette rules describe patterns of relationships, and with norms of eating, four basic domains can be distinguished. First, the relationship between the eater and his food is at stake. How to eat food—including the sequence of ingestion and the handling of utensils involved—is explained. Insofar as foodstuffs are natural substances, the etiquette of eating by extension also touches on the relationship between human beings and nature. As Claude Lévi-Strauss argued, table manners mediate between these two poles by engendering the eater's respect for that sphere of life to which he owes the sustenance of his bodily existence.[68] Conversely, there are indications that norms for eating as mediators protect against substances derived from a world that confronts the human being in both a spiritual and a corporeal dimension as a dangerous source of defilement. To make them safe for consumption, they have to be approached via the proper use of eating utensils that follows established rules and tames the inner as well as the outer nature of the things that are meant to be eaten.[69] The text introduced here does not offer sufficient hints to pursue this issue. What the rules give evidence of is a cultivated, even ritualized treatment of food. It is not only meaningful with regard to the relationship with foodstuffs as an element of the natural world but also acquires its true significance in the context of other patterns of relationships that are given structure by the rules for eating.

The second pattern concerns relations with persons present according to their relative social status involved. Whereas other etiquette manuals contain a number of paragraphs to differentiate attitudes of behavior vis-à-vis the host or (other) guests, this discussion is absent in "How Women Should Eat the Ten Thousand Things." Apart from those passages that focus on an unsavory behavior and thus imagine other people whose feelings have to be respected, the text exclusively introduces rules that address the single eater's behavior.

These rules organize the third and fourth patterns of relationships: Dealings with one's own person—that is, self-constitution—calls for a distinction between the relationship with one's internal personality and one's relation to the (external) body. Norms of eating themselves constitute a "technique of the self" that does not only address the outer appearance; it also affects internal motives, and it subjects dispositions, urges, and emotions to a discipline that is conducive to life in society. Compliance with table manners amounts to not yielding to emotions and urges. Satisfaction of hunger or gratification of the lust to eat are brought into a form that follows established rules of social exchange and acknowledges (and heeds) the feelings, sensitivities, and thresholds of shame and repugnance of others.

Achievement of social competence does not only mean a command of appropriate attitudes (and the inner dispositions they are grounded in) with which a human being enters upon relations of interaction; disciplining the body, too, becomes an indispensable task. However, the internal cultivation can only show itself via external bodily movements. The disciplining regimen that table manners impose upon the body evolves along two tracks. One has to master a large number of motion sequences to be able to handle utensils like bowls, plates, and chopsticks in a manner appropriate for the norm set by the immediate occasion and the given constellation of persons involved. Moreover, the body has to grow accustomed to a mode of control over its natural expressions that—like noises while eating—occur unintentionally through carelessness; even better if this control is internalized so that it becomes a second nature. The internalization of the control function can, as sociologist Norbert Elias (1977) has argued, be achieved by means of the development of shame and repugnance thresholds that have found social acceptance and that are impressed upon the body. Thus bodily discipline is linked to the development of an emotional sensitivity for a certain image of man and his body as agencies fit for social intercourse.

The eighteenth and early nineteenth century witnessed a society that was open and diversified to such an extent that traditional models of life no longer sufficed to answer the needs for morals and social orientation. Growing wealth opened up new areas of activity for those of a certain economic affluence (and male gender) and afforded them the necessary time for (self-) reflection and the active search for answers.

Collections of etiquette rules as part of the advice-book literature exploited a demand for social orientation from below; that is to say, they arose out of the milieu where they claimed validity: the sphere of life of those segments of society that stood outside the circle of political action and decision making—even though for their contents they were indebted to the culture of etiquette that had evolved in the context of a warrior society around the shogunal court during the Muromachi period (1392–1573). In European cultures, drafts of society and concepts for social order are generally linked to notions of law and its materialization in the form of law codices. The model role played by the *Corpus iuris civilis* for European history does not have to be dwelt upon, nor the importance of the *Code Napoléon* for the emergence of the modern nation-state. In the context of the Edo period, the models of human interaction and the expositions of social relationships in advice books and household encyclopedias to a certain degree act in place of law, in contrast to Europe. Etiquette rules—and the rules for eating lie at their heart—are the generally accepted foundation on which a civilized society was able to develop without being in need of a societal and juridical order promulgated by the authorities. Household encyclopedias and advice books are the canon of common knowledge relating to the foundations of society. By recognizing them as relevant for their own life and modeling their behavior on them, Edo-period Japanese integrated themselves into accepted modes of social exchange, thereby proving to be responsible and reliable members of society.

NOTES

1. Cf. Kinski (2003, 123–78). Rather, food and eating culture, beyond the need to satisfy basic needs, developed into a major pastime engaging body and mind. Cf. Harada (1989).

2. The significance of rules for eating in the context of a progressive control of the affects and the body as the result of the growth of population, an intensification of exchange relations, and the centralization of political power was brought into perspective by Elias (1977).

3. The beginning of the trend can already be observed in Thomas Hobbes's (1588–1679) statement: "By Manners, I mean not here, Decency of behaviour; as how one man should salute another, or how a man should wash his mouth, or pick his teeth before company, and such other points of the Small Morals; But those qualities of man-kind, that concern their living together in Peace, and Unity" (Hobbes 1968, 160).

4. This can be deduced from the writings of Japanese "enlightenment" philosophers such as Fukuzawa Yukichi (1835–1901) and their harsh rejection of Chinese culture and Confucianism in particular for the stifling influence they had on the development of "civilization" in Japan. In the early Meiji period, a number of manner books from England and America were translated, and later indigenous publications incorporated elements of European etiquette where the changing conditions of day-to-day life and material culture called for it—European-style attire, concomitant ways of greeting, the encounter with foreign food, and an eating culture—called for adjustments, but

on the whole the contents of concrete rules of behavior and the theoretical passages explaining the necessity of etiquette were indebted to Edo-period precursors. As in the chapters concerning eating, these were often faithfully reproduced until the beginning of the 20th century. See also Kracht (1998, 27).

5. These writings can be characterized as household encyclopedias containing the knowledge of their times in concise form. See Yokoyama (1984, 17–36; 1988, 78–98; 1989, 243–55; 1998, 197–222).

6. Etiquette rule collections are a kind of normative text and as such they tell how one should behave. It is not their purpose to describe how people actually acted.

7. Matsumura adduces a number of works from the late eighteenth and early nineteenth century—for example, Ban Kōkei's (1733–1806) *Biographies of Eccentric Men of Recent Times* (*Kinsei kijin den*) of 1790 (Kansei 2) and Hirose Tansō's (1782–1856) *Evaluation of the Grove of Confucian [Scholars]* (*Jurin hyō*) of 1836 (Tenpō 7)—that introduce Ekiken as a scholar who provided useful knowledge for everyday practice (Matsumura 1997, 115).

8. The library of Sanda Jōken (1666–1733), a merchant of fertilizers from Kashiwara, some kilometers to the south of Osaka, comprised 239 works in more than one thousand volumes (Yokota 1995, 322–23; 2002, 325). At about the same time, the Mori family, headmen of the village Kusaka (east of Osaka), owned 121 works or 394 volumes, the Sasayama family from the village of Minamino had collected 169 works (939 volumes), and the brewer Yao Hachizaemon from Itami (both localities lie west of Osaka) called at least eighty books his own (Yokota 2002, 327).

9. Expanded versions were published in 1849 and 1864.

10. The history of reading—together with the development of printing, bookstores, and commercial lending libraries—has been the subject of a number of studies. To give only a few examples: Konta (1977), Nagatomo (2001), Chibbett (1977), May (1983), and Kornicki (2001). However, reading as an actual practice and the correlation between reading and the application of what has been read—such as in advice books—is still an intangible subject.

11. Muromachi etiquette writings contain provisions concerning the validity of etiquette rules reflecting differences in status, gender, or age. Often persons of high social standing are entrusted with judging for themselves how to behave in certain situations (Kinski 2002, 97–142).

12. For translations into European languages, see Kinski (1998, 2002).

13. The introductory note in the *Great Compilation of [Helpful] Things for the Coming and Going [of Letters]* (*Ōrai mono taikei*) lists Oka Hōmei as the editor of the *Onna chūkyō misao bunko*, and notes that the original printing stocks were carved during the Anei era (1772–81) (Ishikawa 1992–1994).

14. The principles of compilation were eclectic and pragmatic. Later, compilers felt no compunction to draw freely on famous and successful earlier works, often changing nothing except for some words or characters.

15. The description of food consumption has to be seen against the background constituted by the rules of a formal meal known as "meal with a main eating table"

(*honzen ryōri*). See Eric C. Rath's treatment (chapter 1) in this volume. The original text consists of one long paragraph at the beginning and very short ones that follow. All paragraphs are headed by the Chinese character for "one," which I translate as "item." I counted the sentences of the original by putting a number in brackets in front of them.

16. Made from lacquer wood, the "eating table" was either shaped like a serving tray on four feet or had the shape of a boxlike construction with decorative openings on the sides or with drawers. Here, the word *zenbu* is used to refer to a meal.

17. The text states the reading of the Chinese character as *meshi*. In other cases, 食 can also be read *ii*. The word primarily means steamed or boiled rice. Rice can also be replaced by wheat or millet, or a mixture of rice with wheat or millet and/or other substances could be denoted by *meshi* or *ii*. But the connotations of *meshi* are broader, referring to a meal or something to eat in a general sense. Historically, the consumption of rice unmixed with other cereals was a prerogative restricted to social groups of high status.

18. The *Precious Treasures* starts with the sentence: "In case of seven-five-three [meals], five-five-three [meals] and common eating-tables, one should eat rice first." The first two forms of the formal meal are not mentioned here.

19. This could refer to a meal served at a wedding.

20. Illustrations since the Heian period (794–1185) show rice bowls with their contents in smooth piles artfully soaring over their rims.

21. In the Edo period, "soup" could be prepared in two ways; either by using miso, a salty paste of fermented soybeans, grain-carried fungi, and salt that was dissolved in hot water, or as a "clear soup" (*osumashi*).

22. Literally, the verb *suu* means "to slurp/suck something in."

23. The *Precious Treasures* do not allow for more than two kinds.

24. This is one of the most common prohibitions in Edo-period etiquette collections.

25. One of the most prominent aspects of eating subjected to standardization and taboos until present times is the use of chopsticks. The rule against *utsuribashi* is one of the most basic ones. Kaibara Ekiken enumerates five examples under the heading "chopstick taboos" (*hashi no kinkai*). *Teijō zakki* gives more details: This behavior refers to eating from one dish only without letting the chopsticks rest or putting them down (*Teijō zakki* or *Teijō's Mixed Records*, recorded 1763–84, printed 1843; Ise 1985, 157–59); also see Rath (chapter 1) in this book. In addition, Ekiken offers one further bit of information: It is strictly out of the question to use chopsticks for cleaning one's teeth! (From the *Secrets of the Rites for Eating* [*Shokurei kuketsu*, 1699, hereafter referred to as SK]; Ekiken 1910/1973, 310).

26. Generally, *yakimono* relates to grilled fish—but grilled fowl was possible as well. The fact that the expression refers to fish here can be deducted from the context.

27. Ekiken's *Secrets of the Rites for Eating* had given the following rule: "On eating grilled fish: Only the upper side should be eaten. [Thereafter] one has to turn

[the fish] upside down and [thus] cover the traces of eating" (SK 314). Ekiken's advice diverged from what had become the common rule. The *Precious Treasures* stipulated in 1692 that one should only eat the upper side but refrain from turning the fish upside down. This way of eating became standard practice—according to the collections of etiquette rules—and remained like that until the beginning of the twentieth century. Sentence 17 is a shorter version of the description in the *Precious Treasures*: "Something grilled should [already] be plucked apart and served by the serving woman. Even in case one plucks it apart by oneself, it should not be reversed and [then] eaten."

28. I have translated *zashiki* as "reception room" since it is that part of the house where the entertainment of guests took place. (The literal meaning, "laying out seats," refers to the custom of distributing cushions for sitting on the wooden, in later times, tatami-covered floor.) However, *zashiki* not only denotes the room, it can also refer to the entertainment (of guests) or the gathering taking place there itself. Here, a situation is alluded to that allows for some relaxation and does not require the highest formality.

29. The last sentences differ from the *Precious Treasures*. Whereas the latter instruct the serving woman to serve "rice" poured with "soup" in a "cover," the *Onna chūkyō* speaks only of an informal setting where it is allowed to pour "soup" over "rice." The last sentence in the *Precious Treasures*—"It is not appropriate to pour [soup] with the left hand while holding chopsticks like men"—is missing here. In *Precious Treasures*, the introductory paragraph was followed by two brief paragraphs on "hot water." The first tells about drinking it, the second paragraph offers an instruction on how to pour it over "rice" (*yuzuke*). The latter practice is similar to the use of tea for the same purpose (*chazuke*), which began in the Edo period and can still be observed in modern Japan.

30. *Precious Treasures* includes a paragraph about "decorated rice" (*hōhan*) that is missing here. While this rice dish decorated with fresh or dried vegetables cut into small pieces (in other cases, "fish paste" or *kamaboko*, chicken, or eggs could be used) had enjoyed popularity since the Muromachi period, it might be possible that at the time this text was written the dish was not common anymore.

31. Literally, the word means "mixed [things] cooked [together]." As implied by the name, different ingredients were cooked in a broth. While "rice-cake soup" today is a typical New Year dish consisting of a clear broth with only "rice cake," chicken, and one type of green vegetable in it, the Edo-period variant was eaten on ordinary occasions too.

32. The first sentence in the *Precious Treasures* (it suggests to leave the bowl resting on the table while eating the contents) is missing here.

33. "Hard rice," prepared by steaming and served without ingredients, in the formal meal had its place on the "main eating table." For felicitous or religious occasions, it could (and still can) be served as a single dish mixed with red beans (adzuki), taking on a red coloration ("red rice" or *sekihan*).

34. A *kogaku* or *kokaku* is a tray (*oshiki*) three inches square.

35. Muromachi-period etiquette literature included rules for foodstuffs that should be eaten without chopsticks. The *Records of Ise Rokurō Zaemon no jō Sadanori* (*Ise Rokurō Zaemon no Jō Sadanori ki*) gives the following list: "On things that one eats with the hand: hawk-[hunted] fowl, red rice, steamed cakes, [things] baked in rice wine yeast (*kōjiyaki*), fish paste [wine] relish" (from *Zoku gunsho ruijū*, hereafter referred to as ZGR); Hanwa and Ōta (1957–59, vol. 24.2, 23). "Hard rice," too, is mentioned in a number of texts; see Kinski (1999, 74–75). Eating with the hands possibly had the character of a ritual act in decline even in Muromachi times (after eating a bit in this manner, the use of chopsticks is allowed in some writings); see Kinski (1999, 75). It is linked with an expression of gratitude or respect toward the person from whom one received the food in question, and it concerned only dishes that did not soil the hands because of their consistency.

36. "Rice cakes" are made from glutinous *mochigome* that has been steamed and afterwards beaten in a mortar with a wooden mallet into a smooth dough. This is formed into small pieces, either slices or squares.

37. "Steamed cakes" were made from wheat-flour dough that was mostly filled with a red bean paste (called *an*). They were eaten either without or with a soup that could be seasoned in different ways (e.g., with pepper or the peels of mandarins or lime).

38. This dish counts as an early "sweet" (*kashi*) that, for example, was served accompanying tea. Rice, either the whole grain or milled, was steamed and formed like the horn of cattle (geographically different shapes were possible), and wrapped in a leaf that was tied at the ends (thus reminiscent of cattle horns). Besides, the leaves of bamboo grass (*sasa*), reed plants were used. Depending on the region, the rice could be sweetened with sugar. Instead of rice, other ingredients such as kudzu (*kuzu*) were used as well.

39. The proper way to lift chopsticks is to do so from above with the right hand, holding them in the middle between the left thumb from above and the left index finger from below and then grasp their end from below with the right thumb and index finger in a way that it comes to lie between these two fingers.

40. "Thread noodles" or "fine noodles" were made from dough of wheat flour. The dough was drawn out in long threads and hung on poles in the sun for drying. "Fine noodles" were eaten after boiling them in hot water. They were served in a common bowl from which the eaters took small portions with their chopsticks and then dipped in small vessels containing a cold sauce that was served each eater. "Buckwheat noodles" (*soba*; since the end of the seventeenth century wheat flour was added as well), too, were dipped in a sauce, although these could be served in a hot soup as well. Originally, small "buckwheat dumplings" were formed out of the dough and boiled. However, since the turn of the seventeenth century, the dough was rolled out and cut into thin strips. A third type of noodles, called "warm noodles" (*udon*) was—like fine noodles—made from wheat flour and (at least since the Edo period), drawn out in long threads, and dried before being cut into shorter pieces. *Udon* are much broader and thicker than fine noodles and served in a hot soup together with other ingredients.

41. In the *Precious Treasures* this paragraph is part of the preceding one.

42. Ginger in Edo times, like today, was used as a spice or served as a side dish (cut into thin short strips).

43. The use of wasabi has a long tradition in Japanese food culture, and like ginger, is served either in ground or hashed form.

44. Originally indigenous to South America, red peppers were introduced to Japan during the sixteenth century by the Portuguese.

45. In Japan, chestnuts have a long history. Roasted they were eaten as a dessert at the end of a meal.

46. "Baked potatoes," too, count among the desserts. For this purpose, the "sweet potato" (*Satsuma imo*) was used, a South American plant that entered Japan at the beginning of the seventeenth century via the Ryūkyū Islands.

47. Makuwa is a locality in modern Gifu prefecture famous for its melons (*Cucumis melo L.* var. *makuwa Makino*), which became ripe at the beginning of summer. Known as one of the oldest areas for melon cultivation (*uri* reached Japan from China and are mentioned as early as in the eighth-century *Collection of Ten Thousand Leaves, Manyō shū*), "Makuwa melon" became a synonym for melon in general so that other kinds of melon, too, were called by that name, as Ise Sadatake explains (Ise 1985, 154). Melons could be part of a formal meal as dessert.

48. The tea mentioned in the text would have been "pulverized tea" (*matcha*) as used in a formalized tea gathering, prepared by pouring hot water on ground leaves of high quality and stirring with a bamboo whisk until the tea gets foamy. "Parched tea" (*sencha*), made by sterilizing tea leaves with steam and prepared by letting the dried leaves soak in hot water (the most commonly practiced method for preparing tea in everyday life in modern Japan) had just emerged in the second half of the seventeenth century after introduction from China by Chinese monks of the Ōbaku Zen school, and took time to assert its place in the culture of tea drinking.

49. In *Precious Treasures*, this paragraph does not appear in the chapter on eating; it can be found independently as the preceding chapter. Although the text only speaks of "wine cup," it is clear that a drinking event is meant. Rice wine had its place in the opening ceremony of a formal meal, when three courses of simple dishes were served with three cups of wine each (*shiki san kon* or "ceremony of three courses") before the main eating table; see Eric Rath's chapter in this book. Considering that ordinarily one took care to prevent any contact between one's mouth and food or vessels shared by all, this was a strong gesture to strengthen the bonds between those sharing a cup of wine (like in tea drinking).

50. One should not sit in the formal sitting (kneeling) position with one's bottom resting on the heels, but slightly aslant, with the bottom touching the ground.

51. *Itadaku* conveys the idea of raising something that one has received above eye-level in order to express gratitude and respect.

52. *Sakana* is a side dish to go with rice wine. The word consists of the component *saka* standing for rice wine (sake) and *na*, which could mean food served as

side dishes (in modern usage, *na* denotes vegetables, but the word had broader connotations in the past with *mana* or "true side dish" referring to fish). Different kinds (fish, vegetables, fruits, even sweets) went together with different sorts of rice wine and were chosen to accentuate the flavor of the wine they accompanied.

53. That "delicacies" should be received directly with the open hand has a long tradition. See n. 35. Adachi Isamu points out that it had become customary in Nara and Heian times to eat "delicacies" that one had received from high-ranking persons with one's hands (Adachi 1950, vol. 1, 76).

54. Muromachi etiquette literature states that "delicacies" were not eaten on the spot but—as a gift from a higher-ranking person—taken home.

55. *Jōchū* does not denote a maid as in modern Japanese but has to be read as an honorific term for a married woman.

56. In this context, *hasamu* (literally "to hold something between something" or "to squeeze something into something") means to hold food between chopsticks.

57. This kind of meal follows the outline of a "formal meal" as detailed in Eric C. Rath's contribution to this volume, chapter 1.

58. For "thresholds of shame and repugnance," see Elias (1977).

59. Edo-period etiquette rules rarely hint at the sphere of their applicability. The reference to an "unfamiliar place" in sentence 44 may be seen as an indication that these rules were to be observed away from home on formal occasions but did not concern eating daily meals at home. The only example, to my knowledge, suggesting that rules for eating should be followed regardless of context can be found in the *Precious Fabric of the Mirror for Wisdom to Be Used by Women* (*Joyō chie kagami takaraori*, 1769). "During the meals in the mornings and evenings [= the whole day] one should behave properly and eat in such a way that one does not soil the circumference of the eating table. If on a formal occasion suddenly one intends to behave properly and act politely, on the contrary one's heart [attitude] will turn stiff and mistakes will occur" (Ishikawa 1992–94, vol. 94). Etiquette rules, the text seems to say, should be part of day-to-day life so that one has mastered (or internalized) them to such a degree that one can apply them naturally without a second thought when it is called for during, for example, a formal meal.

60. Values are conscious or unconscious basic conceptions of the desirable that influence the aims and ways of behavior and as central elements of culture serve human beings as standards of orientation. Etiquette rules reflect these cultural orientations. I therefore propose to classify these rules into technical prescriptions and those concerning interaction and the reflection of social rank and the forms of respect this entails. The strictly technical rules, too, are to be seen in the context of cultural value orientations as expressed in the form of prohibitions or as expressions of shame and repugnance. Therefore, I call these "value-laden," in contrast to neutral rules that express no such sentiments and that appear as "value-free" in the following. These divisions follow the differences between the respective targets of etiquette rules and make their role as mediators between a number of factors more conspicuous: they concern the relationship of the eating

person involved to "himself" (his urges, feelings, mental disposition), to his body (upon which he or she works consciously as something seen as separate from "oneself"), and to other people included in the interaction, as well as the utensils needed to perform an act.

61. Rules falling under the categories "respect" and "consideration" can be found in Ekiken's *Secrets of the Rites for Eating*. It is an expression of respect when sentence 26 calls for the following: "In front of a noble person one should take the wine cup with the right hand and drink with [also] the left hand supporting it." Among people of the same rank it is only the left hand that holds the wine cup (SK 309). Consideration for others can be noticed when rule 22 urges to leave nothing of "rice" and "soup" as a means to let the host know that his efforts were appreciated or when in rule 17 it says that one should not let the servants wait who want to refill one's soup bowl (SK 308).

62. SK 306–7.

63. Explicit words can, for example, be found in sentences 10 and 57: "it is not allowed" (*shikaru bekarazu*) and "it should not happen" (*aru bekarazu*). In sentence 12 it says "wrong" (*ashiki*). In all other cases, the feeling of shame/repugnance can be deduced from the contents in question.

64. The text does not include any paragraphs on behavior that embarrass the observer through visual impressions. An example from another document is the cleaning of the teeth in front of others (see, for example, SK 311).

65. Cf. n. 25. Yoshikawa (1995, 220–21) counts a total of twenty-four chopstick-related taboos.

66. Ekiken had written that only the upper side of a grilled fish should be eaten and the fish turned upside down thereafter (see n. 27). One can only speculate whether the *Precious Treasures* and its followers considered this handling of the fish unaesthetic, whereas for Ekiken the fish bones were visually objectionable, or if perhaps his case provides a glimpse of an older notion according to which it is embarrassing to harm the integrity of a living being and to allow the eater an unvarnished view on the source of his food. Perhaps respect for the other members of nature can be recognized here that Lévy-Strauss had emphasized as the foundation of etiquette rules among "primitive" people (Lévy-Strauss 1968, 420–22).

67. In fact, other compilations mention just such a behavior. The *Chanoyu kondate shinan*, for example, says that it causes embarrassment to see others cram their mouth full (Kokuhon Edo jidai ryōribon shūsei 3, 29).

68. Lévi-Strauss (1968, 420–22).

69. Elaborate discourses on food and its ingestion as they developed in Western Europe are an eloquent witness to this observation; see Kleinspehn (1987, 111–32); Muchembled (1988).

Primary Sources

Ekiken Kaibana, ed. 1910/1973. *Ekiken zenshū*, 8 vols. Vol. 1: "*Sanrei kuketsu;*" "*Shorei kuketsu;*" "*Shokurei kuketsu;*" "*Charei kuketsu.*" Tokyo: Ekiken Zenshū Kankō Bu.

Hanwa Hokinoichi and Ōta Tōshirō, eds. 1957–59. *Zoku Gunsho ruijū* (ZGR. Vol. 24.2: *Ise Rokurō Zaemon no Jō Sadanori ki.* Tokyo: Zoku Gunsho Ruijū Kansei Kai.

Ise Sadatake. 1985. *Teijō zakki.* Ed. Shimada Isao. Vol. 2. Tokyo: Heibonsha (Tōyō bunko 446).

Ishikawa Matsutarō, ed. 1992–94. *Ōrai mono taikei*, 100 vols. Vol. 90: *Onna chūkyō misao bunko*, 1801. Vol. 94: *Joyō chie kagami takaraori*, 1769. Tokyo: Ōzorasha.

Kinsei Bungaku Shoshi Kenkyūkai, ed. 1981. *Kinsei bungaku shiryō ruijū.* Sankō bunken he . Vol. 18: *Onna chōhō ki.* Tokyo: Benseisha.

Kokuhon Edo jidai ryōribon shūsei (ERS). 1978–81. Ed. Yoshii Motoko, 11 vols. Vol. 3: *Chanoyu kondate shinan.* Kyoto: Rinsen Shoten.

Tanigawa Kenichi, ed. 1982. *Nihon shomin seikatsu shiryō shūsei*, 30 vols. Vol. 30: *Jinrin kunmō zui.* Tokyo: Sanichi Shobō.

Reference Works

Adachi Isamu. 1950. *Kaitei Nihon shokumotsu.* Rev. ed., 2 vols. Tokyo: Yūhikaku.

Bourdieu, Pierre. 1979. *La distinction. Critique sociale du jugement.* Paris: Les éditions de minuit.

Chibbett, David. 1977. *The History of Japanese Printing and Book Illustration.* Tokyo: Kodansha International.

Elias, Norbert. 1977. *Über den Prozeß der Zivilisation. Soziogenetische und psychogenetische Untersuchungen.* Frankfurt: Suhrkamp.

Harada Nobuo. 1989. *Edo no ryōrishi.* Tokyo: Chūō Kōronsha.

Hobbes, Thomas. 1968. *Leviathan.* Ed. C. B. Mcpherson. Harmondsworth: Penguin Books.

Kinski, Michael. 1998. "Eßregeln für Frauen in der japanischen Hausenzyklopädie Onna chōhō ki (1692). Einleitung, Transkription, Übersetzung und Analyse." In *Japonica Humboldtiana: Yearbook of the Mori Ôgai Memorial Hall, Berlin Humboldt University.* Vol. 2, 59–101. Wiesbaden, Germany: Harrassowitz Verlag.

———. 1999. "Bratfisch und Vogelbeine. Frühmoderne Etikettevorschriften zum Verhältnis von Mensch, Tier und Nahrung in Japan." In *Japonica Humboldtiana: Yearbook of the Mori Ôgai Memorial Hall, Berlin Humboldt University.* Vol. 3, 74–75. Wiesbaden, Germany: Harrassowitz Verlag.

———. 2001. "Basic Japanese etiquette rules and their popularization: Four Edo-period texts, transcribed, translated, and annotated." In *Japonica Humboldtiana:*

Yearbook of the Mori Ōgai Memorial Hall, Berlin Humboldt University. Vol. 5, 59–101. Wiesbaden, Germany: Harrassowitz Verlag.

———. 2002. "Rei wa inshoku ni hajimaru. Kinsei Nihon no sahō shū o megutte." *Zinbun gakuhō* 86, 97–142. Kyoto: Kyōto Daigaku Jinbun Kagaku Kenkyū Sho.

———. 2003. "Admonitions regarding food consumption: Takai Ranzan's practical guidebook, Shokuji kai transcribed, translated and annotated, with an introduction." In *Japonica Humboldtiana: Yearbook of the Mori Ōgai Memorial Hall, Berlin Humboldt University.* Vol. 7, 123–78. Wiesbaden, Germany: Harrassowitz Verlag.

———. 2005. "'Kuchioto takaranu kuu beshi.' Reigi sahō no fuhen sei to Edo ki reihō shū ni okeru tokushu sei." *Kokubungaku kaishaku to kanshō* 891:211–22.

Kleinspehn, Thomas. 1987. *Warum sind wir so unersättlich? Über den Bedeutungswandel des Essens.* Frankfurt: Suhrkamp.

Konta Yōzō. 1977. *Edo no honyasan.* Tokyo: Nihon Hōsō Shuppan Kyōkai.

Kornicki, Peter. 2001. *The Book in Japan: A Cultural History from the Beginnings to the Nineteenth Century.* Honolulu: University of Hawai'i Press.

Kracht, Klaus. 1998. "Anstand und Etikette in Japan. Ein Forschungsgebiet. Erster Teil." In *Japonica Humboldtiana: Yearbook of the Mori Ōgai Memorial Hall, Berlin Humboldt University.* Vol. 2, 59–101. Wiesbaden, Germany: Harrassowitz Verlag.

Lévy-Strauss, Claude. 1968. *L'origine des manières de table.* Paris: Librairie Plon.

Matsumura Kōji. 1997. "Yōjō ron teki na shintai e no mannā zasshi." In *Edo no shisō.* Vol. 6, 96–117. Tokyo: Perikansha.

May, Ekkehard. 1983. *Die Kommerzialisierung der japanischen Literatur in der späten Edo-Zeit (1750–1868). Rahmenbedingungen und Entwicklungstendenzen der erzählenden Prosa im Zeitalter ihrer ersten Vermarktung.* Wiesbaden: Harrassowitz.

Muchembled, Robert. 1988. *L'invention de l'homme moderne. Sensibilités, mœurs et comportements collectifs sous l'Ancien Régime.* Paris: Fayard.

Nagatomo Chiyoji. 2001. *Edo jidai no shomotsu to dokusho.* Tokyo: Tōkyōdō Shuppan.

Simmel, Georg. 1957. "Soziologie der Mahlzeit." In *Brücke und Tür. Essays des Philosophen zur Geschichte, Religion, Kunst und Gesellschaft.* Ed. Michael Landmann, 243–50. Stuttgart: K. F. Koehler.

Yokota Fuyuhiko. 1995. "Ekiken bon no dokusha." In *Kaibara Ekiken: Tenchi waraku no bunmei gaku.* Ed. Yokoyama Toshio, 315–53. Tokyo: Heibonsha.

———. 1996. "Kinsei minshū shakai ni okeru chiteki dokusho no seiritsu. Ekiken hon o yomu jidai." In *Edo no shisō: Dokusho no shakai shi.* Vol. 5, 48–67. Tokyo: Perikansha.

———. 2002. *Tenka taihei.* Vol. 16 of *Nihon no rekishi.* Tokyo: Kōdansha.

Yokoyama Toshio. 1984. "The Setsuyōshū and Japanese Civilization." In *Japanese Civilization in the Modern World: Life and Society.* Ed. Tadao Umesao et al., 17–36. Osaka: National Museum of Ethnology.

———. 1988. "Setsuyōshū and Japanese civilization." In *Themes and Theories in Modern Japanese History: Essays in Memory of Richard Storry.* Ed. Sue Henny and Jean-Pierre Lehmann, 78–98. London: Athlone Press.

———. 1989. "Some notes on the history of Japanese traditional household encyclopedias." *Japan Forum* 1, no. 2:243–55.

———. 1998. "In quest of civility: Conspicuous uses of household encyclopedias in nineteenth-century Japan." *Zinbun* 34:197–222.

Yokoyama Toshio, Kojima Mitsuhiro, and Sugita Shigeharu. 1999. *Nichiyō hyakka gata setsuyō shū no tsukawarekata. Ji koguchi shutaku sō no densan gazō shori ni yoru shiyō ruikei sekishutsu no kokoromi.* Kyoto: Institute for Research in Humanities, Kyoto University.

Yoshikawa Seiji, ed. 1995. *Shoku bunka ron.* Tokyo: Kenpakusha.

3 Stones for the Belly
Kaiseki Cuisine for Tea during the Early Edo Period

GARY SŌKA CADWALLADER
AND JOSEPH R. JUSTICE

KAISEKI, A BRIEF DEFINITION

TODAY, THERE ARE TWO WORDS, both pronounced *kaiseki*, that refer to either (1) the meals served during tea functions, or (2) the multicourse meals at Japan's traditional restaurants that originated as a more elaborate form of meal for the warrior elite. These two forms of *kaiseki* are distinguished by many factors but first by the use of different Japanese characters. As the title of this article indicates, tea cuisine today is usually written as "bosom stone" (懐石), or a "stone for the belly" that Zen monks slipped into their robes to warm their stomachs and stop the feeling of hunger while meditating (Anderson 1991, 165–66). This way of writing *kaiseki* and the cuisine it references evokes a Zen aesthetic manifest in a meal said to emulate a monk's fare of "one soup and three side dishes" (*ichijū sansai*) to accompany rice, the basic foodstuff of Japanese cuisine.

The way of writing *kaiseki* as belly stone debuted in the last decades of the seventeenth century, in the lifetime of tea master Sen Sensō, the focus of the first part of this article, although there is no evidence to show that he knew the term. Sensō was a major figure in the revival of the tea style of his great grandfather Sen Rikyū. This style, called *wabicha*, favored the simpler, more spiritually oriented way of tea. Sensō's menus not only reveal a debt to Rikyū's style of tea, but Sensō also consciously evoked Rikyū with food, laying the groundwork to establish both Rikyū and his style of *kaiseki* as the dominant forms of tea cuisine today.

The original way of writing about this meal, *kaiseki* (会席), is actually much older, and it emphasizes the notion of conviviality: literally, enjoying "food" for a "meeting" while "seated" together. In the fourteenth through sixteenth centuries, domainal lords, rich merchants, and aristocrats served tea and food, in many courses and on several trays, in luxurious settings called *kaisho* (会所, such as the Golden and Silver Pavilions) to accompany many days of hospitality for many guests—drinking sake, amusements of all kinds, and gambling. Regional lords (*daimyō*) continued this style of serving several trays of many soups and side dishes as their style of both public and private eating (Ego 2002, 148–51) until the Meiji Restoration in 1868. Modern restaurant *kaiseki* maintains this tradition on a slightly less lavish but more decorative scale.

KAISEKI, A RITUAL FEAST

Eating and drinking, two essentials in life, also provoke a need for specialized or ritual conduct, as Michael Kinski has noted in chapter 2 of this book. Within the framework of the discipline of *chanoyu*, the drinking of green, powdered tea and the sharing of a meal are rituals created from the everyday essential needs of living. These rituals set the stage for *communitas*, which anthropologist Victor Turner defines as relationships among people, "jointly undergoing ritual transition" through which they experience an intense sense of intimacy and equality. People from all levels of society and walks of life may form strong bonds, free of the structures that normally separate them. Not only can a state of liminality (being on or over a threshold) free one from the confines of one's designated role, it can also contain the seeds of the future. In the process of liminality, the pilgrims progressively achieve a release from conformity to general norms and may experience a profound and collective sentiment for humanity that includes or is stimulated by the quest for and presence of a sacred space, god, and spirit (Turner 1974, 166–230).

Indeed, this kind of communication is one of the goals of *wabicha*. *Wabi* is not an easily defined term but may be thought of as combining a number of seemingly contradicting but mutually enhancing features. Asymmetry but balance, naturalness with sophistication, relaxation within dynamic tension, rusticity with depth—all these elements contribute to an overarching system that tries to put the phrase "tea and meditation share one flavor" (*cha zen ichimi*) into some cogent form. *Wabicha* was not the first impulse of the men who drank tea in its early days in Japan but an aesthetic developed over the first three hundred years that powdered green tea was consumed, as an antithesis to the early warriors' devotion to the use of beautiful, valuable Chinese antiques for tea drinking. *Wabicha* first sprang up among the Zen-inspired merchants of Sakai, Nara, and Kyoto, who forsook the pursuit of "exotic" and foreign beauty for the use of the more rustic and humble but equally sophisticated naïve arts and crafts of Korea, Southeast Asia, and Japan. Sen Rikyū (1522–91), in his position as tea master for the hegemon Toyotomi Hideyoshi (d. 1598), introduced his ideas of *wabicha* to the parts of Japan under Hideyoshi's sway. But with Rikyū's death, Hideyoshi fostered a division from *wabicha* and the creation of warlord tea (*daimyō cha*) as described below, and a cool war between *wabi* merchants and *daimyō* tea masters took place along severely restricted class lines.

KAISEKI, A FAMILY TRADITION

Historically, the heads of families (*iemoto*) teaching the way of tea determine the rules for *kaiseki* that accompanies their style of *chanoyu*. Rikyū's *wabicha* ideal for *kaiseki* was just enough to prepare the guests' stomachs and souls for the rather strong effect of the shared thick tea (*koicha*) and was not a place to show off wealth and power. His *wabicha* incorporated the Zen element of minimalist frugality and simplicity in his prescription of "one soup, three side dishes" (*ichijū sansai*). *Daimyō*, however, had social expectations they could not ignore, especially when entertaining. As hereditary governors of large tracts of farm, forest, field, and coast and the people who farmed, hunted, gathered, and fished them, *daimyō* had access to the entire bounty of their domain and were expected to exemplify the enjoyment of that bounty.

This chapter examines *kaiseki* in the records of the youngest of the three brothers in the fourth generation of the Sen family of grandmasters, Sen Sensō Sōshitsu (1622–97), founder of the Urasenke lineage and one of *wabicha*'s chief proponents. His style of *kaiseki* becomes apparent in comparison with the *kaiseki* of selected *daimyō* tea masters, also founders of lineages that continue today. These examples illuminate the early modern history of *cha kaiseki* and reveal its diversity. Furthermore, these menus exhibit the different functions and strengths of *wabi* and *daimyō* teas. The conscious simplicity of *wabi* tea brought attention to the use of certain foods to evoke abstract concepts, and it demonstrated the mastery of the practitioners of this form of tea to use food in this way. Conversely, the luxurious nature of *daimyō* tea provided a way for its select adherents to demonstrate their wealth and privilege.

SENSŌ'S RECORDS

Three major "records of tea functions" (*cha kaiki*) hosted by Sensō hold much information about *chanoyu*, the society in which he lived, and the *kaiseki* of a leading tea master. Sensō founded Urasenke, and his two older brothers founded Omotesenke and Mushanokōjisenke. These three *wabicha* lineages descended from the legendary Sen Rikyū, through their father, Sōtan.

The records examined in this chapter contain a majority of Sensō's known tea gatherings. *The Life of Rōgetsuan, Layman Sen Sensō Sōshitsu (Rōgetsuan Sen Sensō Sōshitsu Koji no shōgai)* (Tsutsui 1996, 90–93) contains the diary of a prosperous merchant from Kanazawa (modern Ishikawa prefecture), Asanoya Jirobei Jōzen (1654–1731). He was probably Sensō's top disciple in Kanazawa. It records ten functions hosted by Sensō that Asanoya attended. *Sensō's Records (Sensō Sōshitsu kaitsuke)* (Yokota 1996, 134–70), details 134 tea functions: 67 morning, 65 noon, 1 evening, and 1 dawn, thought to cover the tenth month of 1681 to the third month of 1688. The third source is a manuscript containing both the *Memorandum for Tea in the Brazier Season (Furo no chanoyu oboe)*, consisting of some 23 records of tea functions held in the summer and fall seasons, and *Memorandum for a Guest Living in Kanazawa, Ishikawa, on Opening of the Tea Jar (Kashū Kanazawa jūko kuchikiri kyaku no oboe)*, with 24 records of teas held in the winter and spring seasons, which is currently owned by Ōhi Chōzaemon XI of Kanazawa (Uejo 1996a, 175–81; 1996b, 182–89).[1]

SENSŌ'S *KAISEKI*

In this section we examine samples of Sensō's menus from each of these sources. We pay particular attention to the metalanguage of the food, that is to say, the various triggers that Sensō hid in the menu that evoked seasonal, topical, or other responses in his guests. There are two ways that Sensō used food to evoke abstract ideas. First, he relied on seasonally appropriate food that incorporated wordplay referencing auspicious symbols and ideas. Second, as Sensō was the last of the Sen family's direct male heirs (his nephews were all born of Sen family mothers and adopted sons-in-law), he utilized utensils and foods to reference his lineal connection to Rikyū, second generation Shōan (1546–1614) and third generation Sōtan (1578–1658), the three preceding generations of the Sen family. Of the descendants of these masters, Sensō was the last and closest to Rikyū. In 1690, as the Sen family's elder, he dedicated the Rikyūdō, a memorial hall to Rikyū, finished to commemorate the 100th anniversary of his death.

The records examined here were not particularly instructive as to how the various foods were served. There was no great consistency in the order foods appeared. Sometimes a "course," or a specific type of food, would be named such as "rice" or "soup" or "things brought out" (*hikide*), but most often only the name of the dish would be recorded, such as "citron [*yuzu*] miso." Modern *cha kaiseki* is made up of fifteen of these "courses," always with a specific mode of preparation (e.g., raw, grilled, fermented) and always in the same order (from the lightest flavors to the strongest). In an effort to make these clear, when a specific dish is listed, it will be called a "course" followed by more specific terms in Japanese. Mention of utensils provided by the record, although few, will appear in the text as well.

In the first menu examined, Sensō established a personal connection with Rikyū. He employed not only one of the first Sen family's namesake tea rooms, Fushin'an (built in Rikyū's style by Shōan [then redesigned by Sōtan] when the Sen family was allowed to return to Kyoto after exile) but also some of his great grandfather's utensils, as well as one of his signature foods, citron (*yuzu*) miso. This dish is a citron, hollowed and filled with various things but mainly sweet, white miso.

1688, 9TH MONTH, 25TH DAY, NOON (SEN SŌSHITSU 1996, 90)
Guests: Asano Jirobei; other guests not listed. Held at Fushin'an
   Pickle Course (*kō no mono*)
   Grilled Course (*yakimono*)[2]
      Grilled dried sea bream
         Hagi ware[3] plate
   Miso Soup Course (*shiru*)
      Vegetables
         Both rice and soup bowls have a design of stylized cherry leaves
            and flowers in cinnabar on a black ground (Rikyū's *Yoshino wan*)[4]
   Citron miso
   Rice Course (*meshi*)
   Raw Fish Course (sashimi)[5]
      Harvest fish (*managatsuo*)
      Octopus
      Ginger vinegar sauce
         Raku plate, diamond shaped
   Thin Soup Course (*suimono*)
      Spiny lobster (*ise ebi*)
   Course of delicacies to eat with sake (*sakana*)
      Nothing specified
   Sweet Course (*kashi*)[6]
      Chestnut rice cake
      Dried gourd

This tea function (*chaji*) was a *kuchikiri*, a celebration of the opening of the tea-leaf jar with the tea master's new, one-year's supply of semiprocessed tea leaves. This is an auspicious occasion, comparable to the New Year, so passing reference to several foods of the New Year—namely the spiny lobster, dried sea bream, and rice cake—was enough to give the meal a holiday festivity.

The next two *chaji* both took place the day after *rōhatsu*, the day the historical Buddha achieved final enlightenment under the *Bodhi* tree. (Zen monks commemorate the eight-day period before this date with a meditation retreat.) The menu features daikon and there are several daikon radish–centered festivals held in Kyoto on this day, for example, at Senbon Shakadō and Kyōkokuji temples, where great caldrons of daikon simmered with tofu soup are distributed to many believers.

12TH MONTH, 9TH DAY, MORNING (SEN 1996, 139)
Guests: two abbots from Myōganji[7]
  Miso Soup Course
    Daikon
    Tofu
  Simmered Course[8] (nimono)
    Burdock
    Lotus root
  Rice Course
  Separately Served Course[9]
    Deep-fried wheat gluten
    Mustard vinegar
  Thin Soup Course[10]
    Kudzu starch-thickened broth
    Leafy vegetable
  Sweet Course[11]
    Adzuki bean soup with rice cake (*zenzai*)
    Salty accompaniment

SAME DAY (12TH MONTH, 9TH DAY), NOON (SEN 1996, 140)[12]
Three guests
  Miso Soup Course
    Tofu
    Leafy vegetable

  "Winter's evening tofu" (*tōyadōfu*)

  Rice Course
  Grilled Course
    Salted salmon

Thin Soup Course
 Same as previous (kudzu thickened broth, leafy vegetable)
Sweet Course
 Rice "brittle"[13]
 Carrot accompaniment

The next tea function took place in Kanazawa, a castle town built around the Maeda castle, dwelling of Sensō's employer; and the tea function, though simple, reflected the status of the guests. Three of the guests for this tea function were officials of the domain, and one, Honda Masanaga, was a high vassal holding the rank of "house elder" (*karō*) (Sen Sōshitsu 2008, 114). Sensō's use of a "later stage" (*godan*), a separate meal later in the tea function, was a holdover from the earliest days of banqueting and tea drinking, while the presence of two helpers was probably in deference to these high-ranking guests.

YEAR OF THE OX, 5TH MONTH, 17TH DAY, NOON (1661)
(SEN SŌSHITSU 1996, 175–76)
In Kanazawa: four guests and two "host's helpers"[14]
 Pickle Course
  Two types
   (on a) leaf
 Miso Soup Course
  Yam root
  Cold pepper; ground
 Namasu Course "Over There"[15] (*namasu mukō*)
  All kinds of things fixed different ways
   Red ark shell
   Sea bream
   Daikon
   Perilla leaf
   Sauce
 Served Separately: the Grilled Course
  Lightly salted sea bream
 Thin Soup Course
  Abalone
  Suizenji nori[16]
 Sweet Course
  Kudzu ball
  Crisped laver
 Later Stage Meal (*godan*)

Mixed Course
  Tofu
  Rice cake
  Kudzu-thickened miso
Hempseed candy[17]
Sugared soybeans
Sugar candies (*konpeitō*)

The feeling of celebration is emphasized by the use of red and white combinations of foods, as in the *namasu mukō* course. Although the use of a *godan* gives an old-fashioned feeling to this tea function, nothing in the tea utensils supports the need for one, so it must have been in deference to the main guest, a house elder of the Maeda domain (and no doubt a practitioner of *daimyō cha*). Earlier tea functions that included *godan* were divided into several parts. The first two consisted of *kaiseki* and thick tea, in a four and a half mat-sized room, using utensils ranked as objects of fame (*meibutsu*) placed on a large, black lacquered stand (*daisu*). The third part, the *godan* featuring the thin tea and objects of less fame, was held in another, larger room with a lighter feeling. A second course of food was served with abundant sake at this time, far from the proximity of the famous objects. In the *wabi* lineages, it was considered inappropriate for tea functions to have a later stage and so was the use of famous objects and Chinese utensils in general.

In another example of a menu from Kanazawa for warrior and merchant guests, Sensō created a less conservative *kaiseki* but one that still used felicitous elements apparent in the colors and variety of foods chosen.

10TH MONTH, 17TH DAY, NOON (NO YEAR GIVEN)
(SEN SŌSHITSU 1996, 182)
Three guests, one of whom was again Honda Masanaga, the Maeda
    house elder, and two "helpers"
Miso Soup Course
  Tofu
  Vegetables
  Fish roe
Pickle Course
Citron Miso
  Lotus leaf plate of Kyoto ware with a cinnabar flat bowl (*hirawan*)
    over it[18]
Rice Course
Course Served Separately

A large layered box brought out[19]
Grilled on Cedar Planks
    Sea bream
    Oysters
    Chestnuts
    Green onions
Sweet Course
    Grilled rice cake
    Cold pepper miso, sugar
    Fermented soybeans
Later Course (*go*)[20]
    Persimmon
    Kelp (*kobu*) roll

Part of the auspicious message of this meal is signaled by the colors balanced against one another and by clever wordplay. The miso soup course here has three things—there are usually only two—in it, one being bright red salmon eggs. Rikyū's signature citron miso is served on a lotus-leaf dish from Kyoto and creatively covered by another bowl, turned upside down. The cedar-plank-grilled sea bream, oysters, chestnuts, and green onions must have been a visual as well as a taste delight. The sweet rice cake (*mochi*) with sugared Japanese pepper (*sanshō*) miso must also have been a tasty treat, complimented by the very strongly flavored fermented soybeans (imagine balls of black salty miso). Sensō also employed minimum wordplay for felicitous effect; for example, the word for kelp is *kobu*, part of the word *yorokobu*, meaning to be joyous.

DAIMYŌ MENUS

In contrast to Sensō's *wabicha*, *daimyō* tea is grander in the amount of food and splendor of utensils but less likely to give rise to feelings of communion among the participants because it highlights differences in status. In this section, we examine representative menus by the most important practitioners of *daimyō* tea as a prelude to a comparison between this tea style and that of Sensō's *wabi* style.

Characteristics of *daimyō* tea evident in the following menus include colorful and valuable utensils, multiple courses of foods, and dishes featuring game fowl that appealed to warrior sensibilities. Customs and warrior prowess with weapons and the pastime of hunting provided them with meat difficult for urban commoners to obtain.

The first proponent of *daimyō* tea was Furuta Oribe (1543–1615), appointed to create it by Hideyoshi himself after Rikyū's death. The following is an example from 1594 of Oribe's *kaiseki* for the wealthy merchant and tea practitioner Kamiya Sōtan (1551–1635).[21] This early example of the post-Rikyū *daimyō* style of edible entertainment (Tsutsui 2002, 171–72) is designed to impress.[22] On the first tray alone there is one soup and three side dishes (*ichijū sansai*) to accompany the rice. While this would be enough food to qualify for a *wabicha kaiseki* in the Sen family tradition, Oribe's menu continued. The second tray had a large platter of tofu, more than one guest could need or want, followed by a third tray with just something to nibble with sake. No second soup or sweet course was listed, and the record ended with pickles.

FIRST TRAY
Miso Soup Course
    Vegetables
Harmonizing Course (*aemono*)[23]
    Not specified
Grilled Course
    Salmon
Rice Course
Sushi
    Fermented crucian carp[24]

SECOND TRAY
    On a large platter
        Tofu in miso with bonito shavings

THIRD TRAY
    Steamed fish cake
    Pickle Course[25]

KOBORI ENSHŪ (1579–1647)

The third shogun, Tokugawa Iemitsu (1604–51), appointed Kobori Enshū, a student of Oribe, as his tea master. Enshū was active in differentiating *daimyō* tea from Rikyū's *wabicha*. In the intimate, unlit rooms Rikyū favored, his dark and rustic utensils evoked a deep and spiritual atmosphere, but the large, bright rooms that Enshū preferred enhanced the utensils he commissioned— gorgeous blue-and-white cobalt underglazed porcelains from kilns in China and ceramics from the Korean kilns in Busan. Enshū also commissioned and fostered several Japanese kilns for the creation of ceramics to be used for his tea as well as presents for the shogun and other *daimyō*.[26] Enshū personally created a whole new order of utensils known as "revitalized objects-of-fame" (*chūko meibutsu*) for the newly created *daimyō* who had risen from lower ranks and did not have family heirlooms. Some of these utensils were Chinese things that had not found favor before, but the greatest number were thick tea containers (mostly made in Seto) ordered by Enshū, who gave them evocative names taken from ancient poetry collections.

On the first tray in the following menu, Enshū listed six, perhaps seven, courses and one course served separately. The second tray has three courses and two courses served separately. Finally, a sweet course appears consisting of a main sweet, a salty accompaniment, and an element unique to the Enshū lineage—raw peeled chestnuts—as a "poison antidote."

1646, 12TH MONTH, 22ND DAY, MORNING (TSUTSUI 2002, 176–77)
In the small drawing room (*zashiki*) in Enshū's Fushimi
    magistrate's estate
Guest: Matsuya Hisashige
Cedar trays with feet
Miso Soup Course
Fresh crane[27]
Fresh sea bass (*suzuki*)
Leafy vegetables
Flat Food Bowl[28]
Steamed bird
Lotus root
Yam
Neri miso[29]
Walnuts
Rice Course
Round cedar chopsticks[30]
Separately Served Course
Various pickles
Grilled shellfish
Dipper shell mollusk (*shakushigai*)
Raw shellfish
Dipper shell mollusk
Acorn[31]

Soup Course
    Tiny white fish[32]
    Rape flowers (in a clear soup) [33]

    Sea cucumber entrails (*konowata*)[34]
Course Served Separately
    White tofu
    Ground black sesame
    Bonito
Served Separately[35]
    Burdock—some were pounded, some were still round/whole[36]
        Soy sauce was sprinkled on it
Wooden Plank[37]
    Grilled bird on skewers[38]
    Salted salmon
Thin Soup Course
    Tuna stomach
Sweet Course
        Square cedar stacked trays[39]
    Cold glutinous rice jelly dumplings dusted with adzuki bean powder
    Daikon salt simmered
    Raw peeled chestnuts[40]
        Sweet pick of camphor wood[41]

This was not the end of hospitality. Enshū continued the feast in the evening on another tray with the pickles omitted previously, rice gruel with sugar, a sweet, two more soups, and yet another serving of rice.

Later that evening, in a large drawing room of the Fushimi estate:

Pickles
Sweet Course
    Rice brittle (*sakobei*)[42]
Rice gruel
    with white sugar sprinkled on
Miso Soup Course
    Yam
    Daikon radish
    Tofu
Thin Soup Course

Japanese honeysuckle leaves
Served Separately
  Shellfish
Rice also Served Separately

KATAGIRI SEKISHŪ (1605–73)

Katagiri Sekishū, lord of the domain of Izumi, inherited Enshū's mantle as a trusted official and tea teacher to the young fourth Tokugawa shogun, Ietsuna (1641–1680) and left us this luxurious and representative *daimyō kaiseki* menu for spring 1641 (Tsutsui 2002, 179–80).[43] Sekishū is considered the first *daimyō* to inject Rikyū's spirituality into his tea (Pitelka 2003, 139). Sekishū learned tea from a disciple of Rikyū's real son (but not spiritual heir) Dōan, so Sekishū felt he was carrying on Rikyū's authentic teachings.[44] That his *kaiseki* did not correspond with modern understandings of Rikyū's legacy does not seem to have crossed his mind.

MENU FOR SPRING 1641 (TSUTSUI 2002, 180)
Sekishū and one more person personally served the two guests.

MAIN TRAY WITHOUT FEET
  Cedar wood utensils: bowls with white lacquered design
    of chrysanthemums
  In a large cobalt underglazed platter[45]
    Japanese parsley (*chisa*)
    Wild endive
    Spinach
    Shiitake mushrooms
    Kelp
      Sauce of miso with vinegar or citrus
  Miso Soup Course
    Sea bass
    Tofu
    Chrysanthemum greens
  Rice Course
  Separately Served Course
    Various pickles

SECOND TRAY—CEDAR WITH FEET
  Small Dish

Horo miso (miso with ground sesame, hempseed, walnuts, and
   Japanese pepper for dipping) in a shallow lacquered bowl
Simmered Course
   Wild yam
   Arrowhead bulb (*kuwai*)
   Dried daikon
Cold soup
   All kinds of things done different ways
   Ginger
Layered box
   Simmered tofu
   Rape
   Slivered burdock harmonized with ground walnut
Split cedar plank
   Grilled tofu with miso topping (*dengaku*)
Thin Soup Course
   Oyster mushroom
   Yam
Course of Delicacies to eat with Sake
   Kumquat
   Bergamot orange (*kunenbo*) with sugar
Sweet Course in a Cedar Box
   Chestnuts
   White rice cake
   Boiled adzuki beans
   Simmered devil's tongue (*kon'yaku*)
Peeled, Raw Chestnut

MATSUDAIRA FUMAI (1751–1818)

Nearly 150 years later, one of the last great *daimyō* tea masters, Matsudaira Fumai, lord of Matsue in Izumo (modern Shimane prefecture), was a follower of the Sekishū's lineage but founded his own substyle. The following *chaji* took place in 1811 in the fifth month for three guests.[46] This meal is very similar in format to modern *wabi kaiseki*: a single tray with rice, miso soup, and raw fish. This was followed by a *wanmori*, which is the "main dish" of a *wabi kaiseki*, served separately. There was also a grilled course, and a *torizakana*, which are delicacies served individually to the guest with sake from a square wooden tray, followed by pickles and a sweet course. Much of the reasoning for so little and yet such simple food is indicative of the Sekishū style and is the same as that of present *wabicha kaiseki*, as the notes, which are part of the menu, explain (Satō, 2002, 267–78).

Rice Course[47]
Raw Fish Course
   "Washed" cod[48]
   Watershield buds (*junsai*)[49]
   Wasabi
   Sauce of denatured sake and soy sauce
     Chokushi, a small bowl, of red and gold over glazed porcelain
       with flying mandarin ducks

Miso Soup Course[50]
   Eggplant
   Mustard
Separately Served Course: the W*anmori* Course
   Salty broth
   Cod
   Snow peas julienne
   Citron flower
     Bowl with a flowering paulownia design[51]
Separately Served Course: the Grilled Course
   Salt-grilled horse mackerel (*sawara*)
   Smartweed vinegar[52]
     Chinese underglazed cobalt dish with spout and handle
Something Taken with Sake Course (*torizakana*)
   Pressed Japanese whiting (*kisu*)
   Chestnut
   Russian olive
     [no utensil listed]

Similar to the *hassun* course in modern *wabi kaiseki*, Fumai gives each guest a "bounty from the mountains and the sea" (also known as "something raw" and something vegetarian or "spiritually advancing," *shōjin*). But unlike the *wabi hassun* course, there is no exchange of sake between host and guests: the first guest serves the host sake as a gesture of appreciation. The exchange of sake known as "plover sake cups" (*chidori sakazuki*) is only thought appropriate between parents and children, brothers, and married couples (three of the five Confucian relationships) and was considered inappropriate between *daimyō* and merchant or monk.

Pickle Course
    Cucumber
        in a bowl decorated with clouds and cranes
Palate Cleanser Course[53]
    Soft adzuki jelly
    Mushroom
        Cinnabar lacquered, lobed tray
Side-sweets[54]
    "Wrung-out pinks"
    Pine wafers
        Chinese underglazed cobalt porcelain of superior manufacture
        (probably an Enshū import) three-legged dish

THE DIFFERENCES BETWEEN *WABI* AND *DAIMYŌ KAISEKI*

Judging from the previous menus, the *daimyō* in Rikyū's following did not retain an interest in *wabi kaiseki* with its emphasis on minimal frugality, simplicity, and *communitas*. The differences between *daimyō kaiseki* and *wabi kaiseki* consist of the names of the courses, the numbers of trays and courses, and, to a lesser extent, the ingredients and preparation methods used. The utensils differed to the same extent that the "cool war of taste" between the *daimyō* lineages and Rikyū's descendants led one side or the other to patronize and use only certain ceramics and types of lacquer both in their tea and in their *kaiseki*. For example, *daimyō* lineages preferred decorated lacquer sets of footed trays and multiple bowls, Chinese celadon, blue-and-white cobalt underglazed (*sometsuke*) and gold and red overglazed (*kinrande*) porcelains, and Korean custom-made stoneware and porcelains. They also favored the gorgeous overglazed stoneware of Nonomura Ninsei (active in the mid-seventeenth century) of Kyoto and the multicolor overglaze enameled porcelains of Kyūshū's Arita, Kutani, and Nabeshima porcelains, but eschewed the dark Raku wares beloved by Rikyū. Several *daimyō* even created and patronized kilns in their own castle grounds for the creation of their own tableware and as gifts to the shogun and other *daimyō*.

The *wabi* lineages preferred monochrome lacquers and now use highly decorated bowls only for the *wanmori* course, which—as the peak of *wabi kaiseki*—comprised the best ingredients cooked to perfection and "mounded in" (*mori*) a bowl (*wan*). They patronize the Ōhi and Raku families and the stoneware potteries of Hagi and Karatsu because of those kilns' *wabi* image (as carriers of the Korean tradition) and the Momoyama period (1571–1600) founding dates, which overlapped with Rikyū's lifetime. As well they used Seto, which included the Mino kilns that made Oribe's wares. Both *daimyō* and *wabi* masters used Bizen, Shigaraki, and Iga wares.[55]

Another difference was the temperature at which the food was served to the guests. A tray of four to seven items could not have been served very hot. In contrast, the present *wabi* style serves everything immediately as it is prepared, course by course, while still hot, ensuring courses are not made in advance and left aside. Hot food meant that the kitchen was close to the teahouse, which was a sign of humbleness, whereas if the food was cold, the food had much further to go, indicating a larger dwelling with the kitchen further away. Hot food was, for a long time, a sign of humbleness and poverty.

For *wabi* masters, *kaiseki* marked the beginning of the *communitas* or union of like spirits, which is the aim of every *wabi* tea function. The sharing of food and the ritual exchange of sake as a source of reinforcing a community was the basis for the ultimate mind-to-mind communication that was sought. The host, in the case of Sensō, was the last direct great-grandson of a famous nonwarrior, political figure, and creative designer, Rikyū, who personally served the Regent and Grand Minister of State Hideyoshi, crown princes, monks, warriors, merchants, and even commoners regardless of their ranks. *Kaiseki* was a convivial and unifying experience for different status groups, although status differences were paid tribute through the use of language and etiquette. Conversation may have revolved mostly around the utensils used but a few bits of gossip were no doubt shared as well. In any case, this intimate atmosphere of conviviality was deepened by the sharing of thick tea drunk in turns by all guests from a single bowl. Thus would the host create a moment of *communitas*. But while the experience lingered in the guests' hearts, the host would serve thin tea and begin to dismantle the communal feeling by providing individual service to the guests, giving each his own bowl of frothy, whipped tea.

Honzen ryōri, as discussed by Eric Rath in this volume (chapter 1), presents an elaboration of trays and side dishes that was also part of *daimyō* tea, but this very richness distracted from the creation of a *communitas*, a concept that was anathema to status-conscious *daimyō* (Satō 2002, 277). In that regard, it seems significant that the main dish of Sekishū's *kaiseki* was not eaten together at the same time as the others, as all dishes are in *wabi kaiseki*, but eaten as soon as it arrived in front of the guests, whose seating order would naturally have been arranged by rank. Awareness of the host's and guests' statuses was also evident in the language that was used and the etiquette required.

Although the accomplishment of tea was still a requirement of elegant living and social interaction throughout the Edo period, *daimyō* tea was only practiced among the few *daimyō* that existed and their families, a few of their closest retainers, and the richest merchants who circulated in those rarified circles.[56] As relations between the individual *daimyō* became more and more elaborate in terms of formality and circumscribed with precedence to prevent any plotting against the Edo government, *daimyō* tea, which had been created in the Momoyama period specifically for *daimyō* to entertain fellow warriors, began losing its vigor, and many *daimyō* left the practice of tea to their retainers until the reintroduction of spirituality to tea by Katagiri Sekishū.[57] The rank-and-file samurai, however, were not bound to *daimyō cha*, and since major *daimyō* like the Maeda family employed both *daimyō* tea experts and *wabi* tea masters, samurai living in proud semi-poverty and seeing that studying something inappropriate to their station could be construed as being improper, found the *wabi* style of tea more to their liking and ability. Who among them could have afforded the required utensils anyway?

In an interesting twist of fate, the fusion of *daimyō* cha and *wabicha* took place in Sensō's lineage just before the end of the Edo period when the heir who became the eleventh-generation Urasenke grand master, known as Gengensai Sōshitsu (1810–77), adopted from a *daimyō* family at nine years old, married a daughter of the tenth grand master. He not only kept up traditional Urasenke relations with the Maeda of Kanazawa and Hisamatsu of Matsuyama, but he also began teaching the Tokugawa lord of Owari, present-day Nagoya (Sen Sōshitsu 1998, 46–47). After the Meiji Restoration in 1868, he petitioned the emperor to prevent the Way of Tea from being labeled an "amusement."

With the Meiji Restoration, all the *daimyō* and samurai lost their status, incomes, and reason for being. However, their philosophy of *chanoyu* and *kaiseki*, which had been developing over the centuries, was not lost but has been actively integrated into the *wabicha* lineages as their own. Present-day *kaiseki* is a vigorous hybrid of merchant and *daimyō* sources, elaborated to what seems to be its maximum extent. New and previously unthinkable ingredients have been joyfully included, such as beef and cheese, and the courses, salads, and different wines to go with them have expanded consciousness while still retaining the basic function of *kaiseki*, which is to produce a coming together of minds in harmony.

Our only fear is that modern *kaiseki* will go beyond even the *daimyō's* luxurious elaboration of gorgeous utensils and use of foodstuff to a new level of tastelessness (artistically) and overconsumption—serving seven to eight different species of fish and shellfish is a bit over the top. When the food is more impressive and more memorable than the tea, something is wrong, and there is something amiss when the guests are groaning and put to sleep by too much food and sake. Having said that, nevertheless, we are confident that in the hands of internationally minded tea masters and the many non-Japanese tea masters who have been nourished over the past fifty years, a glorious future of tea *kaiseki*, taking its place among the great traditional cuisines of the world, may soon become a delicious reality.

NOTES

1. All these records appear in Sen Sōshitsu XV (Hounsai), ed., *Sensō Sōshitsu Koji no ihō, Sensō Sōshitsu Koji Sanbyaku nen ki* (Kyoto: Tankōsha, 1996).

2. The grilled and pickle courses still appear together in Omotesenke and Mushanokōjisenke lineage *kaiseki*.

3. Hagi ware (*Hagi yaki*) is a ceramic ware made in Yamaguchi prefecture, beginning in the sixteenth century by immigrant Korean potters. It is now ranked just after Raku and above Karatsu for tea bowls.

4. Both rice and soup bowls have Rikyū's design of stylized cherry leaves and flowers (*Yoshino wan*) and were served on a cinnabar lacquered tray. The tray in the Yoshino wan set is usually round, but on this occasion Sensō used another, pure red cinnabar lacquered square tray.

5. This dish cannot be considered *mukōzuke* (a utensil and course literally "over there," across the tray from the rice and soup bowls). Today, raw fish is used as the main ingredient for *mukōzuke* at noon tea functions, and the progression of flavors is from lightest (raw fish) to strongest (pickled vegetables), that is, from the freshest to the most preserved. The condiments used, however, range from the strongest, wasabi, to the weakest, hot water.

6. *Mochi* usually refers to sticky rice that has been pounded into a homogenous mass, a "rice cake," but it can also refer to other materials that have had the same treatment. The salty complement to this sweet was dried gourd shavings. The process of making it, called *nishime*, refers to simmering various vegetables and fungus in soy sauce, sake, and *mirin*.

7. This menu, for two abbots of a Nichiren Buddhist temple very near the Sen family's estates in Kyoto, is purely vegetarian.

8. Although both are roots, burdock (*gobō*) represents strength enough to literally "tie an ox to" and is dark and earthy flavored, while lotus root is white, grows underwater, and is a symbol of enlightenment in the physical body—the beautiful

lotus arising from the mud. Also, the holes that run all the way through it are said to reveal the future.

9. Deep-frying *fu*, a wheat gluten product, makes it crispy and puffed, but oily. A mustard vinegar sauce is a very sharp and piquant contrast. Mustard (*karashi*) and vinegar (*su*) are the archetypes of two of the five flavors.

10. Kudzu (*kuzu*) as a starch thickener also tends to hold in the heat and makes for a very warming soup in cold winter mornings in Kyoto.

11. The still very popular *zenzai* is a thick, hot soup of adzuki beans with one or two small rice cakes that are either grilled or boiled. It is one of the few sweets still served with a salty accompaniment, which was not recorded here, but typically these were foods like seaweed (*konbu*) stewed in soy sauce, small mushrooms, Japanese pepper, and dried gourd shavings.

12. Sensō, as did Rikyū before him, often hosted two groups a day for tea. The use of the same utensils and the everyday simplicity of the food made this possible for a single host.

13. One of the more frequently used of Sensō's sweets, *sakobei*, seems to be a kind of "brittle" or *okoshi* made with rice stuck together with malted syrup (*mizuame*), something like a cross between peanut brittle and a popcorn ball (Sue 1982, 715–16).

14. This is neither the first nor the last mention of "host-side staff." Whether they were guests (since they occur in the guest list) who helped the host serve, like the modern "last guest" (*tsume*) or were disciples is unknown. In another record, Sensō's Kanazawa kettle maker, Miyazaki Kanchi, appears as "kitchen-side" in one of the records. Even today at Urasenke, men who have been part of the Urasenke network for years, if not generations, such as utensil dealers, *kaiseki* chefs, and makers of favored utensils are on hand to help at large events.

15. Modern *namasu* ("folk" etymology *nama* = raw plus *su* = vinegar) usually incorporates red and white ingredients such as Japanese carrot or persimmon and daikon radish, served raw in vinegar sauce. *Namasu* is now served at New Years and at congratulatory occasions, such as when a guest attends a tea function for the first time. *Namasu* and sashimi probably combined to produce the *mukōzuke* course, which is often raw fish and complimentary vegetables served with a citrus/soy sauce. The nature of the sauce here is unknown but at least it was mentioned.

16. *Suizenji nori*, also known as congratulatory (*kotobuki*) nori, is a freshwater alga.

17. These candies are the sweets for thin tea served during the later stage meal. *Konpeitō*, now confined to *chabako* use, evolved from the sixteenth century Portuguese sugar confection, *confeitō*. Individually sugared soybeans and hempseed hard candy were also tiny. The liberal use of sugar is impressive for this period.

18. The flat, shallow bowl from the lacquered set is used like a lid on the *yuzu miso*.

19. One of the few "theatrical" dishes recorded by Sensō. The ingredients are placed often on a bed of miso or salt in a cedar box and grilled over a low fire (Sue 1982, 696).

20. Assuming this was a *godan* where thin tea was served in a separate room, these were the sweets. Typically, the tea plantation owner brings a present of fresh, ripe persimmons and fresh chestnuts when delivering the year's supply of tea. Kelp (*konbu*) is often rolled around traditionally sweetened fish like herring at New Years.

21. An important merchant tea master of Kyūshū, Kamiya Sōtan, was cultivated by Hideyoshi to help finance his invasion of Korea.

22. See Slusser (2003) for a more complex analysis of Hideyoshi's conundrum in being both the dominant figure in *wabicha* and the dominant hierarch in warrior society when he ordered Oribe to create a tea for warriors (55–57).

23. *Aemono*, "[a salad of] harmonized things," consists of two to five ingredients—vegetable, fish, or man-made, raw or cooked, dressed with tofu, sesame paste, mustard, vinegar, or a combination of the above.

24. Crucian carp (*funazushi*) stuffed with rice and fermented as something to eat with sake is still a popular delicacy from Lake Biwa.

25. In this menu, pickles come last. Neither the thin soup nor the sweet course is mentioned.

26. Especially well known are still popular kilns like Asahi in Uji, Takatori in Kyūshū, Zeze in Shiga near Lake Biwa, and Akahadayama near Nara. Besides "newer" kilns, Enshū encouraged older kilns to create utensils for him, especially in Seto, Shigaraki, Iga, Bizen, and Tamba. His other achievements include gardens and architectural masterpieces (for example, Kyoto's Sentō Goshō and Katsura Detached Palace, Konchi'in garden in Nanzenji, and Korakuen in Okayama). His political career included inheriting the family estate of Yamato Koriyama, and collecting among his appointments, magistrate of Kawachi and Fushimi, the river port for Kyoto, the heart of a network that ran from the Inland Sea and Osaka by way of the Yodo River to the north shore of Lake Biwa and the Japan Sea. He also oversaw all the construction of "official" buildings and gardens as magistrate of public buildings.

27. Game fowl were popular with warriors and aristocrats, since hunting had been a courtly avocation since the earliest times. The two groups were not as strong in their adoption of Buddhist vegetarian diets. For an overview of the consumption of meat, especially during the Edo period, see Akira Shimizu's treatment (chapter 4) in this volume.

28. The *hirawan* was one of the four bowls used on food trays (*zen*) and on early *kaiseki* trays; it later became the *nimono* course.

29. *Neri miso* has been cooked and blended with sake or *mirin* to make a creamy sauce.

30. In contrast, chopsticks favored by Rikyū (*Rikyū bashi*) have a rectangular cross-section.

31. Although not usual fare, there is a Japanese acorn, eaten for thousands of years that can be made edible by roasting.

32. There are two completely different species of tiny fish that swim upriver in spring, one called whitebait (*shira uo*) and the other, white goby (*shiro uo*). The record is not specific about which one it was.

33. This is clear evidence that the soup (*shiru*) could be either miso or clear (*sumashi*).

34. This is one of the great examples of a "rare flavor" (*chinmi*). When sea cucumbers (*namako*) are threatened, they disgorge their entire digestive system as a form of defense (or offense). A number of these digestive systems are collected, dried, and later consumed with relish.

35. This is a lidded, usually two-layer box, different from a sweet container (*fuchidaka*) in the sense that the bottoms of the levels are indented.

36. A common way to prepare burdock is to beat the roots with a wooden pestle so they are broken lengthwise before cutting them into pieces.

37. A "wooden plank" used for serving food is usually cedar that has been pulled apart like roofing shakes.

38. Fushimi in Kyoto is especially famous for grilled sparrow because the Fushimi Inari Shrine to the rice god is there. The dish is a kind of revenge on sparrows for eating rice.

39. These are stacked sweet trays that originated in Zen temples (for example, Kenninji and Daitokuji) as a way to serve several sweets simultaneously to multiple guests. They are literally trays with "tall edges" and, distinct from the *jubako*, have nothing to keep them from sliding apart except the host's balance and attention. Rikyū favored ones with "cut corners" (*sumikiri*) while Enshū used square ones here.

40. Raw, peeled chestnuts (*mizukuri*) are a special feature of the Enshū lineage's *kaiseki*. Served with the sweet, they are supposed to act as a "poison antidote" (Sue 1982, 704).

41. The *wabicha* lineages use a new pick each time made of spicewood that the guests took home as a memory of the *chaji*.

42. Sensō extensively used rice brittle as well. How it was served or used with the gruel is not apparent.

43. A later generation Kobori tea master was stripped of *daimyō* status for some reason, but the family continued to survive, if not prosper, from teaching tea and appraising tea utensils for other *daimyō*. This family is still very vigorous and active in *chanoyu* both in Japan and abroad.

44. Dōan returned without hindrance to Sakai after Rikyū's suicide to continue to oversee the family business and teach tea, unlike the Kyoto family, which was exiled. Several generations followed before Dōan's line died out.

45. Probably imported by Enshū from kilns in China.

46. The menu with commentary comes from Satō (2002, 268–70).

47. The text calls for three mouthfuls of rice served in a horizontal *ichimonji* (the Chinese character for "one") shape. For Sekishū tea masters, serving the rice still wet before it is steamed was evidence of "unskillfulness." *Wabi* tea masters, in an effort to show every consideration for the guest, do not start cooking the rice or boiling the tea water until the guests have arrived, so neither one has been prepared in advance and just left. The first rice served is soft and wet, the second time drier, and the third time fully steamed and chewy. The last time served (in hot water for pickles), the rice has browned.

48. "Washing" (*arai*) is a preparation technique whereby a very fresh fish, in this case cod, is filleted, sliced, and the meat dipped in iced water to firm it up. The fish was sliced thin and stacked to allow guests to take a piece of fish, dip it in the sauce with a bit of grated wasabi in the soy sauce, and eat it.

49. Crystal clear jelly-covered water shield leaf-buds are a summer delicacy that only grow in ancient, pure ponds. Here it accompanies the fish.

50. The miso soup was probably red and also just three mouthfuls. The main ingredient was a small eggplant, whole but shaved on the bottom to prevent it from being turned over during its transport to the guests.

51. Paulownia flowers in the late spring, and when its first leaf falls it is officially fall. The paulownia is the only tree in which the mythical phoenix will sit. This dish is the high point of the *kaiseki*, like the *wanmori* of *wabi kaiseki*. Rather than waiting to eat it together, each guest is expected to enjoy it as soon as it is served.

52. Smartweed is a very spicy-hot wild herb. Ground fresh leaves mixed with vinegar make a piquant, refreshing sauce for fish.

53. Although called "palate cleanser course," this sounds more like the moist, "main" sweet served after *wabicha kaiseki* in a stacked box (*fuchidaka*). This tray would be used for dry sweets in *wabicha*.

54. These sound like dry sweets but are served on what, for *wabicha*, would be a moist sweet utensil.

55. Shigaraki and Bizen were mentioned by the seminal Takeno Jōō in his call to blur the boundaries between Chinese antiques (*karamono*) and Japanese wares (*wamono*).

56. See Tanimura (2003, 139) for more on the cultivation of the warriors through *chanoyu*.

57. The Sekishū tea lineage itself did not continue directly through bloodlines but through several retainers until there are now several branches (*ryū*) and styles (*ha*).

WORKS CITED

Anderson, Jennifer L. 1991. *An Introduction to Japanese Tea Ritual*. Albany: State University of New York Press.

Chadō Shiryōkan and Raku Bijutsukan. 1993. *Heisei go nen shūki tokubetsu ten: Kaiseki no utsuwa*. Kyoto: Chadō Shiryōkan.

Ego Michiko. 2002. *Daimyō no kurashi to shoku* . Tokyo: Dōseisha.

Fumairyū Daienko Jimukyoku, ed. 2002. *Matsudaira Fumai to chanoyu*. Matsue: Fumaikō Tanjō Nihyaku Jūgo Nen Kinen Shuppan Iinkai.

Harada Nobuo. 2003. *Edo no shoku seikatsu*. Tokyo: Iwanami Shoten.

Ishige, Naomichi. 2001. *The History and Culture of Japanese Food*. London: Kegan Paul.

Pitelka, Morgan, ed. 2003. *Japanese Tea Culture: Art, History and Practice*. London: Routledge.

Satō Yūji. 2002. "Fumairyū to kaiseki ryōri." In *Matsudaira Fumai to chanoyu*. Ed. Fumai-ryū Daienko Jimukyoku, 266–78. Matsue: Fumaikō Tanjō Nihyaku Jūgo Nen Kinen Shuppan Iinkai.

Sen Sōsa, et al., ed. 1983a. *Rekishi. Chadō no genryū: Roku iemoto no keifu*. Vol. 1, Kyoto: Tankōsha.

———, ed. 1983b. *Chashitsu. Chadō no genryū: Roku Iemoto no keifu*. Vol. 2, Kyoto: Tankōsha.

Sen Sōshitsu XIV (Tantansai), ed. 1937. *Chadō zenshū*. Vol. 7. Osaka: Sōgensha.

Sen Sōshitsu XV (Hōunsai), ed. 1996. *Sensō Sōshitsu Koji no ihō, Sensō Sōshitsu Koji Sanbyaku nen ki*. Kyoto: Tankōsha.

———, ed. 1998. *Chanoyu: The Urasenke Tradition of Tea*. New York: Weatherhill.

Sen Sōshitsu XVI (Zabōsai), ed. 2008. *Urasenke Konnichian rekidai*. Vol. 4, *Sensō Sōshitsu*. Kyoto: Tankōsha.

Slusser, Dale. 2003. "The Transformation of Tea Practice in Sixteenth-Century Japan." In *Japanese Tea Culture: Art, History and Practice*. Ed. Morgan Pitelka, 39–60. London: Routledge.

Sue Sōkō. 1982. *Sue Sōkō chosakushū*. Vol. 1, *Chasho no kenkyū*. Kyoto: Shibunkaku Shuppan.

Tani Akira. 2001. *Chakaiki no kenkyū*. Kyoto: Tankōsha.

Tanimura, Reiko. 2003. "Tea of the Warrior in the Late Tokogawa Period." In *Japanese Tea Culture: Art, History and Practice*. Ed. Morgan Pitelka, 135–59. London: Routledge.

Tsutsui Hiroichi. 1996. *"Rōgetsuan Sen Sensō Sōshitsu Koji no shōgai."* In *Sensō Sōshitsu Koji no ihō, Sensō Sōshitsu Koji sanbyaku nen ki*. Ed. Sen Sōshitsu XV (Hōunsai), 90–93. Kyoto: Tankōsha.

———. 2002. *Kaiseki no kenkyū: Wabicha no shokurei*. Kyoto: Tankōsha

Turner, Victor. 1974. "Pilgrimages as Social Processes." In *Dramas, Fields, and Metaphors: Symbolic Action in Human Society*. Ed. Victor Turner, 166—230. Ithaca, N.Y.: Cornell University Press.

Uejo Saori. 1996a. "Furo no chanoyu oboe." In *Sensō Sōshitsu Koji no ihō, Sensō Sōshitsu Koji sanbyaku nen ki*. Ed. Sen Sōshitsu XV (Hōunsai), 175–81. Kyoto: Tankōsha.

———. 1996b. *"Kashū Kanazawa jūko kuchikiri kyaku no oboe."* In *Sensō Sōshitsu Koji no ihō, Sensō Sōshitsu Koji Sanbyaku nen ki*. Ed. Sen Sōshitsu XV (Hōunsai), 182–98. Kyoto: Tankōsha.

Yokota Yaemi. 1996. *"Sensō Sōshitsu kaitsuke."* In *Sensō Sōshitsu koji no ihō, Sensō Sōshitsu Koji Sanbyakunen ki*. Ed. Sen Sōshitsu XV (Hōunsai), 134–70. Kyoto: Tankōsha.

4 Meat-eating in the Kōjimachi District of Edo

AKIRA SHIMIZU

ALTHOUGH PHYSICAL CONTACT with dead animals, including their meat, was considered the cause of defilement during the Tokugawa period (1600–1868), scholars have demonstrated that many Japanese actually ate the meat of four-legged animals (*chiku* as opposed to *kin*, which refers to birds) that were thought to be the most defiled.[1] Such practice, however, had to be clandestine and could not be done in public. In large cities such as Edo (modern-day Tokyo) and Osaka, Japanese ate meat under the pretext of medicinal eating (*kusurigui*) and referred to it with euphemisms such as "*kuroyaki*" (dark baked), "*momonji*" or "*momonga*" (flying squirrel), and "*yamakujira*" (mountain whale). In this way, *on the record*, Japanese did not eat meat, thereby avoiding potential defilement.

In the capital city of Edo, meat was sold at two locations: at the beast market (*kemono dana*) in Kōjimachi (modern-day Chiyoda Ward) and at the east end of Ryōgoku Bridge (modern-day Taitō Ward). Close examinations of existing historical documents that mostly pertain to the beast market in Kōjimachi reveal that meat-eating was an intricate historical practice. Although purportedly eaten for medicinal purposes, not all kinds of meat were served at the beast market. According to historical sources, the range of meat available was consistently selective, with the terms of selection related to a politicized notion of agriculture that conceptually distinguished between draft animals useful to agriculture and game animals inimical to it. Toward the end of the Tokugawa period, the beast market grew in scale and nature and attracted more and more visitors.

This chapter provides an overview of the beast market in Kōjimachi. The historical documents used for this study mainly consist of travel guides and essays written by observers and not of records of those who actually ate meat. In other words, they provide rather nuanced perspectives of the market, mediated by the authors' varying points of view. Because of this, Kōjimachi will not represent the practice of meat-eating in all of Tokugawa Japan. However, this study provides a new perspective for observing early modern Japanese attitudes toward different kinds of meat and animals.

In Edo, Japanese ate game animals such as wild boar and deer but avoided the meat of draft animals such as horses and cows.[2] This was consistent with edicts the Tokugawa *bakufu* had issued to protect cattle and horses, and with the rulings that determined the length of the period of defilement that incurred for contact with an animal's corpse. So-called mourning edicts (*pukki ryō*) stipulated that defilement caused by physical contact with dead cattle and horses was considered a more serious offense than contact with other dead animals. The *bakufu*'s edict of mourning issued in 1688 set a period of 150 days of defilement for physical contact with the meat and corpses of cattle and horses compared to 70 days for those of other four-legged animals such as pigs, dogs, deer, and wild boar. More severe penalties with regards to the consumption of cattle and horses required offenders to stay away from other people for 150 days and may have derived from the fact that these animals were highly valued for their roles in agriculture (Okada Shigeyasu 1989, 304). While these regulations presented ideal guidelines that may not have actually been adhered to, they nonetheless demonstrated official attitudes toward different categories of animals.

Different attitudes toward draft and game animals are also evidenced in the actions of peasants. Peasants often submitted petitions to local magistrates demanding the protection of their farmland from wild boar and deer that would ruin their crops. Magistrates authorized farmers to use muskets to frighten animals, and if this did not have any effect, to shoot and kill them. Unlike cattle and horses, these animals not only ruined agriculture by devouring crops and damaging fields but also threatened the livelihood of farmers (Nobi 1998, 147).

Attitudes that favored the preservation of animals used in agriculture and the destruction of animals that potentially endangered it did not originate in the Edo period. Japanese culinary habits, including the preference for game animals and the avoidance of beef and horse meat, were subject of accounts of foreign visitors who came to Japan prior to the Edo period in the sixteenth century. In 1547, St. Francis Xavier (1506–52), the first European missionary to travel to Japan, was in Portuguese Malacca preparing for his trip to Japan when he met the Japanese convert Angero, who informed him of various aspects of Japanese life.[3] According to Angero, the availability of cattle was "limited" and farmers used horses instead for farming. Also, since chicken meat was considered "not very edible," Japanese hunted "deer and rabbits, as well as a number of quails, pigeons, pheasants, and ducks," and ate their meat. He added that the amount that they actually ate was quite insignificant, and his report only listed deer and rabbits among the four-legged animals that the Japanese consumed. This corresponds with the report filed by Francis Xavier himself in November 1549, in which he wrote that Japanese "do not kill domesticated animals nor do they eat their meat" (Tokyo Daigaku Shiryō Hensanjo 1992, 5, 11, 221).

In 1585, Jesuit Father Luís Fróis (1532–97) recorded the missionary work he and his fellow Jesuits had conducted in Japan as well as Japanese manners and customs in his *Comparison between European and Japanese Cultures*. He remarked that while "Europeans relish hens, quails, pies, and blancmanges, Japanese prefer wild dogs, cranes, large monkeys, cats, and uncooked seaweed [for eating]."[4] Especially notable is the eating of dog meat, to which Fróis added the statement: "We do not eat dog meat but beef; Japanese do not eat beef but dog meat as medicine." He also observed that the Japanese ate wild boar meat as Europeans did. However, while wild boar meat was stewed in Europe, Japanese thinly sliced it and ate it raw (Fróis 1991, 98, 102, 105).

Despite the above accounts of meat-eating observed by foreign visitors, the practice of meat-eating was loaded with religious restrictions throughout Japanese history. According to Buddhist precepts, Buddhists are forbidden from taking life, stealing, engaging in sexual misconduct, and consuming intoxicating substances such as alcohol. Hunting and fishing animals and eating killed animals violated the precept against taking life, including the life of animals. Due to these Buddhist precepts, European beef-eating habits—along with eating other types of meat the Japanese supposedly did not eat—was often criticized by Buddhist monks who perceived the custom of meat-eating as a reason for viewing Christianity as heretical. However, foreign observers such as Alvarez and Fróis pointed out contradictions in the perceptions and practices of meat-eating in Japan. For example, while Buddhist monks remarked that Europeans ate the meat of dogs and other animals, these were practices that Alvarez and Fróis had also witnessed among the Japanese. Citing another example, a Buddhist monk at Mt. Hiei in Kyoto accused Christians of eating the meat of cattle, horses, and dogs as well as other animals (Fróis 2000a, 49).[5] Christian missionaries responded to this accusation by noting the adoption of meat-eating practices by the Japanese, especially the unifier of Japan, Toyotomi Hideyoshi (1536 or 1537–98). According to one missionary, the Christian "dietary practice is well received by Japanese, and they include especially eggs and beef which they had abominated before. Even Taikō [Toyotomi Hideyoshi] relishes them" (Fróis 2000b, 320).[6]

According to Fróis's record, a debate developed between Toyotomi Hide-yoshi, the military hegemon who unified Japan in the 1590s, and Christian missionaries, in the course of which Hideyoshi changed his attitude and came to regard the eating of beef and horse meat as unacceptable because "horses are raised to reduce the burden of human beings by assisting in the transporta-tion of cargo and serving in the battlefield. Cattle are nurtured for agricultural purposes and as tools for farmers. Therefore, eating their meat means the loss of invaluable aids for [the Japanese] people" (Fróis 2000b, 208). Since the protection of cattle and horses was indispensable for agricultural produc-tion, Hideyoshi ordered Christians to hunt game animals instead, including "deer, wild boars, rabbits, foxes, pheasants, monkeys, and other animals" for consumption (Fróis 2000b, 208), the abundance of which the Jesuit Nicolao Lancilotto reported in the summer of 1548 (Tokyo Daigaku Shiryō Hensanjo 1992, 51). However, the missionaries refused this order on the ground that Europeans did not follow the custom of eating the meat of such game animals, noting that even Japanese customarily ate horse meat. They insisted that any decision on abandoning the practice of eating beef among Japanese Christians was a matter that had to be decided by Christians themselves (Fróis 2000b, 208).[7] This debate shows the role of meat-eating practices in the discourse between Buddhists and Christians. The banning of meat-eating by Toyotomi Hideyoshi, who had been positively inclined toward meat-eating before he issued the edict, also signifies heightening tensions against Christianity and underscores the political aspects of meat-eating. While cattle and horses had to be protected since they were useful in agriculture, eating the meat of nondraft animals was permitted.

Hideyoshi's rule was short-lived, but his policies established precedents for the subsequent Tokugawa military rule. Two years after the demise of Hideyoshi in 1598, Tokugawa Ieyasu (1542–1616/r. 1603–5) secured his power over the Toyotomi clan in the battle of Sekigahara (1600), acquired the title of shogun in 1603, and established the Tokugawa *bakufu*. Upon his seizure of power, the political center of Japan shifted from Kyoto to Ieyasu's headquarters in Edo, where he consolidated political and economic structures based on a system in which all agricultural production was calculated for tax-assessment purposes in terms of rice. The Tokugawa *bakufu* built its administration—and that of the regional lords (*daimyō*)—on rice agriculture as the essential foun-dation of Japanese life. Ieyasu issued a decree in 1600 to grant a historically discriminated group known as the "defiled ones" (*eta*) the right of monopoliz-ing the handling and skinning of dead cattle, deer, and dogs.[8] Another edict in 1612 protected the lives of cattle, preventing them from being raised for consumption (Kamo 1976, 189, 190). While the *bakufu* granted the outcasts the right of monopolizing the leather industry, farmers were ordered to concentrate on agricultural production using cattle and horses. Significantly, the right granted to outcasts also helped to confirm their pariah status since they worked in an occupation involving the carcasses of animals that the rest of the members of society were not supposed to handle.

In 1609, the Spanish colonial officer Rodrigo de Vivero y Velasco (usually referred to as Don Rodrigo) had an opportunity to observe some of the effects of these edicts on Japanese manners and customs when his ship, the *San Francisco*, washed ashore on the coast of Iwata village in the Ōkita domain (modern Chiba prefecture). After being rescued by villagers, he was invited by the domainal lord to a banquet that included "a number of delicious dishes featuring meat, fish, and fruit" (Vivero 1966, 14). In Edo, he found many restaurants selling the meat of rabbits, wild boar, and deer (Vivero 1966, 17). However, he added that the Japanese only ate the meat of game animals and cherished their cattle, and that the latter were "so attached to their owners" (Vivero 1966, 96, 101).

Attitudes toward meat consumption slightly differed in the western part of Japan due to the presence of European merchants and their practice of Christianity. According to the English captain John Saris, who visited Japan onboard the commercial ship *Clove* in 1613, the Christian *daimyō* Matsura Takanobu in Kyūshū obtained beef as well as pork from local farmers (Saris 1970, 112). If unable to do so, he demanded these foodstuffs from English merchants (Saris 1970, 112, 205, 206). Also in Fushimi near Kyoto, Saris found a market where the meat of "piglets, fat pigs, and wild sheep" was sold. The city market, he noted, "was filled with chickens, deer, wild boars, wild rabbits, and cattle, the meat of which was cured with salt" (Saris 1970, 168). According to Saris, the habit of meat-eating itself was not particularly offensive to the Japanese, especially for those in the Western part of the country who were more familiar with European dietary habits.

The practice of meat-eating was also reflected in the earliest examples of published cookbooks, especially with regards to medicinal foodways. Japan's first cookbook, *Culinary Tales* (*Ryōri monogatari*) published in 1643, contained a chapter titled "Four-Legged Animals" (*shisoku no mono no bu*).[9] The chapter not only listed the preparation and cooking of different kinds of meat but also elaborated on taboo combinations of meat as ingredients in other dishes. For example, dog meat was either to be stewed or grilled on large seashells whereas the meat of wild boars was not to be eaten with ginger and buckwheat noodles (*soba*). Likewise, the forerunner of Japanese medical books was written in the 1630s by the shogunal doctor Manase Gensaku (1549–1631), who served the Shōgun Tokugawa Ieyasu and his successor Hidetada (r. 1605–23). Manase's *Effects of Everyday Food* (*Nichiyō shokushō*) listed different kinds of meat and described their medicinal values. However, these two books merely replicated Chinese medical knowledge regarding the prescription of the medicinal values of food (Harada 2003, 37, 38). Moreover, it is not entirely clear to what extent Edoites had access to these recipes and prescriptions. Nevertheless, due to the existence of such books, it is fair to assume that information about meat-eating was by no means considered illegal or immoral at this time.

According to the Japanese food historian Harada Nobuo, Edoites stopped referring to meat-eating in written documents between the reign of the fifth shogun Tokugawa Tsunayoshi (r. 1680–1709) and the Kyōhō era [1716–35]. This may have been the result of Tsunayoshi's Laws of Compassion (*shōrui awaremi no rei*), which banned the "killing of all living creatures" (*sesshō*) in any form (Harada 2003, 39). Although his Laws of Compassion are best known for their protection of dogs, Tsunayoshi's purpose in issuing them was to protect the lives of all human beings and animals; however, farmers were not forbidden from shooting wild animals that damaged agricultural land. The Laws of Compassion were firmly based on the idea that agriculture was the foundation of Japanese life.

The Laws of Compassion were the combined expression of Tsunayoshi's belief in the "Buddhist notion of mercy (*jihi*)" and the "Confucian notion of benevolence and humanity (*ren*)" (Kuwata 1975, 99). Initially issued to protect the lives of human beings and draft animals, the laws intensified toward the end of the seventeenth century when Tsunayoshi declared the abolition of falconry in 1693 and ordered the construction of kennels in Edo in 1695 to protect stray and injured dogs (Tsukamoto 1983, 115). In 1687, the *bakufu* recorded that ten men were sentenced to exile for the abandonment of sick horses. On the following day, one samurai retainer was condemned to exile for "assaulting a dog with a sword" (Kuroita 1929, 1213–14). These two instances indicate that the *bakufu*'s attempt to protect horses and other animals was not adhered to on all levels of society. Therefore, the *bakufu* reinforced the following decree:

> Concerning compassion for all living creatures, residents of Terao and Daiba villages of Musashi province were found to have abandoned sick horses. . . . Although [they] deserve the death penalty, [the *bakufu*] benevolently saved their lives by sending them into exile. From this point on,

those who violate [the Laws of Compassion] are subject to severe penalty. (Kuroita 1929, 1213–14)

This announcement was accompanied by additional decrees aimed at protecting birds and cattle by requiring their owners to report injuries inflicted on them by human beings.

To view the Laws of Compassion as the manifestation of Tsunayoshi's belief in the sanctity of all life may obscure the fact that he did allow the killing of animals that threatened agriculture. For example, in 1688, the *bakufu* issued the following edict:

As has been ordered [by the shogun], although it is necessary to uphold mercy for living creatures, matters have arisen concerning wild boars and deer. Should they damage agricultural land and injure human beings, horses, and dogs, such animals may be shot with rifles. However, any misconduct with rifles, such as shooting animals without mercy for all living creatures, shall be subject to severe penalties. (Kuroita 1929, 47)

Even in the year when Tsunayoshi abolished falconry, the *bakufu* decreed that wild boars, deer, and wolves could be shot if they could not be scared off by musket fire (Kodama and Ōishi 1966, 105). These edicts clearly differentiated between animals beneficial to agriculture and animals that were harmful to agriculture and human life.

Nevertheless, the Laws of Compassion did ban the eating and sale of meat of four-legged animals shot dead by farmers (Kuroita 1929, 47). This suggests that people had been eating such meat prior to the decree of the Laws of Compassion. And there is other evidence for such practices. About one hundred fifty years later, the nativist scholar Kitamura Nobuyo (1783–1856) speculated that meat-eating was practiced before Tsunayoshi issued the Laws of Compassion. In his collection of essays *Laughable Views of Happy Plays* (*Kiyūshōran*, 1830), Kitamura stated that it was in the 1670s or 1760s "when a restaurant opened [in the beast market]" (Kitamura 1976, 46).[10] To support this point, Kitamura quoted a passage from *Like Tangerines* (*Ruikōji*), a posthumous collection of poems by Emoto Kikaku (1661–1707) compiled by his students:

As *Ruikōji* puts it: "Monkeys shriek when their intestines are soaked in salt. There are no pleas for mercy. Once upon a time in Yotsuya, there was a restaurant run by hunters. Among the meat they sold—deer, sheep, foxes, dogs, and rabbits—one would find a number of salt-cured monkeys hanging [from the ceiling or beam]." . . . A long time ago in Yotsuya in

Edo there was a market run by hunters. For this reason, the beast market [*kemono dana*] still exists there. (Kitamura 1979, 46)[11]

Emoto died two years before the death of Tsunayoshi in 1709. Since *Ruikōji* has an afterword dated 1707, it is possible that by "once upon a time," Emoto referred to the years before the Laws of Compassion.

Toyotomi Hideyoshi's order against Christians and the 1612 decree of the Tokugawa *bakufu* had sought to protect draft animals, and Don Rodrigo witnessed Japanese eating only game animals. Likewise, Kitamura's reference to *Ruikōji* did not include the meat of draft animals sold at the beast market. This conforms to the treatment of different animals put forth by the Laws of Compassion, which underpinned the attachment of Japanese farmers to draft animals Don Rodrigo witnessed. It is not clear whether the beast market continued its business under the Laws of Compassion. Nevertheless, it is fair to assert that the distinction of draft and game animals was upheld both in politics and in the practice of meat-eating.

According to Harada's observation mentioned earlier, the accounts of the beast market returned to popular publications in the 1730s. The Laws of Compassion had banned the eating of meat, which may have prevented people from discussing it. However, this period witnessed the rise of references to medicinal eating (*kusurigui*) for the first time. The following text examines the beast market roughly from the 1730s to the 1780s, revealing how the medicinal aspect of meat-eating at the beast market was introduced in popular publications.

Medicinal eating was practiced only in one shop in the beast market according to an Edo guidebook. *The Dappled Fabric of Famous Things of Edo* (*Edo meibutsu kanoko*, 1733) contained illustrations and poems to describe places of interest for visitors. In the entry "the Beast Market," the guidebook indicates:

> According to *Grains of Edo Sand* (*Edo sunago*), there is a butcher shop in the third block of Hirakawa District. There is meat hanging every year from winter to spring. *A Brief History of Kōjimachi* (*Kōjimachi ryakushikō*) tells us that there is a butcher shop called *Kōshūya* in the south side of the third block of Hirakawachō. . . . Nowadays, it is only one butcher shop that offers the meat of four-legged animals. In the past, meat eating was referred to as medicinal eating and the restaurant was called "the beast shop" (*momonjiya*). [An illustration of] tinted autumn leaves and two characters reading "mountain" and "whale" mean the meat of wild boars. (Toyoshima and Toyoshima 1959, 8)

This detailed information reveals that there was only one shop called *Kōshūya* in the beast market, which Edoites visited "for medicinal eating." This was confirmed by a guidebook written by the poet Kikuoka Senryō. In his *The Sandy-Detailed Guide of Edo: The Revised and Supplementary Edition* (*Hokō saikō Edo sunago*) written in 1772, Kikuoka also commented that there was only one shop in the beast market (Tōkyōshi Kōjimachiku 1935, 1124). However, the above quote and Kikuoka's description in his guidebook suggest that the beast market was considered a tourist attraction where visitors could experience the meat of wild boars for medicinal eating.

Although there was only one shop in the market, people could purchase virtually all kinds of game animals. As the painter Katsuma Ryūsui testified in the 1780s in his *The Coming and Going of the Variety of Goods* (*Sho shōbai ōrai*), wild boars, deer, foxes, wolves, bears, raccoons, otters, weasels (*itachi*), cats, wild dogs (*yamainu*), and various kinds of fowl were transported to the beast market for sale (Katsuma 1993, 23).

Despite these introductions of the beast market, many people were still reluctant to reveal their experiences of meat-eating. As the nativist scholar Saitō Hikomaro (1768–1854) wrote in his *Reminiscences of the Divine Age* (*Kamiyo no nagori*, 1847), during the period between the early 1770s and the late 1780s, "people of low status" (*iyashiki hito*) in particular ate the meat of wild boars and deer. As such practices were "deemed shameful," many consumers of meat kept their eating habits secret (Saito 1911, 48).

In the years after the 1730s, the introduction of the beast market cast a contradiction. Although the market had become a subject in several guidebooks, people who actually ate meat there were not willing to reveal that they ate meat in publications. As physical contact with dead animals was still considered to be the cause of defilement, these guidebooks merely described the beast market in order to incite public curiosity. One thing we can be assured of is that there was only one shop that sold only the meat of game animals, thus still upholding the political concern for draft animals, which had been protected by the rulers of Japan.

The last two decades of the eighteenth century marked a turning point for the beast market both in terms of quality and quantity of meat and restaurants. While previous accounts mentioned only the availability of meat in conjunction with the practice of medicinal eating, a greater number of authors began to specify the forms in which meat was sold, and they viewed the practice as a challenge to the notion of defilement. This change prompted increasing numbers of writers to discuss the beast market in more critical terms. Curiously, this coincided with a transformation in Edo foodways, such as the emergence of eating competitions and specialty restaurants, as well as the publication of a growing number of cookbooks. Yet historical sources imply that the beast market continued its business by selling only the meat of game animals.

An important shift in the perception of meat-eating occurred in the way meat was served when visitors to the beast market were for the first time able to experience prepared meat in the form of stew, and authors were no longer reluctant to discuss such experiences. Unlike previous authors, who had merely introduced the market and the practice of meat-eating, Kitamura Nobuyo specifically referred to the form in which meat was sold. According to Kitamura, a restaurant served raw meat until the beginning of the 1770s. After that, it began offering stewed meat toward the last quarter of the eighteenth century (Kitamura 1979, 46). With the availability of ready-made stewed meat, the beast market developed into a space in which visitors actually could eat, thereby transforming the market into a locale for restaurants.

This change seemed to have not only offered more opportunities for people to eat meat but also increased the demand, which in turn caused a rise in prices. The Confucian scholar Terakado Seiken (1796–1868) illuminated this point in his controversial *The Record of Edo Prosperity* (*Edo hanjōki*, 1832–36). In the chapter entitled "The Mountain Whale" (*yamakujira*), he described this term as a euphemism to refer to the meat of wild boar. He wrote:

> *Yamakujira* goes well with onions and is served individually to each customer in a pot on a portable charcoal brazier [hibachi]. People eat it together with the hibachi set next to one another. The rich have it with sake; the poor with rice. . . . The meat pot comes in three different sizes. The small one is fifty cash, the medium one hundred, and the large one two hundred. Nowadays, the prices of meat have skyrocketed, and it is almost as expensive as eel. . . . People do not argue about prices. The meat of different animals such as wild boars, deer, otters, wolves, bears, and serows [*kamoshika*] are piled up at the storefront. (Terakado 1989, 49)

Despite the rising prices of meat, gourmands seeking meat did not complain. According to this description, they were in fact even more determined to try out different meat dishes. In comparing them to eels, another Edo delicacy, Terakado's description confirms what Saitō Hikomaro recalled in 1847. According to Saitō, toward the end of the eighteenth century, more and more people began eating wild boar and deer meat and regarded such an experience with "pride and boastfulness" (Saitō 1911, 48). That is, meat-eating was no longer subject to secrecy and embarrassment but was rather an experience in which some people took great pride. According to the recollection of the poet Okada Suketada in 1823, restaurants that specialized in particular dishes such as the charcoal-broiled eel (*unagi kabayaki*) began appearing in the 1760s, and customers spent considerable amounts of money on dishes featuring charcoal-broiled eel. As a consequence, the prices of such dishes rose in accordance with their growing popularity (Okada 1972, 8, 9). Likewise, meat-eating—going to the beast market to visit a beast restaurant to eat *yamakujira*—symbolized a quest for gastronomic pleasure rather than simple nourishment.

Under these circumstances, some authors began to speculate about the origin of the nomenclature. In 1733, *Edo meibutsu kanoko* had already introduced a beast shop under the euphemism "*momonjiya*," and Terakado used another euphemism, "*yamakujira*," to refer to the dishes that featured the meat of wild boar. That is, meat-eating was not stated explicitly, thus blurring the boundary between what was morally acceptable and what was not. The vernacular writer Ryūtei Senka (1804–68) explains that the term *momonji*, derived from the word "flying squirrel" (*momonga*), was used by adults to scare children. In his *Foolish Old Man* (*Oroka oi*), probably written during the last years of his life, Ryūtei speculated about the meaning and origin of this expression. He disagrees with Kitamura Nobuyo's claim that the term *momonji* designated anything covered with hair, rebutting that *momonji* means "filling oneself with wild boar and deer meat." Or it may be "a variation of leg meat [*momo niku*]." He found leg meat to be the tastiest part of a beast (*kemono*) (Ryūtei 1913, 287).

In contrast, the kabuki playwright Nishizawa Ippō (1802–52) and Terakado Seiken both used the same nomenclature. In his *Daylight Slumber in the Imperial Capital* (*Kōto gosui*, 1850), Nishizawa observed that people around Kyoto and Osaka called the meat of both wild boars and deer *roku*, using the character for deer, while in Edo they called both kinds of meat *momonji* or *momonga* (Nishizawa 1976, 709). However, Terakado also notes that "the shop sign features an illustration of autumn leaves and two letters, 'mountain' (*yama*) and 'whale' (*kujira*) . . . [but] people in the capital call [meat] the monster (*obake*)" (Terakado 1989, 50). Since adults also used the word "*obake*" to scare children, this euphemism was employed interchangeably with *momonji*. Finally, according to Kitagawa Morisada, the shop sign "reads '*yama-XX*' or '*yama-kujira*.'" Like "beast," the euphemism "*yamakujira*" referred to the meat of both wild boars and deer, since the colors of these kinds of meat were "likened to peonies and tinted autumn leaves, respectively" (Kitagawa 1996a, 214).

The use of euphemisms seems to have encouraged more and more people to visit the beast market to experience meat dishes because such euphemisms exempted them from admitting that they actually ate meat. This prompted Terakado and two nativist scholars to criticize the practice of meat-eating. For Terakado, such a clandestine naming practice was to ensure the "evasion of state law" (*kokkin o saku*) (Terakado 1989, 50). That is, despite the fact that "state law" banned the practice of meat-eating, those eating meat at the beast restaurants believed that they could avoid defilement by their physical contact with dead four-legged animals because they were actually eating dishes that were compared to peonies and autumn leaves.

Choosing a different approach, two nativist scholars expressed their apprehension for the possibility that meat-eating would undermine Japanese foodways. In his *Essays Written over Years* (*Nennen zuihitsu*, 1801–5), the nativist scholar Ishihara Masaakira (1760–1821) asked if meat-eating was subject to defilement. His answer was: "It has yet to be determined" (Ishihara 1976, 13). He argued that while Emperor Temmu (r. 673–86) had banned the eating of beef, there was no law against the eating of the meat of wild boars and deer. Moreover, some Shinto rituals require leather to be made from the skin of wild boar and deer (Ishihara 1976, 14). According to Ishihara, the ban on meat-eating should apply equally to all four-legged animals, and physical contact with their corpses should be avoided. Moreover, Ishihara believed that people in rural areas refrained from meat-eating and even touching dead animals because they deemed it "shameful." On the contrary, "in places like Edo, people eat meat without worrying about potential problems. There are a number of students who read Chinese books and compose Chinese poems. Viewing defilement as a profane matter, they flatter themselves to think that they are enlightened" (Ishihara 1976, 15). Against Ishihara's wish, so-called enlightened people would convince others of the profane nature of rules regarding meat-eating, thereby undermining the ancient Japanese law that had banned people from any physical contact with dead animals.

Another nativist scholar Okabe Tōkei lamented that those who sought to eat meat had made up another excuse. In his *Essays in Twittering Voices* (*Ōō zuihitsu*, 1842), he wrote: "Nowadays, in the city of Edo, everywhere you'll find people who sell stewed meat on the main street. I hear that [some people] visit [the place] and eat meat after being convinced that the meat is purified through heat."[12] In this way, "[they] do not abstain from eating wild boar and deer meat under the pretext of medicinal eating" (Yamauchi 1994, 243). Okabe sees the practice of medicinal eating as an undermining of the Japanese law of defilement because some people believed that the heating of meat for medicinal eating exempted them from defilement despite the obvious physical contact with dead animals.

Despite such criticisms and fears, the number of restaurants in the beast market increased in the first three decades of the nineteenth century. According to *The History of Kōjimachi Ward* (*Kōjimachi-ku shi*), there had been only one beast restaurant (*momonji-ya*) in the third block of Hirakawa District until the beginning of the 1840s, when the entire block constituted "the beast market" (Tōkyōshi Kōjimachiku 1935, 1124). In his *Record of Edo Prosperity*, Terakado noted: "In the past, there was only one place in Kōjimachi that catered for 'eating for health.' However, looking back to the past twenty years, such places have now become innumerable" (Terakado 1989, 50). Moreover, the painter Kitagawa Morisada, who spent thirty years writing his *Random Writings of Morisada* (*Morisada mankō*) beginning in 1837, noted, "although Edo used to have only one beast restaurant in Kōjimachi, many more have emerged in recent years" (Kitagawa 1996b, 136).[13] Nowadays, many [people] regularly eat the meat of four-legged animals" (Kitagawa 1996b, 384). Likewise, the nativist scholar Takada Tomokiyo (1783–1847) witnessed an increase in the number of beast restaurants in the first three decades of the nineteenth century. While scholars of the Western sciences (*rangakusha*) and retainers of high-ranking samurai households were among the customers, wild boar meat and venison, he emphasized, were sold as *yamakujira*, and these meat dishes were also referred to as "autumn leaves" (*kōyō*) (Kamo 1976, 209; Yamauchi 1994, 243).

In summary, the appearance of the beast market significantly changed in the late Tokugawa period. As the number of beast restaurants grew, different forms of presentation and cooked dishes proliferated, catering to the different needs of the visitors to the beast market. This transformation of the beast market appeared as a challenge to the notion of defilement because the use of euphemisms enabled those who ate meat to avoid potential conflicts, partially obscuring the fact that they had physical contact with dead animals and were subject to defilement. On the other hand, as historical sources imply, the fact that the beast market did not offer beef and horse meat did not change. One may conclude that the edict of mourning issued in 1688 defined physical contact with the meat and carcasses of cattle and horses as a more serious offense than the contact with other four-legged animals. However, the absence of such an argumentation seems to have another reason.[14] That is, animals beneficial to agriculture and human life were protected; however, those potentially harmful could be eliminated from the farmland, justifying the killing of these animals and selling their meat at the beast market.

Beginning in the 1850s, the presence of Western powers in Japan rapidly transformed the life of Edoites. As more Europeans and Americans established settlements, meat was in higher demand, bringing forth merchants who targeted the foreigners and established new types of restaurants that offered novel "Western" dishes. Yet, as the notion of defilement remained strong, especially among high-ranking samurai, meat-eating in public without the use of euphemisms did not quickly permeate into the daily lives of Japanese.[15] This indicates the strong persistence of early modern notion of Japanese foodways, which nevertheless was challenged in the beast market.

NOTES

1. For example, see Kamo (1976) and Harada (1993, 1995, 2003).

2. According to Harada, scholars of the Dutch Learning (*rangaku*) and outlaws preferred beef (Harada 1995, 206). In addition, the Hikone domain sponsored the production of miso-marinated beef it presented to the shogun and high-ranking officials but did not circulate it on the market (Kamo 1976, 199).

3. His Japanese name is Yajirō or Anjirō. Born in Kagoshima, he committed murder and fled Japan with the help of the Portuguese sailor Jorge Alvarez. Having reached Malacca, he converted to Christianity.

4. This title is a translation of the Japanese title that the translator Okada Akio rendered to the Japanese edition. The original is *Tratado em que se contem muito susintae abreviadamente algumas contradições e diferenças de custumes antre a gente de Europa e esta provincia de Japão* and was compiled in Japan in 1585.

5. This is based on the Japanese translation of *Historia de Japam* in twelve volumes.

6. It is well known that Toyotomi Hideyoshi initially tolerated the practice of Christianity when he took over the task of unifying Japan from his predecessor Oda Nobunaga in 1582, who had also supported Christianity. However, this tolerance of Christianity changed significantly. In 1587, Hideyoshi undertook an expedition to unify Kyūshū, the base of a considerable number of Christian *daimyō* and issued an edict that banned Christian missionary activities and banished Jesuits. However, this edict was not thoroughly implemented due to the economic profitability of trade with Spain and Portugal.

7. Under the influence of Christianity, the eating of beef and pork rapidly spread throughout Japan. There is an array of historical sources that reveal the interaction of missionaries and Japanese Christians through the exchange of meat, especially the aforementioned two kinds of meat.

8. It was not until the middle of the seventeenth century that the term *eta* was officially used and systematized in the social structure. Before that, outcasts were referred to as *kawata* and *kawaya* (leather workers).

9. This work is considered to reflect the foodways of the region around Osaka (Kamigata) (Ebara 1986, 17).

10. I designate the term "nativist" to refer broadly to scholars associated with

national learning (*kokugaku*), which advocated a return to the beliefs of ancient Japan before Japan's adoption of foreign knowledge such as Buddhism and Confucianism.

11. Yotsuya was the district next to the Kōjimachi District on the northwest. Both districts are on the Koshū Highway, which connected Edo to modern-day Nagano prefecture through Kai province (modern day Yamanashi prefecture).

12. It is not entirely clear what Okabe meant by "heating it." Perhaps, he meant stewing, as this was the way meat was served in the beast market.

13. The biographical information of Kitagawa Morisada is unclear, except that he was born in Osaka and relocated to Edo.

14. Observing a taboo of the Jews and Muslims on pork, the anthropologist Marvin Harris looks for explanations outside religious discourses. According to Harris, "religiously sanctioned food practices" have "social functions" (Harris 1974, 45).

15. For example, Nakagawaya launched its business in 1866 as the first restaurant to serve beef in Edo. Nevertheless, many people pinched their noses, closed their eyes, and hurried past the restaurant (Nobi 1998, 145).

WORKS CITED

Ebara Kei. 1986. *Edo ryōrishi kō: Nihon ryōri sōso ki.* Tokyo: Kawade Shobō.

Fróis, Luís. 1991. *Yōroppa bunka to Nihon bunka.* Trans. Okada Akio. Tokyo: Iwanami Shoten.

———. 2000a. *Kanyaku Furoisu Nihon-shi.* Vol. 1, *Shōgun Yoshiaki no saiki oyobi jiyū toshi Sakai.* Tokyo: Chūō Kōronsha.

———. 2000b. *Kanyaku Furoisu Nihon-shi.* Vol. 4, *Hideyoshi no tenka tōitsu to Takayama Ukon no tsuihō.* Tokyo: Chūō Kōronsha.

Harada Nobuo. 1993. *Rekishi no naka no kome to niku: Shokumotsu to tennō, sabetsu.* Tokyo: Heibonsha.

———. 1995. *Kinomi to hanbāgā: Nihon shoku seikatsushi no kokoromi.* Tokyo: Nihon Hōsō Kyōkai.

———. 2003. *Edo no shoku seikatsu.* Tokyo: Iwanami Shoten.

Harris, Marvin. 1974. *Cows, Pigs, Wars, and Witches: The Riddle of Culture.* New York: Vintage Books.

Ishihara Masaakira. 1976. "*Nennen zuihitsu.*" In *Nihon zuihitsu taisei, dai 1-ki.* Vol. 21. Tokyo: Yoshikawa Kōbunkan.

Kamo Giichi. 1976. *Nihon chikusanshi: Niku shoku, rakunō hen.* Tokyo: Hōsei Daigaku Shuppan Kyōkai.

Katsuma Ryūsui. 1993. "*Shoshōbai ōrai, zōho.*" In *Ōrai mono taikei.* Vol. 69. Ed. Ishikawa Ken. Tokyo: Ōzorasha.

Kitagawa Morisada. 1996a. *Morisada mankō.* Vol. 1. Tokyo: Iwanami Shoten.

———. 1996b. *Morisada mankō.* Vol. 5. Tokyo: Iwanami Shoten.

Kitamura Nobuyo. 1979. "*Kiyūshōran.*" In *Nihon zuihitsu taisei, bekkan.* Vol. 4. Tokyo: Yoshikawa Kōbunkan.

Kodama Kōta and Ōishi Shinzaburō, ed. 1966. *Kinsei nōsei shiryōshū.* Vol. 1, *Edo bakufu hōrei,* Part 1. Tokyo: Yoshikawa Kōbunkan.

Kuroita Katsumi, ed. 1929. *Tokugawa jikki.* Vol. 5, *Okushitaikei.* Ed. Kuroita Masami and Kokushi taikei henshūkai. Tokyo: Yoshikawa Kōbunkan.

Kuwata Tadachika. 1975. *Tokugawa Tsunayoshi to Genroku jidai.* Tokyo: Akita Shoten.

Nishizawa Ippō. 1976. "Koto gosui." In *Shin gunsho ruijū.* Vol. 1. Ed. Kokusho kankōkai. Tokyo: Daiichi Shobō.

Nobi Shōji. 1998. *Shokuniku no burakushi.* Tokyo: Akashi Shoten.

Okada Shigeyasu. 1989. *Imi no Sekai: Sono kikō to henyō.* Tokyo: Kokusho Kankōkai

Okada Sukekata. 1972. "*Utaku zuihitsu.*" In *Nihon genrin shōsho.* Vol. 10. Tokyo: Ōtori Shuppan.

Ryūtei Senka. 1913. "*Orokaoi.*" In *Shin enseki jusshu.* Vol. 1. Tokyo: Kokusho Kankōkai.

Saitō Hikomaro. 1911. "Kamiyo no nagori." In *Enseki jusshu.* Vol. 2. Tokyo: Kokusho Kankōkai.

Saris, John. 1970. "The voyage of Captain John Saris to Japan." Ed. Ernest Satow. Trans. Kawamura Kengo. In *Shin ikoku sōsho.* Vol. 6. Tokyo: Yūshōdō Shoten.

Terakado, Seiken. 1989. "*Edo hanjōki.*" In *Shin Nihon koten bungaku taikei.* Vol. 100. Tokyo: Iwanami Shoten.

Tokyo Daigaku Shiryō Hensanjo, ed. 1992. *Nihon kankei Iezusukai Nihon shokan shūyakubun hen.* Vol. 1. Tokyo: Tokyo Daigaku Shuppankai.

Tōkyōshi Kōjimachiku. 1935. *Kōjimachikushi.* Tokyo: Tōkyōshi Kōjimachiku.

Toyoshima Jizaemon and Toyoshima Yaemon, ed. 1959. *Edo meibutsu kanoko.* Tokyo: Kinsei Fūzoku Kenkyūkai.

Tsukamoto Manabu. 1983. *Shōrui o meguru seiji: Genroku no fōkuroa.* Tokyo: Heibonsha.

Vivero, Rodrigo de. 1966. "Don Rodrigo Nihon kenbunroku." Trans. Murakami Naojirō. In *Shin ikoku sōsho.* Vol. 9. Tokyo: Yūshōdō Shoten.

Yamauchi Hisashi. 1994. "*Shoku*" no rekishi jinruigaku: Hikaku bunkaron no chihei. Kyoto: Jinbun Shoin.

5 Wine-drinking Culture in Seventeenth-century Japan
The Role of Dutch Merchants

JOJI NOZAWA

ONE MIGHT ASSUME THAT the history of wine-drinking in Japan began in the Meiji period (1868–1912) accompanied by other imports to the diet, such as beef and Chinese dishes as described by Shimizu and Kushner in this volume, but this is only partially correct. The history of viniculture in Japan did indeed originate in the Meiji period when occidental methods of wine grape production were introduced and wine production became part of national agricultural and academic research within that field.[1] However, earlier studies of the history of wine in Japan that begin with the Meiji period neglect the fact that the beverage had not only been introduced centuries prior to that period but that wine drinking had also become popular among some groups in Japan as early as the seventeenth century.[2] Before the Meiji period, Japanese obtained wine from Dutch merchants whose trade options in Japan were so restricted that they were forced to live on Deshima, an artificial island in Nagasaki Bay. Previous studies of Dutch–Japanese relations in the seventeenth and eighteenth centuries occasionally refer to the presence of European wines in Japan, but these references are few and in passing. Moreover, wine had almost no economic impact on the Dutch East India Company (*Verenigde Oost-Indische Compagnie*) [hereafter VOC] or on Japan, which is why historians have not included wine as part of the historical trade accounts between these two countries in the early modern period.[3] Yet the Dutch Republic was one of the major wine importers in the seventeenth century and was well known for its intermediary role in the European wine trade. The redistribution of and the demand for all these imported wines carried by the Dutch has yet to be fully investigated, particularly the matter of their export to overseas countries.[4] In short, there is a need to extend the historical narrative of wine-drinking in Japan back to the early modern period with the goal to explore the role of the Dutch as wine promoters more fully. This chapter considers the consumption of European wines in Japan during the first half of the seventeenth century, with particular focus on the Dutch merchants who lived there and brought the wines to Japan's shores.

The central focus of this chapter is a discussion of trends in the consumption of wine in Japan on the basis of the "daily records" (*dagregister*), which were the official accounts written by the heads of the Dutch factory (*opperhoofd*) in Japan.[5] The detailed descriptions in these records provide us with answers to the following questions: (1) On which occasions did Dutch merchants drink wine with the Japanese? (2) Who were the Japanese they shared wine with? and (3) Did the Japanese purchase European wines? "Trade journals" (*negotie journal*), which are financial accounts of day-to-day transactions, allow us to look at the same questions from a more quantitative perspective.[6] Combining daily records and trade journals enables us to understand a range of issues with regard to the consumption of European wines in early modern Japan.

These sources reveal that wine was not only meant for the enjoyment of the Dutch merchants residing in Japan but was also circulated among the Japanese elites. This chapter traces the evolution of wine consumption by the Japanese in three distinct phases: (1) in entertaining, (2) as a gift, and (3) for purchase. This is the order whereby Japanese consumers shifted from a passive to a more active approach toward the consumption of wine.

WINE FOR ENTERTAINMENT: THE HIRADO PERIOD (1609–41)

In 1609 Tokugawa Ieyasu (1542–1616) granted the VOC the right to establish its first local trading post in Hirado. During this early stage of the company's history, European wine in VOC shipping had no commercial value. It was imported for the daily consumption of a dozen employees residing there. According to the trade journal, the Dutch factory in Japan received on average approximately 540 liters of wine per year in the 1620s, 1,700 liters in the 1630s, 2,300 liters in the 1640s, and the figures remained between 2,000 and 3,000 liters per year for the rest of the century. Dutch merchants were certainly the first to have access to wines available at their factory in Japan, but the records hardly provide any mention of wine consumption among the Dutch merchants themselves. In principle, the company's records in Japan focused primarily on trade issues. The internal use of wines was not considered significant.

Dutch merchants brought different types of wine to Japan, each of which had a different value and was consumed on different occasions. Between 1620 and 1652, the trade journals record five different types of wine: Spanish, "tent,"[7] French, Rhine, and Portuguese. All wines came from European vineyards, and the first three wines were shipped to Deshima on a regular basis. This variety in the composition of wines was characteristic of the Netherlands, whose climate and high latitude did not favor the domestic production of wine. In other words, the Dutch relied on an extensive network for purchasing wines from a variety of neighboring European countries.

Spanish wine maintained the steadiest supply both in terms of volume and continuation. It accounted for more than three quarters of the total wine consumption between 1620 and 1652. Although there has been no indication of its color, several daily records imply that it was more likely to be white wine. The conspicuous consumption of Spanish wine is all the more curious given the fact that the homeland of the Dutch merchants was struggling for independence from the Iberian Catholic nation during this very period.

Tent wine also showed a very steady supply albeit in smaller quantities. It seems that this type of wine was a multipurpose brand that the Dutch merchants reserved for particular occasions such as festivities. The daily records show that Dutch merchants tended to choose tent wine for the Japanese. In the trade journals, tent wine was often listed as a "non-evaluated" good and scarcely given an indication of its cash value, but judging from its selling price, it became the most expensive brand closely followed by Spanish wine.[8] An important implication in this context is that the Dutch merchants always used more valuable wines in their interactions with the Japanese.

The last of the three regular brands was French wine. Its supply was fairly intermittent, but in total quantity it matched tent wine. Unlike the other two brands, French wine scarcely appeared in the daily records. We can assume that French wine was by and large limited to consumption among the VOC employees. In addition, contrary to its reputation in contemporary times, French wine was by far the cheapest of the three wines.

In contrast to the consumption by members of the VOC, when wine was shared with their Japanese counterparts, suddenly a considerably greater amount of information appeared in the daily records as the act of consumption came to be considered part of commercial activities. Many examples of the Hirado period (1609–41) fall into two categories. First, wine was served to entertain guests. Dutch merchants frequently entertained high-ranking officials and regional lords (*daimyō*) with wine, not only at their factory in Hirado but also in Edo during trips made to pay ceremonial visits (*hofreis*) to the shōgun.[9] For instance, in February 1638, Matsura Shigenobu (1622–1703), the *daimyō* of Hirado, went on board the flute-ship (*fluitschip*)[10] *Petten* with a number of his principal vassals. The chief of the Dutch factory entertained his guests first on board with wine, liquors, and preserved fruits and then again at the company's lodgings with wine, sake, and snacks (*sakana*).[11]

Second, Dutch merchants employed European wines as gifts.[12] According to the trade journal, during a journey to Edo in 1627, six small barrels of Spanish wine and another six barrels of tent wine—approximately 480 liters in total—were registered as an expense, part of which was offered to the shogun as well as to some of his entourage.[13] The invoice shows that these wines were already designated to be offered as gifts when they were shipped from Batavia (present-day Jakarta). In other words, Dutch merchants did not improvise wine as a spontaneous gift, but it was agreed upon in advance through prior consultation. However, the existing documents do not necessarily prove the regular use of wine as an official gift during the Hirado period. In 1636, for instance, wine was deliberately avoided. When Nicolaes Couckebacker prepared some wine as part of an annual gift to the shogun, Matsura Takanobu (1592–1637), the *daimyō* of Hirado, declined by pointing out that "the Majesty does not drink any foreign wine."[14]

Dutch merchants also began to employ wine in order to improve relations with the Japanese. However, due to the use of wine in the Eucharist and the highly symbolic meaning of wine as the metaphorical blood of Jesus, the custom of drinking wine was perceived to be a contradiction to the anti-Christian policy of the Tokugawa government. The earlier success of the propagation of Christianity familiarized many Japanese with the religious connotation of the beverage.[15] During the Shimabara Rebellion in 1637–38, which has often been considered as a key turning point of the anti-Christian policy in seventeenth-century Japan, rebels used a large chalice as a motif on the battle flag with a wafer above it.[16] Since many peasants turned out to be Japanese Roman Catholics converted by Iberian missionaries, the *bakufu* responded by strengthening their enforcement of an already existing ban on all Christian beliefs and activities. Likewise, the list of "prohibited Christian goods" became more extensive. Consequently, the incident also led to a reconsideration of food generally consumed by Europeans. Thus, on the first day of the eighth month of 1641, the governor (*bugyō*) of Nagasaki notified Maximiliaen Lemaire, the chief of the Dutch factory in Japan at that time, of the following order:

ORDINANCE
No meat, bacon, arrack,[17] Spanish and French wine, olive oil, and other foodstuffs—which the Christians are accustomed to eat—that have been

brought here on the first and second Dutch ship this southern monsoon may be sold, presented, bartered or given by anyone of that nation to any Japanese, Chinese, or foreigner. Should this ordinance not be strictly obeyed, the captain, who has also signed this ordinance, will be arraigned about this breach and will be punished according to the laws of the land.[18]

The above ordinance, which lists European wines as one of the prohibited goods, reveals some implications that appear to have effected this announcement. First, the ordinance suggests that the Japanese authorities were fully aware of the highly symbolic value of wine. Second, the ordinance also alludes to the fact that some Japanese had previously had access to European wines. Although it is not certain whether this decision was only provisional or limited to certain localities, for a number of subsequent years the daily records confirm that even some Japanese officials in Edo resolutely refused any offer of European wines.[19]

THE DESHIMA PERIOD: WINES AS GIFT AND COMMODITY

In 1641, two years after the exclusion of the Portuguese from Japan, the Dutch factory was transferred from Hirado to Nagasaki, to the well-known small artificial island Deshima, which resulted in closer Japanese surveillance of VOC merchants. Despite the recent ban on European foodstuffs, wine did find its way out into the Japanese population, and the consumption of wine continued in a discreet and hesitant fashion that can be traced to the early 1640s.

As early as October 1641, Maximiliaen Lemaire, the chief of the factory, welcomed a number of Japanese officials to his new residence in Deshima and served them wine. He wrote, "in the afternoon, the Lord of Arima [the *daimyō* of Shimabara] came, accompanied by Commissioner [*ōmetsuke*] Chikugo-no-kami [Inoue Masashige], the two governors [*Nagasaki bugyō*], and many other nobles to visit the island. . . . We treated them to wine and pastries. They had many questions and remarks about the wine, arrack, butter, cheese, and other things set before them."[20] A barrage of questions on the prohibited foodstuffs might imply a mixed feeling of suspicion and curiosity. Wine's "forbidden" flavor may have made the delicacy all the more appealing to people in the context of the *bakufu*'s anti-Christian campaigns. Descriptions of such visits to Deshima by Japanese officials were repeatedly documented in the daily records throughout the year.

Just as in the Hirado period, Dutch merchants continued to serve wine during their journey to Edo. While waiting for an audience with the shogun, they busily received numerous visitors at their inn. When the families of the governor of Nagasaki came to visit the foreigners out of curiosity, accompanied by a large entourage, Wilhem Versteeghen observed that "Seven sons and two grandsons of Governor Gonpachirō [Yamazaki Gonpachirō Masanobu], who has eight children, including one daughter, from only one mother, visited me with their father's secretary and many other nobles. I let them have a look at everything and treated them to wine and sakana. Thus the whole day I have not had a moment's rest with visitors all day."[21]

The practice of gift giving was increasingly systematized at this stage and had become an integral part of diplomatic protocol. However, it was not until 1645 that wine for the first time was recognized as a suitable official gift for the shogun.[22] Soon thereafter wine began to be offered to the two governors of Nagasaki who were under immediate surveillance of the *bakufu* and were in charge of the city's municipal administration and foreign relations.[23] At first, only tent wine was offered, but Spanish wine was added to the list from 1653 onward. These two types of wine presumably resulted in a combination of red and white varieties. The use of wine as a gift became a regular practice and was repeated every year. In the 1640s, the shogun and the governors of Nagasaki were the only people who were chosen to receive wine as an official gift. European wines were offered only to those of higher rank. And the higher their position, the greater the quantities they received. Accordingly, the quantity for the governors of Nagasaki never exceeded that of the shogun.[24]

Only a few options remained for those who did not rank high enough to receive European wines as a gift but who desired to drink wine more often than on the occasions that they were entertained by the Dutch. One possibility was to purchase wine, although this was not an option for everyone. As early as the mid-1630s, records show that the *daimyō* of Hirado, Matsura Takanobu (1592–1637), tried to order some tent wine and Spanish wine, as well as peacocks, "if they were not so expensive."[25] Yet it is not clear whether this transaction was ever completed. Eventually, according to the trade journal, the first sale of European wine occurred on the twenty-fourth day of the first month in 1644 during a journey to Edo. Johan van Elseracq sold fifteen *flapkan* of tent wine (approximately 22.5 liters) in exchange for an immediate payment of 85.5 guilders (30 taels).[26] These wines comprised part of what had originally been a gift. The first Japanese buyer was registered as Inspector General (*ōmetsuke*) Inoue Chikugo no kami Masashige (1585–1661), who is known to be a leading figure of the anti-Christian policy from the late 1630s to 1660.[27] He was also responsible for the Dutch–Japanese relations at that time. As Leonard Win-nincx correctly pointed out, in Edo "no one can visit us without Chikugo no kami's permission."[28] Inoue Masashige would continue to purchase European wines and guide their circulation. In later years, he even entertained Dutch merchants with European wines from his own private cellar.

In the following year, a wine sale took place in Nagasaki. The trade journal indicates that European wines were sold at an auction on Deshima for the first time in 1647.[29] Sixty *flapkan* (approximately 90 liters) of tent wine at 855 guilders (300 taels) and 45 *flapkan* (approximately 68 liters) of Spanish wine at 385 guilders (135 taels) were sold to those who made the highest paper bids. The records identify the Japanese bidders only as anonymous merchants.

By comparing two types of transactions in the trade journal—namely, the expenses for wine used as gifts and the revenue from the sales of wine—we can perceive a slow but gradual transition during which European wines were transformed from being gifts to more marketable products. From the late 1620s, Dutch merchants began to employ wine as official gifts approximately once every five years and more frequently after the 1640s. Recorded for the first time in 1644, wine sales showed a gradual growth toward the end of the decade. While the quantity of wine used as a gift remained stable around 170 liters per year in the 1640s, sales increased rapidly from 22 liters in 1643–44 to 180 liters in 1647–48. During the year 1651–52, sales surpassed gifts in quantity: 320 liters in sales and 210 liters as gifts. The increase of wine sales and the subsequent transformation from wine being a gift to a marketable product represents the commodification of European wines by the VOC merchants in Japan by the middle of the seventeenth century.

JAPANESE CONSUMERS OF WINE

The consumption of European wines in Japan during that time was certainly limited to a small number of people but included Japanese of different socioeconomic groups. Some had the status to receive wine as a gift whereas others held the privilege of being able to purchase the beverage, and again others had the opportunity to drink wine on various occasions. Although most consumers of wine remained anonymous in the Dutch records, these sources often provide their status or occupation. Such indications allow us to specify a number of categories of wine consumers in Japan.

The Tokugawa family members were the noblest consumers of wine. Besides the shogun who received wine as an official gift every year, members of two of the three branches of the Tokugawa successor houses (*gosanke*), Mito and Owari, were regular customers. Inoue Masashige often confirmed that the VOC's remaining stock of wine would be sufficient to meet the demands of these honored Tokugawa families. Zacharias Wagenaer, the chief of the Dutch factory then, wrote one evening in Edo, that "it was very late when Chikugo no kami [Inoue Masashige] let me know that, considering that people are sending for tent wine and Spanish wine every day, we should keep at least five *gantang* [approximately 12 liters] in reserve, so that when Mito-sama [Tokugawa Yorifusa] or Owari-sama [Tokugawa Mitsutomo] sent for some, we could oblige them at least with this much."[30]

One particularity of the process of selling wine to the Tokugawa families was the ritual of poison testing. Gabriel Happart described vividly how the representatives of the *daimyō* of Mito, for example, came and purchased wine:

> One was the senior chamberlain and the other the taster of the King [*daimyō*] of Mito and both were his confidants. They brought a special license from the commissioner [Inoue Masashige] for two *gantang* of tent wine [approximately 4.8 liters] for their lord. I had to pour it while they were watching. I had to drink some first and they followed suit before the bottle was sealed and stamped with their chop and with my seal. It appears that not only in Europe are the great lords and kings on their guard against poison.[31]

Such procedures were regularly observed in the records. In the following years, Dutch-language Japanese interpreters (*Oranda tsūji*) and the landlord of the Dutch inn (*Oranda yado*), which was the temporary residence of the Dutch in Edo, were obliged to participate in the poison testing in order to demonstrate the safety of the beverage.[32]

Certain *daimyō* of Kyūshū, particularly those from the neighboring domains of Nagasaki, were also among the regular wine consumers and customers. Having gradually formed close contacts with the VOC merchants, they had relatively frequent and easy access to European wines. To name but a few, the names of the *daimyō* of Shimabara, Saga, Fukuoka, and Kokura often appear in the documents. The *daimyō* house of Hirado, despite their long contact with foreign merchants, was excluded from entry to the new Dutch residence at Deshima for over a decade. Leonard Winnincx testified in 1654 that the *daimyō* of Hirado had "never visited the island in all of the fourteen years that we have resided here."[33] Moreover, for him, the sale of European wines had long been refused "either because of the unwillingness of the governors [of Nagasaki] or for another reason."[34] It was not until the mid-1650s that they managed to normalize these contacts again.

Nagasaki, the city of Dutch residence, had the widest variety in terms of the different social standings of wine consumers. In the course of their duties, administrative officers often had the chance to enjoy European wine. Their professional duties facilitated access to this foreign beverage. The governors of Nagasaki continued to purchase wine in addition to the wine they had received as gifts; the intendant (*daikan*), town officials (*machi doshiyori*), and village headmen (*otona*) were the primary beneficiaries of wine. Each of these officials played a role in relation to the Dutch presence in Japan. Other anonymous local officers were in charge of tasks such as the inspection of ships and cargos, the supervision of auctions, and the transmission of messages, all of which were occasions when the Dutch often served wine as a token of their gratitude.

As trade became more institutionalized, wine tended to appear more regularly during certain transactions with Japanese merchants. One example was price negotiations over specialized commodities such as Chinese silk. Among merchants "the heads of the five shogunal cities (*gokasho shōnin*)," namely, Sakai, Nagasaki, Kyoto, Edo, and Osaka, which comprised the largest cities in Japan at this time, were directly involved in trade with the VOC. Less frequently, copper merchants were also found in the records as being treated to wine. Other ordinary merchants also came to Deshima for public bidding on newly arrived imported products. Part of this bidding process often included the consumption of European wines. Another group of merchants consisted of owners of inns where Dutch merchants stayed during their journeys to Edo (*Oranda yado*). Not only did these innkeepers have the chance to partake in wine consumption, but Dutch merchants often consigned them the remaining wine stocks for sale.[35]

The last category of wine consumers was intellectuals, especially Dutch-language interpreters (*Oranda tsūji*) whose presence was indispensable in the communication between the Dutch and the Japanese. The nature of their duty obliged them to be involved in every aspect of the lives of Dutch merchants in Japan. Likewise, they were present on numerous occasions when wine was consumed. In fact, Japanese–Dutch interpreters were the hidden but grand connoisseurs of European wines in Japan.

In this context, it is noteworthy that no Dutch records reveal the consumption of wines by Japanese women during this period, although it seems most conceivable that Japanese prostitutes (*yūjo*) often tasted wine in the course of their professional responsibilities.

There were several reasons for the gradual increase in demand for wine in Japan over the course of the seventeenth century. First, a number of *bakufu* officials began to purchase European wines because they could not receive them as gifts. Such is the explanation given by Wilhem Versteeghen, who referred to the example of Inoue Masashige, identified as the first buyer of wine according to VOC records. "He is not allowed to accept any presents, for which the shogun remunerates him with a large sum of money every year. Nonetheless, all that we bring him he accepts, against payment, but not for the full value."[36] Likewise, other officials tended to follow the same practice in order to "relieve their consciences."[37] Having vaguely alluded to the "illegality" of this process, Wilhem Versteeghen was convinced that the company should continue to provide as many gifts as possible to the Japanese because these would all be paid for in the end with other rewards.

Second, it is possible that wine was sought for medical purposes. Though no descriptions in Dutch records explicitly point to the medicinal use of wine by the Japanese, the fermented grape juice often appears in references to the treatment of the sick. On his way back from a visit to Edo, when one of the retainers of the governor of Nagasaki was badly wounded in his arm by a pike, the VOC surgeon administered first aid using some Spanish wine as a tonic to restore him.[38] Another example from Dutch records shows how warmed wine was recommended to accompany medicine.[39] Such uses explain why the Japanese sometimes purchased wine along with medicinal goods. The contemporary Chinese medical book *Compendium of Materia Medica* (*Bencao gangmu*), originally published in 1596 and translated into Japanese as *Honzō kōmoku* in the early seventeenth century, also lists wine and its properties in the section on fermented products.[40]

Third, wine was presumably favored simply because of its taste. When Ogasawara Tadazane (1596–1667), the *daimyō* of Kokura, requested a reimbursement for tent wine that he considered "too thin," Zacharias Wagenaer made a rare remark on the Japanese taste for wine: "It is true that the tent wine which was brought here last year is rather bad and thin, which is the reason that less than ten gantang [approximately 24 liters] have been sold in the entire year. These people like it thick and black." He concluded sarcastically, saying, "I would know how to please them if only we had enough ink available."[41]

Similarly European wines also appeared to be a useful diplomatic tool for Dutch merchants to ensure good relations, especially with the *bakufu* in Edo. Successive chiefs of the Dutch factory understood the necessity of such expenses. Wilhem Versteeghen noted in 1647 that "every person gets the small things he requests, and by doing so we shall also win their affection. I think that this stratagem should be pursued in the future, for it only costs the Company a handful of spectacles, some telescopes, butter, tent wine, almonds, cheese, and other such trifles."[42] Likewise, Johannes Boucheljon observed that the only reason for such expenses is "to become acquainted with these gentlemen and encourage their favorable disposition towards the company."[43] It is possible that the Dutch merchants initially did not have the intention to commercialize European wines in Japan, but the repeated use of wine on various occasions inside and outside the factory provided a potential market. Such early "marketing" strategies bore fruit in the mid-1640s.

Most importantly, the rationale behind the Japanese consumption of wine until the mid-seventeenth century was not a thirst for European civilization but rather a desire to create distinctions within a stratified society. European wine represented a privilege that was only available to a few. When Gabriel Happart witnessed a former governor of Nagasaki's persistent request for tent wine, he observed, "it is surprising that gentlemen of such distinction have to request such a small thing in this way and that this juice remains in such high esteem with them as a second nectar that even the enjoyment of a *gantang* or two [approximately 2.4 to 4.8 liters]—which is a measure somewhat larger than a *flapkan*—and that at 5 taels each, is considered a prerogative."[44] The capacity for acquiring this exotic beverage itself was an important sign of distinction. Luxury goods are powerful markers of social differences, following the observation of Pierre Bourdieu, "the relationship of distinction is objectively inscribed within it [i.e., the world of luxury goods], and is reactivated, intentionally or not, in each act of consumption, through the instruments of economic and cultural appropriation which it requires" (Bourdieu 1984, 226).

By the mid-seventeenth century, European wines were exported to Japan to meet the demand of precocious amateur connoisseurs. The consumption of wine in Japan first appeared as an independent phenomenon, but it can be understood in a national and a global context.

The regular supply of European wines in Japan coincided with the rise of sake consumption in Edo. In the second half of the seventeenth century, brewers in the Kinai region, the area around the cities of Osaka and Kyoto, took the initiative to export their products to the shogunal capital (Yuzuki 2005, 73–75, 241–48, 277–79). Behind the development of this new trade was the centralization of distribution networks and subsequent flourishing of urban culture. Although quantities were limited, European wines circulated on a similar basis as sake, which also remained a luxury item during that period. Since rice was a staple food that influenced the nation's economy, the government kept close control over its production and consumption (Yoshida 1997, 95–112; Yuzuki 1990).

Another reason for the acceptance of European wines in Japan might have been the fact that the consumption of alcoholic beverages such as sake was already an established practice by the time European wines first reached Japan. The new alcoholic beverage made of fermented grape presented a possible alternative to sake. It is speculative whether the Dutch merchants first used wine in a similar way as the Japanese, who served sake on social and political functions. Although such a process of assimilation appears to be natural in the establishment of a new food product, it is important to note that the distribution of alcoholic beverages from Europe could have had the opposite effect and had a disruptive impact, as had sometimes been the case with certain indigenous societies outside Europe.[45] The existence of a mature drinking culture was a key element that facilitated the moderate acceptance of this new alcoholic beverage from Europe.

Conversely, it might also be possible to situate the consumption of wine in seventeenth-century Japan in the context of European wine history. As a number of classic works in this field repeatedly illustrate, even in a country like France, the consumption of wine as a commodity had for centuries been limited to persons of a certain rank with fortune and distinction (Lachiver 1998, 307–14). The consumption of wine had represented prestige for a long time. It was only during the course of the seventeenth century that wine gradually became a popular drink in Europe, particularly in metropolitan areas. Roger Dion claims that it was not uncommon until the end of reign of Louis XIV (1715) for peasants in the Burgundy region to never have tasted the main food product of their region (Dion 1959, 472–73). Moreover, it seems probable that the Sun King drank very little wine (Enjalbert 1975, 104–6). These facts suggest that wine consumption in Edo could be understood against European consumer societies in Paris and Amsterdam.

In that regard, the seventeenth century witnessed more and more wine consumption outside religious contexts and institutions. Under the ancien régime, monarchs and their courts, as well as emerging bourgeoisies, increasingly enjoyed wine. In Japan, mercantile Dutch Protestants reincarnated this sacred beverage that had originally been introduced by religious Portuguese Catholics. The Japanese accepted it by completely transforming it into a secular beverage void of any religious connotations characteristic of a Christian context.

European wine culture expanded to different parts of the globe from the late Middle Ages to the early modern period through the activities of merchants and missionaries. Countries such as South Africa that started the production of wine in that period are nowadays challenging traditional European vineyards on the global wine market, while a country like Japan that began to consume wine at the same time is one of the major export markets for classic European wines today. The evolution of wine in Asia in general has certainly been slow, but at the same time it has made a gradual progress over the course of the centuries (Pitte 2009, 253–70). A study of wine consumption in early modern Japan helps us to understand the initial stage of the globalization of wine consumption more thoroughly. The seeds of the current wine market and industry were sown during this period in history.

NOTES

1. Asai's study (1992) is a prominent example of a historical investigation of wine in Japan that begins in the Meiji period. The term *wine* will be used, unless otherwise indicated, as "the fermented juice of the grape used as a beverage" (*Oxford English Dictionary*, 1989). The term *budōshu* (grape wine) appears in a number of Japanese works such as *Encyclopedia of Food in Japan* (*Honchō shoku kagami*), published in 1697 (Hitomi 1976, 129), but the liquors referred to in these works defined a different type of alcoholic beverage that was made of grapes and sugar soaked and blended in old liquor.

2. Pitte (1990) also addresses the lack of historical research on wine in the premodern period. Popular historians have so far demonstrated better than academics their interests in the history of foreign alcoholic beverages in Japan. See Fujimoto (1992) and Maniwa (1976).

3. See Bruijn, Gaastra, and Schöffer (1987) and Gaastra (2003) for the general aspects of the company. The emphasis on production and the indifference toward consumption (as well as distribution) is not unique in the history of wine in Japan. We can also see these tendencies in historical research on wine in Europe. The fact that the history of wine has been predominantly studied in wine-producing countries seems to offer a plausible explanation for this. Hancock (2009) provides an inspiring example that attempts to bridge such lacuna in historiography.

4. Two of the most recent theses on this topic are by Bruyn Kops (2007) and Wegener Sleeswijk (2006).

5. Blussé and Viallé (2001/2005) and Historiographical Institute (1974–2007). Any Western names mentioned will be the names of Dutch factory heads unless otherwise indicated.

6. For financial data, see the National Archives (hereafter NA); *Nederlandse Factorij in Japan* [hereafter NFJ], inv. no. 829–851, *negotie journal*. All trade journals between 1638 and 1641 have completely been transcribed by Kazuhiro Yukutake; see

Hirado City Historiography Committee (1998/2000). Yukutake (1992) serves as one of the best introductions to the bookkeeping system of the VOC.

7. The term *tinto* certainly signifies the color of red wine, and *tinto* often means simply red wine, particularly in Iberian languages. However, no records or relevant descriptions about the place of origin are available thus far. According to a contemporary Dutch medical book, tent wine is defined as a Spanish red wine produced in the Mediterranean area, particularly in the hinterland of Alicante (Beverwijck 1642, 140).

8. This calculation is based upon NFJ 839 from the year 1639. The price of tent was approximately 0.59 guilders per liter, Spanish wine 0.41 guilders, and French wine 0.16 guilders.

9. The annual journey to Edo was regularized after 1633. The official purpose was to have an audience with the shogun to show gratitude for the permission of trade. In the first half of the seventeenth century, the entire journey took twelve to thirteen weeks, lasting from the twelfth through the third months. During their stay in Edo for a few weeks, the Dutch merchants were kept busy in meetings with the Japanese.

10. A flute is a type of transport ship in high demand, particularly in the seventeenth century (Kooijmans and Ellen 2000, 44).

11. Historiographical Institute, *Diaries Kept by the Heads of the Dutch Factory in Japan* (hereafter DFJ). Vol. 3, p. 101, dated 8 February 1638.

12. Viallé (2006) offers profound insight into the practice of gift-giving conducted by VOC. See also Kato (1998) and Chaiklin (2003).

13. NA, NFJ 831, dated 26 December 1627.

14. DFJ. Vol. 2, p. 18, dated 21 March 1636. The "Majesty" mentioned here is the third shogun, Tokugawa Iemitsu (1604–51).

15. For instance, Oze Hoan (1564–1640) described in his famous *Biography of Toyotomi Hideyoshi* (*Taikōki*) (1625) that Christian missionaries often treated Japanese, particularly public servants, to wine and confectionary (in the case of nondrinkers) with the objective of proselytizing them (Oze 1996, 9). According to estimates, the Christian population in Japan at that time consisted of 300,000 people (Boxer 1951, 320–21) and the number of Jesuit churches amounted to around two hundred (Takase 1993). The influence of Christianity spread widely, especially in Nagasaki, whose population amounted to approximately 40,000 people in 1626 (Kato and Yamada 1981, 288). Almost the entire population of Nagasaki was Christian, at least in the first decade of the seventeenth century (Elisonas 1991, 368).

16. Shimabara is in the southern region of Nagasaki. At the request of the Tokugawa *bakufu*, VOC vessels assisted in suppressing the rebellion, an act that demonstrated the Dutch intention to show loyalty to the Japanese on the one hand and to eliminate the influence of the Roman Catholics on the other.

17. Arrack can be "any strong drink, distilled spirit, essence" (Yule and Burnell 1903, 36). It is made from different grains and fruits, sometimes flavored with aniseed. The spelling also reflects the regional variety of the production. The arrack mentioned here likely came from Batavia.

18. Blussé and Viallé, *The Deshima Dagregisters* (hereafter DD). Vol. 11, 14 and NA, NFJ 55, dated 1 August 1641.

19. See, for instance, DD. Vol. 11, 155, dated 23 December 1643

20. DD. Vol. 11, 40–41, dated 24 October 1641.

21. DD. Vol. 11, 262, dated 5 January 1647.

22. NA, NFJ 1163

23. See Suzuki (2007) for the evolution and importance of this post.

24. In February 1653, the shogun received 40 *kan* each of Spanish and tent wine, approximately 144 liters in total, and each governor of Nagasaki received 21 *gantang* of only tent wine, approximately 50 liters. NA, NFJ 1171.

25. DFJ. Vol. 1, 257, dated 1 August 1635.

26. NA, NFJ 844, dated 24 January 1644. Thirty taels is the equivalent of 5 *ryō*.

27. See Nagatsumi (1975) and Blussé (2003) for this prominent and curious personage.

28. DD. Vol. 12, 195, dated 16 February 1655.

29. NA, NFJ 847, dated 22 October 1647.

30. DD. Vol. 12, 292, dated 28 February 1657.

31. DD. Vol. 12, 133, dated 4 February 1654.

32. DD. Vol. 12, 42, dated 2 February 1652.

33. DD. Vol. 12, 180–81, dated 5 November 1654.

34. DD. Vol. 12, 136, dated 18 February 1654.

35. See Katagiri (1984) for the sales of remaining commodities through the Dutch regular inns.

36. DD. Vol. 11, 261, dated 2 January 1647.

37. DD. Vol. 11, 261, dated 2 January 1647.

38. DD. Vol. 12, 54, dated 3 March 1652.

39. DD. Vol. 12, 137, dated 18 February 1654.

40. Iwashita (1998) also argues for the possible medicinal use of wine in seventeenth-century Japan.

41. DD. Vol. 12, 394, dated 9 September 1659.

42. DD. Vol. 11, 269, dated 11 January 1647.

43. DD. Vol. 12, 241, dated 11 February 1656.

44. DD. Vol. 12, 132, dated 2 February 1654.

45. Marshall (1979, 452). Examples in Africa and America prove that alcohol was even a tool for colonial expansion.

WORKS CITED

Manuscripts

National Archives, The Hague, Nederlandse Factorij in Japan te Hirado en Deshima
NFJ 55   Dagregisters

NFJ 829–851   Journalen
NFJ 1163—1171   Specificatie, Jedosche en Nangasaquische geschenken

Bibliography

Asai Usuke. 1992. *Nihon no wain tanjō to yōran jidai.* Tokyo: Nihon Keizai Hyōronsha.

Beverwijck, J. van. 1642. *Schat der ongesondheyt, ofte geneeskonste van de sieckten.* Dordrecht: n.p.

Blussé, Leonard. 2003. "The grand inquisitor Inoue Chikugo no kami Masashige, spin doctor of the Tokugawa *bakufu.*" *Bulletin of Portuguese/Japanese Studies* 7:23–43.

Blussé, Leonard, and Cynthia Viallé. 2001/2005. *The Deshima Dagregisters.* Vols. 11 and 12. Leiden: Institute for the History of European Expansion/Leiden University. [DD].

Bourdieu, Pierre. 1984. *Distinction: A Social Critique of the Judgment of Taste.* Cambridge, Mass.: Harvard University Press.

Boxer, C. R. 1951. *The Christian Century in Japan: 1549–1650.* Berkeley: University of California Press.

Bruijn, J. R., F. S. Gaastra, and I. Schöffer, eds. 1987. *Dutch-Asiatic Shipping in the 17th and 18th centuries.* Vol. 1. The Hague: Martinus Nijhoff.

Bruyn Kops, Henriette de. 2007. *A Spirited Exchange: The Wine and Brandy Trade between France and the Dutch Republic in Its Atlantic Framework, 1600–1650.* Leiden: Brill.

Chaiklin, Martha. 2003. *Cultural Commerce and Dutch Commercial Culture: The Influence of European Material Culture on Japan, 1700–1850.* Leiden: CNWS.

Dion, Roger. 1959. *Histoire de la vigne et du vin en France des origines au XIXe siècle.* Paris: Author.

Elisonas, Jurgis. 1991. "Christianity and the Daimyo." In *Early Modern Japan.* Vol. 4 of *The Cambridge History of Japan.* Ed. John Whitney Hall, 301–72. Cambridge: Cambridge University Press.

Enjalbert, Henri. 1975. *Histoire de la vigne et du vin, l'avènement de la qualité.* Paris: Bordas.

Fujimoto, Giichi. 1992. *Teihon yōshu denrai.* Tokyo: TBS Britannica.

Gaastra, Femme, S. 2003. *The Dutch East India Company: Expansion and Decline.* Trans. Peter Daniels. Zutphen: Walburg Pers.

Hancock, David. 2009. *Oceans of Wine: Madeira and the Emergence of American Trade and Taste.* New Haven: Yale University Press.

Hirado City Historiography Committee. 1998/2000. *History of Hirado City: Historical Documents in Foreign Languages.* Vols. 2–3. Hirado: Author.

Historiographical Institute, ed. 1974–2007. *Diaries Kept by the Heads of the Dutch Factory in Japan,* 11 vols. Tokyo: University of Tokyo Press [Original Texts]. [DFJ]

Hitomi, Hitsudai. 1976. *Honchō shoku kagami*. Tokyo: Heibonsha. Vol.1. Translated with notes by Isao Shimada. Originally published in 1697.

Iwashita Tetsunori. 1998. *Kenryokusha to Edo no kusuri: Ninjin, budōshu, osoba no kusuri*. Tokyo: Kitaki Shuppan.

Katagiri Kazuo. 1984. "Ranjin ni yoru kenjō, shinmotsu zanpin no hanbai to Oranda tsūji." *Aoyama shigaku* 8:91–111.

Kato Eiichi. 1998. *Bakuhansei kokka no seiritsu to taigai kankei*. Tokyo: Shibunkaku.

Kato Eiichi and Yamada Tadao, eds. 1981. *Kōza nihon kinsei shi*. Vol. 2. Tokyo: Yuhikaku.

Kooijmans, Marc, and Judith Ellen. 2000. *VOC-glossarium: verklaringen van termen, verzameld uit de Rijks Geschiedkundige Publicatien, die betrekking hebben op de Verenigde Oost-Indische Compagnie*. The Hague: Instituut voor Nederlandse Geschiedenis.

Lachiver, Marcel. 1988. *Vins, vignes et vignerons*. Paris: Fayard.

Marshall, Mac, ed. 1979. *Beliefs, Behaviors and Alcoholic Beverages: A Cross-Cultural Survey*. Ann Arbor: University of Michigan Press.

Maniwa Tatsuzō. 1976. *Nanbanshu denrai shi*. Tokyo: Shibata Shoten.

Nagatsumi Yoko. 1975. "Orandajin no hogosha to shite no Inoue Chikugo no kami Masashige." *Nihon rekishi* (Tokyo) 327, no. 8: 1–17.

Oxford English Dictionary. 1989. 2nd ed. Ed. J. A. Simpson and E. S.C. Weiner. Oxford: Clarendon Press.

Oze Hoan. 1996. *Taikōki*. Rev., annotated Teruhiko Hinotani and Hiroshi Emoto. Tokyo: Iwanami Shoten. Originally published in 1625.

Pitte, Jean-Robert. 1990. "Vignobles et vins du Japon." In *Les vins de l'impossible*. Ed. Alain Huetz de Lemps et al., 37–50. Grenoble: Glénat.

———. 2009. *Le désir du vin. À la conquête du monde*. Paris: Fayard.

Suzuki Yasuko. 2007. *Nagasaki bugyō no kenkyū*. Kyoto: Shibunkaku.

Takase Kōichirō. 1993. "Iezusu kai Nihon kanku." In *Iwanami kōza Nihon tsūshi*. Vol. 11. Tokyo: Iwanami Shoten.

Viallé, Cynthia. 2006. "In Aid of Trade: Dutch gift-giving in Tokugawa Japan." *Tōkyō daigaku shiryō hensanjo kenkyū kiyō* 16:57–78.

Wegener Sleeswijk, Anne. 2006. *Franse wijn in de Republiek in de 18e eeuw: Economisch handelen, institutionele dynamiek en de herstructurering van de markt*. PhD diss., University of Amsterdam, Amsterdam.

Yoshida Hajime. 1997. *Edo no sake: Sono gijutsu, keizai, bunka*. Tokyo: Asahi Shinbunsha.

Yukutake Kazuhiro. 1992. "Account books of the Dutch factory at Deshima: The accuracy of the recorded figures of the commercial transactions between Japan and the Dutch East India Company through their analysis." *Socio-Economic History* (Tokyo) 57, no. 6: 793–831.

Yule, Henry, and A. C. Burnell. 1903. *Hobson-Jobson: A Glossary of Colloquial Anglo-Indian Words and Phrases, and of Kindred Terms, Etymological, His-*

torical, Geographical and Discursive. New ed. Ed. William Crooke. London: J. Murray.

Yuzuki Manabu. 1990. "Inshu to sesshu ron: Sono rekishi teki kōsatsu." *Keizai gaku ronkyū* (Nishinomiya: Kwansei Gakuin University) 44, no. 2: 39–58.

———. 2005. *Sake tsukuri no rekishi.* New ed. Tokyo: Yūzankaku. Original edition in 1975.

PART II   *Modern Japan*

6 The History of Domestic Cookbooks in Modern Japan

SHOKO HIGASHIYOTSUYANAGI

THE MODERNIZATION OF JAPAN, especially after the Meiji Restoration of 1868, involved the creation of new gender roles often modeled on the Western ideal of domesticity.[1] Accordingly, the education of women focused on practical knowledge in household management in order to produce "good wives and wise mothers" (*ryōsai kenbo*), idealized paragons able to maintain a harmonious household.[2] Beginning in the 1880s, practical guides to housekeeping—including books on cookery, clothing, housing, and child-rearing—were published in increasing numbers. This essay examines the history of domestic cookbooks during the Meiji period (1868–1912), years of rapid change in all areas of society and the years when domestic cookery came to be entirely entrusted to women. Following Stephan Mennell, I define the modern domestic cookbook as an "English kind of book" aimed specifically at a female audience. He compares English and French cookbooks of the late sixteenth century and notes that almost all French cookbooks were written for "male chefs" or "members of the nobility and *haute bourgeoisie* seeking guidance in the ordering of meals *a la mode*," whereas "English" books were intended to satisfy the needs of a new breed of "housewives who busied themselves with all aspects of household work" (Mennell 1996, 87). The Japanese experience in the late nineteenth century follows a similar pattern but makes a dramatic leap into national kitchen politics in the early twentieth century. An analysis of domestic cookbooks can help us to understand the modern transformation of the Japanese housewife.[3]

THE RISE OF COOKBOOKS IN JAPAN

The history of cookbooks in Japan can be traced to the end of the beginning of the thirteenth century; however, these early compendiums of menus, cooking, and presentation skills were compiled as secret books (*hidensho*) intended as instructions for specific male cooks who served court nobles and samurai households. It was only in the Edo period (1600–1868) that cookbooks were published and readily available for an expanded reading audience. In conjunction with the growth of Japan's printing industry in the late seventeenth century, involving woodblock printing rather than movable type, and advances in commoner literacy, an abundance of books was available in Japan's urban centers, including Edo, which reached a population over one million. In addition to travel guides, play scripts, advice manuals, art books, and stories, cookbooks were an established and popular genre (Harada 1989, 104–42). These new cookbooks made recipes and menus public and were a departure from earlier traditions of secret transmission of cooking knowledge. Moreover, the popularity of the genre demanded the birth of new and unique publications. Some books specialized in recipes for individual foodstuffs; for example, there were specialty books for cooking tofu, sea bream (*tai*), Japanese radish (daikon), citron (*yuzu*), egg, sweet potato (*kansho*), and devil's tongue (*kon'yaku*). These cookbooks were classified as "books for 100 rarified tastes" (*hyakuchin mono*) and included many brand-new recipes, hoping to please the palates of a demanding and ever-growing number of readers. Additionally, cookbooks were issued by some of Edo's most famous restaurants, including the super-expensive Yaozen. Famous chefs published their recipes, providing a feast for the eye—and serving as advertisements for their culinary establishments. And despite Japan's limited contact with the outside world during the Edo period, books specializing in Chinese cooking were published that included instructions on how to eat in the Chinese style and information on Chinese cooking tools and ingredients (Higashiyotsuyanagi 2005, 2–29).

For most of the Edo period, cookbooks were intended for a male audience and were more voyeuristic than practical. They were not intended for home cooking; rather, they described the preparation of formal sumptuous banquets and served the purposes of hobby reading. All authors and editors were male, and in cases where the books did provide practical information, the target audiences clearly were male professional cooks and dilettantes. The first cookbooks aimed clearly at female readers appeared in the first half of the nineteenth century, just before the opening to the West. Two books stand out: *How to Receive Sudden Guests* (*Rinji kyaku ashirai*, 1820) and *Dishes for All Seasons* (*Nenjū bansai roku*, 1849). Both books were intended as practical guides for home cooking. The introduction to *Dishes for All Seasons*, for example, noted that sometimes even experienced wives and cooking maids, let alone novice cooks, were occasionally at a loss about what and how to cook. Accordingly, the book offered easy-to-prepare recipes in order to relieve their stress and strain of their daily cooking duties. In fact, these cookbooks directed at women offered an array of reasonable recipes capitalizing on low-cost ingredients such as bracken (*warabi*), burdock (*gobō*), cucumber (*kyūri*), dried radish (*kiriboshi daikon*), and small fish (*zako*). These books represented the dawn of domestic cookbooks that came to dominate the market in the later part of the nineteenth century.

NEW COOKBOOKS AND THEIR READERS

New types of cookbooks gained popularity after the Meiji Restoration, particularly books on Western cuisine and domestic cookbooks for the woman of the house. Japan resumed active contact with the West after the visit of Commodore Perry in 1853; the opening of a foreign settlement in Yokohama in 1859 further integrated Japan into international trade networks. Rapid Westernization followed the Meiji Restoration of 1868, symbolized by the introduction of the steam locomotive, gas lamps, and the eating of beef. Indeed, a popular novel, *Sitting around the Stewpot* (*Ushiya zōdan agura nabe*, 1871–72), declared that beef-eating was a true mark of becoming a civilized country.[4] Around the same time, numbers of Western cookbooks went on sale. They were used by cooks and maids who sought employment in the houses of foreigners, people who sought to learn about the West through its food, or by some enterprising men who dared to open up restaurants serving beef. Government propaganda promoted beef-eating and milk-drinking as one way to add strength and height to the Japanese physique, in the end hoping that a Western diet would make Japan's military force more formidable. Actually most cookbooks published in the 1870s and 1880s introduced Western cuisine (and table manners), reflecting more the concerns of the state than the taste buds of its people (Steele 2003, 110–32).

Aside from the hope that beef and milk would strengthen the national body, the new government used familiarity with Western cuisine and social etiquette as a means to advance negotiations intending to revise the unequal treaty system imposed on Japan. In 1883, the government built a lavish Western-style ballroom and social center, the Deer Cry Pavilion (Rokumeikan), close to the Japanese Foreign Ministry in Hibiya, where government dignitaries held banquets and balls to entertain Western guests (Takeuchi et al. 1978, 109). To this end, knowledge of Western cookery and table manners were matters of national urgency.

These Western cookbooks were necessarily directed at a male audience; it was only in the 1890s that women began to experiment with Western menus in response to a new series of cookbooks aimed at home cooking. Most of these domestic cookbooks explicitly targeted female readers; the writing style was easy to understand and included phonetic symbols (*furigana*) alongside difficult Chinese characters. Recipes were not only easy to prepare but also inexpensive. They pointed out that previous Western cookbooks had been difficult and complicated for female Japanese readers. In order to demystify foreign menus, familiar Japanese equivalents were assigned to Western dishes: soup = *suimono*, beef steak = *yakiniku*, rice curry = *meshi no ankake*, croquette = *kizaminiku iri no tempura*, sandwich = *seiyō bentō*, in order to allay any apprehensions (Wilson and Ōmachi 1903). The low-cost recipes proved especially attractive to women readers, prompting them to experiment with Western dishes in their homes and then to cook them on a more regular basis. In short, Western cookbooks had two aspects: one aiming at professional cooks in the public sphere and another aiming at female readers who were in charge of daily cooking in domestic situations.

Indeed, beginning in the 1890s, women became the central audience for cookbooks in general, both Japanese and Western cuisine. These domestic cookbooks included daily menus and home recipes, and were intended for "amateurs" (*shirōto*), women engaged in home cooking as opposed to professional male chefs who worked outside the ordinary home in restaurants or the kitchens of the upper class (Ehara and Higashiyotsuyanagi 2008, 52–53).

Meiji period social and economic change gave birth to new gender roles; the state gave its moral and legal backing to division of patriotic duties, men serving the state in public, women as "good mothers and wise wives" in private. Accordingly, newly established schools for women, many set up by Christian missionaries, placed great emphasis on practical knowledge, "home economics," where women could learn skills such as cooking, sewing, and bookkeeping that were necessary for efficient and rational home management. This curriculum, aimed primarily at upper-class women who could afford higher education, was mirrored in the publication of domestic cookery books that presented an innovative variety of recipes and suggestions to meet the needs of a growing number of female readers who cooked for their family every day (Higashiyotsuyanagi and Ehara 2003, 225–40).[5] By the 1890s, domestic cookery was entrusted entirely to women, who came to rely upon domestic cookbooks for the planning and preparation of daily meals and for general information on how to manage their households. Like Mrs. Beeton's famous book so popular in Victorian England, the Japanese domestic cookbook served as a guide of reliable information for aspirant middle-class women.

The first domestic cookbooks, however, did not necessarily deal with the preparation of daily home meals. Instead, many of the cookbooks tended to recommend special recipes for the entertainment of guests. Increasing levels of affluence, both among the upper and middle classes, allowed families to enjoy food from outside the house, either in the form of catering services (*shidashi*) or visits to restaurants. In 1910, for example, a young Kyoto housewife writes in her diary of a special New Year's party: "The parlor had been prepared for the occasion and the dinner was catered by *Harisei* for 90 sen per guest. . . . A *nakai* [professional server] came to help serve the meal. Everyone got drunk and had a wonderful time—there was plenty of laughter" (Nakano 1995, 59).[6] Domestic cookbooks, however, cautioned against dependence on these food services, citing extravagance and waste, encouraging the dutiful housewife to entertain guests at home with the skills of her own kitchen.

The number and variety of domestic cookbooks, some appearing in magazine format, increased suddenly after the turn of the century. Any housewife uncertain of her abilities to run a "modern" household could turn to these for advice. Ogawa Toramatsu, for example, published a cookbook on *Japanese and Western Home Cooking* (*Wayō nichiyō ryōri*) in 1901, targeting young housewives in need of practical information on cooking, sewing, and economy (Ogawa 1901, i–ii). Domestic and Western cookbooks alike were published in uncomplicated and simple language. In 1905, for example, Kamei Makiko, one of the first women to author a cookbook, complained that previous cookbooks were too difficult for beginners, making it clear that her cookbook was meant to meet the simple needs of everyday life (Kamei 1905, 1–2). Kamei asserted that her book, *Practical Domestic Cookery* (*Jitsuyō katei ryōrihō*) was intended for those who do not even know how to hold a kitchen knife or how to cut carrots or burdock root (Kamei 1905, 1–2). Her book did provide much practical advice: how to stock a pantry, which tools to have on hand, how to sharpen knives, how to use dusters, how to buy ingredients, how to deal with kitchen waste, how to use various stoves and ovens, how to cut ingredients, and so on. Indeed, the book was intended for beginners, teaching inexperienced housewives, often termed "amateurs" (*shirōto*), the very basics of cooking and household management.

THE TRANSITION FROM THE "SUPERVISORY HOUSEWIFE" TO THE "PRACTICAL HOUSEWIFE"

How did the role of women in the kitchen change over the course of the Meiji period? One popular cookbook published in 1898, *All-Year Delicacy Cooking for Amateurs* (*Chinmi zuii shirōto ryōri*), makes the following assertion:

The History of Domestic Cookbooks in Modern Japan 133

This book was compiled for people who preside over an ordinary kitchen. Cooking methods are explained in simple and minute detail, making it easy for even amateur cooks to make delicious dishes. Even people who do not cook themselves, but only employ servants, will read this book and supervise their servants accordingly, and become able to transform the terrible into the delicious! (Nakamura 1898, 1)

According to this book, the supervision of servants was an important part of a housewife's expected repertoire of skills. The image of the "supervisory housewife" is borne out on the frontispieces of several cookbooks from the 1890s. For example, the cover of *How to Cook Meals for All Seasons* (*Shirōto ryōri nenjū sōzai no shikata zen*, 1893) depicts a woman who is instructing a servant on how to cook using a cookbook (Hananoya 1893). This illustration is evidence of the existence and role of the "supervisory housewife," a reader who does not cook herself but was nonetheless fully involved in the preparation and presentation of foods through the supervision of her servants.

Also in the 1890s, the term "housewife" (*shufu*) came into common use, appearing regularly in books and magazines intended as practical instruction for a new generation of brides and stressing the female role in the overall management of household affairs (Muta 1996, 65–67). The proper instruction of servants was a central theme, even surpassing the necessity of gaining practical cooking skills. At this time, authors and publishers of domestic cookbooks assumed that their readers belonged to an upper class of women who were able to employ servants in their role as a "supervisory housewife."

In the 1900s, however, a publication boom in cookbooks betrayed change on the horizon. The titles of many of these new domestic cookbooks included words such as "practical" (*jitsuyō*), simple (*otegaru*), easy (*kantan*), and useful (*katsuyō*), foreshadowing the appearance of the "practical housewife." Even the joys of Western cookery, as the instructions in the 1905 publication *Domestic Western Cookery* (*Katei seiyō ryōri*) proclaimed, were well within the reach of the ordinary housewife.

On the other hand, authors of many domestic cookbooks insisted emphatically on the intrinsic significance of cooking for women. The introduction of *Domestic Japanese-Western Cookery for Amateurs* (*Katei chōhō wayō shirōto ryōri*) declared that the act of cooking is by no means vulgar but a desirable occupation that respectable ladies (*fujin*) and daughters (*reijō*) should never disregard; indeed, Japanese women should follow the model of ladies in the West, who were reputed to be actively engaged in cooking classes (Okamoto

A supervisory housewife and a servant from *How to Cook
Meals for All Seasons* (*Shirōto ryōri nenjū sōzai no shikata zen*,
1893) (Ajinomoto Dietary Culture Center).

1904, 1). Other cookbooks evoked the Western woman and her passionate
concern for cookery as a model for duplication in Japan.

Moreover, the introduction of *The New Cookery Guide* (*Shinsen kappō
tebiki*, 1901) argued that kitchen management is an important household
duty of the modern housewife (Inoue 1901). This book notes that housewives
usually entrust their servants with daily duties in the kitchen and sometimes
order foods to be delivered from restaurants and catering services when

entertaining guests, but it also warns that an ignorant housewife's mismanagement of the kitchen can easily lead to financial problems. At the very least, a housewife was expected to have mastered the basics of cooking and know how to instruct servants on how to construct a menu. The introduction to *A New Practical and Economical Vegetable Cookery* (*Jitchi keiken saishin yasai ryōrihō*, 1911) maintained that a lack of sewing and cooking knowledge should be considered a housewife's disgrace; the ability to read Western books or play the piano or violin could provide no consolation to a family in need of a good cook and overall household manager. The book also noted that cooking (*kappō*) was a subject of supreme importance in girls' schools, the mastery of which should place the woman where she squarely belongs—in the kitchen. A woman, the 1911 cookbook declared, must acquire unerring skills in the kitchen and must know how to economize in order not to enrage her mother-in-law. Cooking skills were essential because a woman must eventually marry into another household (Tanaka Seiko 1911, 1–3).

The practice of cooking was eagerly encouraged as an essential subject for women in the early twentieth century. As domestic cookbooks indicate, cooking held no less importance than the study of the liberal arts. More specifically, the acquisition of cooking skills was seen as a sort of barometer in determining family harmony. There was a clear shift in the perception of the housewife's role in the home and in the kitchen. In the 1890s, it was believed that a housewife must be well informed about kitchen matters in order to give proper instructions to servants; however, by the early 1900s, "modern" domestic cookbooks began to emphasize the necessity of practical cooking skills.

The new emphasis on practical skills can be seen in illustrations and photographs found in domestic cookbooks in the 1900s. The image of the "supervisory housewife" gave way to a woman who worked actively and personally in managing the household. The frontispiece of *Lessons on Daily Food Preparation* (*Sōzai ryōri no okeiko*, 1907) depicts three women: an older woman in the center of the picture seems to be the housewife; she is surrounded by two younger women who appear to be servants (Kaetsu and Asao 1907). As can be seen, the housewife is cooking something independently of the servants.

In summary, a housewife not only had to equip herself for supervising her own servants, but she also had to be prepared and able to personally participate in cooking and other household arts and economies. The cookbooks of the early 1900s give evidence of a shift from a "supervisory housewife" to a "practical housewife." The following decades witnessed even further increases in the number of such modern women (Imai 2002, 84–96).

An old housewife and two servants from *Lessons on Daily Food Preparation* (*Sōzai ryōri no okeiko,* 1907) (Ajinomoto Dietary Culture Center).

THE PROSPERITY OF DOMESTIC COOKBOOKS FOR "PRACTICAL HOUSEWIVES"

Rapid industrialization after the Russo–Japanese War (1904–5) was the cause of drastic changes to the expected roles of women in society. Jordan Sand has examined these changes of house and home and ideas of domesticity (Sand 1998). Dina Lowy has noted the emergence of the Japanese "new woman" in her study of the Japanese bluestocking movement (Lowy 2007). Barbara Sato has examined this phenomenon through an exhaustive study of Japanese women magazines, seeking to understand the links between modernity and women in the 1920s (Sato 2003). The examination of cookbooks published in the Taishō period (1912–26) is an equally appropriate method to analyze the changing role of women in Japanese society, especially the rise of what might be called "the new housewife." Increased opportunities for women to enter the workforce beyond the thread mills and home service was certainly a major factor in the rise of the independent, professional, and even stylish "new woman" (Tsurumi 1990; Bernstein 1991; Imamura 1996; Molony and Uno 2008). The rise of a new middle class of working women, however, meant a decline in the number of women willing to work as servants, forcing new demands upon the woman of the house. This new type of housewife, an avid consumer of cookbooks and other books and magazines on home management, was increasingly obliged to do the housework alone.

Additionally, the target of many domestic cookbooks came to focus more on younger housewives or unmarried girls.[7] An illustration in Koboso Takako's *Home Western-style Cookery* (*Katei yōshoku ryōrihō kan*, 1921) makes this point: servants are absent, and a woman is shown standing alone in the kitchen (Koboso 1921). As Jordan Sand notes, cookbooks in the Taishō era were aimed at "young women experiencing in the kitchen without the supervision or help of another woman" (Sand 2003, 83).

Furthermore, the worries of the new housewife were reflected in domestic cookbooks of the Taishō period. For example, the introduction to *Domestic Practical Menus and Cookery* (*Katei jitsuyō kondate to ryōrihō*, 1915) suggested that new housewives might be puzzled over what to cook everyday within the bounds of a limited budget (Nishino 1915, introduction by Miwada Masako). The book suggests that the dilemma of constructing an economical menu is a perennial problem, confronting women throughout history. There were, however, economic difficulties unique to the Taishō period, especially to the working classes, causing many domestic cookbooks to include low-cost recipes and hints about how to cut household costs.

A young housewife in a kitchen from *Home Western-style Cookery* (*Katei yōshoku ryōrihō*, 1921) (Ajinomoto Dietary Culture Center).

The Japanese economy grew spectacularly as a result of the First World War, making the years after the war an age of upstart millionaires (*narikin*). At the same time, however, the rapid appreciation of food and commodity prices meant that the livelihood of ordinary people was depressed. Wages increased, but not in pace with inflation. For example, the price of rice declined sharply right after the beginning of the First World War but rose sharply after 1917, in the end resulting in the mammoth rice riots of 1918, the largest popular disturbance in modern Japanese history (Lewis 1990). In response to these years of economic hardship, domestic cookbooks placed more and more emphasis on economical cookery and useful recycling of waste (Ehara and Higashiyotsuyanagi 2008).

The introduction to *Five Hundred Delicious, Nutritious and Cheap Meals* (*Bimi eisei anka ryōrihō gohyakushu*, 1916) alerts its readers that monotonous menus create waste in the home economy. The book states: "It is true that bad housekeeping destroys a family harmony and comfort. Boring meals, repeated ad infinitum are the cause of a lackluster life. Therefore, this book recommends to take the time to cook three delicious, appetizing meals per day" (Kuma 1916, 2).

This book and others attempted to make a patriotic connection between low-cost cookery and national economic stability. The frugal housewife could thus contribute to national prosperity.

This point is made ever clearer in the introduction to *Cheap Life Cooking Methods* (*Anka seikatsu kappōhō*) published in 1917 by Iwai Ken. The author described the postwar economic crisis that confronted Japan and urged housewives to initiate efficient and economic kitchen management (Iwai 1917). Iwai especially directed his attention to cutbacks in spending for food, urging housewives, as patriotic citizens, to do what they could to help with the national debt. Living frugally was thereby turned into a virtue. Nonetheless, Iwai echoed the author of *Five Hundred Delicious, Nutritious and Cheap Meals* (*Bimi eisei anka ryōrihō gohyakushu*, 1916), in calling upon the inventiveness of women in the kitchen. He also appealed to women to devote their energies in devising well-balanced meals that would ensure national longevity. By cooking economically, while still maintaining taste and variety, housewives could guard against the fear that lackluster households would lead to a lackluster country.

Japan's women's liberation movement traces its origin to the Taishō period. The Japanese Bluestocking Society (Seitōsha) was founded in 1911. Its founder, Hiratsuka Raichō, declared herself to be a "new woman" and began to improve women's position in society. Begun as a literary movement, Hiratsuka and fellow activist Ichikawa Fusae gradually become more militant; in 1920 they established the New Women's Association (Shin fujin kyōkai) and called for equal political rights. There has been much scholarship written on the women's movement, but emphasis on the "modern girl" (*moga*) has tended to obscure the sorts of problems that ordinary women encountered as a result of their encounter with modernity.

A look at Taishō-period domestic cookbooks provides insight into the thought and behavior of the "new housewife" who was forced to struggle to make ends meet. The cookbooks invariably included key words such as "cheap" (*anka*) and "economical" (*keizai*). A book published in 1916, *Five-sen a Dish, Today's Meal* (*Ippin gosen kyō no ryōri*), concentrated on low-cost cooking; it became a best-seller and went through over sixty editions. The book warned against an extravagant lifestyle and stated, "to cook without considering economic constraints will lead to an unhappy household" (Sakurai 1916). This book recommended against the use of sweet sake (*mirin*) in Japanese dishes and the use of butter in Western cooking. *Five Hundred Delicious, Nutritious and Cheap Meals* (*Bimi eisei anka ryōrihō gohyakushu*, 1916) included some sections on "tasty, cheap and nourishing sardine cookery" and a selection of recipes using "delicious economical nutritious tofu" and "side dishes of potato" (Kumma 1916). New low-cost substitute foods were encouraged, such as pork, mutton, potatoes (*jagaimo*), and even bread. These examples show how different Taishō domestic cookbooks were compared to their Meiji forerunners; supremely practical and economical, the cookbooks rarely mention special dishes for guests.

Taishō cookbooks constantly urged housewives to use substitutes as a means of economy. Hayashi Sueko, for example, held potato cookery lessons and published several potato cookbooks (Hayashi 1910, *inter alia*). She was particularly known for her "potato rice" (*bareisho-mai*) recipe that was able to stretch a household's rice budget without sacrificing nutritional value.[8] Another key spokesman for frugal cooking was Tanaka Hiroshi, a professor at Tokyo Imperial University, who championed the eating of pork. His *Tanaka-style Pork Cookery* (*Tanakashiki butaniku chōrihō*, first published in 1916) became a best-seller, going through many editions (Tanaka 1916). He also, like Hayashi, held special pork cookery lessons for housewives in line with the general appeal to housewives to take up low-cost cooking appropriate to those difficult times.

The introductions of many Taishō-period domestic cookbooks universally adopted a political message: The urgent task for women was to master domestic cookery in order to alleviate the national economic crisis. This pattern would only be exaggerated in the 1930s when the sense of crisis spread into other spheres. In other words, modern domestic cookbooks offered practical advice on how and what to cook, but at the same time, in accordance with the changing times, they mirrored a national discourse connected mainly to aspirations to build up Japan's wealth and power (*fukoku-kyōhei*). Even from the early Meiji period, the eating of beef and drinking of milk was connected with military power. Domestic cookbooks were nonetheless published first to satisfy curious taste buds and later redefined as guidebooks for domestic harmony. In the early twentieth century, however, domestic cookbooks pursued higher goals: Proper cooking and housekeeping would lead to national stability and progress. Women, moreover, were not simply confined to house and home; as "new housewives," they were part and parcel of a sort of national kitchen politics that sought to play a role in the creation of modern Japan.

NOTES

I am grateful to Professor M. William Steele of International Christian University for his advice and help in improving the English of this essay.

1. Eminent studies on modern Japanese women include Ochiai (1989), Bernstein (1991), Ueno (1994), Imamura (1996), Nishikawa (2000), and Molony and Uno (2008), among others.

2. In her study of female education intended to create "good wives and wise mothers" (*ryōsai kenbo*), Koyama Shizuko points out that the duties of "good wives and wise mothers" evolved to include household management and sewing (Koyama 1991).

3. For another study of cookbooks and what they can imply and create, see Appadurai (1988). He examines the role played by cookbooks in creating a national cuisine in postcolonial India, especially in the 1960s and 1970s.

4. *Sitting around the Stewpan* (*Ushiya zōdan agura nabe*) was written by an author of popular stories, Kanagaki Robun (1829–94). This humorous book consists of five volumes that depict various guests' conversations in restaurants serving beef stew (*gyūnabe*) in the early Meiji period. The lively situations depicted in these restaurants were often cited as an example showing the revival of beef-eating in Japan. The modern dish sukiyaki derives from *gyūnabe*.

5. In Japan, the first cooking textbook for women is *Kitchen Hints* (*Kuriya no kokoroe*) published by the first teachers' school in Kanazawa in Ishikawa prefecture in 1874 (Ishikawaken 1874). This text emphasized the necessity of learning cookery as part of female education. Although it is uncertain whether this text was actually used in girls' schools, the connection between cookery and female education is clear.

6. According to Makiko's diary, Harisei was a neighborhood restaurant frequently patronized by the Nakano family (Nakano 1995, 60). It continues to operate in Kyoto.

7. In the early Meiji period, after the abolition of the status hierarchy of the Edo period, three status groups (*zokushō*) existed: *kazoku, shizoku,* and *heimin. Kazoku* referred to the emperor, his family, and the court nobles, while *shizoku* meant the former samurai class, and *heimin* meant the other people such as farmers and townspeople. Members of these status groups were prohibited from intermarriage. With the expansion of the capitalistic system in the latter half of the Meiji era, wageworkers became a more recognizable group, and people were allowed the freedom to choose their own employment. These wageworkers derived from poorer *shizoku* and *heimin*; and it was not long after that they were called a new

middle class. This rise of the middle class caused a more specific difference between the male domain and the female domain: namely, the male "work sphere" and the female "domestic sphere."

8. "Potato rice" (*bareisho-mai*) is made by peeling potatoes, cutting them into the size of rice grains, and soaking them in water. The potatoes are then placed in boiling water to make them soft-boiled. Then, they are soaked in water again for twelve hours and dried.

WORKS CITED

Appadurai, Arjun. 1988. "How to make a national cuisine: Cookbooks in contemporary India." *Comparative Studies in Society and History* 30, no. 1: 3–24.

Bernstein, Gail, ed. 1991. *Re-Creating Japanese Women, 1600–1945*. Berkeley: University of California Press.

Ehara Ayako, and Shoko Higashiyotsuyanagi. 2008. *Kindai ryōrisho no sekai*. Tokyo: Domes Shuppan.

Hananoya Kochō. 1893. *Shiroto ryōri nenjū sōzai no shikata zen*. Tokyo: Jōkandō.

Harada Nobuo. 1989. *Edo no ryōri shi: Ryōribon to ryōri bunka*. Tokyo: Chūō Kōronsha.

Hayashi Sueko. 1910. *Shokumo tsukai daikakushin bareisho seizō oyobi chōrihō zen tsuki bareisho saibaihō oyobi chozōhō*. Tokyo: Kyōdō Shuppan.

Higashiyotsuyanagi Shoko. 2005. "*Edo ryōrisho ni miru chūgoku ryōri kondate no juyō*." In *Fūzoku shigaku*, no. 30. Tokyo: Nihon Fūzokushi Gakkai.

Higashiyotsuyanagi Shoko, and Ayako Ehara. 2003. "*Kaidai kindai Nihon no ryōrisho 1860–1930*." *Tōkyō kasei gakuin daigaku kiyō*, no. 43.

Imai Miki. 2002. "Ryōri zasshi kara mita Meiji kōki no shoku jōhō." *Chōri kagakkaishi* 35, no. 2.

Imamura, Anne E., ed. 1996. *Re-Imaging Japanese Women*. Berkeley: University of California Press.

Inoue Zenbei. 1901. *Shinsen kappō tebiki*. Unknown publisher.

Ishikawaken Daiichi Shihan Gakkō, ed. 1874. *Kuriya no kokoroe*. Tokyo: Masuchikan.

Iwai Ken. 1917. *Anka seikatsu kappōhō*. Tokyo: Shokumotsu Ryōyōin.

Kaetsu Takako (supervisory editor) and Tomotsu Asao, ed. 1907. *Sōzai ryōri no okeiko*. Tokyo: Hōeikan.

Kamei Makiko. 1905. *Jitsuyō katei ryōrihō*. Tokyo: Hakubunkan.

Kanagaki, Robun. 1871–72. *Ushiya zōdan agura nabe*. Tokyo: Seishido.

Koboso Takako. 1921. *Katei yōshoku ryōrihō kan*. Tokyo: Okada bunshōdō.

Koyama Shizuko. 1991. *Ryōsai kenbo to iu kihan*. Tokyo: Keisō Shobō.

Kuma Moriyuki, ed. 1916. *Bimi eisei anka ryōrihō gohyakushu*. Tokyo: Dainihon Ryōri Kenkyūkai.

Lewis, Michael. 1990. *Rioters and Citizens: Mass Protest in Imperial Japan*. Berkeley: University of California Press.

Lowy, Dina. 2007. *The Japanese "New Woman": Images of Gender and Modernity*. New Brunswick, N.J.: Rutgers University Press.

Mennell, Stephen. 1996. *All Manners of Food*. Urbana: University of Illinois Press.

Molony, Barbara, and Kathleen Uno, eds. 2008. *Gendering Modern Japanese History*. Cambridge, Mass.: Harvard University Press.

Muta Kazue. 1996. *Senryaku tositeno kazoku—Kindai Nihon no kokumin kokka keisei to josei*. Tokyo: Shinyōsha.

Nakamura Ryūu, ed. 1898. *Chinmi zuii shirōto ryōri*. Osaka: Yajima Seishindō Shoten.

Nakano, Makiko. 1995. *Makiko's Diary: A Merchant Wife in 1910 Kyoto*. Trans. Kazuko Smith, Stanford, Calif.: Stanford University Press.

Nishikawa Yuko. 2000. *Kindai kokka to kazoku moderu*. Tokyo: Yoshikawa Kōbunkan.

Nishino Miyoshi. 1915. *Katei jitsuyō kondate to ryōrihō*. Tokyo: Tōukadō.

Ochiai Emiko. 1989. *Kindai kazoku to feminizumu*. Tokyo: Keisō Shobō.

Ogawa Toramatsu. 1901. *Wayō nichiyō ryōri*. Tokyo: Ogawa Shōeidō.

Okamoto Kiyoshi, ed. 1904. *Katei chōhō wayō shirōto ryōri*. Tokyo: Hagiwara Shinyōkan.

Sakurai Chikako. 1916. *Ippin gosen kyō no ryōri*. Tokyo: Jitsugyō no Nihonsha.

Sand, Jordan. 1998. "At home in the Meiji period: Inventing Japanese domesticity." In *Mirror of Modernity*. Ed. Steven Vlastos, 191–207. Berkeley: University of California Press.

———. 2003. *House and Home in Modern Japan*. Cambridge, Mass.: Harvard University Asia Center.

Sato, Barbara. 2003. *The New Japanese Woman: Modernity, Media, and Women in Interwar Japan*. Durham, N.C.: Duke University Press.

Steele, M. William. 2003. "The emperor's new food." In *Alternative Narratives in Modern Japanese History*, 110–32. London: Routledge Cruzon.

Takeuchi Riso, Akira Tanaka, Shunichi Uno, and Ryuji Sasaki, eds. 1978. *Nihon kingendaishi shō jiten*. Tokyo: Kadokawa Shoten.

Tanaka Hiroshi. 1916. *Tanakashiki butaniku ryōrihō*. Tokyo Shuppansha.

Tanaka Seiko, ed. 1911. *Jitchi keiken saishin yasai ryōrihō*. Tokyo: Tanaka Shoseki Shuppanbu.

Tsurumi, E. Patricia. 1990. *Factory Girls: Women in the Thread Mills of Meiji Japan*. Princeton, N.J.: Princeton University Press.

Ueno Chizuko. 1994. *Kindai kazoku no seiritsu to shūen*. Tokyo: Iwanami Shoten.

Uno Yatarō and Kamakichi Watanabe. 1905. *Katei seiyō ryōri*. Tokyo: Okura Shoten.

Wilson, Mary M., and Sadako Ōmachi. 1903. *Yōshoku no okeiko*. Tokyo: Hōeikan.

7 Imperial Cuisines in Taishō Foodways

BARAK KUSHNER

AS JAPAN'S EMPIRE EXPANDED from 1895 through the 1910s and began to encompass large swaths of East Asia, as well as islands in the Pacific, the Japanese began to import more rice from abroad (Francks 2003, 133).[1] In the early twentieth century, little distinction had been made of the origin of foodstuffs; but as colonial possessions became more of a standard barometer to measure progress, the Japanese began to debate more vociferously the virtues of pure white rice produced domestically and the supposedly less tasty granules from "backward" nations. National food and cuisine became a marker of civilization.[2]

In this chapter I argue that Japanese foodways grew out of both a dialogue within Japan's colonial empire and a discourse bent on separating the concept of national food away from and in distinction to China.[3] For post–Meiji Restoration (1868) Japan, we cannot understand "Japanese cuisine" in a geographical and historical vacuum as a product that grew up in isolation. Indeed, one of the major ideological shifts in identity during the Taishō era (1912–26) was the incorporation and consumption of Chinese food and its influence on Japanese cuisine and diet, even as the very concept of Japanese cuisine was forming. This is not to say that the Japanese had not appreciated or dined on Chinese cuisine previously. They had, as the work of Higashiyotsuyanagi Shoko in chapter 6 of this volume and her research with Ehara Ayako elsewhere reveal.[4] However, I aver that these changes can be understood in the broader context of how the economic and social changes affected the national diet during the Taishō period. Knowledge of China through cookbooks did not necessarily always translate into respect for East Asian cultures in other venues; this interaction between the cooking world and political world is partly the focus of this essay.

Chinese cooking (*Shina ryōri*) began to be seen as tasty or worthy of emulation, but the process required time.[5] Japan's first modern book about Chinese cooking was published in 1886, but Chinese cooking as practiced by the Japanese and Chinese immigrants only hesitantly caught on as Japan industrialized decades later. This relatively small number of these cook-books can be contrasted with 130 cookbooks on Western food produced for eager Japanese readers in the same period.

Establishing this barrier between China and itself, or distinguishing Japan away from China in the minds of outsiders and foreigners, propelled Japanese to shun Chinese cuisine in the early years of the new regime. The late Meiji and early Taishō Japanese government and oligarchs were deeply worried about the international image of Japan. Early Meiji laws known as the *Petty and Misdemeanor Ordinances* (*Ishiki kai'i jōrei*) quickly attempted to stave away poor initial impressions by focusing on cleanliness, smell, and proper physical appearance so as not to cause embarrassment to foreign visitors. One key area for these efforts stood in the realm of hygiene as a way for Japan to separate itself from the Western view of an unclean and backward Asia.

FOOD AND EXCREMENT

Japanese initially hesitated to experiment with and appreciate Chinese cook-ing during the Meiji era because they associated such cuisine with a dirty and dystopian East Asia. This strategy stood, of course, completely in the opposite direction of pre-Meiji Sino–Japan relations where Japan borrowed heavily from China in the realm of cooking and eating.[6] National cuisine was a marker of civilization, but so was hygiene. Colonized nations did not just appear socially and politically backward: what they ate was poor and how they disposed of their effluvia was even worse.

Japanese travel books, prolific during the beginning of the twentieth cen-tury, discussed aspects that Japanese tourists believed represented the back-wardness of East Asian society. China was not the only sector targeted for abuse. Japanese intellectuals and officials also held strong views of Korean cuisine and hygiene. One book, Okita Kinjō's *The Backside of Korea*, lam-basted the small huts Koreans lived in as "pigsties" and reported that the Koreans' way of defecating everywhere made Seoul the "shit capital" of the world, with a corresponding stench (Duus 1995, 401–3). Okita almost held an even lower opinion, if that were possible, of Korean cuisine. "There are people who imagine pig, dog, it's all the same in Korean food . . . it more or less seems like you are picking up horse dung and eating it, but that would be judging it too quickly because we know they are after all a rice eating people," he wrote (Okita 1905, 76). Arakawa Gorō, in his travelogue *Contemporary Korea*, expressed similar distaste that everything was so dirty that Koreans could not distinguish Japanese soup (miso) from shit (*kuso*) (Duus 1995, 403; Arakawa 1906, 89).

The Japanese government had grown concerned about how its domestic food culture and that of its colonies was perceived internationally, so officials conducted a two-year study of Korean cuisine. The report summarized that Koreans mostly ate rice mixed with some grain or cereal but that in the countryside, away from urban areas, people who ate rice were pretty "rare." Choice words in the report were reserved for Korean kitchens, or "what you could call such a room are rare, and usually just a dark and unclean place to cook" (Murakami 1916, 88).

Japanese preoccupation with the association between bowel movements and national stature did not necessarily reflect poorly on their general perceptions. Japan was still largely agricultural, and night-soil fertilizer had been integral to Japanese agriculture since the seventeenth century. In addition, the topic of toilet activity ranked very highly in all sorts of intellectual and popular literature. Agriculturists paid close attention to excrement, and its collection, treatment, and distribution were serious endeavors in pre–WWII East Asia.[7] In 1909 the *Journal of Japanese Agricultural Studies* discussed how closely connected the act of eating and excreting was in an article, aptly titled "Excrement and Rice—Which Is More Valuable?" In direct language, the author voiced what was probably on the mind of many of his compatriots: "That which exits from people's buttocks we all know as excrement, but that feces is the treasure of farmers. We should look to it as the predecessor to rice, or as the successor of what rice once was." Summing up his views, the author concluded, "Feces is created and depends on people and rice depends on feces. Rice is excrement and in a way excrement is rice." The article ended by encouraging readers that "If we think about the connection between the two, you are indirectly consuming feces when you eat rice" (Yazaki 1909/2003, 46–47).

Taiwan offered another example of Japanese views of their own colonial cuisine.[8] The experiences of a young policeman who was elected to go and work in Taiwan in the mid-1920s are informative in this regard. In his recollections about early colonial life in Taiwan, the officer discussed smell. He admitted that garlic was healthy and full of vitamins but recalled, "I can't stand the odor but the people who eat it can't smell it themselves." He elaborated, "Because of that, when you enter a Taiwanese house there is some indescribable stench. It's really a huge problem." The first time the young man came into personal contact with the smell and entered a villager's house, he thought he was going to vomit due to what he termed the overpowering reek of garlic

(Aoki 2002, 84). The smell of a culture, not only its hygiene but also how it tasted in the physical sense, was a powerful signal to officials and intellectuals of the importance of Japan's plan of imperial progress and how such a project was linked to what colonials and Japanese consumed in their diets.

RAISING THE STANDARD

Taishō-era Japan experienced both the economic boom due to World War I market expansion and consumer demand and the later economic bust due to a hungry and growing population that did not always find food for its table. Japan was growing more sophisticated in parts, lusting after cuisine with taste and nutritional value, not just something to fill the belly.[9] Poverty remained a serious economic anchor that stymied future growth, but Taishō was also a period of deep transformation in Japan. Labor unions grew in number and strength and attempted to secure better wages and a reasonable workday, and to break traditional patterns of employment while raising the political consciousness of the working poor. The conditions for laborers, even after the implementation of the Factory Law (Kōjōhō) in 1916, were not ideal. The law, for places that employed more than fifteen workers, set the working day at twelve hours. Little quarter was given to sex and age—conditions were equally injurious to all. Women and children were guaranteed two holidays a month and about a half hour of rest after a half day of labor (Gowen 1925, 161–62). Suzuki Bunji, an early labor rights advocate, in 1917 described mines that employed 70,000 women as an environment where "they work in the bowels of the earth, naked like the men, wearing only a little breech-clout. . . . They are so like animals they can hardly be called human" (Gowen 1925, 162–63).

While Japan slowly modernized and Tokyo stood as one of the most advanced cities in East Asia at the time, on a daily basis most people in Japan still ate poorly. To investigate these matters, the Ministry of Home Affair's Bureau of Hygiene completed a survey in 1918 examining what people consumed from day to day. As the target audience moved from cities to the rural areas, the amount of rice people ate dropped precipitously (Segawa 1983, 18). In early Taishō, the country's ability to provide enough food without importing more supplies became less and less tenable, and prices for most goods had already started to rise.

Those who worked in urban areas as day laborers experienced economically rough times, and their numbers grew enormously throughout the 1910s and 1920s. During the late 1880s, most urban incomes had only allowed a family to purchase enough rice to survive on for a year; but as industries changed the manner and structure of employment, income expanded and "by 1930, in terms of rice and its quality, the average poor were absolutely much better off than the poor a generation before, though remaining underprivileged relative to contemporary standards" (Chūbachi and Koji 1976, 408). An article from the September 1914 issue of *Housewife's Companion* (*Shufu no tomo*) highlighted the poor state of caloric consumption with a dramatic example. A family of seven detailed in the article lived in a two-tatami-mat room and supposedly existed on one bowl of rice for everyone (Shōwa joshi daigaku shokumotsu kenkyūshitsu [hereafter SJDSK] 1971, 391).[10] Exact prices are hard to gauge given the shifting values of Japanese currency but food occupied a large portion of the working-class budget.[11]

A nutritious and filling recourse for the lower classes, during the day or on the way home and mostly for men, were "one-meal stands" (*ichizen meshiya*) that began to proliferate in areas where the working classes congregated to eat, drink, and rest from working. These stands were a slight improvement over the mid-Meiji "leftover food stalls" (*zanbanya*) because the food was made fresh to order. At such enterprises you could order a bowl of rice topped with a sprinkle of vegetables or some other topping for a slightly higher price. Noodle stands, *sobaya*, were also inexpensive places to eat away from home (SJDSK 1971, 391–92). Portable noodle stalls had flourished during the Edo period but now expanded to serve a more varied offering with the noodles. Unlike the period after WWII when Japanese believed foreign white rice to be less tasty than their own, during the Taishō era, Taiwanese and Korea rice imports steadily increased, feeding the growing Japanese population. People voiced some opposition, but the fact that imports from the colonies provided cheap and affordable rice diminished the outcry (SJDSK 1971, 409). Hunger cares little about the national origin of the ingredients.

The real social sticking point for bureaucrats bent on modernizing Japan and rendering it the most advanced country in Asia was the hygiene of kitchens. The Taishō population fretted over what was termed "cultured living" (*bunka seikatsu*). During the First World War era, with bounding industrialization and a growing number of urban laborers, the majority of Japan was still agriculturally based, but bread offered a more convenient manner to eat breakfast than rice. Bread was not extensively consumed in prewar Japan but it was making inroads along with wheat products such as noodles that mirrored what was available in Chinese cuisine.[12] Traditional Japanese meals were labor intensive. The maid (*jochū*) or lady of the house had to get up two hours early to cook rice and miso. Bread proved a time saver where you just cut a slice, slapped on butter, drank some coffee, and went to work.

One woman wrote in the April 1913 issue of *Housewife's Companion* (*Shufu no tomo*) that her kitchen stocked only a fry pan and a single pot, so having bread at her disposal greatly diminished her time in the kitchen because now she had to cook rice only once a day (SJDSK 1971, 443). There were no electric kettles or rice cookers in those days, so rice was made by boiling water over a small coal stove that required heating, constant attention while cooking, and then vigilance when cooling down the contents. If rice were eaten at night, the same time-consuming actions had to be repeated, fuel had to be gathered anew for the fire, and the ashes once more cleaned. The *Ladies' Companion* (*Fujin no tomo*) ran a monthly series of articles in 1913 concerning how long it actually took to make these types of dishes (SJDSK 1971, 461). Cooking was not easy work.

Maids were an indispensable part of early twentieth-century cooking for the simple fact that cheap labor in urban areas was readily available and food preparation took an inordinate amount of time when everything had to be made from scratch. Even though Japan was relatively poor, as soon as any family could theoretically afford domestic help, they often hired a housemaid. The first national census, conducted in 1920, calculated that there were slightly more than 580,000 young women working as house servants (Kiyomizu 2005, 88). A Japanese manual from 1907, *Renovating Kitchens* (*Daidokoro kairyō*), explained in great detail how to demand the most work from your maid for the least amount of money. The chapter on hiring maids suggested that you ask them straight out, "Do you have any kitchen experience?" If not, you could pay them less the manual recommended. If they responded that they did have experience, you could make them produce written proof from a previous employer and use that as the basis for their reduced wages (Amano 1907, 177).

By the early part of the century, the kitchen had now become a center for scientific experimentation. It was not enough to know *how* to cook; it now had to be clean, safe, and nutritious. Cleanliness was important because the authorities began to realize that unclean kitchens could cause the nation's health to suffer and this was a main source behind public disdain for Chinese food, argued some authors (Yamagata 1907, 439).

Early Taishō demonstrated advances in Japanese food science and tremendous progress in general science as well. These inventions promoted the idea of "delicious" (*umai*) food to a wider audience. This was also the time of the invention of food additives that changed the face of all Asian food. Ikeda Kikunae, the University of Tokyo professor who invented monosodium glutamate, more commonly known now as MSG, started his studies in the Satsuma domain in

A housewife and maid discussing kitchen tasks from *Renovating Kitchens* (Amano 1907).

Kyūshū. Ikeda's discovery of isolating the element behind the taste of "savory," or *umami* in Japanese, and his chemical patent led to the manufacture of a new food additive. MSG, when added to food, brought to life its inherent taste and thus further enhanced the palatability of Japanese dining.

TIME IS THE METER OF CIVILIZATION

Ajinomoto, "the essence of taste," the first company to produce MSG, began operations in 1909 only a few years after Japan's victory in the Russo–Japanese war. The seasoning was also the archetypal colonial food product. Japan required mass amounts of soy, rice, and other cereals to sustain its population, and imported larger quantities each year from China and its more formal colonies of Taiwan, Korea, and the South Pacific. MSG in the strict sense has no flavor, and only serves to enhance an inherent taste so it is technically not a spice but rather an additive. Ironically, Japanese cuisine historically does not champion thick or meaty flavors, but the country was home to extensive use of kelp (*konbu*), often used to make soup stock and by itself a natural source of *umami*. What is fascinating is why people crave the *umami* flavor, and Ikeda hypothesized that "the taste of glutamate is closely associated with animal food" so people are drawn to the flavor almost physically because it leads to an intake of "nutritive foods" (Ikeda 1909/2002, 820–36). A savory taste also synthesized better with the increase of noodle and wheat dishes that were gradually being imported from China and consumed beginning in the 1910–20s. As late as 1915, Chinese laborers made up the largest foreign population residing in Japan (Vasishth 1997, 108).[13]

MSG was not used in the early years of making rāmen, the Japanese version of a popular Chinese noodle soup, but its arrival on the market altered the taste that Japanese consumers demanded. Since the 1910s, workers, farmers, and urban residents clamored for savory dishes. MSG offered the means to make the less delectable savory and increased the market demand for a rich and meaty flavor. Rāmen and other postwar dishes responded to these economic forces. The patent makers intended the additive to be sprinkled onto food to enhance its "natural" flavor or made into a broth (*dashi*) and served as soup or gravy.

Ajinomoto conducted intensive research on colonial markets, such as Korea, to sell MSG. The company gave away gifts, and it was also used in *seolleongtang*, a thick soup made with beef stock. Korean cold-noodle shop owners formed an association to link up with Ajinomoto and received direct distribution. It is unclear if the Japanese administration of Korea formally supported Ajinomoto, but the company president was a school friend of the one-time governor general of Korea, Yamanashi Hanzō (Jung 2005, 32).

Even though most people, especially in contemporary Japan, use a variety of spices and industrially produced flavors in their kitchens, this was not yet the case in the early twentieth century. Japanese were not convinced that industrial flavors were necessary, and in response the Ajinomoto Company realized that such ignorance necessitated a campaign to teach the public to appreciate convenience. Several antiseasoning campaigns spread rumors that the spice was made from snake and at first people avoided using it (Ema 1985, 210). Ajinomoto resorted to public tastings and paying performers (*chindonya*) to march around the country touting the new product's arrival. *Chindonya* were popular forms of amusement/entertainment bands that marched around towns drawing attention to whatever brand or product they were paid to tout. It is difficult to gauge the success of the early campaigns because at the same time chemists and pharmacies stocked the product in a medicinal-looking glass bottle (Ōtsuka 1969, 111).[14] Sales increased more rapidly, however, once MSG began to be marketed more as an additive for cooking.

The Chinese had also long been keen on discovering the chemical composition of savory flavors, and many entrepreneurs spent countless hours trying to match Japanese industrial know-how. Wu Yunchu (1891–1953) succeeded. Wu was a significant business entrepreneur in Republican-era China, and MSG was excellent product on which to base Chinese nationalist pride. Wu was born in the 1890s outside of Shanghai and later studied at a school attached to the Jiangnan arsenal. In the 1920s while living in Shanghai, he managed to chemically formulate the Japanese product MSG that was proving popular with Shanghai restaurants and patrons. He labeled his product *weijing*, in Chinese, similar in meaning to the Japanese label of "the essence of taste," and applied for a patent. Both the Chinese and Japanese factories used starch derived from wheat and then treated the gluten with acid and soda to form it into a salt. Ajinomoto protested that its patents were being infringed upon, but Wu's plants kept producing; by 1928, domestically manufactured Chinese MSG outstripped Japanese imports. By the mid-1920s, Chinese in Shanghai and other modern cities immensely enjoyed the flavor that MSG brought out in cuisine to the tune of $1 million annually (Reardon-Anderson 1986, 188–89).

The 1920s in China was a time of Chinese boycotts against Japanese and European goods. The movement in support of nationally produced goods at one point drew so many people wishing to purchase *weijing* that demand outstripped supply, so Wu's company "bought Ajinomoto and then repackaged and sold it under its own brand" (Gerth 2003, 346). Wu Yunchu and his staff took "advantage of the national products movement by advertising their product as a 'completely Chinese product'" (Gerth 2003, 344).

The speed with which Japan transformed from the nineteenth to the twentieth century took the breath away of the elder generation, accustomed to the slower patterns of Meiji life (Tamura 1920/1980, 219). New mass media developing during the Taishō era, with an increasing number of magazines targeted at a larger body of consumer groups, and more aggressively marketed advertising campaigns also led to a change in how the population conceived of Japanese cuisine. Nowhere was this more evident than in the home, among those who were now burdened with the task of producing these new meals. This "discourse shaped the national standard of the home meal, which would be put into practice by future generations of housewives" (Cwiertka 2006, 99–100). Dominant themes in women's magazines, where a growing sector of ladies gained new knowledge about such matters, now centered on food and cooking with a similar focus on hygiene, nutrition, economy, convenience, and novelty. This attention declined briefly during World War II, but suffices to say by the 1960s, this trend had thoroughly solidified, and "cooking was projected as a way of showing every woman's affection for her family" (Cwiertka 2006, 113).

WOMEN'S ROLE IS TO COOK

Not only were late Meiji and early Taishō-era scientists deciphering the chemical codes for taste, but Japanese imperial subjects were also busy developing different modes of conduct for household duties. These changes included the realm of cooking and cleaning. This sudden effort to get women cooking in the kitchen was a relatively new trend, and now women required instruction in nutrition as well as texts that could teach them the recipes to create wholesome meals of Western and increasingly Chinese meals as well.[15]

Before the 1880s, the term *shufu*, the contemporary term for "housewife," did not exist in the common lexicon. By the turn of century, women began to be tied to the kitchen—where "good" housewives demonstrated their talents. The government promoted programs such as nutritional guidelines and the publication of recipes, while women's groups and journals urged families to eat at the same time around the same table—all part of the national "Lifestyle Improvement Campaigns" (*Seikatsu kaizen undō*) that included the rationalization of eating and personal finance (Cwiertka 2006, 91–92). "On the order of maintaining the health of family members," wrote one author in a 1923 book about the new education necessary for women, "direct and indirect responsibility falls on women. To meet this duty requires us to deepen and expand education about managing a house more economically and efficiently" (Ishizawa 1923, 23). Education and the media would have to supplement this knowledge since women could no longer acquire it while spending all their days cooking and sewing if the nation at large expected to raise its standard of living, the author suggested (Ishizawa 1923, 24). The Japanese government specifically targeted women and their education about home economics in its numerous Taishō-era campaigns to improve the nation's lifestyle. Convenient cooking methods, dishes with meat, and quick menus were the order of the day to feed a family within budgetary constraints, in a healthy manner, now seated together at the dinner table.

The kitchen, hygiene, personal health, and the stability of the family were all now tied together around the time of World War I into an important feature for a modern, civilized, and advanced country. One author in *Housewife's Companion* (*Shufu no tomo*) explained the situation as such. Germany, he said, is fighting many other countries. The men have left for the front and the women are taking care of the house while working away from home. The home is the center of national society, the writer concluded, and so an orderly family home with no waste is necessary. We need to do away with rooms we do not need, he said, and put in Western-style doors so we are safe when we leave. "Of second order are Japanese kitchens, they are dark and very unhygienic. We really must improve this situation. Kitchens are like peoples' stomachs, the place for providing nutrition and thus a most important space," he added (Yamawaki 1980, 180).

Hani Motoko (1873–1957), a noted liberal educator, publisher, and feminist, promoted in her main journal, the *Ladies' Companion* (*Fujin no tomo*, 1908–present),[16] the idea of keeping household account ledgers to encourage people to save money since many "were not yet accustomed to living on salaries" (Ambaras 1998, 25).

IMPERIAL FOODS

Japan saw imperialism and British strength through the possession of colonies not merely as a symbol of international prestige but also as a steady pipeline of food for the mother country. A Japanese treatise on opening up China for trade published in 1903 noted, "Even during times of peace, it is of the utmost importance to maintain a strong national supply of food (*minshoku no jūjitsu*) to serve as the base in supporting flourishing commerce and industry." Furthermore, "by opening sea lanes between the Qing Empire and Japan within a few days it is not difficult to ship enormous amounts of foodstuffs." And so, the book concluded, "we must work toward the development of China (*Shina*) to assiduously meet this end" (Satō 1903, 81).

To many Japanese in the early twentieth-century, China was a source of natural resources, but while its cuisine was largely ignored, the import of Chinese ingredients was an accepted practice. China, or *Shina* as the country was frequently referred to then in Japan, was seen as a haven of repellent corruption and degeneracy. Kodama Kagai (1874–1943), a well-known author and poet, in 1911 typified this disdain when he wrote about the cramped housing, undersized venues devoted to entertainment, and small restaurants squished together in quarters where Chinese conglomerated in Tokyo. "There were many Chinese restaurants—*Shina ryōri*," he said in a displeased voice. "They are covered with a sort of rodent-colored patina of dirt; when you open the door smoke billows out with the stench of pig fat and you get the feeling it is a sad and decrepit place. Pork is tasty but it's the food of an indolent and withering people," Kodama opined (1911, 80).

Yet, regardless of how the Japanese denigrated the Chinese, Japan itself was still far from being a utopia for a majority of the population. Even by 1921 only 10 percent of the population could be classified as middle class, and the 1918 rice riots "stand out as a sign of women's frustration and rage in the economic and political realms, capitalism, which made leaps during the war, changed the face of urban life" (Sato 2003, 30).

APPEARANCE OF RĀMEN

Consumers in Taishō Japan were feasting on a symphony of new tastes. These changes in living standards, consumption attitudes, and desires for different foods were, in part, produced by the growing presence of Chinese immigrants who spurred the opening of restaurants and the rise of an urban consumer class. It is from this class that rāmen, the archetypal Asian noodle soup, emerged. The spread and popularity of rāmen was not limited to the capital or the international city of Yokohama. Rāmen was a national phenomenon. The noodle soup arrived in slightly different forms in a variety of venues prompted by similar conditions all over Japan. In 1911, a shop in Sapporo, the Takeya Cafeteria, tentatively offered Chinese food. The cafeteria served many of the Chinese exchange students flooding into the newly established Imperial Hokkaidō University to learn the process of Japan's quick modernization. To meet the new demand, proprietor Ōhisa Masaji hired Wang Wencai, an itinerant Chinese laborer with cooking experience in the Russian Far East, as a short-order cook and switched the menu over to "Chinese food" (*Shina ryōri*). Wang quickly produced a new stream of meat and noodle dishes and one dish that he called "Chinese noodles" (*Shina soba*). The noodles were dissimilar to thick Japanese *udon*, or the more easily chewed and traditional favorite in pre-Meiji Tokyo, *soba*, *buckwheat noodles*. Wang's noodles had an al dente consistency and he bathed them in a meaty broth soup, a savory new taste.

The new dish flummoxed customers a bit when they tried to order. What to call it? The term "Chinese noodles" satisfied many, and well into the 1930s, peddlers on carts would call out in the late afternoons and early evenings, announcing their arrival with a mournful tiny trumpet and chanting,

"Chinese noodles! Hey there! Chinese noodles for sale!" (Yonezawa 1989, 86). But many of the Japanese who ate in noodle shacks merely resorted to saying, "Gimme some of that Chinky soup (*chankoro men*)." Such language was derogatory, and Ohisa's wife thought of calling the noodle soup *ryūmen* (willow noodles), in reference to the willow trees across the street from her store.[17] Another theory holds that while Wang was cooking the noodles, he would yell to the front in Chinese "*hao le*" but with his Shandong pronunciation it sounded more like "*hao la*," or "all ready!" The term for noodle in Chinese and Japanese shares a similar reading for the same character, *mian* in Chinese and *men* in Japanese. Uncouth customers would joke and demand some of the "*la-men*," or "la noodles." In Mandarin Chinese the actual word for pulled noodles is "*la-mian*" which over time ended up being the resultant term used for the new dish, written at least onto the Sapporo menu. The term failed to be adopted nationally, and most customers continued ordering "chink noodles" until Japan rebuilt during the postwar era. On postwar menus store owners used *katakana*, the Japanese alphabet for foreign words, instead of Chinese characters, and clients slowly began to order the noodle soup by name (Okuyama 2003, 57). A new dish was born, *rā-men*, because the Japanese language does not distinguish between the pronunciation of "l" and "r" (Okada 2002, 91–93).

Rāmen shops sprang up all over, demonstrating the penetration of the countryside by Chinese traveling laborers and market desires for new tastes broadly across the nation. In 1925, in the city of Kitakata in the central northern prefecture of Fukushima, a popular rāmen shop dominated the marketplace near the rail station. Kitakata is not a large city but currently houses the greatest number of rāmen shops per capita in Japan, eighty rāmen houses for a population of approximately eighty thousand. A Chinese peddler from Zhejiang province, Fan Qinxing, opened the noodle shop and called it The Original Come and Get It Shop (*Genraiken*), in homage to a similarly labeled predecessor in Tokyo (Okada 2002, 97). Fan's shop still stands in Kitakata, but it is far from the only game in town today as the popularity of rāmen has drawn in dozens of competitors to build on neighboring streets.

It was during the early Taishō era when the roots of what we could consider the Japanese taste and diet finally embraced Chinese cuisine and gave birth to something closer to contemporary Japanese national cuisine. One important ingredient in this process was an urbanized labor force looking for fattier foods. The Chinese food boom of the 1920s was due in part to an increasing number of factory and day laborers moving into the urban areas and a larger body of foreign populations, mostly from the Asian mainland, preparing and consuming cheap and convenient meals for these blue-collar workers. The living standards and aspirations of the masses of Japanese society were on the rise, and they accepted the more proletarian ideal of Chinese cuisine that emphasized taste over presentation in the opposite way of traditional Japanese cuisine. By 1923 there were about twenty thousand eating and drinking establishments in Tokyo, including maybe one thousand Chinese restaurants (SJDSK 1971, 643).

By the 1920s, some Japanese appreciated Western food, but more enjoyed Chinese food because it was eaten with rice like Japanese cuisine so it provided a supposedly more digestible combination. Not everyone disdained Chinese cuisine, and many Japanese who frequently traveled there acclaimed the food in the same breath that they disparaged China's supposedly backward culture. Venerated novelist of prewar Japan Tanizaki Junichirō (1886–1965) waxed poetic about Chinese food long before it became socially acceptable. In a 1919 newspaper article in the Osaka *Asahi* newspaper, Tanizaki said that he had always felt that Chinese cuisine was the tastiest (Tanizaki 1968, 78–83). Tanizaki did not, however, appreciate all aspects of Chinese cuisine. In general, "I like Chinese food and garlic is ok, but the day after I eat it my piss stinks so it's a bit annoying," he wrote (Chiba 2004, 43). Even by the 1920s with all the changes in lifestyle Taishō prosperity had initiated, Japanese still ate a fairly bland diet that even the pungent flavor of garlic disturbed.

As a corollary to concerns about national cuisine, the Japanese government and military were very cognizant of the shortages that Britain had endured with its food supply while fighting the Germans during World War I. They therefore focused their own attentions toward the issue of nutrition.[18] Nutrition in the 1920s was now a watchword for a strong and healthy country. A daily column appeared in the newspaper, the "Economic and Nutritious Daily Menu." In 1922 the Ministry of Education conducted the first national inquiry into school lunches and this launched the movement "to establish a nutritious nation" (*eiyō rikkoku suru*), a phrase politicians employed (Hagiwara 1987, 12). Saeki Tadasu proposed the idea to establish a National Institute for Nutrition Research (*Kokuritsu eiyō kenkyūjo*), and a bill quickly passed. By the time of Japan's war in Asia in the 1930s, the government had already pushed for the building of a Ministry of Health and Welfare and had drafted policies promoting national strength and military power. The army deep-fried or breaded everything because it was economically cheap and such meals provided heavy calories to soldiers who needed them (Cwiertka 2006, 82).[19]

As Japan moved into the 1930s, life in the rural areas and cities was almost of two different worlds (Itagaki 2004, 180–224). Village life was rough and far from the idyllic image often depicted in novels. "It was not unusual for men to eat as much as three pounds of rice in a day," but life grew quickly monotonous, and "only on rare occasions did the family eat pure white rice," said one author depicting that decade's standards (Partner 2004, 13). Hygiene had arguably not improved much either. A 1934 survey in Aomori prefecture, in the deep north, found that "out of 44,000 households 17,500 bathed only once or twice a year, and 13,500 bathed less than once a year" (Partner 2004, 25).

In contrast to dull rural offerings of cuisine in prewar Tokyo, Chinese sellers of noodles proliferated in the major cities and metropolitan areas. By the 1930s, as Japan's empire increased in parallel with its interest in Chinese continental culture, the 1930 diary of Matsuzaki Tenmin, a popular journalist who pioneered new forms of reportage, is revealing. He, as many other urban intellectuals, appreciated Chinese cuisine because "it gave off the amalgamated character of an acculturated mix of eastern and western" (Minami 1987, 174).[20] Yamada Masahei's newspaper columns on Chinese food in the magazine *Ladies' Companion* (*Fujin no tomo*) also became a book and best-seller between 1931 and 1932 (SJDSK 1971, 782–83).

Japanese acceptance of Chinese cuisine reflected the general tenor of the new consumerism transforming Japan. From the ashes of the Great Kantō earthquake (1923) arose new department stores, complete with mass restaurants (*taishū inshokuten*) for eating and drinking. In a sense, the Kantō earthquake eradicated so much of old Tokyo that merchants could break free with the past and invent new tastes and sites for consumption. Rail transport was on the move, and local flavors were no longer regionally confined. Kansai preferences, what Osaka and the Kyoto basin ate, began to float upriver and cruise north on steel tracks to compete in the new and open market in flourishing Tokyo, creating an entirely new, more homogenized national taste (SJDSK 1971, 711). This was also the era of the China boom and Japanese interest in Chinese popular culture: the songs, movies, and clothing of the 1930s. It is no wonder that Chinese cuisine became an area of interest as well.

Radio, inaugurated in 1925, also helped advance cuisine and a new image of the family in home cooking shows started in 1926. Moves to advance culture and render daily life more hygienic were part of the government's Lifestyle Improvement Campaign to rationalize and scientifically calculate women's household chores. These moves to ameliorate women's domestic industry spurred a secondary market for instant products (*sokuseki*). By the middle to late 1920s, the market already consumed instant curry and the "essence of taste" Ajinomoto additive, which at first marketed its product as "instant seasoning" for cooking—the point being that you did not have to spend hours in the hot and dark kitchen to make savory and nutritious meals for your family (SJDSK 1971, 713–15).

In 1926, the start of the new imperial Shōwa reign, many Japanese household activities remained the same as they had since traditional times: You still made your own fire in the kitchen and hauled your own water to cook and wash. Around 1930 some houses had sinks with faucets but plumbing in Japan spread slowly—only 29.1 percent of the population installed indoor piping in kitchens by 1935 (Nihon shokuryō shimbunsha 1990, 194–95). People started to dine out more, especially those who lived near expanding urban markets. By the 1930s there were 800 cafés and 10,000 waitresses in Osaka alone, 112,000 nationally by 1936 (Silverberg 1998, 213). In the 1930s, as Japan's empire extended its borders, people in the urban areas ate more in restaurants or at simple street stalls often run by fringe members of the Japanese imperial project—colonists, Koreans who emigrated, Taiwanese, Chinese, and others (Silverberg 1998, 221). While the Japanese empire gave precedence to Japanese employment, it also created new markets and drew labor and capital from around East Asia. The tastes that grew popular and that Japanese consumers eagerly produced had quietly and yet steadily shifted radically from their Tokugawa and Meiji predecessors. The terms used to describe them, *Nihon ryōri*, *washoku*, or *Nihon shoku* might have remained, but the contents, recipes, and presentations had permanently changed as a by-product of Japan's imperial expansion into East Asia.

By the time Japan entered the 1930s and began to mobilize the national diet for war in China, the Chinese had been working and living in Japan for decades and Japanese cuisine itself had already turned into a hybrid. By the autumn of 1931, Japan's preparation for war and empire stunted the initial forays Chinese cuisine made in Japan, and the full effect of the prewar cultural exchange over cuisine would not be felt until the close of the American occupation in 1952. The Taishō reign set the stage for a food revolution in the Japanese diet, but the militarism of the 1930s partially obstructed the process. It would not be until the mid-1950s that hybrid foods like rāmen returned, but for the immediate future what preoccupied most inhabitants of the empire was the increasingly loud noise of gunfire in the distance.

NOTES

This research was assisted in part with a grant from the Japan Foundation Endowment Committee, U.K.

1. The amount of rice imported from Taiwan to Japan, 1903–33, rose about four times and from Korea about twenty-one times, mostly after formal colonization. But this rice was still sold at different prices, about 70–80 percent of the price of domestically produced rice.

2. In Natsume Sōseki's turn-of-the-century novel *The Miner* (*Kōfu*), laborers debate the merits of the two strains of Japanese and Chinese rice (Ohnuki-Tierney 1990, 203).

3. The discussion of how to label post-Meiji Japanese cuisine—*washoku*, *Nihon ryōri*, or *Nihon shoku*—is a debate without end. For the sake of brevity, I have chosen to use the term *Nihon ryōri* with the understanding that it sets off a discussion of Tokugawa-era *kaiseki* cuisine and other traditional cuisines usually related to the pre-Meiji eras. As soon as they colonized other areas or grew wealthy enough, European powers behaved in a similar fashion. The French in the early twentieth century were well known for "asking for white bread no matter what the latitude" (Peters 1999, 150–51).

4. See Shoko Higashiyotsuyanagi's chapter in this book (chapter 6) as well as her co-authored work with Ehara Ayako, *Kindai ryōrisho no sekai* (Ehara and Higashi-yotsuyanagi 2008).

5. For a discussion of the word *Shina* as a referent for China, see George's Solt's chapter in this volume (chapter 9).

6. The list of scholarship on this topic is immense. For a good overview, see the six-volume series edited by Ishige (1999). For a complete one-volume overview, see Ehara, Ishikawa, and Higashiyotsuyanagi (2009).

7. This was equally the case in the major urban zones within China as well during the late nineteenth and early twentieth centuries. The collection of night soil was not only crucial to the smooth operation of a clean city and home but also an obligatory ingredient to prime the fertilizer necessary to supplement fields to produce crops. For a detailed look at how the situation operated in early modern China, see Lu (1999, 189–98).

8. This is not to say that Europe was somehow pristine and sterile. Britain and other Western countries had only more recently learned about the science of hygiene the hard way. The disastrous death rates during the Crimean War (1853–56) against Russia helped alert British and French to their lack of understanding regarding health and hygiene (Ponting 2005, 334). Ponting notes that "during the Crimean War about four times as many men died from disease as from military action," and he adds that "the two main killers were cholera and typhus." See also Alain Corbin's *The Foul and the Fragrant: Odor and the French Social Imagination* for insight concerning how early modern French conceived of hygiene (Corbin 1986).

9. Murai Gensai typified these changes with his best-selling novel about the new

Japanese gastronomy in *The Gourmand* (*Kuidōraku*), originally published in 1903 (Murai 1913).

10. Sugimoto Tōzō states the average working Japanese male required approximately 2,445 calories for his ten-hour workday (1925, 73).

11. Food purchases occupied about one third of the average working family's monthly budget, and rice alone itself consumed about one third of that budget, according to historical Japanese statistics (Nihon Tōkeisha 1987, vol. 4, 475). The fact that salaries were low and working hours long made the appearance of cheap, tasty, and filling Chinese noodle and similar dishes quite popular with the working classes who were increasingly gaining wealth, albeit slowly.

12. Soba, made from buckwheat, had been the hands-down favorite noodle dish of early modern urban residents of Edo, later renamed Tokyo.

13. This number excluded Koreans since they were at the time of Japanese colonial management legally defined as Japanese. According to the *Historical Statistics of Japan*, in 1913 the foreign population legally registered in Japan was 18,763 people, of whom 11,869 were Chinese, about 63 percent of all foreigners. By the end of Taishō, there were 31,140 foreigners with 22,272 Chinese, an increase to 71.5 percent of the foreign population in Japan being Chinese (Nihon Tōkeisha 1987, vol. 1, 52).

14. See also Sand (2005, 38–49).

15. For a discussion of cookbooks written in this period, see chapter 6 by Shoko Higashiyotsuyanagi in this volume.

16. The journal was originally called *Katei no tomo* (*Home Companion*) and was established in 1903.

17. *Ryū* is a Japanese reading of the Chinese character for willow.

18. Ina Zweiniger-Bargielowska (2000) notes that after 1850, Britain began importing more foodstuffs, and thus by the time of the First World War, the nation had to ration consumption to fight against German military attempts to shut off supplies. In response, the British government created the Ministry of Food and reestablished the same institution during the early years of World War II to harness public consumption and allow the country to survive on fewer food supplies arriving from abroad. Avner Offer argues that the conclusion of World War I had less to do with weak military strategy and more to do with poor German agricultural infrastructure and the propaganda value of getting food on the table as causes for the kaiser's defeat (Offer 1989).

19. Saeki Tadasu, a noted scientist with a degree from Yale University, also repeated what had come to be common knowledge by the mid-1920s that, in his words, "people and nations are built on food" (Saeki 1926, 215).

20. Matsuzaki Tenmin (1878–1934) was a popular journalist whose personal travels and visits to the exotic or the underground of society earned him accolades from readers who devoured his writings. His travels and experiences made him the perfect editor for seven years of the magazine *Gourmand* (*Kuidōraku*), starting in 1928.

WORKS CITED

Primary Sources

Amano Seisei. 1907. *Daidokoro kairyō*. Tokyo: Hakubunkan.

Aoki Setsuzō. 2002. *Harukanaru toki Taiwan: Senjūmin shakai ni ikita aru Nihonjin keisatsukan no kiroku*. Osaka: Kansai Tosho Shuppan.

Arakawa Gorō. 1906. *Saikin Chosen jijō*. Yamagata: Shimizu Shoten.

Chiba Shunji, ed. 2004. *Tanizaki Junichirō Shanhai kōyūki*. Tokyo: Mimizu Shobō.

Ikeda Kikunae. 1909/2002. "New seasonings." Trans. Yoko Ogiwara and Yuzo Ni-nomiya. *Journal of the Chemical Society of Tokyo* 30 (1909): 820–36, in *Chemical Senses* 27 (2002): 847–49.

Ishizawa Yoshima. 1923. *Bunka chūshin kaji shinjugyōhō*. Tokyo: Kyōiku Kenkyūkai.

Kodama Kagai. 1911. *Tōkyō inshōki*. Tokyo: Kanao Bunendō.

Murai Gensai. 1913. *Kuidōraku*. Tokyo: Hōwasha.

Murakami Tadakichi. 1916. *Chōsenjin no ishokujū*. Seoul, Korea: Tosho Shuppanbu.

Nihon Tōkeisha, eds. 1987. *Chōki tōkei sōran*. Vol. 4. Tokyo: Nihon Tōkeisha.

Okita Kinjō. 1905. *Rimen no Kankoku*. Tokyo: Kōbunkan.

Saeki Tadasu. 1926. *Eiyō*. Tokyo: Eiyōsha.

Satō Torajirō. 1903. *Shina keihatsuron*. Yokohama: Yokohama Shinpōsha.

Shōwa Joshi Daigaku Shokumotsu Kenkyūshitsu, ed. (SJDSK). 1971. *Kindai Nihon shokumotsushi*. Tokyo: Daibundō.

Sugimoto Tōzō. 1925. *Ichō no shineisei*. Jitsugyō no Nihonsha.

Tamura Kikujirō. 1920/1980. "Seikatsu kaizo no dai ippo wa nani zoya." Originally published in 1920, reprinted in *Nihon fujin mondai shiryō shūsei*. Ed. Maruoka Hideko. Vol. 7. Tokyo: Seikatsu Domesu Shuppan.

Tanizaki Junichirō. 1968. "Shina no ryōri." In *Tanizaki Junichirō zenshū*. Vol. 22. Tokyo: Chūō Kōronsha.

Yamagata Kōhō. 1907. *Ishokujū*. Tokyo: Jitsugyō no Nihonsha.

Yamawaki Gen. 1980. "Katei seikatsu o keizaiteki ni kairyō seyo." Reprinted in *Seikatsu*, vol. 7 of *Nihon fujin mondai shiryō shūsei*. Ed. Maruoka Hideko. Tokyo: Domesu Shuppan.

Yazaki Ihachi. 1909/2003. "*Fun to kome to wa izure ga tattou ka*." In *Nihon nōgaku zasshi* (April 1909): 46–47; reprinted in *Kawaya to haisetsu no minzokugaku*. Ed. Koishikawa Zenji. Tokyo: Hihyōsha.

Secondary Sources

Ambaras, David. 1998. "Social knowledge, cultural capital, and the new middle class in Japan, 1895–1912." *Journal of Japanese Studies* 24, no. 1: 1–33.

Chūbachi, Masayoshi and Koji Taira. 1976. "Poverty in modern Japan: Perceptions and realities." In *Japanese Industrialization and its Social Consequences*, 391–437. Ed. Hugh Patrick. Berkeley: University of California Press.

Corbin, Alain. 1986. *The Foul and the Fragrant: Odor and the French Social Imagination*. New York: Berg.

Cwiertka, Katarzyna J. 2006. *Modern Japanese Cuisine: Food, Power and National Identity*. London: Reaktion Books.

Duus, Peter. 1995. *The Abacus and the Sword: The Japanese Penetration of Korea, 1895–1912*. Berkeley: University of California Press.

Ehara Ayako, Ishikawa Naoko, and Higashiyotsuyanagi Shoko. 2009. *Nihon shokumotsushi*. Tokyo: Yoshikawa Kōbunkan.

Ehara Ayako and Higashiyotsuyanagi Shoko. 2008. *Kindai ryōrisho no sekai*. Tokyo: Domesu Shuppan.

Ema Tsutomu. 1985. *Shoku no fūzoku minzoku meicho shūsei*. Vol. 1, *Tabemono no konjaku*. Tokyo: Tokyo Shobōsha.

Francks, Penelope. 2003. "Rice for the masses: Food policy and the adoption of imperial self-sufficiency in early twentieth-century Japan." *Japan Forum* 15, no. 1: 125–46.

Gerth, Karl. 2003. *China Made*. Cambridge, Mass: Harvard University Press.

Gowen, Herbert H. 1925. "Living conditions in Japan." *Annals of the American Academy of Political and Social Science* (The Far East) 122:160–66.

Hagiwara Hiromichi. 1987. *Jissen kōza gakkō kyūshoku*. Vol. 1, *Rekishi to genjō*. Tokyo: Meicho Hensankai.

Ishige Naomichi, ed. 1999. *Kōza, shoku no bunka*. Tokyo: Ajinomoto Shoku no Bunka Sentā.

Itagaki Kuniko. 2004. "Kessenka kokumin seikatsu no henyō." In *Dainihon teikoku no hōkai*. Ed. Yamamuro Kentoku. Tokyo: Yoshikawa Kōbunkan.

Jung, Keun-Sik. 2005. "Colonial modernity and the social history of chemical seasoning in Korea." *Korean Journal* 45, no. 2: 9–36.

Kiyomizu Michiko. 2005. "*Shakai chōsa ni miru jochū.*" *Kansai kokusai daigaku kenkyū kiyō*, dai 6 gō: 87–98.

Lu, Hanchao. 1999. *Beyond the Neon Lights: Everyday Shanghai in the Early Twentieth Century*. Berkeley: University of California Press.

Minami Hiroshi, ed. 1987. *Kindai shomin seikatsushi*. Vol. 6. Tokyo: Sanichi Shobō.

Nihon Shokuryō Shimbunsha. 1990. *Shōwa to Nihonjin no ibukuro*. Tokyo: Nihon Shokuryō Shimbunsha.

Offer, Avner. 1989. *The First World War: An Agrarian Interpretation*. Oxford: Clarendon.

Ohnuki-Tierney, Emiko. 1990. "The ambivalent self of the contemporary Japanese." *Cultural Anthropology* 5, no. 2: 197–216.

Okada Tetsu. 2002. *Rāmen no tanjō*. Tokyo: Chikuma Shinsho.

Okuyama Tadamasa. 2003. *Bunka menruigaku rāmenhen*. Tokyo: Akashi Shoten.

Ōtsuka Tsutomu. 1969. *Shoku seikatsu kindaishi*. Tokyo: Yūzankaku shuppan.

Partner, Simon. 2004. *Toshie: A Story of Village Life in Twentieth-Century Japan*. Berkeley: University of California Press.

Peters, Erika. 1999. "National preferences and colonial cuisine: Seeking the familiar in French Vietnam." *Proceedings of the Western Society for French History* 27:150–59.

Ponting, Clive. 2005. *The Crimean War: The Truth behind the Myth.* London: Pimlico.

Reardon-Anderson, James. 1986. "Chemical industry in China, 1860–1949." *Osiris,* 2nd series, 2: 177–224.

Sand, Jordan. 2005. "A short history of MSG: Good science, bad science, and taste cultures." *Gastronomica* 5, no. 4: 38–49.

Sato, Barbara Hamill. 2003. *The New Japanese Woman: Modernity, Media, and Women in Interwar Japan.* Durham, N.C.: Duke University Press.

Segawa Kiyoko. 1983. *Nihon no shokubunka taikei.* Vol. 1, *Shoku seikatsu no rekishi.* Tokyo: Tokyo Shobō.

Silverberg, Miriam. 1998. "The café waitress serving modern Japan." In *Mirror of Modernity: Invented Traditions of Modern Japan,* 208–25. Ed. Stephen Vlastos. Berkeley: University of California Press.

Vasishth, Andrea. 1997. "A model minority: Chinese community in Japan." In *Japan's Minorities: The Illusion of Homogeneity,* 108–39. Ed. Michael Weiner. London: Routledge.

Yonezawa Mengyō Kumiai Kyūjūnenshi Kankōi'inkai, ed. 1989. *Yonezawa mengyōshi.* Yonezawa City: Yonezawa Mengyō Kumiai.

Zweiniger-Bargielowska, Ina. 2000. *Austerity in Britain, Rationing, Controls and Consumption, 1939–1955.* Oxford: Oxford University Press.

8 Beyond Hunger

Grocery Shopping, Cooking, and Eating in 1940s Japan

KATARZYNA CWIERTKA

AND MIHO YASUHARA

"THE SACRIFICE OF ONE Who Refused to Eat on the Black Market" proclaimed a headline of *Mainichi shinbun* on October 12, 1945. The newspaper reported the case of Kameo Hideshirō, a language teacher at Tokyo Higher School, who died of starvation in consequence of refusing to buy food on the black market. A similar tragedy caught the attention of the media again two years later when Judge Yamaguchi Yoshitada of Tokyo District Court starved himself to death out of principle of obeying the law (Griffiths 1999, 45–46). Cases like these were relatively rare and, generally speaking, Japan managed to escape mass starvation during the 1940s.[1] Nevertheless, memory of the period is intricately interwoven with hunger.

Food shortages and malnutrition feature prominently in the (oral) historical accounts of the decade (for example, Havens 1978; Cook and Cook 1992; Yamanaka 1989; Gekkan 2007). The quest for food comes into sight as the preoccupation of practically every individual, especially among the urban population for whom the conditions deteriorated particularly rapidly in the early 1940s. This is definitely true for the middle years of the decade. However, a closer examination reveals that the reality of the 1940s was far more complex than the prevailing myth. First of all, food shortages did not develop overnight but unfolded gradually and improved gradually as well. Furthermore, the situation varied considerably depending on the local conditions at different times. All in all, mundane activities such as cooking and eating family meals, and even occasional dining out, did in fact continue, even after the crisis reached a peak in the mid 1940s, forcing on most Japanese the hand-to-mouth existence described in the mainstream accounts of wartime misery. Moreover, some Japanese, though definitely in the minority, continued to eat relatively well even during the crisis years of 1944–47.

This chapter is an attempt to bring some nuance into the stereotypical view of wartime Japan as a nearly lifeless "dark valley" (*kurai tanima*). There was much more to this experience than hunger alone, and we aim to bring those aspects to light. The same holds true for the years that followed directly after the capitulation. Behind the lethargic images of the middle of the decade, life did continue, regardless of hardships and deprivations. The focus on food will help us to illuminate the complexity of the transwar reality of the 1940s. These were not simply the "lost years" of disruption but rather the point of origin for Japan's postwar history. Despite a broad spectrum of changes, there was a considerable degree of continuity before and after 1945.

SAKAMOTO TANE'S DIARY

At approximately the same time Judge Yamaguchi of Tokyo District Court literally gave up his life to obey the law, his colleague at the District Court of Kōchi, a provincial town in southern Shikoku, was hale and hearty. According to the account of his wife Tane, Judge Sakamoto Tetsuaki (1897–1982) celebrated his fifty-second birthday in June 1948 more or less as usual with festive adzuki beans and rice (*sekihan*) and a selection of delicacies (Kodera 2005, 255).

Sakamoto Tane (1900–1982) kept a diary for the span of fifty-two years, from January 1929 to December 1981, nearly her entire married life. The entries of the first twenty-two years (from 1929 to 1951) were edited by her nephew Kodera Yukio, who inherited the Sakamoto's possessions, and were published as *Daily Life of Wartime: A Judge's Wife's Diary* (*Senji no nichijō: Aru saibankan fujin no nikki*). Except for a few interruptions, of which the most extensive were the periods 1931–33 and 1944–46, Sakamoto Tane on a regular basis recorded daily matters of her family, not infrequently supplementing them with remarks and observations concerning public events and wartime news. Most importantly for our purpose, Tane's diary is brimming with depictions of foods she cooked and the ways in which she acquired the ingredients. Her records provide us with a glimpse of daily life that is difficult but not glum, at times anxious but never despondent.

It goes without saying that the diary by no means conveys a reality representative of an average Japanese family. The middle-class status and financial security of the Sakamotos protected them from the hardships that their less-affluent compatriots were forced to endure. We may also presume that wartime life in a provincial town was somehow more sheltered than in the large cities that suffered from strategic bombing. Yet the fact that the diary was discontinued in October 1944 to be resumed only two years later indicates that the mid-1940s were indeed a critical time for Sakamoto Tane and her family. The reasons are not explicitly mentioned in the diary, but we may surmise that preoccupation with practical problems did not allow her to devote time and attention to diary writing. Another possible explanation might be the shortage of paper, notorious during the time in question.

A particularly valuable aspect of the diary, despite its incomplete nature, is the fact that it brings to light the routine of interwar life that is characterized by unpredictability of supplies, hours of standing in lines, and worries about soaring prices. The entry from autumn 1943, for example, is very telling in its matter-of-fact tone when recounting the bizarre mixture of household chores, patriotic activities, and wartime propaganda:

> *November 24, Wednesday, clear*
> The weather was pleasantly warm. It was quite a busy day: laundry, delivery of rationed fish, seeing-off soldiers [departing for the front], delivery of rationed fruit et cetera. The day was all gone before I was able to write a letter to father in Kobe. The Imperial General Headquarters announced that great military results were achieved yesterday in the vicinity of Gilbert Islands—four aircraft carriers and three submarines sunk. (Kodera 2005, 176)

The accounts of food appear in Tane's diary regularly from the very beginning.[2] Throughout 1938, her entries contain particularly detailed accounts of family menus,[3] carefully filled in separate space provided for this purpose by the *Housewife's Diary Book* (*Shufu nikkichō*), which she used.[4]

APRIL 3RD, SUNDAY
Breakfast: miso soup with cabbage
Lunch: tofu lees (*okara*)
Dinner: clear soup with pike and trefoil (*mizuna*)[5] and *abura age*[6] simmered with soy sauce

MAY 1ST, SUNDAY, CLEAR
Breakfast: miso soup with tofu and green onion
Dinner: young burdock root simmered with sugar, deep-fried breaded prawns

MAY 15TH, SUNDAY, CLEAR
Breakfast: miso soup with sweet potatoes and green onion
Dinner: curry

MAY 21ST, SATURDAY
Dinner: *tamagoyaki,*[7] broad beans simmered with sugar

Lunch: bread, butter, black tea
Dinner: *kamaboko,*[8] broad beans

JUNE 3RD, FRIDAY
Breakfast: miso soup with lettuce
Dinner: *kamaboko*, grated giant white radish, clear soup with tofu

JUNE 11TH, SUNDAY
Breakfast: Miso soup with *wakame* seaweed[9]
Dinner: salt-grilled barracuda, cucumber dressed with vinegar, clear
    soup with tofu (Kodera 2005, 80)

The first remarks related to the wartime food shortages began to appear in the diary in February 1940, when the family still resided in Sendai, a city in the northern part of the main island. Tane complained about shortages of charcoal and matches; and she stockpiled sugar, anticipating that it would soon become difficult to obtain (Kodera 2005, 92). By then sugar had acquired an important role, particularly in urban Japan, not only as an ingredient for confectionery but also as a flavoring in home cooking. Between the 1910s and the 1930s, its per capita consumption increased threefold, reaching approximately 14 kg at the time of the outbreak of the Sino–Japanese War (1937–45). The rising demand for sugar in interwar Japan was secured mainly by imports from Taiwan. These were dramatically reduced after 1937, dropping by the end of the war to one fourth of the prewar level. Moreover, the priority allocation of imported sugar, along with the small quantities produced in Okinawa and (from sugar beets) in Hokkaidō, was for industrial rather than household use. The quantities destined for household consumption plunged from 285 thousand tons in 1941 to scarcely 3 tons four years later (Johnston 1953, 42, 89, 159–60).

Sugar was to become the first item to enter the nationwide rationing system, effective on November 1, 1940 (Shimokawa and Katei 1997, 114–16). It was soon followed by a wide range of other foodstuffs, from luxuries such as sake, confectionary, and fruit to daily necessities like fish, eggs, and vegetable oil. The rationing of rice, introduced in the six largest cities in April 1941, was extended nationwide in February the following year.[10] The daily ration of 2.3 *gō* (approximately 322 g) of partly polished rice was determined by the cabinet as the national standard (Imada 2002, 139).[11]

Various forms of rationing and purchase-permit systems had already been introduced on a local level by regional municipalities as early as 1939. For example, in Sendai, where the Sakamotos remained until the autumn of 1940, rationing of sugar had been enforced a few months before the national system became active, and Tane immediately purchased and stocked two thirds of the monthly quota (Kodera 2005, 98). Moreover, the implementation of nation-wide measures remained diverse, depending on the administrative capacities as well as consumption practices of each locality. For instance, the nationwide rationing of sugar entitled the citizens of large cities to purchase 60 g (0.1 *kin*) more sugar per month than those residing elsewhere (Shimokawa and Katei 1997, 114–16). The quantities of rationed food also depended on the type of employment of an individual and his or her age. For example, the allotment of rice for workers classified as "heavy laborers" was 240 grams per day higher than the regular adult ration, but was in turn reduced by 90 g if the laborer in question was older than sixty (Cohen 1949, 375).

After the early 1940s, the food rationing system of wartime Japan expanded, gradually tightening the grip of the state over the consumption practices of its citizens. Taste and eating were thereby transformed from a strictly personal to a public matter, since the maximum use of limited resources was considered of great import for national security (Yamanaka 1989, 142). Documenting the institutional growth of the food rationing system and examining how it (mal)functioned will remain outside the scope of this chapter. Studies to date have largely covered this terrain.[12] Instead, we look at how daily life continued regardless of the tightening controls—the everyday reality concealed behind the public memory of hunger.

THE NEW REALITY OF SHOPPING FOR GROCERIES

As a growing number of groceries entered the ranks of rationed goods, the daily routine of housewives like Sakamoto Tane became increasingly com-plex. The so-far straightforward task of shopping became more bothersome, including repetitive trips to rationing points. Standing in lines, sometimes for hours, to return home empty-handed was by no means unusual. For ex-ample, on January 15, 1942, early in the morning, Tane stood in line to buy fish, but it was sold out before her turn came. Another trip to town later in the afternoon proved more successful and resulted in acquiring half a pound of butter (Kodera 2005, 121).

The entries related to food in Sakamoto Tane's diary become markedly anxious after the autumn of 1941, soon after the family moved from Sendai to Kōchi.[13] For instance, Tane complained that the culinary preparations for the celebration of New Year were considerably less festive. She was unable to obtain either beef or pork, so had to make do with rationed shrimp and swordfish. On January 7, 1942, she served traditional "seven-herb gruel" (*nanakusagayu*) without the customary rice cake (*mochi*), but noted the feeling of pride about this patriotic sacrifice the moment she heard on the radio the news about the glorious successes of the Imperial Army (Kodera 2005, 88, 118–19).

The irregularities of supplies come strikingly to surface in the entries for the summer and early autumn of 1942. On August 12, Tane made stew for the first time in a long time, since rationed beef was unexpectedly delivered on that day. Two days later she managed to acquire two watermelons. Yet in the entry for September 3, she complained again about the ongoing scarcity of fish. Consequently, the following day the Sakamotos were forced to consume yet another vegetarian dinner (Kodera 2005, 133–36). However, acquiring rationed groceries was not always as bothersome, and at times even went quite smoothly. For example, on March 12, 1942, Tane reported enthusiastically that together with Ms. Shimamura she managed to acquire beef, tofu, and sake all in one day (Kodera 2005, 126).

Interestingly, the overall tone of the diary improved considerably by the end of 1942. It is unclear whether this indicates improvement in the food supply situation in Kōchi in comparison to a year earlier or simply means that Tane became accustomed to the circumstances. At any rate, on December 31, she proudly recorded two ingredients perfectly fit for the New Year's feast that she managed to acquire that day: five small sea breams through rationing and 100 *momme* (375 gram) of beef "thanks to the kindness" of her husband's superior (Kodera 2005, 147). A few months later, in April of 1943, Tane again noted that the supply of fish and vegetables greatly improved. She was even able to obtain bamboo shoots of very good quality—a seasonal delicacy. She simmered these in soy sauce and some sugar from Ms. Konishiike's stockpile, which the latter was kind enough to trade with her (Kodera 2005, 154).

By the summer of 1943, rice became practically unattainable in Kōchi, but the Sakamotos were by no means hungry. On August 23, Tane reported that she ran out of her stock of rice and switched to bread and other types of recommended substitutes. For the evening meal that day she prepared sweet adzuki-bean soup (*zenzai*) with wheat dumplings. She remarked that it turned out quite well, since she used quite a generous amount of sugar (Kodera 2005, 206).

As time went by, the records of rationed groceries appeared in Tane's diary almost on a daily basis: fish and fruit on November 24, sweet potatoes and *konbu* seaweed[14] on November 29, sweet potatoes and fish on December 1, *chirimenjako*[15] on December 3, tangerines on December 5, banded blue sprat (*kibinago*) and taro on December 6 (which required a one-hour wait to obtain), sugar on December 8, sweet potatoes on December 9, tangerines and apples on December 14, herring roe and *konbu* seaweed on December 22, and sake and grilled fish on December 31 (Kodera 2005, 176–84). Again, it is difficult to assess whether the supply improved or that hunting for groceries had turned into Sakamoto Tane's daily obsession. Whatever the case, the list does imply that even at the dawn of 1944, the deliveries of rationed food took at least partly into consideration the holiday season. Herring roe and *konbu* seaweed, for example, played an important role in the culinary celebrations of the Japanese New Year. The supply of rationed sake frequently coincided with the holiday seasons as well and was often attuned to the military successes of the Imperial Army. For example, on February 26, 1942, Tane recorded that around 7 A.M. the head of the "block association"[16] announced through the megaphone that celebratory sake would be rationed that day to rejoice in the fall of Singapore.[17] Tane embarked to town in search for groceries to prepare a meal to go with the festive drink, but since she was unable to find any beef or fish, there was nothing else to do but to open a can of eel that she had stocked earlier for emergencies (Kodera 2005, 123).

Celebratory deliveries of rationed sake continued after Japan's surrender as well. For example, Tane reported that 2 *gō* (360 ml) of sake was distributed to each household at the occasion of the proclamation of the new constitution on May 3, 1947. Still, *Tango no sekku* (Feast of Banners), a seasonal festival that fell two days later, was celebrated at the Sakamotos yet again without the customary "rice cake in oak leaves" (*kashiwa mochi*) (Kodera 2005, 230).[18]

It is important to mention at this point that only a few months earlier, in November 1946, when Sakamoto Tane resumed her diary after nearly a two-year break, she declared that the anxiety concerning food had disappeared and it was no longer necessary to leave one's house in order to hunt after groceries (Kodera 2005, 224–25). Instead, her main worry was now the skyrocketing prices. It goes without saying that she referred to the black market prices, which rose in a dramatic tempo between 1945 and 1948, when Japan was caught in an inflationary spiral inflamed by the incompetent financial reforms of the postwar governments (Cohen 1949, 447–68). Interestingly, Tane only very sporadically refers to the black market in her diary. In the summer of 1943, she mentioned buying groceries through the so-called *jiyū hanbai*, or "free sale," but used the word black market (*yamiichi*) only in her postwar accounts: on November 9, 1946, she recorded buying 200 *momme*

(750 g) of mackerel; on July 17, 1947, fish, vegetables, and 50 *momme* (187.5 g) of beef; on September 4, two mackerels; and on August 8, 1948, 8 *shō* (14.4 liter) of rice and 5 *gō* (0.9 liter) of *mochi* rice (Kodera 2005, 160, 162, 226, 234, 235, 257). Unfortunately, the diary does not clarify how much she relied on the black market for her supply of groceries before and after 1945, and whether her husband's social position had any impact on the Sakamotos' dietary security.

BACK-BURNER MILITARISM

In February 1941 the cookery section of the popular women's magazine *Housewife's Companion* (*Shufu no tomo*) included an article with the title "Seven Tasty Recipes for Sweets without the Use of Sugar." The subject was clearly a response to the rationing of sugar that had been implemented only three months earlier. The seven recipes introduced in the issue claimed to have four things in common: they were tasty, economical, easy to make, and could be prepared entirely without the use of sugar. Indeed, *Manjū* with Persimmon Filling, Small Pancakes Sandwiched Together with Sweet Filling (*Dorayaki*), Steamed *Kasutera* with Persimmons, Fried *Manjū*, German-style Deep-fried Sweets, Potato Roll with Apple, and a doughnut-like snack with the name "Parōn" relied solely on persimmons, bananas, apples, sweet potatoes, and honey.[19] An article on the following page was similar in tone, aiming to aid Japanese housewives in their struggle with food shortages.[20] It included detailed advice from Yamamoto Keizō—a chef at the famous elite restaurant Yaozen in Tokyo—on how to prepare a superb tempura, as well as how to economize on sugar and other seasonings when cooking classics from the repertoire of Japanese cuisine, such as *nimono*,[21] *sunomono*,[22] and *dashi*. In May, the magazine shifted attention to rice, which began to be rationed in large cities the previous month.[23] "Forty Economical Recipes to be Prepared from Rationed Rice" declared a headline in the cookery section of the May issue, introducing dishes such as Dumplings with Vegetable Filling, *Oden*,[24] Vegetable Omelet, Fish Croquettes, Deep-fried Tofu Lees, Vegetable Soup with Curry-flavored Gnocchi, Steamed Macaroni in White Sauce, and Fried *Udon*.[25] Interestingly, the core advice outlined in the introduction to this section of *Shufu no tomo* urged Japanese housewives to shift the focus of their meals from rice to "nourishing" (*eiyō tappuri*) side dishes. By serving a variety of side dishes, argued the editor, the consumption of rice could be easily reduced.

Thus, in the long run, the chronic shortage of rice that began at the dawn of the 1940s set the stage for the postwar transformation of the Japanese diet, which was characterized by the diminishing quantitative importance of rice (Cwiertka 2006, 157–59). The call for curtailed rice consumption during the 1940s clearly contradicted earlier projects undertaken with the war effort in mind, emphasizing the need for the reduction rather than extension of side dishes. The most symbolically potent initiative belonging to this genre was definitely the "National Flag Lunch" (*hinomaru bentō*) that originated in 1937, shortly after the outbreak of the Sino–Japanese War. A dried, salt-pickled Japanese apricot (*umeboshi*) placed in the center of a rectangular lunch box packed with boiled rice constituted the sole side dish of this meal. Its chief function was to be a powerful and visceral reminder of the hardships that the Japanese troops fighting in China allegedly experienced, and thus unite the nation at war. An additional ideological bonus was provided by the visual resemblance of the box to the Japanese flag, greatly enhancing the patriotic overtone of the entire initiative (Cwiertka 2006, 117–18). The point at stake here is the contradiction between the 1937 emphasis on limiting side dishes and the 1941 stress on extending their consumption. Both recommendations stemmed from the principle of easing the war effort but attuned to the changing circumstances.

The "National Flag Lunch" is perhaps the best well-known but not the only example of culinary patriotism thriving in wartime Japan. In May 1941, the very same edition of the magazine *Shufu no tomo* that included advice on the conservation of rationed rice suggested to its readers a festive menu that was to be prepared especially for the aforementioned *Tango no sekku* festival. The menu vividly reflects the spirit of the times—deeply immersed wartime ideology not yet bruised by the hardships of economic chaos and dearth. Fanatically labeled "Dishes to Raise the Fighting Spirit in the Era of Rising Asia," the menu contained dishes with no less militant names, such as Submarine Salad and Rising Asia Rice Dumplings. Similar to the case of *Hinomaru bentō*, the visual aspect played a vital role in conveying the ideological message. For example, the main course featured mashed potatoes arranged in the form of a helmet (covered with cinnamon powder for more effect) and a hamburger glazed with a white sauce "cloud" topped with three tiny airplanes skillfully arranged from pieces of sugar peas (Saitō 2002, 40–43).

Another ideological trend that prevailed in early 1940s cookery columns was an increased presence of recipes inspired by German cuisine. Dishes such as Fried Fish German Style, German-style Potato Dish, German Beef, German-style Stew with Ham and Cabbage, German-style Deep-fried Sweets, and Potato Roll with Apple were very well suited to the Japanese principles of wartime cookery. They relied heavily on potatoes and fried cabbage, which constituted a cheap source of calories. Moreover, they made extensive use of stewing, which was a very efficient technique in utilizing small amounts of meat for making large quantities of vegetables more palatable.[26] The connection with Nazi Germany was a bonus that provided these recipes with an ideological flair. One may wonder whether their proliferation at this specific time was directly stimulated by the Tripartite Pact, a formalized agreement of partnership between the Axis powers signed between Japan, Germany, and Italy on September 27, 1940. Although German-inspired recipes were not entirely absent in the Japanese cookery columns of the 1920s and 1930s, they evidently increased in spring and summer of 1941.

The above-mentioned instances of culinary militarism are by no means surprising when placed in the larger context of wartime propaganda. Since the outbreak of the Sino–Japanese War, the use of military images in the media steadily increased, and ties between advertising and propaganda strengthened. As Barak Kushner astutely observed, a desire to increase profits conveniently merged with patriotic sentiments, and "advertising executives and the industry in general recognized they had a window of opportunity to join with the government" (Kushner 2006, 68). Not only did private advertising agencies produce government propaganda, but also the opposite development took place—propaganda was recycled by private companies manufacturing products with no implicit connection with militarism or warfare. In the late 1930s, war was "hot" and helped sell commodities. For example, in 1938 Matsuda advertised its radio tubes with a background image of soldiers in combat,[27] a photograph of a jet fighter in the air was utilized in a salad oil advertisement, and one for curry powder pictured a tank in action (Cwiertka 2006, 127). By the early 1940s, the encroachment of the economy of dearth rendered advertising groceries unnecessary, but ideologically correct culinary messages were still utilized by the media. Perpetuating patriotic messages through cookery columns was of great importance for the morale of the population, since these provided advice and moral support for women responsible for feeding the nation. This tactic was also an important survival strategy for dieticians, journalists, and publishing houses such as *Shufu no tomo*, which endured the war without missing a single edition (Saitō 2002, 50). As the food supply dramatically deteriorated by the mid-1940s, ideological connections like the ones described above were overshadowed by anxiety and hunger and consequently removed from public memory. However, they are an equally valid aspect of Japanese wartime history as rationing coupons and sweet potatoes.

DINING OUT

In interwar Japan, dining out belonged to the favorite leisure activities of the urban middle class. Cafés, lunchrooms, and, above all, dining halls in department stores thrived during the 1920s and 1930s, offering "recreational spaces that celebrated a notion of leisure built around consumption" (Young 1999, 62; Moeran 1998). On top of that, railway terminals that offered commuters quick and convenient dining facilities, as well as a great array of new and old street stalls and other eating places, had by the 1940s become part of a daily routine for practically all urbanites (Cwiertka 2006, 50–55).

Although successively affected by wartime food shortages, the restaurant business kept on functioning, gradually adjusting to changing conditions. One of the first measures that affected the sector was the retail price control promulgated by the cabinet on October 18, 1939. The Price Control Ordinance was commonly known as "9–18 price-freeze ordinance" (kyūichihachi kakaku teishirei) or "9–18 stop ordinance" (kyūichihachi sutoppurei), because it froze retail prices, including those of food and drink offered at restaurants, cafeterias, and street stalls, at the level of September 18, 1939—a month earlier from the day of its promulgation (Nagahara 1999, 363, 413). Retailers were obliged to mark their merchandise as "frozen-price goods" (kakaku teishihin), usually abbreviated by the so-called freeze mark (marutei māku)—a circular stamp with the tei ("suspension") character in the center. Certain products that were approved for sale at prices higher than the September 18, 1939, level were indicated as "officially priced goods" (kōtei kakakuhin), usually abbreviated by the so-called permission mark (marukō māku)—a circular stamp with the kō ("official") character in the center. These measures were aimed at keeping the prices of restaurant meals under control, but in reality proved quite ineffective. As ingredients became increasingly difficult to acquire and entered the black market where they were sold at higher prices, restaurateurs were forced to be creative in order to stay in business and still elevate profit. The least drastic measures included cutting down the portions, lowering the quality of the food served, and abandoning certain items on the menu. Gradually, however, entering the undercover world of illegal dining seemed the only option for survival.

In December 1941, for example, a renowned economist and politician Kawakami Hajime (1879–1946) mentioned in his diary that, under the pressure of price control, restaurants were no longer able to maintain their standards. In spite of this, he remarked, if one was willing to pay 2.5 yen for tempura on rice—instead of the official "frozen" price of 0.35 yen—the food served would be as delicious as ever before (Kawakami 1997, 200–203). In other words, from the early 1940s onward, legally operating restaurants already served "undercover" menus at illegal prices.

A more drastic measure, the ultimate step for a restaurant in wartime Japan, was to go "underground." The usual tactic was to pretend that the restaurant was closed down or the food was sold out, and only let in customers who were willing to pay black-market prices. In a January 1944 entry of his diary, the famous prewar comedian Furukawa Roppa (1903–61) provides us with a detailed description of exactly such an instance. Yōshokuya Kinbō, a restaurant that operated near the Shinagawa station in Tokyo, used to draw the curtains and hang a "Closed" sign at the entrance. Only initiated customers knew that the "real" entrance was at the back. Kinbō provided a service of calling its regular diners to inform them whether the food would be served on the specific day or not. Since the owner of the restaurant suspected that his telephone was being tapped by the police, a secret code was used. "The weather is fine today" meant that the ingredients were secured and the customers were welcome (Furukawa 2007, 15).

Throughout 1944, Furukawa's diary brims with the accounts of good food he sampled, perhaps because such occasions became increasingly scarce (see Table 1). It is not entirely clear whether all the food he ate outside the home was illegal, since he did not always indicate it as such as explicitly as he did in the case of Kinbō.

The diary of the renowned actor and silent film narrator Tokugawa Musei (1894–1971) also contains a number of menus served in 1944. For example, on May 14 he recorded a dinner of chicken sukiyaki (including a raw egg!) and sake at an inn in the city of Himeji. On November 8, he described a superb dinner served at Hiroshimaya Inn in Tokuyama, including a squid dish, *nimono*, and sashimi of blowfish or sea bream,[28] and a soup with *matsutake*[29] and sea cucumber (*namako*) (Tokugawa 1977, 209, 233). However, these meals served at legally operating inns were incomparable to the food prepared at an illegal restaurant in Fukui prefecture a few weeks later, approximately nine months before Japan's capitulation. The bill of fare included sashimi, shellfish *sunomono*, soy-simmered fish, white fish tempura, meat stew, crab, beef sukiyaki, and rice curry (Tokugawa 1977, 231–33).

Diaries are an important source for the study of wartime dining because very few printed menus survived those turbulent times. Mitsukoshi Department Store managed to preserve a few used from 1941–42 at its posh dining hall on the sixth floor of its store in Tokyo (see Table 2).

The wartime influence is clearly visible not only through the presence of

Grocery Shopping, Cooking, and Eating in 1940s Japan 177

Table 1. Restaurant Meals Recorded in the Diary of Fukukawa Roppa between January 1 and December 30, 1944

Date/Type of Meal	Place	Restaurant Name/Type	Menu
13 January/lunch	Tokyo	"Kinbō"/ an illegal restaurant	Cream soup, beef stew, cauliflower in cream sauce, beef steak, breaded cutlet, rice curry
25 January/lunch	Tokyo	"Kinbō"	Cream soup, hamburger steak, beef steak, breaded pork cutlet, Irish stew, rice curry
3 February/lunch	Kobe	"a cafeteria on the 8th floor of a building"/unclear	Tomato soup, bastard halibut fried in butter, pork stew, lettuce
5 February/lunch	Osaka	"Tanaka shokudō"/ unclear	Thin beef steak, breaded cutlet
4 March/not recorded	Tokyo	"Kinbō"	Cream soup, beef stew, breaded pork cutlet, hamburger steak, beef steak
21 May/lunch	Aizu Bange (Fukushima prefecture)	"Kawakatsu shokudō"/ most probably a legal restaurant	Omelet, fried egg, rice curry
22 May/ lunch	Aizu Bange (Fukushima prefecture)	"Kawakatsu shokudō"	Breaded chicken cutlet, omelet, white rice with vegetables flavored with soy sauce
22 May/dinner	Aizu Bange (Fukushima prefecture)	"Kikusuiken"/a legal restaurant	Sweet-simmered taros and lotus root, miso soup with taros and bracken, *sunomono* with wild *udo*,[1] *ohagi*[2]
23 May/lunch	Aizu Bange (Fukushima prefecture)	"Kawakatsu shokudō"	Beef steak, breaded chicken cutlet, boiled eggs
2 July/breakfast	Tsuchiura (Ibaraki prefecture)	unknown/most probably a legal restaurant	Chicken sauté, *tamagoyaki*, boiled egg, chicken broth, fried chicken liver, white rice with raw egg on top
26 July/dinner	Osaka	"Kamigata"/most probably an illegal restaurant	Sashimi, prawn tempura, beef steak, beer
29 July/lunch	Osaka	"Suikōsha"/a club for Navy officers	Onion au gratin, shrimps dressed in mayonnaise, breaded beef cutlet with mashed potatoes, melon, sweet adzuki-bean soup, ice tea
2 September/ dinner (the price of this meal is recorded: 15 yen)	Tokyo	"New Castle"/ most probably an illegal restaurant	Soup, breaded beef cutlet, chicken stew, white rice, real coffee, hot cakes, watermelon

Source: Furukawa Roppa, *Roppa no hishokki* (Tokyo: Chikuma Shobō, 2007), 13, 15, 18, 19, 27-28, 36-38, 50, 54, 59.

1. *Aralia cordata*, a fragrant plant reminiscent of asparagus (Hosking 1996, 163-64).
2. Rice cake that resembles the flowers of bush clover (*hagi*). Dough made from steamed pounded mixture of glutinous and nonglutenous rice is shaped into balls and covered with unsieved adzuki-bean jam (Hosking 1996, 113).

Table 2. The Menu of Mitsukoshi Department Store in Nihonbashi, Tokyo, Sixth-Floor Restaurant, April 1942

	Price (Yen)
Western Cuisine ("frozen-price items")	
Lunch (with bread)	0.50
Tairagai[1] au Gratin (with bread)	0.50
Tairagai Fried in Butter (with bread)	0.50
Macaroni and Cheese	0.40
Cream Soup	0.30
Chinese Cuisine ("frozen-price items")	
Chinese-style Lunch (with noodles)	0.60
["permission mark"] *Yakisoba*[2]	0.30
Sushi ("frozen-price items")	
Deluxe Sushi Set (rice substitute)*	0.50
Popular Sushi Set (rice substitute)*	0.35
Gomokuzushi[3] (barley and vegetables)	0.35
Three Types of Sushi (rice substitute)*	0.35
Regular Sushi Set (rice substitute)*	0.30
Osaka Sushi (rice substitute)*	0.30
"Golden" Sushi (rice substitute)*	0.30
Japanese Cuisine ("frozen-price items")	
Set Menu (with soup)	0.85
"Japan-Manchuria" Lunch Box (rice substitute)*	0.50
Sashimi Lunch Box (rice substitute)* with soup	0.50
Western-style Lunch Box (salt-grilled)	0.50
Eel Lunch Box (rice substitute)* with soup	0.50
Regular Lunch Box (rice substitute)*	0.50
Stew (with steamed bread)	0.40
Tempura on Rice (rice substitute)*	0.40
Red Rice Lunch Box with Simmered Vegetables (barley)	0.35
Suiton[4]	0.35
Noodles ("officially priced items")	
Curried *Udon* with Meat	0.25
Hot *Udon* with a Dipping Sauce	0.20
Japanese/Western Desserts, Fruit ("officially priced items")	
Mitsumame[5]	0.15
Cake (one piece)	0.08
Fruit Punch	0.15
Tangerine	0.15
("freeze-mark") Pineapple	0.15
("freeze-mark") Pudding	0.15
("freeze-mark") *Tokoroten*[6]	0.10
Drinks ("officially priced items")	
Soda (all varieties)	0.15
Grape Juice	0.15
Orange squash	0.15
Chocolate	0.15
Coffee	0.10

Table 2. (cont.)

	Price (Yen)
Tea	0.10
Ice Cream	0.13
Amazake[7]	0.15

*rice cooked with barley or with broken *udon*
Source: Courtesy of Mitsukoshi Department Store.
1. More commonly known as *tairagi*, this is a saltwater clam *Atrina (Servatrina) pectinata* (Sugahara and Inoue 1974, 112). In English referred to as pen shell, wing shell, fan shell, or fan mussel.
2. Noodles fried with vegetables and meat, flavored with soy sauce; a dish of North Chinese origin that became popular in Japan during the 1940s (Igarashi et al. 1998, 1091).
3. Also known under the name *chirashizushi* or *barazushi*, these are various toppings scattered on top of a bed of sushi rice (Hosking 1996, 223).
4. Wheat flour dumplings served in a soup (either clear or with miso); a relief meal consumed at impoverished rural areas since premodern times, which spread in Tokyo in the years following the great Kantō earthquake (1923) and nationwide during the 1940s (Igarashi et al. 1998, 567).
5. Cubes of seaweed gelatin served in a syrup with sweet beans and pieces of fruit (Hosking 1996, 96).
6. Thin noodles made of seaweed gelatin, served chilled in a dressing made of soy sauce, vinegar, and mustard (Hosking 1996, 159).
7. A hot drink made by fermenting cooked rice, water, and the fermentation starter (*kōji*) for twelve to twenty-four hours, sweetened and often flavored with ginger (Hosking 1996, 21).

marutei and *marukō* symbols but also by the fact that a rice-barley mixture, rice-noodle mixture, and steamed bread were served instead of the orthodox white rice. However, the elaborate drink and dessert menu, as well as the elegant distinction between Japanese, Western, and Chinese cuisine, is in discord with the established images of the wartime years of hunger and deprivation. It needs to be kept in mind, however, that without the testimony of a contemporary, whether a customer or a staff member, it is practically impossible to know whether the food that appears on the printed menu was indeed served in April 1942. For example, the fact that *yakisoba* and the two types of *udon* are the only dishes indicated as "officially priced items," might imply (but not necessarily) that in practice these were the only meals that were actually served.

The records of dining out are relatively scarce in Sakamoto Tane's diary, but her account does indicate that restaurants kept operating even in provincial cities like Kōchi. For example, she recorded her husband socializing with the head of the local police at the restaurant Ōion on December 2, 1942, and returning home with a selection of wrapped delicacies (Kodera 2005, 139).

On the following day, the Sakamotos ordered food at the occasion of a visit of Mr. Sano, Judge Sakamoto's old friend. Tane was displeased with the fact that she could not rely on her favorite caterer, Nagayama, and had to order the food elsewhere (Kodera 2005, 140). We may surmise that the activities of popular caterers such as Nagayama were somehow restricted by the irregular supply of ingredients.

Five days later, on December 7, 1942, Tane dined out with Ms. Matsumura. The two went to see the war exhibition organized at the occasion of the first anniversary of Japan's attack on Pearl Harbor, and on the way home had lunch at a renowned sushi restaurant. Tane ordered a portion of takeout packed for her husband as well (Kodera 2005, 141). The accounts such as this one help us realize that war, with all its ideological baggage and practical inconveniences, was closely interwoven with ordinary lives of people like Tane throughout the 1940s. Particularly striking is the entry of January 1944, which emanates a bizarre mood of joyful delight undisturbed by the harshness of wartime reality:

JANUARY 23, SUNDAY, FINE WEATHER

It was a pleasant, spring-like warm Sunday. We ran out of rice in the end, so husband suggested we have lunch at Kogetsu. Afterwards we visited the Hachiman shrine and strolled in the direction of the Red Cross Hospital. We were back home around 3:00. It has been so long since I was able to enjoy a Sunday like this. Husband also seemed quite content. (Kodera 2005, 188)

As Owen Griffiths masterly describes, in post-surrender Japan, the black market became "the principal social space in which the drama of daily life was played out" (Griffiths 2002, 825). Most people had little choice but to participate in black-market transactions—attempts to remain beyond its reach ended tragically, as the cases of Kameo Hideshirō and Yamaguchi Yoshitada illustrate. While it continues to be projected as the symbol of post-surrender Japan, it was in fact "a structure of continuity linking war and defeat as a single historical era" (Griffiths 2002, 825). These markets had functioned since 1938, ignited by the economy of dearth that developed as a direct consequence of the mobilization for total war.

The focus on food, perhaps even more so than the black market, is a useful tool in tracking down transwar continuities because food was a daily necessity. The chaos and disruption of war may halt certain economic activities and render many aspects of life insignificant. For example, social rules and conventions tend to loosen at times of conflict, not to mention trends and fashions becoming nearly irrelevant. The need for food, however, cannot be ignored and the social actions that it requires continue in all circumstances.

The end of the war being the point of origin for the postwar history of the Japanese people, documenting it in a balanced way is of great importance not only for the study of Japan's past but also of its present. In this chapter, we have attempted to demonstrate various aspects of wartime life that tend to be overshadowed by the mainstream account of hunger and deprivation. The focus on food can help us illuminate the complexity of wartime experience and prevent the danger of public memory overcoming the historical truth.

NOTES

Research for and writing of this article has been financially supported by the Netherlands Organization for Scientific Research (NWO), VIDI grant no. 276–53–003.

1. Starvation did occur during the first months after capitulation but not on a mass scale. See, for example, Dower (1999, 93).

2. The calorific intake of food and the consequences of diminishing availability of nutrients on the health of the Japanese population lie outside the scope of this study. Per capita daily calorific data is included here only as an indication; 1937: 2181 calories (cal); 1938: 2185 cal; 1939: 2131 cal; 1942: 2080 cal; 1943: 1877 cal; 1944: 1939 cal; 1945: 1677 cal; 1946: 1587 cal; 1947: 1822 cal; 1948: 1943 cal (Kenkō Eiyō Jōhō Kenkyūkai 1998, 63; Hagiwara 1987, 62; Nōrinshō Sōmukyoku Chōsaka 1948). When dealing with this data, one needs to be aware of the fact that it by no means reflects the reality. Among other difficulties, it is usually based on surveys conducted in a particular geographical area and/or in a specific community, and therefore does not reflect the specific situation of food supplies in various localities.

3. The menus list only side dishes, which were to be served with boiled white rice.

4. This was a special format of a household account book (*kakeibo*) preprinted by the publisher of the magazine *Fujin no tomo* (*Ladies' Companion*). The leading women's magazines in interwar Japan, such as *Shufu no tomo*, *Fujin no tomo*, and *Katei no tomo* (*Home Companion*), printed account books in order to encourage frugality and the rationalization of housework (Ishikawa et al. 1994, 139). See also Sand (2003, 55–94).

5. Pot herb mustard *Brassica campestris* var. *lanciniifolia* (Hosking 1996, 96).

6. Thin, deep-fried slices of tofu (Hosking 1996, 19).

7. Japanese-style omelet flavored with soy sauce, stock, and sugar or *mirin*, which is a sweet liquid flavoring containing 14 percent alcohol, often translated as "sweet cooking sake" (Hosking 1996, 94, 154).

8. Fish paste thickened with starch, molded into pillows and steamed (Hosking 1996, 70).

9. *Undaria pinnitifida* (Hosking 1996, 169).

10. Tokyo, Yokohama, Nagoya, Osaka, Kobe, and Kyoto.

11. Throughout the diary, Tane uses traditional units of measurement: 1 *gō* = 0.18 l; 1 *shō* = 1.8 l (= 10 *gō*); 1 *momme* = 3.75 g; 1 *kin* = 0.6 kg (= 160 *momme*). Even today, rice and sake are customary measured using these traditional units.

12. See Cohen (1949, 374–79), Johnston (1953, 165–212), and Pauer (1999, 89–102) for details concerning the Japanese food rationing system. For a detailed account on the black market, see Griffiths (2002) and Scherer (1999).

13. A transfer to Kōchi was clearly a promotion for Judge Sakamoto, who assumed the position of department chief in a district court (Kodera 2005, 109).

14. Kelp, *Laminaria* spp. (Hosking 1996, 82).

15. Small young sardines, less than 3 cm long, which are boiled and then dried (Hosking 1996, 33).

16. Beginning in 1940, towns and villages were divided into "neighborhood associations" (*tonarigumi*), comprising approximately 10–20 households, and "block associations" (*chōnaikai*) consisting of approximately twenty neighborhood associations. Food rations were allocated not to individuals or families but to neighborhood associations. The land for vegetable gardens and the seeds were also allotted to the neighborhood association as a unit. See also Pauer (1999, 96–98).

17. Singapore surrendered to the Japanese forces on February 15, 1942, in the midst of a kind of "Oriental blitzkrieg." The fall of Singapore followed shortly after that of Hong Kong and the Philippines, and preceded the surrender of the Dutch East Indies only by a few weeks (Ienaga 1978, 143).

18. Round-shaped rice cake (*mochi*) filled with adzuki-bean jam and wrapped in an oak leaf. An obligatory component in the celebration of *Tango no sekku* (Hosking 1996, 74).

19. "Satō irazu de oishii okashi no tsukurikata nanashu," *Shufu no tomo* 1941, no. 2: 300–302.

20. "Zairyō fusoku demo oishium dekiru fuyu no katei ryōri no tsukurikata hiketsu," *Shufu no tomo* 1941, no. 2: 303–5.

21. A major category in Japanese cookery, which is prepared by simmering vegetables and/or seafood, usually in stock flavored with soy sauce, sake, and sugar. Variations in flavoring may, for example, include miso with ginger root (for seafood), or stock (*dashi*) with salt and sugar (for vegetables).

22. Vegetables and/or seafood in a lightly sweetened vinegar dressing. A major category in Japanese cookery (Hosking 1996, 149).

23. "Haikyūmai de makanaeru keizai ryōri yonjūsshu no tsukurikata," *Shufu no tomo* 1941, no. 5: 306–15.

24. A variety of ingredients simmered in a large container of hot stock, *dashi* (Hosking 1996, 112).

25. Soft, thick wheat noodles traditionally served in hot broth (Hosking 1996, 164). In this recipe, which is inspired by the Chinese-style fried noodles (*yakisoba*),

udon is fried with bamboo shoots, carrots, shiitake mushrooms, and other ingredients, and flavored with sugar and soy sauce.

26. "Natsu no kenkō ryōri to eiyō pan no tsukurikata sanjūsshu," *Shufu no tomo* 1941, no. 7: 273, 276, 277; "Natsu no eiyō ryōri no tsukurikata sanjūsshu," *Shufu no tomo* 1941, no. 8: 231; "Satō irazu de oishii okashi no tsukurikata nanashu," *Shufu no tomo* 1941, no. 2: 300–302.

27. *Asahigurafu* (1938, no. 15, back cover).

28. Furukawa was not sure himself which fish was served.

29. A type of mushroom highly valued for its aroma, *Tricholoma matsutake* (Hosking 1996, 92).

WORKS CITED

Cohen, Jerome B. 1949. *Japan's Economy in War and Reconstruction*. Minneapolis: University of Minnesota Press.

Cook, Haruko Taya, and Theodore F. Cook. 1992. *Japan at War: An Oral History*. New York: New Press.

Cwiertka, Katarzyna J. 2006. *Modern Japanese Cuisine: Food, Power and National Identity*. London: Reaktion Books.

Dower, John W. 1999. *Embracing Defeat: Japan in the Wake of World War II*. New York: W. W. Norton.

Furukawa Roppa. 2007. *Roppa no hishokki*. Tokyo: Chikuma Shobō.

Gekkan Bōsei Henshūbu, ed. 2007. *Ano hi, ano aji: "Shoku no kioku" de tadoru Shōwashi*. Tokyo: Tōkai Kyōiku Kenkyūjo.

Griffiths, Owen. 1999. The Reconstruction of Self and Society in Early Postwar Japan 1945–1949. PhD diss., University of British Columbia, Department of History.

———. 2002. "Need, greed, and protest in Japan's black market 1938–1949." *Journal of Social History* 35, no. 4: 825–58.

Hagiwara Hiromichi. 1987. *Jissen kōza gakkō kyūshoku dai ikkan: Rekishi to genjō*. Tokyo: Emti Shuppan.

Havens, Thomas. 1978. *Valley of Darkness: The Japanese People and World War II*. New York: Norton.

Hosking, Richard. 1996. *A Dictionary of Japanese Food: Ingredients and Culture*. Rutland, Vt.: Charles E. Tuttle.

Ienaga, Saburō. 1978. *The Pacific War, 1931–1945: A Critical Perspective on Japan's Role in World War II*. New York: Pantheon Books.

Igarashi Osamu et al., eds. 1998. *Maruzen shokuhin sōgō jiten*. Tokyo: Maruzen.

Imada Setsuko. 2002. "Dainiji sekai taisen to kibishii shokuseikatsu." In *Kingendai no shokubunka*. Ed. H. Ishikawa and A. Ehara, 133–53. Kawasaki: Kōgaku Shuppan.

Ishikawa Hiroshi et al., eds. 1994. *Taishū bunka jiten (shukusatsuban)*. Tokyo: Kōbundō.

Johnston, Bruce F. 1953. *Japanese Food Management in World War II*. Stanford, Calif.: Stanford University Press.

Kawakami Hajime. 1997. *Jijoden 5*. Tokyo: Iwanami Shoten.

Kenkō Eiyō Jōhō Kenkyūkai, ed. 1998. *Sengo Shōwa no eiyō dōkō: Kokumin eiyō chōsa yonjū nen o furikaeru*. Tokyo: Daiichi Shuppan.

Kodera Yukio, ed. 2005. *Senji no nichijō: Aru saibankan fujin no nikki*. Tokyo: Hakubunkan.

Kushner, Barak. 2006. *The Thought War: Japanese Imperial Propaganda*. Honolulu: University of Hawai'i Press.

Mitsukoshi Department Store. 1942. Menu, April. Translation of the original menu served at the 6th floor restaurant, Nihonbashi store in Tokyo. Public Relations and Archives Section, Mitsukoshi Department Store.

Moeran, Brian. 1998. "The birth of the Japanese department store." In *Asian Department Stores*. Ed. Kelly L. MacPherson, 141–76. Richmond, Va.: Curzon Press.

Nagahara Keiji, ed. 1999. *Iwanami Nihonshi jiten*. Tokyo: Iwanami Shoten.

Nōrinshō Sōmukyoku Chōsaka, ed. 1948. *Nihon ni okeru shokuryō nōgyō jijō ni kan suru FAO ate 1948 nendo nenji hōkokusho*. Chōsa shiryō dai 25 gō (bugaihi).

Pauer, Erich. 1999. "A new order for Japanese society? Planned economy, neighbourhood associations and food distribution in Japanese cities in the Second World War." In *Japan's Wartime Economy*. Ed. Erich Pauer, 85–105. London: Routledge.

Saitō Minako. 2002. *Senka no reshipi: Taiheiyō sensōka no shoku wo shiru*. Tokyo: Iwanami Shoten.

Sand, Jordan. 2003. *House and Home in Modern Japan: Architecture, Domestic Space, and Bourgeois Culture, 1880–1930*. Cambridge, Mass.: Harvard University Asia Center.

Scherer, Anke. 1999. "Drawbacks to controls on food distribution: Food shortages, the black market and economic crime. In *Japan's Wartime Economy*. Ed. Erich Pauer, 106–23. London: Routledge.

Shimokawa Akifumi and Katei Sōgō Kenkyūkai, eds. 1997. *Shōwa, Heisei kateishi nenpyō, 1926–1995*. Tokyo: Kawade Shobō.

Sugahara Tatsuyuki and Inoue Shirō. 1974. *Genshoku shokuhin zukan*. Tokyo: Kenpakusha.

Tokugawa Musei. 1977. *Musei sensō nikki*. Vol. 4. Tokyo: Chūō Kōronsha.

Yamanaka Hisashi. 1989. *Kurashi no naka no taiheiyō sensō*. Tokyo: Iwanami Shoten.

Young, Louise. 1999. "Marketing the modern: Department stores, consumer culture, and the new middle class in interwar Japan." *International Labor and Working Class History* 55: 52–70.

9 Rāmen and U.S. Occupation Policy

GEORGE SOLT

*My wish is that we return to a situation consistent with the funda-
mental laws of economics, where people with lower levels of income
eat more wheat, and people with higher levels of income eat rice.*
—Ikeda Hayato, Minister of Finance, December 7, 1950

THE SCARCITY OF FOOD, particularly rice, and the necessity of securing
substitute staples such as sweet potatoes, soybeans, squash, and wheat flour
were the central concerns for the vast majority of people in Japan during the
final year of the Pacific War and the first two years of the U.S.–led Allied occupation. After treating the acute food shortage as a matter of low priority
in terms of the overall management of the occupied areas to be resolved by
the Japanese themselves, policymakers in Washington changed course and
began supplying large quantities of wheat flour to rehabilitate the Japanese
economy for strategic cold war purposes beginning in mid-1947. At the same
time, Japanese government attempts to control the production and distribution of all staple foods and other basic necessities produced a sizeable black-
market economy, which became the primary source of subsistence for most
city-dwellers during the occupation.

Rāmen, or Japanese-style Chinese noodle-soup (still primarily referred
to as *Shina soba* or *Chūka soba* in this period), played a key role in both of
these areas, as noodles made of wheat flour served as one of the primary
substitute staples for rice, and one of the foods most commonly found at
black market *yatai* (pushcart stall) operations. In addition, the majority of
people serving *Chūka soba* at the *yatai* were Korean and Chinese laborers
out of industrial work, returnees from the colonies, or decommissioned
soldiers, illustrating the ways in which the noodles reflected the population movements and geopolitical changes of the early postwar period. The
rāmen chefs of the black market usually relied on government supplies of
imported U.S. wheat flour, which was in high supply after the Truman administration's decision to prioritize food aid to Japan over other occupied
areas in desperate need, such as Okinawa and Korea.

WARTIME/OCCUPATION RICE SHORTAGES, SUBSTITUTE STAPLES, AND SURVIVAL FOODS

One of the primary causes of the wartime/occupation food crisis in Japan was the shortage of rice and other staples due to the Allies' denial of access to food imports from both Japanese and European colonies in Asia. Between 1931 and 1940, for example, people in the Japanese home islands depended on imports for roughly 20 percent of their total food supply, including 19 percent of rice, 67 percent of soybeans, 84 percent of sugar, and 21 percent of wheat. Rice was primarily imported from Korea and Taiwan; sugar from Taiwan and the Dutch East Indies; wheat from Australia, Canada, and the United States; and soybeans from Manchuria. After 1943, however, blockades, ship sinkings, and crop failures in the colonies reduced imported food to 9 percent of total calories consumed, roughly half of the pre-1941 level (U.S. Strategic Bombing Survey 1947, 2).

Meanwhile, domestic food production dropped by an estimate of 26 percent between 1943 and 1945 due to a diversion of resources away from agriculture and toward war production. Specifically, the conscription of 874,000 able-bodied farmworkers into the army between February 1944 and February 1945, the redirection of ammonia supplies from agricultural use as nitrogenous fertilizer to munitions manufacturing in the form of nitric acid, a 75 percent reduction in the amount of iron allocated to farm-tool production, and a requisitioning of farm horses by the army all severely hampered the ability to grow food (U.S. Strategic Bombing Survey 1947, 9).

With the home islands largely cut off from Korean, Taiwanese, and Southeast Asian imports of rice after 1943, the government turned to Manchuria, to which shipping access was still more secure, for more imports of soybeans and other grains. Thus, while rice imports from Korea fell by 90 percent between 1939 and 1945, soybean imports from Manchuria increased by 30 percent between 1941 and 1945 (U.S. Strategic Bombing Survey 1947, 2). The added imports from Manchuria, as well as a vigorous drive to boost small-scale staple food production on school grounds, home gardens, and other public land, somewhat offset the enormous loss in imported food from the colonies. However, the substitution of potatoes, soybeans, sweet potatoes, and coarse grains for rice in the government's staple food rations after 1943, and the decrease in ration volumes, clearly signaled to the people that the war was not unfolding in Japan's favor.

Okumura Ayao, a Japanese food scholar born in 1937, describes his memories of alimentary scarcity toward the end of the war as follows:

> From 1944 on, even in the countryside, the athletic grounds of local schools were converted into sweet potato fields. And we ate every part of the sweet potato plant, from the leaf to the tip of the root. We also ate every part of the *kabocha* pumpkins we grew, including the seeds and skin. For protein, we ate beetles, beetle larvae, and other insects that we found at the roots of the plants we picked, which we roasted or mashed. Even in the countryside, food was scarce.
>
> That year, "victory provisions" (*hisshō shokuryō*) became the most commonly used phrase throughout the country to refer to the changing and dwindling food supplies. The Minister of Agriculture at the time, Ishiguro, urged the populace to abandon the notion of rice as the primary staple of Japan and instead to eat any and all edibles available, including the leaves of previously uneaten plants and parts of vegetables. (Okumura 1998, 174)

The rationing of food and other basic materials was a part of the wartime economic controls that the Konoe cabinet first implemented under the National General Mobilization Law (*kokka sōdōinhō*) in 1938 and expanded incrementally to include almost every basic necessity by early 1942. The mobilization of the economy for total war with China created a surge in demand for food due to the swell in the ranks of the military and the industrial workforce, as the state allotted soldiers and heavy laborers significantly higher rations than the average civilians. Concretely, the state was to provide soldiers, heavy industrial workers, and average civilians with 600, 420, and 330 grams of rice or rice equivalents per day respectively (U.S. Strategic Bombing Survey 1947, 18).

The large-scale rationing of foodstuffs such as rice, wheat flour, eggs, fish, vegetable oil, and sugar began in 1941, and became codified under the Food Management Law (*shokuryō kanrihō*) of February 1942. By 1944, however, the production and importation of controlled foodstuffs could not keep pace with their allotted rationing to households, and the urban population was forced to support itself through bartering with farmers, collective gardening, and the ingestion of unfamiliar foods such as insects, boiled leaves, and tree roots in many cases.

The wartime food crisis only worsened after the conflict officially ended. The decolonization of the Japanese empire produced a massive influx of roughly six million returnees and a corresponding surge in demand for food just as supplies from the colonies and home production were dwindling. Poor rice harvests in 1944 and 1945 due to weather and war compounded the direness of the situation, resulting in widespread malnutrition and starvation, particularly among children.

Although the food situation in urban Japan had already deteriorated to bare subsistence levels for most residents by the end of the war, the situation worsened during the initial two years of the Allied occupation due to a shortfall in global food production and poor oversight of the rationing system by both the Japanese and American authorities. Furthermore, the average civilian's ration, which was already inadequate for survival, did not arrive with the regularity that the government promised. Beginning in March 1946, residents in Tokyo and Yokohama began experiencing long delays, reductions, and even cancellations of their rations. The average Tokyo resident, for example, received 70 percent of the official ration, or roughly 775 calories per day between March and June of 1946 (National Diet Library U.S. Occupation Archives Microfilm [NDL] 1946a, 9).

In February 1946, the U.S. Combined Food Board (consisting of the secretaries of the War Department, Commerce Department, Department of Agriculture, and Department of State) met to discuss the matter of feeding the populations under Allied military occupation. Japan, however, was only one of many occupied areas on the verge of famine, and the U.S. administration did not treat it as a higher priority over other territories that fell under its command. Cables exchanged between the secretary of war, Robert Patterson, and the supreme commander for the Allied powers, Douglas MacArthur, from February to May 1946 indicate that the Truman administration considered Japan's situation to be no more urgent than other occupied areas in need of food, and that the onus of feeding the population rested upon the Japanese themselves. A February 28 cable from Secretary Patterson to MacArthur states:

1. What are conditions in Japan as compared with those in other areas?
2. What are the capabilities of the Japanese to provide for themselves?
3. How can the available resources be increased?
4. How can transportation problems particularly in internal transport in the U.S. be resolved to increase shipments of foodstuffs?

     [R]igid controls of rationing should be exerted at once to reduce the rate of consumption to the lowest possible level consistent with the present directives to prevent mass starvation and widespread disease and unrest (Ara 1995, 9).

In short, the U.S. administration proposed that the primary solution to the food problem in Japan was reduction of the rate of consumption to the lowest level possible without spawning a humanitarian or political crisis, and to increase production in Japan.

The shortage of food became so severe in Tokyo that by early May, hundreds of thousands of men, women, and children began protesting the inadequacy of food rations and the scale of black-market corruption. While the protests did not turn into violent uprisings, as the supreme commander and War Department officials had feared, they signaled to the Americans that hunger had brought the urban masses of Japan to the brink of an uprising. The possibility that food shortages in Japan and Germany would lead to violent rebellion against the Allied troops appeared high enough in late April 1946 to warrant a top-secret memorandum from the Joint Chiefs of Staff, Dwight Eisenhower, to President Truman warning of the need to increase either the amount of food or the number of troops in these two areas. The last two paragraphs relate the urgency of the situation from the army's point of view:

> Reduced German and Japanese food rations will be well below the bare subsistence level, in which case disease and widespread unrest will develop in both occupation areas. From the military point of view, without regard to the long-term political consequences of such a development, requirements for major increases in the size of our occupation forces, to control unrest and preserve order, must be anticipated as an inevitable consequence.
>
> It is understood that the Secretaries of State, War and the Navy are presenting urgent proposals designed to alleviate this extremely grave situation. From the military point of view, immediate and drastic action is clearly indicated. (NDL 1946b, 3)

The document confirms that Eisenhower requested the emergency food shipments in order to quell the possibility of violent mass rebellion, which would have required additional combat forces from the United States that were not readily available. Furthermore, the U.S. government provided the emergency food shipments as loans, not aid, and expected the Japanese government to pay the full price as soon as it recovered its ability to do so. As the report "Food Year during the First Year of Occupation" states, "It should be pointed out that the food imports to Japan during the past year have not been in the form of direct relief. They have been commercial exports for which Japan is being charged in full at current U.S. prices" (NDL 1946a, 11).

In the spring of 1947, the U.S. government shifted its policy from one of expecting the Japanese economy to recover on its own to one of actively aiding its reindustrialization. The shift was the result of the Truman administration's policy of containment toward the Soviet Union by means of German and Japanese economic revival. Diplomatic historian Michael Schaller observes, "As the European 'containment program' took form, the United States determined that Japan, like Germany, must serve as a bastion against Soviet expansion and, more positively, a catalyst sparking regional recovery. . . . In simplest terms, containment meant putting 'Japan, Germany, and other affiliates of the Axis . . . back to work.' . . . Without full recovery, the occupied nations would drain American resources, stifle prosperity among their neighbors, and devolve into economic chaos that would entice the Soviet Union" (Schaller 1985, 77–78).

In April 1947 the Joint Chiefs of Staff issued a report titled "Assistance to Other Countries from the Standpoint of National Security," which stressed America's strategic interest in rehabilitating the Japanese economy and military above all others in the region. The report noted, "Of all the countries in the Pacific area Japan deserves primary consideration for current United States assistance designed to restore her economic and military potential" (Schaller 1985, 90). This was a notable departure from the initial approach of occupation leaders of taking no responsibility for Japan's economic recovery, as asserted in the February 1946 cable mentioned above.

American food imports were the most basic component of the U.S. cold war strategy of reindustrializing the Japanese and German economies. The restoration of productive capacity clearly could not occur without the United States first addressing the shortage of food among workers in key industries such as coal mining. An occupation document titled "Supplementary Distribution of Commodities for Workers," dated 1949, details the history, purpose, and specifics of a wartime supplementary ration program for heavy industrial workers that the Americans enhanced to jumpstart reindustrialization. The report states:

> The system of special allocation of commodities for workers has been in effect since 1941 when the shortage of essential commodities was widespread. Its objective was to increase worker efficiency and reduce absenteeism.
>
> After the Surrender the already war-disrupted living conditions deteriorated still further. Hence the importance of supplementary distribution

of commodities to workers increased. In November 1946 the Japanese Government adopted a policy of strengthening the existing supplementary distribution program for workers in industry. Since June 1947 this policy has been recognized not only as a measure for the protection of the worker's livelihood but also as an important means in accomplishing the national economic stabilization objectives.

In May 1948 the present organization and procedure for the distribution of supplementary commodities for workers was introduced.

The most important commodities distributed through the national programs are staple foods, sake (Japanese rice wine), tobacco and textile products. . . .

The supplementary allotment of staple food is essential to the supplementary distribution plan. The special food program covers almost all establishments engaged in mining, manufacturing, gas and electricity supply, land and maritime transportation, construction and public works activities. A few manufacturing activities of minor importance are excluded. Protective service workers, such as hospital nurses, are included in the program. The total number of workers receiving supplementary rations of staple food approximates 7.3 million. (NDL 1949, 1)

The document highlights the connection between workers' nutrition and national economic recovery, and marks June 1947 as the beginning of the U.S. government's adoption of a policy recognizing this point. The timing is noteworthy, for it came shortly after the Truman administration finalized its decision to hasten the recovery of the Japanese economy. Furthermore, the report shows that the U.S. government began administering the new system for distributing food aid to high-priority population groups in May 1948, averting a third consecutive summer of severe food shortages and resultant protests.

In addition to continuing the wartime rationing using imported food, the occupation authorities implicitly condoned the black market that grew out of price controls by allowing the police to punish consumers and petty vendors instead of large-scale suppliers of goods. John Dower, the preeminent U.S. scholar of the American occupation of Japan, asserts, "While industrialists, politicians, and former military officers made killings on the black market, while government officials lavishly wined and dined their American overlords, some 1.22 million ordinary men and women were arrested for illegal black market transactions in 1946, a number that rose to 1.36 million and then 1.5 million in the next two years" (Dower 1999, 100).

For those who did not receive supplementary rations from the government or who were not connected to the criminal suppliers of basic goods, the black market became the only means of survival. Thus, obtaining basic subsistence required engagement in criminal behavior for the vast majority of people in Japan. The prevalence of the black-market economy challenged the image of a democratizing Japan and lent credence to the notion that the same coterie of industrial and military leaders who led the country during the war indirectly controlled the economy. Christopher Aldous argues, "Throughout the Occupation the police were controlled by an alliance of politicians, bureaucrats and criminal elements. . . . The natural inclination for the police to look to their traditional masters was reinforced by the latter's ties to prominent black marketers. . . . Those who appropriated the military's huge stockpiles of food, clothing, and other necessities controlled the police on both an individual and a corporate level" (Aldous 1997, 213).

The dependence on American wheat flour imports during the occupation fundamentally transformed the dietary patterns of people in Japan. In mid-1946, as rice rations disappeared, the government announced, "The era of flour has arrived" (Dower 1999, 169). Crude forms of bread (referred to as "hardtack" by the Americans), plain dumplings (*suiton*), and homemade *udon* noodles became a prevalent form of sustenance, making use of the occupation flour for many malnourished Japanese in the initial postwar period. The increase in wheat flour consumption in the form of bread, however, was the most drastic. According to Ōtsuka, a historian of wheat flour, the amount of bread consumed in Japan increased from 262,121 tons in 1948 to 611,784 tons in 1951 (Ōtsuka 1989, 79).

The attempt to reshape Japanese dietary patterns based on the newfound importance of Japan as a strategic U.S. ally was also evident in the high priority afforded its school lunch program. School lunches thus became a primary vehicle for absorbing U.S. food imports, as bread and powdered milk became staples of the daily meal guaranteed initially only to elementary-school-aged children in large cities but later to all schoolchildren. Not only was the school lunch program vital in creating a healthy workforce for a strategic anticommunist ally, it served as a powerful propaganda device to legitimize the occupation in the eyes of the occupied. In addition, the program was an important publicity tool for the administration vis-à-vis Congress in securing funding for aid to a still unpopular Japan. A memorandum concerning the allocation of imports for the school lunch program from the Public Health and Welfare Division, dated May 25, 1948, illustrates both the program's usefulness in helping the occupation obtain funding from Congress, and the high-level

U.S. involvement in seeing through its success, as represented by ex-president Hoover's personal participation:

> General Sams contended that a feeding program for children has a universal appeal and it is of particular importance as it relates to the reaction of the U.S. Congress when considering and approving appropriations. A review of congressional action, he further stated, will reveal that one of the last appropriations to be reduced in any "cut-back" is an appropriation dealing directly with the welfare of children. . . . •
>
> Prior to conference with Mr. Pate, and at Mr. Pate's request, Chief, WD/PHW, conferred with ex-president Hoover, who according to Mr. Pate, maintains a genuine interest in all child feeding programs worldwide. Mr. Hoover's advice was to the effect that indigenous products and necessary imports be earmarked for a School Lunch Program, and the experience that obtained in the German School Lunch Program was outlined wherein a definite allocation for the school feeding program was devised so that any cut-back in imports to sustain the indigenous food economy would not affect the school feeding plan. (NDL 1948a)

As mentioned earlier, ex-president Hoover was one of the key planners at the cabinet-level meetings where the Truman administration developed the postwar strategy of Soviet containment through the accelerated reindustrialization of the former Axis powers. His direct personal involvement in the school lunch program in both Japan and Germany highlights the elementary importance of food in executing U.S. cold war policy.

BLACK-MARKET NOODLE-VENDING

As the Americans imported sizeable amounts of lard and flour, which Japanese authorities regulated less stringently than rice, noodle soups became a food more easily to obtain than rice for most urban Japanese. A notable increase in noodle soup sold at small *yatai* occurred as a result of a swell in open-air food vending, despite a prohibition against all such activity between July 1, 1947, and February 15, 1950, stipulated by the Emergency Measures Ordinance for Eating and Drinking Establishments (*inshoku eigyō rinji kiseihō*). Culinary scholar Okumura Ayao notes that the *Shina soba* and *gyōza* dumplings sold at the *yatai* carts became increasingly popular in the immediate postwar period because of their perceived nutritional value in providing stamina.

The war ended. Yet, the scarcity of food was even more pronounced than before, as returnees from the war zones increased the population beyond prewar levels, and outings to the countryside to procure food became common. Out of the ashes rose black markets, where people formed long lines for rice gruel and *suiton* (dumpling) soups. Anything was fine, as long as it would fill the people's stomachs sufficiently. . . .

In the cities, many returnees began operating *yatai* serving *gyōza* and *Shina soba* (which would eventually become *Chūka soba*), at which long lines of customers would form. The idea that the people above all needed to absorb more nutrition led to the popularity of these foods, which were relatively cheap and considered nutritious. The reason that Japanese *gyōza* dumplings are so garlicky is that garlic was thought to provide high levels of stamina, which fit the early postwar era of empty stomachs.

The soup in the *Chūka soba* of that time was not of the settled, attractive style found today, but contained floating shiny fat, gave off a strong odor of chicken bones, and the smell of the alkali-water, and the body odor of the many people waiting would combine together to give anyone who ate a bowl an energized feeling. (Okumura 1998, 175)

Okumura's argument that Chinese food became popular in the immediate postwar period because of its perceived high energy value illustrates the extent to which the popular perception of Chinese food as nutritious and filling had been established by military-affiliated nutritionists in the prewar period (Cwiertka 2006, 113). The occupation also embarked on public relations campaigns propagating the superiority of wheat flour and animal-derived protein, which also bolstered the perception of Chinese food. At bottom, however, the desperateness of the food situation heightened the desirability of foods considered filling and nutritious such as *Chūka soba*, and the occupation's heavy importation of wheat flour turned noodles, bread, and dumplings into central features of postwar Japanese dietary practices.

Okumura also explains why so many small business operators chose Chinese noodle-soup as opposed to other ventures:

In 1950, the government eliminated controls on the exchange of wheat-flour, which led to a sharp increase in the number of *Chūka soba* shops. These shops were also relatively easy to start up. Large corporations began to rent out *yatai* startup sets inclusive of noodles, soup base, hot water, toppings, bowls, and chopsticks, which operators would rent and walk around town blowing their *charumera* flute, keeping a given percentage of the sales. Even then, the *hikiko* (one who pulls a *yatai* cart around) earned plenty of money. This *Chūka soba* was made from surplus (*yojō*) American wheat flour. (Okumura 1998, 176)

As Okumura notes, postwar returnees also contributed to the initial revival of *Chūka soba* during the occupation period. Many of the returnees who repatriated from the colonies took up noodle-making, opening small *yatai* operations. The relatively low cost of establishing a *yatai*, as well as the availability of flour and lard as compared with rice, made noodle-making a viable option for many returnees with no other source of revenue.

Chinese and Korean laborers also formed a large portion of vendors serving *Chūka soba* in the black markets of Tokyo and other large cities. Occupation arrest records for unlicensed vending reveal a high frequency of non-Japanese names among the arrestees selling food, particularly *Chūka soba*. For example, an occupation record of arrested vendors dated September 18, 1948, reveals that of the 191 names registered, 20 were arrested solely for serving food, while the 171 others were arrested for serving some form of alcohol. Of these 20, nine were detained for the sole offense of serving *Shina soba* (or *Chūka soba*), two for serving *wantan*, two for serving *udon*, two for serving *soba*, two for serving sushi, and three for serving "rice with dishes." All but one of the nine serving *Shina soba* had non-Japanese names. (30 of the 191 arrestees in this sample have non-Japanese names, and after taking into account the fact that some of the arrestees with Japanese names were also Koreans and Chinese who had changed surnames under pressure during the colonial era, it is evident that non-Japanese comprised a considerable portion of small vendors in the black market) (NDL 1948b).

One point worth noting is that the established historical narrative concerning rāmen as offered by the Rāmen Museum of Shin Yokohama, Nissin Foods Corporation, and food authors such as Okumura tend to emphasize the role of Japanese returnees from "war areas" in popularizing *Chūka soba* at the expense of recognizing the Korean and Chinese laborers who, by all indications, were central to the repopularization of Chinese noodle-soup in the early postwar era. In this way, the story concerning returnees opening *yatai* serving *Chūka soba* after the war has the effect of eliding the immense and underappreciated role of non-Japanese in popularizing the dish *after* the war. The established narrative thus confines the influence of foreigners to the earliest phase of the dish's introduction, conveniently omitting the interconnected problems of decolonization and ethnic discrimination in postwar Japan. The focus on the hardships and resilience of Japanese returnees from "war areas" (a term that displaces "colonies") actively overlooks the history of colonial subjugation and its ramifications, which were central to the popularization of *Chūka soba*.

THE ORIGINS OF INSTANT RĀMEN

The long lines of hungry customers found forming around Chinese noodle-soup vendors during the U.S. occupation also served as the inspiration for the invention of instant rāmen. Andō Momofuku (born Pu Wai-fu), the Taiwanese-Japanese founder of Nissin Foods Corporation and the inventor of the first instant and cupped rāmen, claims that the sight of starved customers of all ages standing in front of *yatai* serving Chinese noodle-soup sparked his interest in developing mass-produced, instant forms of the dish (Andō 1992, iii). According to his autobiography, the mission to create an instant form of rāmen derived from meetings with bureaucrats from the Ministries of Agriculture and Health and Welfare, who were looking for new ways to make use of the U.S.-imported wheat flour. He writes:

> At the time, rāmen and Japanese udon were solely the domain of small-scale businesses. There was no pipeline connecting U.S. flour surpluses with the structures necessary to produce and distribute noodles. The lack of adequate manufacturing facilities amounted to a bottleneck.
>
> The Ministry representative recommended that if I was so keen on the idea, I should do the research myself. This suggestion was to later become one of my incentives. . . .
>
> What I wanted was to launch a factory production of rāmen that could easily be eaten at home. I also wanted to supply the rāmen to school lunch services. . . .
>
> As shown by the long lines that once formed in front of rāmen stands, rāmen is a food that appeals to the masses. . . . I pondered how to mass-produce rāmen and give it a homemade flavor. (Andō 1992, 35–37)

Andō's story illustrates the deep connections between U.S. wheat-flour imports during the occupation, the Japanese government's efforts to absorb the flour on a mass scale, and the subsequent invention of instant rāmen. Andō's desire to distribute instant rāmen through the school lunch program is also indicative of how profitable that outlet became for large-scale food processors, and how indispensable intimate government connections were to establishing such distribution channels. The birth of instant rāmen in 1958, therefore, was the culmination of a process that was spawned from Andō's interest in Japanese government efforts to utilize U.S.-imported wheat flour during the occupation period.

Andō also asserts that the invention of instant rāmen contributed to the preservation of Japanese food culture by allowing wheat flour imports to be used for noodles rather than bread. Andō repeats this argument at various points in his autobiography, and the same idea is presented at the Nissin Corporation's food library's permanent exhibit, located at its Tokyo headquarters in Shinjuku. The framing of the instant rāmen invention narrative as resistance to Western hegemony for the purpose of safeguarding Asian cultural autonomy is ironic considering the role of American wheat-flour imports in supplanting demand for domestically produced rice in this period.

FROM *SHINA SOBA* TO *CHŪKA SOBA*

The postwar popularization of Chinese noodle-soup coincided with a modification in the dish's name, which itself reflected the changed geopolitical relationship between Japan and China. The term *Chūka soba* came into popular use among noodle makers, and the term *Shina soba* went out of circulation during the early postwar years, coinciding with the shift away from the use of the word *Shina* and its replacement with the word *Chūgoku* in mainstream politics. The discursive transition indicates a shift away from words tainted with the memory of imperialism and war, and an attempt to remake Japan through a remaking of its Others. Along with *Chūka soba*, the word *rāmen*, which some shops had already begun using in the Taishō period, became the dominant signifying term for the dish after the war. Many in Japan, however, continued to use the term *Shina soba* to refer to the ostensibly Chinese dish, as seen in early postwar films depicting the dish.[1]

As *Chūka soba* consumption began to reappear as a constitutive part of the planned industrial recovery of Japan's urban areas, one finds the beginning of the dish's frequent use in radio, film, and popular music. The dish often appeared as a way to represent various aspects of everyday life in early postwar Japan, such as the desperate food situation, the growing generation gap between the dietary habits of the young and old, and the marking of gender and class differences between certain characters.[2]

The increasingly frequent appearance of Chinese noodle-soup in early postwar popular culture illustrates the dish's availability in relation to other foods as a result of U.S. occupation food policy. At the same time, its Chinese symbolism became increasingly thin, reflecting the attenuation of China in Japan's foreign imaginary overall as a result of the U.S.-imposed Pax Americana. The dish thus became a staple of postwar Japanese fast food and was recognized as such in studies of Japanese food history, government statistics, as well as works of popular culture.

At the most basic level, though, *Chūka soba* made of U.S.–imported wheat flour served the function of an emergency food for the fortification of the Japanese workforce and, in turn, the reindustrialization of the postwar economy. Japanese-style Chinese noodle-soup reemerged in a moment of alimentary scarcity to provide nutrition for those charged with rebuilding the nation into a strategic U.S. ally for cold war purposes. In this way, Prime Minister Ikeda's proposition for "people with lower levels of income [to] eat more wheat" in line with the "fundamental laws of economics" was realized in part through the mass consumption of Japanese-style Chinese noodle-soup.

NOTES

1. For example, see the film *Sanma no Aji* (dir. Ozu Yasujirō, 1962, Shōchiku).
2. Examples include the films *Bangiku* (dir. Naruse Mikio, 1954, Tōhō) and *Ochazuke no aji* (dir. Ozu Yasujirō, 1952, Shōchiku), as well as the song *Charumera soba ya*, popularized by *enka* singer Misora Hibari in 1953.

WORKS CITED

Aldous, Christopher. 1997. *The Police in Occupation Japan: Control, Corruption, and Resistance to Reform*. London: Routledge.

Andō, Momofuku. 1992. *Rising to the Challenge: Living in an Age of Turbulent Change*. Tokyo: Foodeum Communication.

Ara, Takashi, ed. 1995. *GHQ/SCAP Top Secret Records*. Set 1, vol. 2. Tokyo: Kashiwa Shobō.

Cwiertka, Katarzyna J. 2006. *Modern Japanese Cuisine: Food, Power, and National Identity*. London: Reaktion Books.

Dower, John. 1999. *Embracing Defeat: Japan in the Wake of World War II*. New York: W. W. Norton.

National Diet Library (NDL), U.S. Occupation Archives Microfilm (Tokyo). 1946a. General Headquarters, Supreme Commander for the Allied Powers, Economic and Scientific Section, Price Control and Rationing Division. "Food situation during the first year of occupation." Undated. (Declassified E.O. 12065 Section 3–402/NNDG #775024)

——. 1946b. Joint Chiefs of Staff, JCS 1662, Memorandum by Chief of Staff, U.S. Army. "Food crisis in Germany and Japan." April 27, 1946. (Declassified E.O. 12065 Section 3–402/NNDG #775027)

——. 1948a. General Headquarters, Supreme Commander for the Allied Powers,

Public Health and Welfare Section. "Allocation of imports for Japanese school lunch program." May 25, 1948. (Declassified E.O. 12065 Section 3–402/NNDG #775024)

———. 1948b. General Headquarters, Supreme Commander for the Allied Powers, Government Section. "Report on arrest of violators of emergency measures ordinance for eating and drinking business." September 18, 1948. (Declassified E.O. 12065 Section 3–402 NNDG #775009)

———. 1949. General Headquarters, Supreme Commander for the Allied Powers, Economic and Scientific Section, Labor Division. "Supplementary distribution of commodities for workers." Undated. (Declassified E.O. 12065 Section 3–402/NNDG #775017)

Okumura Ayao. 1998. *Shinka suru menshoku bunka.* Tokyo: Foodeum Communication.

Ōtsuka Shigeru. 1989. *Shushoku ga kawaru.* Tokyo: Nihon Keizai Hyōronsha.

Schaller, Michael. 1985. *The American Occupation of Japan: The Origins of the Cold War in Asia.* New York: Oxford University Press.

U.S. Strategic Bombing Survey. 1947. *The Japanese Wartime Standard of Living and Utilization of Manpower.* Washington, D.C.: Manpower, Food, and Civilian Supplies Division.

10 *Bentō*

Boxed Love, Eaten by the Eye

TOMOKO ONABE

They say that a Chinese dish you eat by taste, a Western one you eat by aroma, and a Japanese one you eat by color. When you make a bentō, it has to be tasty of course. But more than that, the bentō has to be beautiful in color so that by only looking at it you will have appetite. —Mikuriya 1952, 18–19

MAKING A TRADITIONAL BOX LUNCH called a *bentō* has long been a major source of complaint, especially among Japanese mothers of young children. In recent years, there has been an added emphasis in boxed-lunch making on color balance and the combination of foods. A Japanese traditional lunch box is said to be "eaten by the eye" rather than the mouth, as the book *All about Bentō* (*Obentō no iroiro*) (Mikuriya 1952, 19) characterized them half a century ago. For housewives who are the chief preparers of *bentō* in families, this focus on appearance only adds new challenges to making *bentō* for children and husbands. Housewives must concern themselves with the ingredients' overall color combination and presentation while reasonable cost, easy preparation, tasty recipes, children's pickiness, seasonal appropriateness, and potential spoilage remain daily concerns. Packing all these elements neatly into a little lunch box certainly seems to be a challenging task.

In this chapter, I first explore the history of *bentō* from the Meiji era (1868–1912), focusing on traditional values of *bentō* as symbols of commensality and products of the balance between contrasting "secular" and "sacred" ingredients. Then I concentrate on the elements of multipolarizing colors, analyzing the puzzling rise of attention to (and consequential diversification of) visual elements in the ingredients. Finally, I present a feminist critique of *bentō* by examining the lunch box as a communication tool (between mother and child, and school and mother), as well as a vehicle for expressing domestic devotion. Two major questions are considered: how and when the appearance of a *bentō* became important in Japan, and how the *bentō* became a key symbol of communication between the maker and the eater.

THE TRADITIONAL DICHOTOMY AND PRIMACY
OF INVISIBLE BALANCE

The vital equilibrium of Meiji period cooking was not gustatory (aroma, taste, color) but that of secular and sacred. Contemporary cookbooks and journal articles of the Meiji period emphasize balance in bentō, but visual attractiveness was not at all a major concern—or rather, it could not be. Instead, the cook's principle concern was taste and aroma, balancing the symbolic dichotomy of the sacred and the secular. Most foods were essentially labeled either as "secular" foods (namagusa) or as "sacred" foods (shōjin).[1] In practice, this meant distinguishing between namagusa (fish, meat) and shōjin (vegetables, tofu, beans). After frying or baking, often with soy sauce, however, all ingredients became similarly brownish in color and they did not possess the visual contrast so vital to contemporary bentō. (Japanese did not develop the custom of eating raw vegetables until the introduction of Western-style salad during the Meiji period by elites, and then more commonly after 1945.) A striking difference compared to contemporary bentō-making, this emphasis on equilibrium was unrelated to either nutrition or color combination but strictly limited to the symbolic level of the secular/sacred. This reflects a more ritualistic notion of food presentation, even in a light lunch box.

The secular/sacred balance was the invisible determinant of a properly balanced lunch box. According to a typical bentō cookbook, Lunchbox Cooking Guide for Everyday Use (Bentō ryōri annai nichiyō benri) (Fujimura 1905), when preparing a bentō, the cook's emphasis was on the balance of aroma and taste. This cookbook indicates that for everyday bentō, one only needs some rice, pickles, and one main dish (fish, egg, or meat), avoiding any extravagance. Furthermore, when serving fish (or meat), "it is better to be accompanied by a sacred (shōjin) dish," which is believed to symbolically absorb the fishy aroma and neutralize the "secular" aspect of the fish (Fujimura 1905, 2). One might interpret this to be a contrast of meat versus vegetables, but this refers purely to the balance of symbolic scents and tastes. These two contrasting elements, the binary of secular fishiness versus sanctity in the traditional style of preparation of a meal, is key to understanding future emphasis on the colorful bentō. In other words, this strong traditional sense of the balance of food, quite apart from nutritional considerations, persists today as articulated in the contemporary valorization of color variety, contrast, and balance.

The secular/sacred discourse shifted from aroma to taste, while assigning somewhat arbitrary designations for ingredients along the continuum.

Originally taste-oriented words were substituted for aroma-oriented words. The secular was referred to as strong-taste (*nōkō*, heavily seasoned) versus sacred as mild-taste (*tanpaku*, lightly seasoned). But again, this remained at the metaphoric level of taste, since in fact food was not seasoned accordingly. All vegetables were automatically labeled mild, whether seasoned or not. The book lists more examples of mild foods: flowering fern (*zenmai*), hijiki seaweed (*hijiki*), lily bulb (*yurine*), wheat gluten (*fu*), and *kon'yaku* noodles (*shirataki*) (Fujimura 1905). The following ingredients were typical dishes for Buddhist ceremonies, so they were viewed as mild, pious foods yet sometimes criticized as tainted with sacred connotations:

- flowering fern (*zenmai*): delicious and mild, good for *bentō*, although sometimes reeking of sacred abstinence (*shōjin*) because of its frequent use in Buddhist ceremonial menus (Fujimura 1905, 142). [Note: Here, "reeking" is used metaphorically, since it is a sacred food without the taint of fish and blood.]
- Hijiki seaweed (*hijiki*): different from flowering fern in terms of taste, but since it is often used in Buddhist cuisine, people criticize that it is full of the smell of sacred abstinence (*shōjin-kusaki*) (Fujimura 1905, 143).
- lily bulb (*yurine*): for *bentō* maybe too mild in taste, but when accompanying meat, creates a good balance (Fujimura 1905, 41).

Here, meat was considered "more secular" than fish, so the super-negative (a super-mild pious vegetable) achieves equilibrium with the "stinking" secular meat dish.

The categorization of food along the secular/sacred continuum is unrelated to nutritional or color elements. Food in one category (lily bulbs, hijiki seaweed, and flowering fern) are presented as being similar, yet they possess no common nutritious elements from a contemporary point of view. Their color after being boiled or fried is subdued, making no seeming contrast with meat or fish that are similarly brownish in color. When placing actual food from each category side by side—flowering fern with cooked fish, or lily bulb with meat—the appearance is often an unappetizing juxtaposition of different shades of brown. Only with this insight into the traditional dichotomy between pious and secular foods are clear contrasts visible.

With the importation of new foods and knowledge of Western cuisine, cookbooks shifted emphasis from secular/sacred to taste, yet not color, as determinants of a balanced meal. In 1908, a domestic science teacher, Kaetsu Takako, emphasized the balance of taste, or a new version of the balance of strong taste/mild taste (secular/sacred) in her book, *Lectures on Domestic Science* (*Kaseigaku kōwa*): "The strong-taste of beef stew with mild-tasting mashed potato, Western dishes with salad at the end of the meal, protein food with fat or carbohydrate, are all considerations for balance" (Kaetsu 1908, 183–84). The traditional strong/mild taste balance is applied here to Western cuisine. Significantly, taste and nutrients—rather than color—are mentioned as vital elements of balance. In a newspaper contest in 1905 featuring rather extravagant *bentō*, even the first-place menu for one week looks brownish, and the emphasis of the reviews were on the balance of taste.[2]

In summary, by the early twentieth century, the appearance of the *bentō* was not as important as today, especially its colors. The balance of food was limited to the symbolic and somewhat arbitrary interpretation of secular or pious food, and later Japanese/Western, or nutritious components, articulated mainly through aroma and taste. Consumption of food was enjoyed accordingly through appreciation of symbolic contrasts between the senses of smell and taste.

We can find a remnant of the traditional dichotomy between secular and pious foods in the contemporary ingredients for sukiyaki, indicating that the traditional contrast described in the previous section persists. Sukiyaki is a typical hot-pot dish with sliced beef and various other ingredients cooked in a big pot. When sukiyaki is cooked, everything is of a uniform, unappetizing brownish color with a lack of apparent color balance. Yet decoding it from the standpoint of the traditional balance between the ideals of secular versus pious foods, we can discover a remarkable contrast counteracting each other in any sukiyaki pot. The aggressively secular meat is neutralized by all other traditionally Buddhist-laden ingredients (tofu, *shirataki* [*kon'yaku* noodles], wheat gluten [*fu*]), in addition to a "deodorant" (*kusami-keshi*) herb of spring onion. When I discovered such traditional contrasts for the first time while researching this topic, I was stunned by the significance of the traditional and historic concepts that I had followed unwittingly. (For older generations, this balance may be more self-evident.) Some sukiyaki aficionados may see the contrast; most people never do.

Foods thus appear to have objectively discernible characteristics with regards to color, nutrition, smell, and taste. Shifts in the perception of food, however, may be followed by a public unawareness of the original concept for their creation. Therefore, the evaluation of the correct equilibrium of food continues to be historically subjective, shifting according to tastes, changes of philosophy, common custom, and the importation of new scientific theories of diet.

THE RISE OF VISUALITY AND THE PRIORITY
OF THE VISIBLE

The increasing importance of visuality in *bentō*-making dates to the 1950s, and became more prevalent in the 1970s when Japan was experiencing a period of high economic growth (*kōdo seichō ki*). This period was accompanied by the introduction of visual media, including color television and broadcasting, and colorful print magazines filled with photographs.

Until the 1950s, the discourse on food was mostly verbal, leaving far more room for rhetorical description or imagination. In the summer of 1905, the *Niroku* newspaper (*Niroku shinbun*) sponsored a contest called "menu for a hot summer *bentō*" (1905, July 2, 3). The organizers conducted three different contests according to various budgetary limits of different socioeconomic groups: twenty sen, ten sen, and six sen for each *bentō* (one sen was 1/100 yen). The main focus of the jury was on the upper-class twenty-sen *bentō*. The ideas collected from readers were deliciously described in a weekly menu, followed by an expert's meticulous critique.

FIRST PLACE MENU OF TWENTY-SEN BENTŌ
Monday: Teriyaki sea bream (*tai*), sugar-glazed arrowhead (*kuwai*) and gingko nuts, red pickled ginger, vegetables pickled in sake lees (*Narazuke*).
Tuesday: Ham sandwiches of Kamakura ham, milk chocolate.
Wednesday: Beef omelet, melon salad, toasted bread. (*Niroku shinbun* 1905, August 15, 3)

The menu continues in a similar fashion. This first-prize menu seems so extravagant in terms of ingredients and description, and it is unrealistic for a hot summer in terms of keeping the food fresh and safe. Yet this exercise of creating extravagant fantasy menus serves exactly the same purpose as colorful food photographs do in contemporary women's magazines. These menus appeal to the imagination of domestic *bentō* cooks, who perhaps enjoyed reading about this upper-class, Western-style cuisine. Clearly, the purpose of the contest was not pragmatic at all but rather to offer readers an imaginary picture of a fancy lifestyle. Few readers would have dared to try to realize the menu. There is a clear sense of distinction between fantasy and the real world; these menus were meant for savoring on the page.

The first introduction of visual descriptions of food in a woman's magazine occurred in the 1930s. In 1938, black-and-white photographs appeared occasionally in the menu of *Illustrated Woman's Magazine* (*Fujin gahō*) (1938, April, 164–67). Yet it is very hard to tell what we are seeing just by glancing at the pictures. With very close study and the help of captions, it might be possible to discover what they represented—but the food still looks uninviting. When we stop and reflect that this must have been very attractive for readers in 1938, it is surprising how drastic the shift of popular perception has been. After experiencing the influence of colorful media, it seems far more challenging for us to "read" or decode the supposedly clear message of those monochrome cookery photos as people seventy years ago apparently did. In short, we have unwittingly developed illiteracy toward reading black-and-white photos.

Despite such illustrated recipe sections, only in the 1950s with the advent of color photography did visual appearance become critically central to *bentō*. From the late 1930s until the end of World War II in 1945, there was no substantial rise in the visuality of food in public displays, simply because of wartime restrictions on available media for leisure and shortages of food. After the war, the first example of a *bentō* cookbook stressing the importance of colorful combinations, *All about Bentō* (*Obentō no iroiro*), was published in 1952. After acknowledging the value of colorfulness in *bentō* as a particularly Japanese phenomenon, Mikuriya Yoshiko continues:

> To make a colorful *bentō*, when choosing the ingredients, you must consider the combination of colors very carefully. For example, if you choose meat with shiitake mushrooms and burdock on the side, the color combination is monotonous. But if you choose meat with snow-white steamed potatoes, and with fresh green vegetables or spring beans, it looks more delicious just by its appearance. (Mikuriya 1952, 19)

Mikuriya thus criticizes the appearance of the traditionally perfect combination of meat with shiitake mushroom and burdock as unappealing. Then, after offering tips on making a *bentō* look more charming and attractive, she concludes:

> When you make a positive effort to beautify your *bentō*, such efforts effectively will make your *bentō* look more delicious (*oishiku suru*) than it actually tastes. Please remember that not only *bentō* but every dish is "eaten by the eye," as well as for its taste. (Mikuriya 1952, 19)

While the Japanese love of color contrast and balance may appear to be of ancient origin, this is the earliest example I have found that clearly places visual attractiveness over the traditional sacred/secular (mild/strong taste) balance. The *bentō* tips in this book, *All about Bentō* (*Obentō no iroiro*) are also the earliest examples that introduced *bentō* that look similar to those of today. This turning point marked one of the most remarkable changes in the rise of the visual consciousness of food. By the 1950s, the appearance of food with an emphasis on color combination, which had not been important earlier in the twentieth century, emerged to gain equal or greater importance over taste. Despite the substitution of the secular/sacred balance with color as essential to its success, this new trend remained faithful to the old concept of the ideal *bentō* as a balance of diverse elements.

THE RISE OF COLOR AND THE FALL OF NUTRIENTS

The postwar history of *bentō* is marked by a tension between the government's emphasis on nutrients versus a journalistic and societal stress on appearance. Curiously, an attempt to visualize the nutritional components through somewhat arbitrary colors led inadvertently to a greater emphasis on color combinations, often at the nutrients' expense.

Thus the first shift of perception of food, and accordingly the attention paid to *bentō*-making, occurred on the eve of the period of high economic growth (*kōdo seichō ki*) in the early 1950s, while the balance of color in *bentō* became more important later in the 1970s. Many factors contributed to this stress on appearance and especially color contrast after the period of high economic growth from the mid-1950s to the early 1970s. A greater variety of foodstuffs became available, making it easier to express color contrasts in a *bentō*. And certainly the rise of cheap color printing, photography, and later color television and movies contributed to the development of more colorful *bentō* in the 1970s and 1980s. Despite this new interest in color, the most essential element for health in any *bentō* is undoubtedly the food's nutritional value. The following section describes how the national government after the war tried to educate people about the importance of a nutritious food balance.

In the 1970s, the Ministry of Education advocated a popular theory of the tricolor balance of nutrients (*eiyō sanshoku undō*) that had been established and advocated by Kondo Toshiko, a nutritionist and former bureaucrat who had retired from the Ministry of Public Welfare. Kondo associated nutrients with three colors in 1953, well before the government had shown any interest in the use of color.[3] The grassroots food education (*shokuiku*) private association she founded in 1953, the Association for the Improvement of Nutrition (*Eiyō kaizen fukyūkai*), led the tricolor movement. Their members employed the tricolor balance of nutrients to encourage people to form good habits of eating balanced meals; Kondo continued to be the leader of the tricolor movement until her death in 2008. For each meal, people were encouraged to take an item of food from three different nutritional categories, represented by different colors. It was no surprise at the beginning when the familiar words of colors were applied to represent the then-unfamiliar terms for nutrients. But it was a historical coincidence that the fictitious notion of balanced colors, a mere symbol for educational and communicative convenience, eventually swept away the most significant aspect of food: the balance of nutrients.

There are, of course, other options to classify necessary nutrients for balanced meals, but using colors for the grouping of food is somewhat intuitive, a simple and easy mnemonic. In the system, the three categories are represented by red, yellow, and green: red for protein, yellow for carbohydrates and oils, and green for vegetables and fruits. Each category has two subcategories:

RED (TO FORM BLOOD AND MUSCLES)
subcategory 1: milk, other dairy products, eggs
subcategory 2: fish, meat, beans

YELLOW (TO SUPPLY STRENGTH AND MAINTAIN
BODY TEMPERATURE)
subcategory 1: wheat, potatoes, sugar
subcategory 2: oils and fats

GREEN (TO PROMOTE FITNESS)
subcategory 1: green-yellow vegetables
subcategory 2: light-green vegetables, seaweed, fruit (Mori 1977, 83)

By the mid-1970s, the tricolor movement had not only reached enormous popularity among educators but had also gained the authority of official governmental sanction. In 1977 the Ministry of Education adopted this color categorization of food for home economics courses in the primary school curricula, a public theory of nutrients taught to every primary school pupil.

Yet from the beginning, the theory of the tricolor balance of nutrients was potentially misleading, because food itself has its own natural color, which often differs from the color of its symbolic category. Yellow eggs and cheese, for example, were classified as red. Subcategories became even more confusing when dark-green peppers or dark-red tomatoes were placed in the group of light green because of their lack of vitamins to qualify them as green-yellow. The appearance of food did not represent invisible nutrients; in fact, normally one cannot judge food's nutritional value by its appearance.

Yet by using colors symbolically, the three color categories invited confusion when these somewhat arbitrary labels conflicted with the natural colors of vegetables and fruit.

The confusion of the symbolic color with the natural color can be found as early as 1977 in the curriculum guidelines of the Ministry of Education published in that year: "*Stir-fried green-yellow vegetables.* When choosing the vegetables, select from both the green-yellow and light-green categories in order to provide pleasant variations of color as well as easy cooking with natural moisture (of light-green vegetables)" (Mori 1977, 76). Light-green and green-yellow are the names of two subcategories that do not represent actual colors; therefore, their inclusion cannot make any "pleasant variation in color" except in a symbolic sense. For example, cabbage and *komatsuna* leaves (a popular green leafy vegetable used for stir-frying) are included in two separate categories, albeit they look similar in color. The tricolor scheme, while handy and easy to remember, can just as easily confuse essential nutrients with superficial colors.

This confusion of superficial colors and nutrient symbols make the categories inherently unstable. Two popular deep-color ingredients for *bentō*, green peppers and tomatoes, were in the subgroup of light-green vegetables, according to the nutrients they actually contain, until 1982 when the Ministry of Education authorities finally gave in and made exceptions to negotiate between actual and symbolic (nutritional) colors. Finally, green peppers and tomatoes were listed under yellow-green vegetables. In the explanation of the change for the categories, ministry officials defended their unusual compromise by stating that those vegetables could be de facto yellow-green vegetables since if people eat them frequently, their total intake of vitamin increases substantially.[4] This decision conveniently harmonized the symbolic color of the foods with their actual color. But the fact remains that the invisible nutritious symbolism conceded to superficial color in the supposedly scientific definition of food in 1982, and it hints at the contemporary overwhelming persuasive force of surface colors and appearance.

As we have seen, the 1980s marked a paradigmatic shift in the visuality of food. The 1950s witnessed the first shift, from a balance of sacred and secular foods to a visual color balance. But the traditional sense of balance survived this change, seeking harmony by opposing elements in a lunch-boxed menu, and the emphasis in *bentō*-making was still on nutrients. Then, the introduction of the tricolor balance occurred from the 1950s to the 1970s. The subsequent change in the 1980s marked the confusion of the essential and the arbitrary. Trivial colors win over vital nutrients, reinforced by the misleading popular belief that achieving a good food balance could only be realized by a superficial color balance. As a result, the *bentō* is seen to be eaten only by the eye.

THE MYTH OF GENUINE AFFECTION

Our discussion so far suggests why *bentō*-making can be such a physically time-consuming and complex task today. If one seeks to achieve both nutrition and color harmony in lunch boxes every day, making *bentō* soon becomes an arduous chore, as anthropologist Anne Allison discovered: "[The] key element is appearance. Food must be organized, reorganized, arranged, rearranged, stylized, and restylized to appear in a design that is visually attractive. Presentation is critical: not to the extent that taste and nutrition are displaced . . . but to the degree that how food looks is at least as important as how it tastes and how good and sustaining it is for one's body" (Allison 1997, 298). Yet mothers of young children, who are the ones principally responsible for creating such fancy *bentō*, face a number of additional psychological pressures with regards to *bentō*-making. In the world of kindergarten, a *bentō* becomes a legitimate and crucial symbol of whether or not motherly affection is genuine. In other words, *bentō* is simply boxed love.

There are three factors that contribute to such a far-fetched psychological argument. First and foremost is the historical change in the notion of the *bentō* as a communication tool (from school to mother, mother to child). The second is the *bentō*'s exposure to and evaluation by the eyes of other people. The third factor is navigating the space between the ideal and the real. From the mothers' perspective, the practical negotiation of these combinations of vectors of public discourse and peer pressure has transformed *bentō*-making into a stressful homework assignment. The task is packed with intricate puzzles, ones that they must solve under pressure every morning before sending their child to kindergarten.[5]

Kindergartens (*yōchien*) have always distinguished themselves from nursery schools as middle- to upper-class institutions. On a purely institutional basis, the *yōchien* is administered by the Ministry of Education (*monbukagakushō*) while the nursery school (*hoikuen*) is administered by the Ministry of Public Welfare (*kōsei rōdōshō*). Joseph J. Tobin explains the social distinction: "The most basic distinction is that *yōchien* tend to serve the children of women who define themselves as full-time mothers and *sarariman* [salaried businessman] wives, and *hoikuen* serve the children of women who work and who for economic or ideological reasons are not involved in the *sarariman* family life-style described by Ezra Vogel in *Japan's New Middle Class* [1971]"[6] (Tobin 1989, 47). Therefore, the staffs of kindergartens feel entitled to demand more tasks from homemaking mothers than nursery schools do. Through such demands, and the mother's submission to them, kindergartens and parents have constructed an institutional ideology of being committed to child rearing.[7] So, for mothers of kindergarteners, semipublic displays of caregiving, including the *bentō*, are semipublic proof of their social status.

Accompanying the emphasis on *bentō* colors and general appearance from the 1950s to 1970s, making *bentō* became an important ritual to reflect their social identity as devoted middle-class homemaking mothers. But this trend was contagious, and also affected schools such as nursery schools for working mothers, where *bentō* were not required on a daily basis; however, when *bentō* did become a requirement, they were especially inspected by teachers.[8] Gradually the distinction between nursery school and kindergarten blurred, as demands on everyone became similar. Most primary schools provide school lunches, so for entrepreneurial publishers of *bentō* cookbooks, the commercial target has been the caregivers of preschool-age children.[9] Since the years of preschool are limited, mothering as expressed through *bentō*-making becomes more important.

Communication through *bentō* was much weaker before the Second World War, due to the general poverty of people's diets and the social structure of large, extended families. Before the school lunch system was launched in 1946, there were many households that could not provide their school-age children any lunch. The major homemaker was often not the young mother but the mother-in-law, who did not pay much attention to each individual in the extended household. Often *bentō* were made for working parents and children using the same ingredients, so that all members of a family, even stay-at-home grandparents or ancestors, who would be provided a daily offering, might partake of meals "together." The young and the old may have collaborated or taken turns in order to make these communal lunches. Like feasts that invariably accompany the rites of passage in Japanese tradition, shared meals symbolically unify the partakers as a family.

I propose the following types of communication through *bentō*. The traditional custom followed the second type, the homemade group-shared *bentō*. Since the identity of the *bentō*-maker is uncertain, we can assume that the provider of *bentō* is the household as a general entity. According to folklorist Yanagita Kunio, writing in *A Record of the Meiji and Taishō Era* (*Meiji Taishō shi sesō hen*) (1931), the original principle of *bentō* was perhaps very similar to *kagezen*, the custom of offering some portion of a meal at the altar in the hope that traveling members of the family could share the same meal in the imagination with the rest of the family. Yanagita explains: "The very nourishment of a *bentō* depended on the imagination of the eater who appreciated the sense of virtually sharing food with the rest of the family at about the same time as they were having a meal back home. In other words, the *bentō* was invisibly seasoned by the sense of confirmation that the family was taking part in the ritual of shared meals" (Yanagita 1931/1993, 97). Yanagita depicts the *bentō* as a form of virtual commensality created and partaken by the household, which is quite distinct from its present type of communication shown in the third type, where unique *bentō* are made by individuals for particular members (see Table 3).

When a *bentō* is made for an individual child, its preparation becomes an indication of the affection of a mother. The mother crafts a custom-made *bentō* of deliberately unshared food, for an individual child, with supposed total affection. In fact, she is obliged to do the same for every member of the household, including her husband. When newlywed, she is supposed to make totally devoted "affectionate-wife *bentō*" (*aisai bentō*) for her husband; when a child is born, she makes an "affectionate-mother *bentō*" (*aijō mama bentō*) for the child. In sum, the *bentō* mirrors the stereotyped, beautified identity of a middle-class nuclear family homemaker, with her value reduced to being an affectionate producer.[10] In this ideal, the maker of a *bentō* is clearly identified, as well as her particularized love. The pleasure of sharing food has been forgotten as attention shifts toward the maker's unique relationship with a particular individual recipient.

Educational anthropologist Lois Peak correctly pinpoints the importance of the daily chore: "In preschools these box lunches (*obentō*) assume a symbolic significance far beyond their nutritional value. In part, they represent a concrete manifestation of the mother's love and concern for the child and

Table 3. Three Types of Communication about *Bentō*

Type	Maker	Eater/Potential Eaters	Number of Eaters	Indication of Affection
Store bought	unknown	general public	infinite	none
Homemade group/shared	household	family members	several	some
Custom made for each member	specified family member (mother)	specific individual (each child or working parent)	one	total

form a symbolic bond between the mother at home and the child at school" (Peak 1991, 59). In fact, the director of the Tokyo preschool at which Peak researched makes this unique, custom-made, and mutually satisfying exchange quite explicit:

> By taking the trouble to make a nice lunch each morning, the mother communicates her feelings for her child. It's only during preschool that the mother will have this chance to get up a little early and do something nice for her child. . . . It's also important that *obentō* be made especially for the child, not food left over from dinner or the adult's *obentō*. . . . It should be nutritious, be the kind of food children enjoy, look colorful, and be cutely prepared. When the child removes the lid of his lunch box at lunchtime, his mother's love and feelings for him should pop out of the box. Children should feel, "My mother made this just for me." (quoted in Peak 1991, 59–60)

The media, too, takes up this element in a way sure to stimulate feelings of inadequacy in most mothers. The need for earnest love in communication through food is typically promulgated in *bentō* cookbooks such as *The Complete Guide for Lunchbox-making for Kindergarten* (*Yōchien no obentō zensho*) in 2002 by Naitō Akira: "Oh, you need not worry so much [about making *bentō*]. There is only one point to check. If you succeed in this, your *bentō* will be fine and pass the test every time you make it. What is that point, then? Affection!" (Naitō 2002, 149). The cookbook concludes, "So never forget to check whether you boxed enough love into it. Please make sure every *bentō* is an affectionate *bentō* (*aijō bentō*)." According to the prerequisites that we have discussed so far for making a satisfactory lunch box, *bentō*-making requires a depth of knowledge of nutrients and color, of the art of cooking, of the recipient's likes and dislikes and overall appetite that day, as well as time and energy. Yet the author patronizingly declares that love is everything. This message is hardly good news for *bentō*-making mothers. It does not literally mean that any *bentō* will do as long as you pack enough love into it. On the contrary, the statement invokes an eternal domestic aspiration for the myth of a genuinely affectionate *bentō*.

The true meaning of this message seems to be the threat that now the *bentō* reflects who you are and how affectionate a mother you are. Since the identity of the maker is more obvious due to the trend toward the nuclear family, the *bentō*-maker boxes lunch as earnestly as possible in hopes of seeing her own identity as "a good mother" mirrored in the care, control of contrasts, and time-consuming labor of creating the *bentō*.

The second pressure vector comes from the fact that *bentō* is "eaten" and judged by observers' eyes. Japanese preschool or kindergarten education typically focuses on encouraging children to form healthy habits in all aspects of everyday life. Inevitably, teachers tend to pay a great deal of attention to what children eat in a *bentō*. As a result, teachers feel entitled to critique a *bentō* and its maker, and do so openly. According to Peak and Allison, suggestions from other mothers were mainly about making bite-sized portions, how to wrap them in foil, decorate them with seasonal ornaments, or cut them in cute ways, and make them appealing to young children.

Sometimes other children make fun of a child's *bentō*. When playtime follows lunchtime, group ethos demands that the entire class wait until the last child has finished his or her *bentō* before the class goes outside. All eyes turn to the slow or picky eaters. The children of international mothers often experience teasing from peers because of a nonstandard *bentō*, who then complain to their mother that she created a funny *bentō*. Here is an experience of an American mother living in Japan whose son's lunch was made fun of at the local kindergarten.

> The next day I made him a Japanese lunch, a *bentō*. But he came home from school again unhappy, again about his lunch. I said, "Now what's wrong? I made you a Japanese lunch." He said, in tears, "But you didn't cut the apple slices so they look like bunny rabbits like the other mothers do." I was sure this was an exaggeration on his part. I thought, "All the other mothers can't be cutting apples to look like rabbits." But I checked around a bit and discovered that children's lunches really do look great—the apples and carrots are cut up like rabbits and flowers and whatnot. I just don't have the time to be a professional lunch maker. (quoted in Tobin 1989, 67)

The burden of *bentō*-making partially comes from peer comparisons as illustrated above. The *bentō*—and by extension, its maker and consumer—faces the inevitable exposure to the eyes of others and evaluation by them.

The third factor arises from the dilemma of how to find a compromise between the ideal and the real. A *bentō* that satisfies the teachers' eyes often differs from what pleases a child's palate. As we all know, children love peanut butter sandwiches or the equivalent in Japanese lunch, say, fried noodles (*yakisoba*). Yet such a lunch would surely receive harsh comments from teachers, even with an excuse that one happens to have nothing else to serve one busy morning. Thus even having perfected a few recipes will not resolve the challenges of *bentō*-making, which demand variety according to the weather, age of child, gender, and changing tastes of the child.

Seasonally appropriate ingredients give *bentō*-makers further challenges between the real and the ideal. In summer, for example, to make *bentō* stay fresh in room temperature for four hours one needs to be very careful to make sure that utensils are perfectly clean and the ingredients fresh. The *bentō* manuals preach that the menu has to be carefully chosen, and the foods carefully arranged in the box to minimize potential spoilage. But in real-life situations, there needs to be some compromise. Such incoherence in *bentō*-making makes the task an everyday stressful obstacle course, full of complex barriers to surmount at every turn.

It is a sort of bittersweet game, and in Japanese comic books for young mothers, the gap between the real and the ideal *bentō* is a favorite topic. Comic book writers depict and make fun of their own experiences with kindergarten or nursery authorities over the gap between the ideal that the school demands and the reality they cope with. One of the best-selling comics for mothers of young children, *Moms Love Flabby Monsters: Volume Two* (*Mama wa poyopoyo zaurusu ga osuki: Futatabi*) by Aonuma Takako, has a story entitled "I Hate Making *Bentō!*" It continues "And I am sure I'm not the only one who is crying out like this!"

> I chose that kindergarten for Ryu [her son] because it was within three-minute walking distance. But—wait for this—you need to make *bentō* as many as four days a week! Monday, Tuesday, Thursday and Friday!! Before he entered the kindergarten, I was pretty optimistic, thinking "Well, it'll be just a tiny *bentō* for a kid who eats tiny portions! Easy, easy!!" But once you actually start making *bentō*, the number of dishes you have to make for a tiny little *bentō* could add up to way over that of a dinner menu. "Wow, it took forty minutes to make!" And after all, you know, it will be exposed to the public eye (*yososama no me ni fureru*). (Aonuma 1995, 109–10)

After Aonuma lists the unexpected challenges she faced, she continues:

> When I took making *bentō* so seriously and repeated it day after day, I found myself hesitant to wake up in the morning. When I did not have to make *bentō*, I could wake up happily and pleasantly early in the morning. One morning I found myself standing and staring at the frying pan on the stove for thirty minutes, doing nothing. I think I was suffering severe "*bentō*-phobia" (*obentō-kyōfushō*). (Aonuma 1995, 110)

This is a comical but not unusual situation of an earnest and sincere mother caught up in the dilemma between the prescribed and the practical.

CONCLUSION

In summary, we can draw conclusions about why mothers of young children consider it stressful to make a *bentō* today. The secular/sacred dichotomy held residual sway beyond the Meiji period, when it transformed into a more general demand for the balance of tastes, and later colors. This change of perception was further complicated by the government's attempt to match actual colors to the arbitrary symbolic ones in the tricolor nutrient system of red-green-yellow. On top of that, with the advent of the modern nuclear family and the reduction in the number of children, despite the hard work and time of its creation, the art of making *bentō* was mystified and reduced by self-proclaimed authorities into "measurable affection." This myth prevails.

Our discussion suggests reasons why *bentō*-making can be such a challenge today. Primarily, this comes from a forced sense of obligation to create a nutritious and colorful harmony in a lunch box every day. Second, mothers of young children face additional psychological pressures in *bentō*-making stemming from the historical changes of attitude toward *bentō*, from virtual commensality to custom-made affection-bearers. Severe critiques from observers of *bentō* (teachers, children's peers and their mothers), and strong and unreasonable attacks that a *bentō* is judged by the amount of its boxed love, are two among them. In that regard, the initial complaints by mothers seem absolutely legitimate. Putting all these requirements neatly in a little lunch box cannot merely be challenging but also a next-to-impossible task of endless striving to achieve an equilibrium amid historically unstable and shifting perceptions of nutrients, color, variety, seasonal appropriateness, and taste.

NOTES

1. Literally "fishy, stinking of fish or blood," *namagusa* refers to nonsacred foods. Literally "pious, religious purification, abstinence from fish and meat," *shōjin* refers to the diet of priests or those on an observant Buddhist diet.

2. *Niroku* newspaper (1905, July 2 and August 15).

3. Kondo Toshiko was born in 1913. In the prewar era she worked as a nutritionist for factory lunch meals, and taught dietetics at schools. After the war she continued teaching dietetics and was involved in labor movements, and then worked for the Ministry of Public Welfare. When she resigned from the ministry in 1953, she founded the Association for the Improvement of Nutrition and started the tricolor movement of nutrients. She published several books on her activities and food education, including *A Japanese Style Diet* (*Nihongata shoku seikatsu*, 1982).

4. For a brief history of the yellow-green category, see Ministry of Education (2005, chapter 3, section 6, page 1).

5. Allison picked up principles for *bentō*-making from manuals, other mothers, and school newsletters that included nonfood decorations and elaborations: adding toothpicks, seasonal decorations, cute and varied containers for soy sauce and ketchup, and other nonfood items to make the *bentō* appealing to the child (1997, 306–7).

6. Vogel describes the life of salaried workers and their families based on research from 1958 to 1960 in Mamachi, a section of a Tokyo suburb, selected by Japanese social scientists as typically middle class. "Few Mamachi women are aware of any conflict between home and work or between home and personal enjoyment. The Mamachi wife is pleased that in comparison with poorer families she is able to devote herself to her home and family" (Vogel 1971, 189).

7. Anne Allison sees the elaborate *bentō*-making demands as part of the state ideological apparatus for ensuring the role of professional housewives (1997).

8. At my daughter's nursery, teachers even posted pass/fail grades with comments by teachers, such as the "overall balance is fine, but needs more work to make meatballs tender. We suggest simmering them in soup after stir-frying." I was stunned not only by the fact that the teachers actually gave grades for *bentō* but also that they posted such grades publicly.

9. *Bentō* cookbooks and magazine columns, which were geared toward creating the general family *bentō*, began in the 1980s to categorize *bentō*-making by age (kindergarten, junior high, and husband). The emphasis is on the most complicated: the kindergarten lunch box.

10. There are numerous *bentō* cookbook titles indicating affection as the key. See Yanagisawa (2003).

WORKS CITED

Allison, Anne. 1997. "Japanese mothers and *obentōs*: The lunch box as ideological state apparatus." *Food and Culture: A Reader*. Ed. Carole Counihan and Penny Van Esterik, 296–314. New York: Routledge.

Aonuma Takako. 1995. *Mama wa poyopoyo zaurusu ga osuki: Futatabi*. Tokyo: Fujin Seikatsusha.

Fujimura Munetaro. 1905. *Bentō ryōri annai nichiyō benri*. Tokyo: Daigakukan.

Fujin Gahō. 1938, April.

Kaetsu Takako. 1908. *Kaseigaku kōwa*. Tokyo: Dōbunkan.

Mikuriya Yoshiko. 1952. *Obentō no iroiro*. Tokyo: Nihon Kyōikukai.

Ministry of Education. 2005. *Gotei zōho Nihon shokuhin hyōjun seibun hyō*. 5th rev. ed. Tokyo: Ministry of Education.

Mori Yoshichi. 1977. *Kaitei shōgakkō gakushū shidō yōryō no tenkai: Kateika-hen*. Tokyo: Meiji Tosho Shuppan.

Naitō Akira. 2002. *Yōchien no obentō zensho*. Tokyo: Butikkusha.

Niroku [*Niroku shinbun*]. 1905, July 2 and August 15.

Peak, Lois. 1991. *Learning to Go to School in Japan: The Transition from Home to Preschool Life*. Berkeley: University of California Press.

Tobin, Joseph. 1989. *Preschool in Three Cultures, Japan, China, and the United States*. New Haven, Conn.: Yale University Press.

Vogel, Ezra F. 1971. *Japan's New Middle Class: The Salary Man and His Family in a Tokyo Suburb*. Berkeley: University of California Press.

Yanagisawa Hideko. 2003. *Aijō obentō*. Tokyo: Fusōsha.

Yanagita Kunio. 1993. *Meiji Taishō shi sesō hen*. Tokyo: Kōdansha.

PART III   *Contemporary Japan*

11 Mountain Vegetables and the Politics of Local Flavor in Japan

BRIDGET LOVE

VITALIZATION (*KASSEIKA*) WAS THE theme of an early fall symposium held in 2003 in a weather-stained municipal building in the mountainous interior of Japan's northeastern Iwate prefecture. Seated in rows of folding chairs, an audience of around eighty men and women faced a low stage flanked by banners; one announced the afternoon's panel discussion, "Bringing the Region to Life—Discussing Nishiwaga's Future" (*Chiiki o ikasu—Nishiwaga no shōrai o kataru*). The future was an anxious topic for the gathered audience of local residents. The Nishiwaga region, comprised of neighboring Yuda town and Sawauchi village, each with roughly 3,500 residents, has lost three generations of young natives to urban outmigration that fueled the nation's postwar miracle and decades of rapid economic growth. As in much of rural Japan, the downturn of the 1990s, following the collapse of the nation's economic "bubble," has further sapped local industries, hastening the exit of area youth in search of better opportunities elsewhere. In response to these trends, municipal officials organized the day's symposium to mobilize local energies and boost morale by showcasing grassroots efforts to awaken area vitality.[1]

A middle-aged farmer named Keiko participated in the symposium as a panelist representing a group working to transform area culinary traditions into heritage food commodities. Hers was one of nearly a dozen neighborhood female farm groups in Nishiwaga to form within the past decade in order to produce and sell foods using local ingredients. Female farmers' groups like Keiko's proliferated in the 1990s as Japan's Ministry of Agriculture, Forestry, and Fisheries (MAFF) and Japan Agriculture (JA), the national agricultural cooperative, sought to foster a more active role for women in reviving Japan's farm sector (Okabe 2000, 18).[2] Within Nishiwaga, groups like the Makino Wives Pickle Interest Association and the Nagaseno Food Culture Study Association formed at the district (*chiku*) level with names that indicate their neighborhood affiliations. Collectively, they are celebrated as a force of local vitality. *The Taste of Snow Country* (*Yuki guni no aji*), a catalog produced by Sawauchi village, compiles the gustatory offerings of municipal groups (*Sawauchi bussan* 2001).

On successive pages, each appears in matching aprons and accompanied by its trademark jarred sauces, preserved mountain vegetables (*sansai*), and snow country pickles, including whole daikon pickled in brine (*daikon no ippon zuke*) and freeze-dried daikon (*shimi daikon*).

With their work smocks and rustic preserves, Keiko and her elderly colleagues are agents of an active civic movement to invigorate Japan's regions by putting the appeal of local character to use as an area resource. The cultivation of local resources is a timely priority. Economic reform policies introduced in the early 1990s under the banner "regional decentralization" (*chihō bunken*) and implemented in the new millennium seek to cut government spending by demanding that local government, civic groups, and private enterprises assume greater responsibility for the needs of regional citizens. Measures include a 2002 Municipal Merger Law to promote greater local self-sufficiency through the reorganization of Japan's municipalities into larger, more fiscally efficient cities and towns.[3] The day's symposium was part of two years of active deliberations over whether Yuda and Sawauchi might best weather impending policy changes by merging into a unified town.[4] Yet discussions of how to streamline the region into a self-sufficient municipality seemed only to highlight the dire circumstances of town and village. Both Yuda and Sawauchi have booming elderly populations with growing social welfare needs; they shoulder municipal

Members of a neighborhood farm group preparing mountain vegetable steamed buns appear in a municipal pamphlet for Nishiwagan products. (Courtesy of Sawauchi Bussan 2005)

debt accrued through past revitalization schemes and must stretch waning tax revenues to maintain vast rural infrastructures, including country roadways clogged by 10 meters of winter snowfall (Yuda chō sawauchi mura 2003, 6).

Given the fiscal predicaments facing the area and its households, it was noteworthy that the economic promise of enterprises showcased at the symposium was not a central emphasis of the afternoon's presentations. Keiko introduced her group's mission not as that of boosting household incomes but of fostering appreciation for her hamlet's food traditions in order to "transmit" (*denshō suru*) and "preserve" (*hozon suru*) them for future generations. Her concern with continuities measured through food traditions resonated within a larger national discussion over the future of domestic culinary culture in Japan. Faltering family food habits, an increase in lifestyle diseases, and the nation's growing dependence on foreign imports have stoked popular debate and inspired recent government policy. This includes a measure to require "food education" (*shokuiku*) as part of national school curricula to build student awareness of food origins and native food traditions. As Japan's birth rate falls, it is the nation's productive-aged women who face criticism for their failure to reproduce and nourish future generations. At a Kyoto forum on local food traditions, nutritionist Yamashita Machiko articulated the link between domestic culinary heritage and gendered responsibility for Japan's future. Lamenting that today's mothers are unable to produce for their children the home-cooked regional dishes their own mothers skillfully made for them, she observed, in one generation "tradition has been severed" (*Mainichi shimbun* 2008, 27 May).

Regional producers like Keiko enter this conversation by offering an antidote to the perceived deterioration of food consciousness and growing culinary homogeneity in Japan. Keiko noted, "Today every [food] is available year-round in the grocery store, so young people have lost an awareness of local and seasonal flavors." To these young and largely urban consumers, her group's regional food products offer a concentrated dose of locality and seasonality exported from Nishiwaga in the form of mountain vegetables (*sansai*), greens plucked from area forests in the spring and early summer to feature in seasonal menus. For enterprise participants, mountain vegetables have lucrative commodity potential: Their soothing associations to native food traditions nurtured in the intimate terrains of Japan's mountain villages and embodied in the rustic home cooking of rural grandmothers lend appeal and moral salience to their consumption. Area producers, in turn, are eager to claim these associations as positive local attributes.

This chapter explores heritage food initiatives in Nishiwaga as forums where interested residents work to stake out an advantageous position for the region on the margins of the nation. Celebrating a rustic regional culture borne of a harsh terrain and climate, they aim to spin selected area attributes into unlikely sources of income and local cohesion. While participants and supporters, from municipal bureaucrats to farmers and local activists, seek the seeds for Nishiwaga's regeneration in the contours of area microclimate and ancestral experience, their efforts respond to contemporary trends: a national demographic slowdown, changing farm and municipal subsidy structures, and national demands for greater regional self-sufficiency. Although Nishwagan initiatives tap into the popularity of regional food cultures among today's Japanese consumers, they do more than cash in on local character to offset area decline. They are forums for forging generational continuities and sustaining human and environmental relationships rendered tenuous by the upheavals of depopulation and economic uncertainty.

HERITAGE HARVEST

As I watched the symposium from a seat in the audience, Keiko's concluding remark took me by surprise. Though born and raised in Sawauchi, she explained, she did not grow up eating most of the food items that her group produces. Instead, she and her colleagues enlisted local grandmothers to familiarize them with the sauces and preserves that they now market as heritage commodities. In the context of the panel discussion, her comment served as encouragement to audience members that even overlooked features of local life can serve as potential springboards for vitalization. More importantly, Keiko's acknowledgment that the area's food culture is not seamlessly communicated between generations of local inhabitants highlights the perceived role of human effort in its transmission. In this sense, local food traditions are not only vulnerable to passive neglect but also available to be strategically deployed in conscious efforts to shore up generational continuities.

In her multisited survey of culture tourism, art historian Barbara Kirschenblatt-Gimblett asserts that heritage offers hope to places on the verge of extinction, where it can make undervalued assets economically productive "by adding the value of pastness, exhibition, difference and where possible indigeneity" (Kirschenblatt-Gimblett 1998, 150). Kirschenblatt-Gimblett emphasizes the generative potential of heritage industries that reference the past as a means of creating something new in the present; however, she suggests that rather than fostering actual vitality, local heritage industries often reproduce sites as hollow exhibits of themselves. As she describes, "Dying economies stage their rebirth as displays of what they once were, sometimes before the body is cold" (1998, 151). In Nishiwaga, farmers and other participants do not recognize their activities as circumscribed by this kind of ironic dilemma. Rather, traditional food industries in Nishiwaga, as conceived by their founders, aim to foster a mode of local stewardship that prizes the expression and fulfillment of local character as a path to area regeneration.

Since 1950, Yuda town and Sawauchi village have lost 60 percent of their combined resident base to the outmigration of young residents to urban Japan. In 2003, nearly 40 percent of Nishiwagan residents were sixty-five years old or older (Yuda chō sawauchi mura 2003, 6). The area reflects to an exaggerated degree Japan's rapid aging and low birthrate, trends unfolding most dramatically in the mountainous interiors of the nation's northeastern and southwestern peripheries.[5] Sawauchi, with a large agricultural base, has experienced slow but steady outmigration since the 1950s, while neighboring Yuda has had a more turbulent demographic history. Booming copper mines that swelled Yuda's wartime population to over 12,000 collapsed in the 1960s as international metals prices fell. During this same period, a national dam project submerged five hamlets of the then-village, sparking a dramatic exodus of area households. By the early 1970s, a municipal development plan observed the dire need to develop "responses to depopulation that makes the continuation of hamlets more and more difficult as they gradually 'hollow' (kūdōka suru)" (Yuda chō 1971, 3). Hollowing is an apt description of depopulation in Nishiwaga, where young outmigrants leave behind small "aged households" (kōrei setai) living in homes that become "vacant houses" (akiya) once their elderly inhabitants pass away.[6]

As Japan's rural population flowed toward urban centers, governmental efforts to halt rural decline in the 1970s and '80s entailed channeling monies back to the regions under the auspices of "native place-making" (furusato zukuri). A political platform of Prime Minister Takeshita, furusato zukuri aimed to foster the sense of a shared national past rooted in nostalgically remembered old villages as the "native place" (furusato) of, and model for, the contemporary urban nation (Figal 1996, 903; Robertson 1991). Furthermore, the marketing of this past by rural localities was promoted as a route to restored socioeconomic health. Programs to attract tourist and consumer income by enhancing the nostalgic charms of village Japan entailed what historian Karen Wigen has aptly phrased "cultivating native-place distinctiveness as a resource for regional development" (Wigen 1996, 493). Despite their emphasis on regional character, projects often adhered to cookie-cutter templates to package local appeal in easily consumable formats. A 1993 *Town-making Handbook* compiles the development concepts of various government ministries, packaged as models to be handily adopted by local municipalities. For picturesque rural towns, options included a "Refresh *Furusato* Promotion Model" to foster rural recreational opportunities that allow weary city-dwellers to relax in and breath temporary life into villages rendered spacious through depopulation (Chiiki kasseika sentā 1993, 22).

In the late 1980s, anthropologist William Kelly documented the tightrope tread by residents of the Shōnai region in Yamagata prefecture as they attempted to use nostalgia as a resource for economic advancement without "falling prey to a cloying sentimentality" that might undermine the area's valued local traditions (Kelly 1986, 614). Two decades later, tensions between regional integrity and economic development have assumed new salience in the context of regional decentralization as struggling municipalities strive to stave off extinction by organizing themselves more efficiently. Proponents predict that decentralization will allow diversity and vitality to blossom throughout the nation's regions as they become more self-sufficient (Ōyama 2000). However, because it strips away subsidies that rural towns and villages depend on, decentralization is viewed by critics as government divestiture, a "throwing away [of] the regions" (Kaneko 2005) that some argue will hasten the decline of the countryside (Tanaka 1999, 14).

Navigating these extremes, Yuda's and Sawauchi's municipal offices organized the public symposium as a forum for contemplating ways to positively enact the mandate of decentralization. The invited keynote speaker, an elderly agricultural economist, gave a rousing lecture on the topic "Looking for Regional 'Treasures' and Creating a 'Face' for the Region" (*Chiiki no "takara" o sagashi, chiiki no "kao" o tsukuru*). He described local initiatives from around Japan that utilize area resources as the basis for tourism and agribusinesses. In order to spark positive local change in a period of subsidy cutbacks, he urged, Nishiwaga must also look within its boundaries to inventory its own resources—whether geographical, cultural, or historical—and decide how best to put them to use.[7] Municipal health and survival, he suggested, hinge on bringing local character to life. Keiko and her colleagues, whose presentations followed his lecture, work toward this goal; they capture local flavor in a line of products featuring mountain vegetables (*sansai*), edible wild greens hand-gathered from local mountain forests, then preserved, pickled, or prepared into sauces. Sold in jars or sealed plastic pouches at local souvenir venues or through mail and Internet order, their products embody the rustic appeal of regional food and lifeways. Producers envision them as a way of safeguarding the future of the area's living traditions, albeit in commodity form easily disseminated to urban palates hungry for localized flavors.

In developing saleable specialty products, Nishiwagan farmers and officials enlist understandings of the local past to lend stability to an uncertain future. Analyzing the use of timelines by feminist groups in Japan to organize their histories, anthropologist Tomomi Yamaguchi contrasts concepts of *nagare* (flow) and *ugoki* (movement) as alternate modes of conceiving history as a progression through time: *ugoki* denotes "an active, agent-informed process of change in contrast to the agent-less *nagare* that 'flows naturally' from one point to another . . . without disruption" (Yamaguchi 2005, 51). As Yamaguchi notes, the contrast is also illuminated by the concepts of *naru* (to be or become) and *tsukuru* (to create or make): *tsukuru* implies "intentional purposeful action," while *naru* "elides or renders unproblematic the process and conditions of production" (Robertson 1991, 30). Nishiwagan food heritage enterprises blur the distinction between "making" and "becoming" as modes of historical unfolding. As organizers and participants work to regenerate their locality over time, they stake out a role for themselves as agents engaged in the strategic making of the area *and* as caretakers of a local tradition that emerges and flows from area microclimate and ancestral experience. Depopulation and economic decline complicate their efforts, impeding the capacity of resident-activists to assertively shape the area's future and threatening understandings of Nishiwaga as perduring through succeeding generations. Rather than marking a retreat to nostalgia, then, activities to celebrate the region's culinary culture are high-stakes efforts to reassert continuities with the past that might invigorate the hollowing area.

MOUNTAIN BOUNTY

Seated to Keiko's left on the symposium panel was Takeshi, the manager of a small local company called Kingdom of Mountain Bounty (*Yama no sachi ōkoku*). The company was launched in the spring of 2003 with funding from Yuda's town office and run as a third-sector enterprise.[8] With a small staff of three part-time female employees and its manager, the company worked to transform Nishiwaga's mountain vegetables into local specialty products with nostalgic and seasonal appeal. Company mission and name were derived from a municipal "Kingdom of Mountain Bounty Concept" (*yama no sachi ōkoku kōsō*), an orientation devised by interested area residents and bureaucrats for developing new industries to revamp the demographically distressed town into a kingdom (*ōkoku*) built upon the area's rich resources, its "mountain bounty" (*yama no sachi*). Inspired by this concept, the company's mission extended beyond product sales. It aimed at renewing historical consciousness and community spirit through the revival of gendered know-how and ancestral practices linked to local mountain vegetables.

Mountain plant guidebook author Ōsawa Akira defines mountain bounty as "mountain vegetables, tree fruits and nuts, mushrooms, tree buds, mountain and field grasses, river grasses and river fish. [However,] it is generally represented as mountain vegetables (*sansai*)" (Ōsawa 2003, 10). *Sansai* is a catchall term for edible vegetation that grows in Japan's highland forests in the spring and early summer; popular varieties in northeastern Japan include ostrich fern fiddleheads (*kogomi*), giant butterbur (*fuki*), hostas (*urui*), angelica tree buds (*taranome*), and a range of coarse ferns, like bracken (*warabi*) and royal fern (*zenmai*). They begin sprouting underneath heavy layers of winter snow and are gathered in the early spring. Elderly residents of Nishiwaga fondly recalled the first taste of spring mountain vegetables after a long winter without any fresh foods. During postwar food shortages, gathered mountain plants were staples of subsistence, referred to as "edible field grasses" (*taberareru yasō*) or "famine relief foods" (*kyūkō tabemono*) (Ōsawa 2003, 10).

Today, mountain vegetables are no longer dietary necessities borne of deprivation but a reflection of refined food sensibilities. They epitomize a food culture that prizes "seasonal flavor" (*shun no aji*). Unlike the four seasons of spring, summer, fall, and winter, *shun* is reckoned by the division of months into an early season (*jōjun*), middle season (*chūjun*), and late season (*gejun*) during which quality of fruits, vegetables, fish, and flowers peak. A culinary calendar organized around the seasonal peaks of food items has long shaped consumer tastes and the business of food distribution in Japan (Bestor 2004, 167). Today, complex considerations about the healthfulness, safety, and sustainability of food heighten consumer interest in seasonality. Agricultural scientist and local food advocate Sōma Satoru identifies ten features of seasonal vegetables (*shun no yasai*) that combine these concerns; he explains, "1) In each region, in suitable soil and 2) in the most suitable season, 3) without unreasonable effort, *shun no yasai* are 4) produced safely with few chemical pesticides or fertilizers. This means of production is 5) good for the natural environment and 6) good for people. It creates [produce] that 7) at the best time for eating 8) is harvested in a fresh condition, so 9) is full of nutrients and 10) delicious." While he does not directly condemn global food systems that displace food in time and space, Sōma asserts the morality of local and seasonal consumption as "a way of living that is good for the planet . . . the direct opposite of the arrogant lifestyle of a person who in February eats bright red strawberries cultivated by burning fossil fuels" (Sōma 2004, 114).

In discussions of food in Japan, consciousness of locality and seasonality is not only a matter of ethical consumer choice; it is also evoked to define domestic culinary sensibilities or, by extension, mark their decline. At a recent conference on community food traditions in Kyoto, author Arashiyama Kōzaburō criticized contemporary eaters for judging food based only on whether or not it tastes "delicious" (*Mainichi shinbun* 2008, May 27). In an age of imported ingredients and international cuisines, he lamented the lost ability of Japan's eaters to discern and value within food ingredients the diverse places and relationships that produced them. Mountain vegetables, on the other hand, epitomize the very capacity for food to rouse consumer interest in its temporal and spatial origins. Ōsawa argues in the preface to his mountain plant gathering guide that the subtle local flavors, wild origins, and hand-picked variety of mountain vegetables are perfectly suited to a Japanese palate sensitive to the complexities of food fragrance, sweetness, age, heat, and moisture. Citing a final reason for the contemporary "boom" in mountain vegetables, Ōsawa explains, "as urbanization progresses and the population concentrates in cities, there is a strong trend of people seeking *furusato no aji*" (the taste of native place) (Ōsawa 2003, 11).

"The taste of native place" is a nostalgic reference to foods that evoke the warm human networks, local traditions, and healthful environments associated with quintessential old villages in Japan. As Jennifer Robertson argues, "*Furusato* appropriates a special past: *mukashi* 昔. *Mukashi* signifies a past of indefinite chronology and duration. . . . [It] alludes to the Good Old Days—to modes and contexts of sociability long since transcended, abandoned or dismantled, but reconstructable and revivifiable in a selective form through nostalgia" (Robertson 1991, 15). The flavor of home-cooked local dishes provides one point of access to this native past, and rural women are its gatekeepers. The phrase "taste of mother" (*ofukuro no aji*), a gendered counterpart to the "taste of native place," (*furusato no aji*) summons up a powerful nostalgia for the remembered tastes and sensations of being with one's mother in one's old hometown. *Ofukuro*, a term that attaches an honorific "*o*" to "*fukuro*" (bag), is affectionate slang used by men to refer to their mothers, at least metaphorically, as receptacles.

If the "taste of mother" evokes a sensory longing for a lost closeness to one's hometown and the warmth of motherly affection, the trope also suggests the role of rural women as conduits of localized food culture through time.

These associations propel regional cookbooks like *Taste of Mother, Taste of Hometown* (*Ofukuro no aji, furusato no aji*) in which author Ishizaka Satoko instructs readers how to prepare Nagano prefecture dishes as a way of imparting "a precious food culture with values borne of the wisdom of lifeways of people from the distant past [*mukashi no hito*]. You can say that it's been developed over time by the power of women" (Ishizaka 1996, i). Nishiwagan food enterprises harness both the affective potential and technical know-how of area grandmothers to utilize local food culture as a resource.[9] The Kingdom of Mountain Bounty company, for example, recruited elderly local women to help with the time-consuming and labor-intensive work of processing and preserving mountain vegetables and teaching its methods to the company's younger female staff. While some mountain vegetables are simply sautéed or fried and eaten, others must be soaked and boiled with ash or baking soda to draw out bitter flavors and soften tough fibers. Some varieties may be preserved in salt, and others dried and reconstituted; the bulbs of certain mountain plants can be dried and pounded into starchy flour.

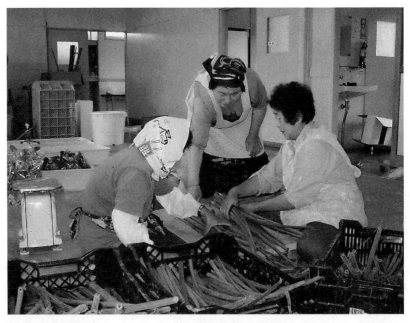

Local female farmers work part-time at company headquarters to prepare and preserve the spring crop of mountain vegetables. (Photograph by author)

A 2003 winter issue of Nishiwaga's agricultural co-op newsletter celebrates several female farm groups who translate this labor into efforts to renew area vitality and morale. It begins:

> Just when cold weather and damage from crop blight have made this a very severe year for agriculture in the Nishiwaga region, an extremely spirited voice has sounded at all kinds of events. This voice comes from our area's mothers. They've been working proactively to develop special products from Nishiwaga, and turn them into commodities. Their actions have put smiles on the dark faces of area fathers, and given them courage. (*Megumi meru* 2003, December)

The cheerful visibility of women in Nishiwagan agriculture is a relatively new phenomenon in Japan where female farmers have long performed the majority of labor on Japan's family farms, but as an "invisible presence" (Mitsuoka 2001, 31; Miyaki 2001, 9).[10] Their prominence in farm revitalization today is an emerging phenomenon but one that belies perplexing rural trends. In Nishiwaga, despite a booming population of elderly widows who outlive and outnumber their male counterparts by over three to two, area farm households are vexed by a shortage of brides willing to marry male farm successors. In addition to reproducing area households, rural wives are caregivers for elderly in-laws and household ancestors (Martinez 2004, 179; Traphagan 2004, 99). Their absence, therefore, poses a threat to the future of both area households and districts.[11]

Nishiwagan wives' associations, once forces of district activity and industry, began to lose luster in the 1970s, disappearing entirely from parts of the region as aging members "retired" without a younger cohort to replace them. In this context, female farm groups are celebrated as proactive forces in rural Japan, and not only because of their economic potential. Scholarly assessments of "rural women's start-up enterprises" (*nōson josei kigyō*) to promote local food products note that their role in building supportive relationships within and between neighborhood households outweighs their modest economic impacts (Makidaichi 2001, 99; Okabe 2000, 34). Improving the cohesiveness of local districts and their ability to undertake shared goals is a priority of vitalization enthusiasts in Japan. It is primed by folkloric visions of rural hamlets as integrated and organic sodalities: MAFF official Nagaya Matsurō likens rural districts (*chiiki*) to organisms that age and die over time as members and their approaches become old and rigid (Nagaya 1999, 17). Unlike living organisms, however, he argues that hamlets and districts can be restored to their youthful

A female farmers' group from Yuda's Makino district is pictured in Nishiwaga's agri-coop newsletter to promote the proactive work of "area mothers" to transform local products into commodities. (Courtesy of *Megumi mēru*, December 2003)

vigor through care and attention. Female farm initiatives represent the collective effort and civic action that might restore neighborhood morale and vitality.

Revitalization enthusiasts in Nishiwaga agree with this vision of community regeneration and seek its seeds in the ancestral past. Supporters of the Kingdom of Mountain Bounty concept cite Yuda's and Sawauchi's hefty volumes of municipal history, commissioned in the late 1970s as part of village- and town-making projects. Nishiwaga suffered frequent crop failures that plagued the Tōhoku area in the premodern era: Between the first year of Genroku (1688) and the final year of the Edo period (1868), one in four local harvests produced under half its expected yield. Statistics indicate that the region experienced lower mortality rates than towns and villages in the Kitakami plain that borders the area because local practices of mountain plant gathering helped residents avoid starving (Yuda-chō 1979, 312). Evoking this history as evidence of the spirit of ingenuity and forbearance of area ancestors, Takeshi explained at the symposium that the company Kingdom of Mountain Bounty originates "ultimately in a very old industry. It aims to excavate [*horidasu*] and bring back [*horiokosu*] Nishiwaga's old food culture." As they revive food traditions and the values of resilience and industry that shaped them, enterprise participants tap into potential excitement for mountain vegetables in a complex consumer landscape. They would transform Nishiwaga's distinctive climate, elderly populations, and history of deprivation from evidence of the region's marginality to markers of distinction. In doing so, they suggest modes of local continuity and coherence independent of the area's precarious demographics, rooted instead in ancestral histories and gendered nostalgia for local flavor.

LOCAL FLAVOR

Despite the origins of Nishiwaga's *sansai* in area terrain and tradition, efforts to shape them into brand-name products entailed negotiating complex contemporary considerations that implicated issues ranging from food safety and changing farm policy to the politics of environmental sustainability in Japan. As it contemplated the possibilities of its Kingdom of Mountain Bounty concept in 2000, Yuda's town office commissioned a regional university to undertake a study of local mountain vegetables. The study report noted low levels of harshness (*aku*) and high levels of stickiness (*nebari*) in area bracken (*warabi*). Company supporters seized upon these qualities as evidence of the superior taste and texture of Nishiwaga bracken. In a Kingdom of Mountain Bounty company advertisement, manager Takeshi explained that these positive attributes are rooted in the cyclical seasonality of area terrain. He noted, "The secret of the company's mountain vegetables is 'soil.' The Nishiwaga region has long winters, when its soil rests for almost half the year under heavy snows. During that time its nutrients flourish, and when spring comes, sweet . . . moist mountain vegetables grow" (Sawauchi bussan 2005). The local character of Nishiwaga's greens, in other words, is expressive of the area's microclimate in all its regional distinctiveness.

Sansai are also vehicles for more broadly considering the politics of environmental change and stewardship in urbanized Japan. In the words of mountain plant guidebook author Okuyama Hisashi, *sansai* convey "the flavor of flora that grows wild in the hills and fields" in contrast to a normal fare of cultivated vegetables with their uniform taste and availability (Okuyama 2003, 4). Theirs is neither the flavor of cultivated farmland nor of a remote wilderness, but of Japan's *satoyama* or village-mountain, a historical landscape defined by Arioka Tatsuyoshi as the perimeter of forested land that surrounded human settlements and upon which "village people" (*satobito*) relied for the raw materials they needed to survive (Arioka 2004, 3). *Satoyama* denotes a terrain created and managed by local human populations, a "'mosaic' of sustainably maintained environments" that includes rice paddy, grassland, mountain forest, and settlement (Takeuchi et al. 2003, 22). Contemporary conservationists evoke *satoyama* as a native model of environmental health, biodiversity, and the responsible human stewardship of nature (Kobori and Primack 2003, 309–11; Takeuchi et al. 2003, 24). Melding politics and consumerism, some citizen-led conservation movements are inspired by Totoro, a popular cartoon figure who inhabits a *satoyama* woodland (Kobayashi 2000, 204).[12]

While national revitalization enthusiasts and rural tourism promoters playfully invoke *satoyama* to mobilize new appreciation for the nation's forests as sites of play, learning, and healthfulness, local residents in Nishiwaga express their own concerns over the local stewardship of area mountains.[13] In a region where many labored in a now-defunct forestry industry, elderly and middle-aged residents often commented on the changing texture of the area's surrounding mountain forests as they thicken and darken into unfamiliar and unused terrains. Their observations are expressive of pervasive anxieties over the decrease in local *ninaite*, literally "hands to shoulder" the area's natural environments and cultural traditions. Importing vacationing urban outsiders to use area mountains as sites of recreation is not in itself a satisfying solution for everyone. Nishiwaga's residents are generally good-natured about the spring day-trippers who visit on outings to gather mountain vegetables. However, experienced gatherers guard their favorite sites with care; some complain that many nonlocals don't understand "mountain rules," and destroy plants by breaking off all their emerging shoots, or even pulling them up by their roots.[14] By organizing the sale of locally harvested mountain vegetables, Kingdom of Mountain Bounty staff and supporters conceived the company as a means of protecting area flora from grasping tourist hands, while putting the environmental and cultural riches of the area to sustainable use under a banner evocative of the area's local offerings.

The complex politics and consumer promise of products suffused with local identity is illuminated by the case of France, where the notion of "products of the soil" (*produits du terroir*) situates and fixes agrifood products in the local terrains and life ways that generate them. Scholarship such as Barham's analysis of the contested designation of *appellation d'origine contrôlée* (AOC) labels (2003, 131) and Hodges's case study of troubled efforts to promote village heritage food tourism in the Languedoc region point to a hotly political, rather than mystical, relationship between locality and traditional foods (Hodges 2001). French anthropologist Michele de la Pradelle further complicates the link between products and local origins by considering the local as both a marketing strategy and compelling consumer orientation. In her study of Provencal market culture, she describes the work of vendors to arrange their market displays to imply associations between products and localized traditions in order to heighten consumer desire for products that are "localizeable, if not [actually] local" (la Pradelle 2006, 109). Market shoppers, in turn, are drawn to items they associate with localized traditions, even when their specific places of origin are unidentified or even unidentifiable.

Appealing to consumer enthusiasm for "localizable" products in Japan, the Ministry of Agriculture, Forestry and Fisheries (MAFF) promotes the development of locally defined brand names that "embody culture, nature and history, a region's unique resources . . . in order to inspire consumer confidence and awareness" (Nōrinsuisanshō 2005, 20). Evoking localized terrains and traditions in consumer consciousness, local brand names—according to ministry officials and regional activists in Japan—are a potential means of boosting the sales of domestic agrifood products. Brand-naming also appeases darker anxieties involving food safety and security that stem from concerns over Japan's dependence on scandal-tainted foreign import foods, as Stephanie Assmann describes in this volume (chapter 12). As news of *bovine-spongiform-encephalopathy* (BSE) infected cattle feed from the United States and Europe, avian flu in Southeast Asia, and pesticide-laden vegetables from China flooded Japan's news media, Kingdom of Mountain Bounty founders envisioned their rustic mountain vegetables would satisfy demand for foods that provide consumers with "safety and peace of mind" (*anzen anshin*), a ubiquitous buzzword that tacitly reassures consumers of domestic food origins.

Notably, however, the company's plan entailed more than organizing the mass gathering of wild local mountain vegetables. It centered on plans to transfer mountain plant varietals from local forests for cultivation in converted rice paddies. One goal of this experiment was to help diversify Yuda's rice-centered farm sector, following a MAFF announcement of plans to reverse its long-standing policy of rice acreage reduction (*gentan*). This reversal marked the phasing out of an entrenched system that subsidized Japan's farmers to let paddy land lie fallow in an effort to control rice surplus and price, in order to shift to a merit-based subsidy structure that rewards farmers for producing crops with high consumer demand.[15] The new policy aims to foster the emergence of a smaller and more entrepreneurial agricultural sector made up of larger-scale farms that can compete with foreign producers on an open market.

With a large number of its small, part-time family farms squeezed into narrow mountain valleys, many Nishiwagan farmers fear that the government's focus on efficiency will force elderly farmers out of production and drive young part-time farm families away from Nishiwaga. Kingdom of

Mountain Bounty represents one municipal attempt to mitigate the risks that a new subsidy system poses to farmers. The company aimed to enlist a large number of households to convert a small amount of farmland to mountain vegetable cultivation. In turn, company staff assumed responsibility for developing a brand name and sales routes for area mountain vegetables, particularly the company's focus crop of bracken (*warabi*). Bracken is a simple fern that emerges from the ground in single shoots, each with a beaded head that uncurls into a triangular frond; it is edible when boiled, but only in the spring. In its first season, the company delivered bracken bulbs and a manual of growing instructions to seventy-four farm households (Yuda-chō 2002). Some were attracted by the low labor demands of bracken, which requires neither pesticides nor elaborate maintenance to flourish. Well suited to the capabilities of elderly male and female producers as well as the area's cold climate, bracken is also an ideal crop to grow in the uneven and irregular farm plots common in mountainous Nishiwaga.

Yet even with help from the local branch agricultural extension office, the company found it difficult to streamline methods of transplantation and cultivation so that farmers could consistently produce the quality crops they needed to maintain regular clients in urban Morioka, Sendai, and Tokyo. Hearty weeds quickly overtook and stunted many bracken fields, while other farmers produced plots lush with healthy plants of uniform height. Watching these developments, a number of young farm households expressed concern that the Kingdom of Mountain Bounty concept was merely a stopgap plan to bolster a geriatric farm sector, rather than a comprehensive strategy for fostering a vital agricultural sector. There were concerns that despite its rhetorical emphasis on the continuity of local tradition and know-how, plans to revive local agriculture through mountain vegetable cultivation would not actually induce a new generation of successors to take over local family farms. Despite the enthusiasm of some area farmers for the company's work, others reserved judgment or voiced outright skepticism as they waited to see results.

The goal of developing agriculture suited to local character, nevertheless, remained a shared local priority. The association of local places and signature products is not a new invention in Japan. It was famously appropriated beginning in the late 1970s as a domestic development strategy (and international export) in the "one-village one-product" policy of Oita prefecture's Governor Hiramatsu (Hiramatsu 1990). As Japan's ongoing economic downturn and depopulation persist in its rural regions, the development of regionally diverse farm products expressive of local terrains and climates is viewed still as one key strategy to boost the income of local farm households and strengthen municipal economies. A mandate shaped by changing subsidy structures and regional policy, it is further complicated by the morality implied by rhetoric that equates the work of economic revitalization with that of assuming stewardship for resources expressive of human ancestry and local character. Municipal officials and resident activists engaged in the revitalization of Nishiwaga wrestle with the difficult work of uniting these goals as a way to mobilize the community labor needed to sustain the area.

"MAKING" AND "AWAKENING"

In his keynote speech at the symposium that begins this chapter, agricultural scientist Mori Iwao spurred Nishiwagans to summon local energies needed to awaken the region's dormant potential. In doing so, he sketched a contrast between the work of "town-making" or *machi zukuri* (and its counterpart village-making) and "town-revival" or *machi okoshi*. The former implicates municipal strategies of place-making and the agency of bureaucratic officials. Mori's conception of *machi zukuri* encodes a critique of the failures of Japan's local and central governments to stem rural socioeconomic decline despite spending lavishly on public works and revitalization projects. In contrast, for Mori, *machi okoshi* connotes positive change "from inside, from below, with [local] volition" (Mori 1992, 15). The term points to latent human energies and local potentials that might be channeled into grassroots activities to enact positive change, while implying that regional citizens adopt a more self-reliant approach to solving their own problems.

I introduce these terms here to indicate the contentious political field in which Nishiwagans engage in vitalization activities. The rhetorical opposition between making (*zukuri*) and (re)awakening (*okoshi*) as alternate routes to community vigor is evoked—in governmental debates, academic argumentation, and local activism—to address questions about who is ultimately responsible for the costs of regional decline and rejuvenation, and who is authorized to plot local change. However, for many Nishiwagans, who acknowledge the practical need for government intervention to augment local residents' efforts at community revival, the terms are not in particular tension. "Making" and "awakening" are used alternately by many residents to refer to community activity aimed at sustaining local vigor, whether planned by officials or local residents.

The context of decentralization calls for new terminologies and designations. Contemporary revitalization activists apply the term *chiiki zukuri* or "region-making" to connote activities that emerge organically from shared community goals and utilize existing human resources. *Chiiki* designates a more neutral "region" than terms like "town" (*machi*) or "administrative district" (*gyōsei chiku*) with their bureaucratic overtones and links to centralized authority. It also avoids the associations of terms that allude to "natural villages" (*shūraku* or *shizen mura*) either with their folkloric overtones as organic sodalities or rigid gender and kin hierarchies (see Fukuta 1984; Yasui 2002). "Region-making" is evoked in praise of revival projects fueled by local impetus and with "area people" (*chiiki no hito*) as their agents. But even with its grounding in local volition, the project of *chiiki zukuri* is easily adapted to state interests: As local boundaries are redrawn in compliance with decentralization policies, for example, *chiiki* handily refers to regions of flexible size, scale, and definition.

Discussions about shifting local boundaries and definitions of regional character took on new practical significance in the public debates that preceded the amalgamation of Yuda and Sawauchi into the new town of Nishiwaga in the fall of 2005. While fiscal and administrative logistics plagued area administrators, questions about the fundamental compatibility of Yuda and Sawauchi persisted in the final lead up to the merger. Residents of town and village cited differences in municipal character, economic orientation, and historical experience that separated the two entities. At the same time, the historical unity of town and village was regularly invoked as the return to a past order: Before the establishment of municipal Yuda and Sawauchi, the area comprised a series of village hamlets occupying a region called the Sawauchi Road (Sawauchi dōri) under the oversight of a domainal magistrate in the Edo period (1600–1868). As the merger became inevitable, Kingdom of Mountain Bounty supporters referenced this period as the origins of local mountain vegetable culture, and rationale for the expansion of the company's mission as an industry outlook to unify the new town.

Nishiwagan heritage-food industries represent locally motivated efforts to transform the area's heavy snows, rustic food culture, and elderly know-how into resources that might foster local vitality. Yet harsh weather, remoteness, and aging are the very attributes that limit Nishiwaga's ability to organize itself into the efficient municipality demanded by decentralization policy. Ominously, the Kingdom of Mountain Bounty did not survive Yuda's and Sawauchi's merger. Nishiwaga's first mayor closed the company down in 2005, citing its inability to produce sufficient profit to cover its own operating costs; the company's business model ultimately failed to cohere as seamlessly as its optimistic vision for the town. However, the work of female farm enterprises to transform mountain vegetable culture into stronger community bonds and local vitality continued. In crafting their commodities, they assert stewardship over the region and craft a tentative generational continuity—one freed from the logistical constraints of the region's aging population, depopulating landscapes, and budgetary cutbacks, to be summoned up and savored as ancestral flavor.

NOTES

1. This chapter is based on twenty months of ethnographic field and archival research in Nishiwaga between 2002 and 2005. I use pseudonyms to refer to all individuals in Yuda and Sawauchi.

2. Miyaki (2001, 10) and Kawade (2007, 4) explain the 1990s "boom" in female farm start-up enterprises (*nōson josei kigyō*) as a response to MAFF policy, while popular how-to manuals like *You Can: Female "Food" Enterprise Revival* (*Gambare, josei no 'shoku' gyō okoshi*) offer detailed advice to prospective participants (Higuchi and Adachi 1995).

3. The Great Heisei Amalgamation is the latest in a series of mergers implemented by Japan's central government. A wave of amalgamations in the 1880s dubbed the Great Meiji Amalgamation consolidated over 70,000 towns and villages into around 14,000 municipalities (Ōta 2000, 3). The postwar Great Shōwa Amalgamation further reduced the number of municipalities in Japan from 12,000 to around 3,400 by the 1960s (Ōta 2000, 3). The current merger law aims to streamline Japan's municipalities into just 1,000. See also Mabuchi (2001).

4. Yuda and Sawauchi were established as administrative municipalities through the merger of dozens of hamlets during the Meiji Amalgamation. The two entered into merger negotiations in the mid-1950s during the Shōwa Amalgamation, but were unable to reach agreement: Sawauchi welcomed the idea of merging with its (then) larger and more prosperous neighbor, while Yuda objected on the grounds that an amalgamation would create a municipality of unwieldy size and render local government less (rather than more) cost effective.

5. Japan has one of the most rapidly aging populations in the world: according to a Ministry of Health, Labor, and Welfare (*Kōseirōdōshō*) 2007 white paper, 21 percent of Japan's 2006 population was sixty-five years of age or older, while the nation's birthrate fell steadily from 1.38 in 1999 to 1.26 in 2005. For regional breakdowns and projections of population loss, see Kokuritsu shakai hoshō, jinkō mondai kenkyūjo (2007, 11).

6. Statistics compiled by Yuda's Social Welfare Association chart a doubling of aged households from 155 in 1990 to 289 in 2005.

7. The speaker reiterates and expands upon this argument in Mori (1992).

8. The "third sector" refers to joint public–private enterprises that emerged as

popular development tools in 1990s rural Japan. Public government offices cannot legally operate moneymaking ventures but may use municipal funds to establish independently managed companies. Unsuccessful ski facilities, convention centers, and theme parks built with borrowed funds comprise a huge source of debt for many municipalities. The question of "what to do about the troubled management of the third sector" has become a national dilemma (*Asahi Shimbun* 2007, September 5).

9. Robertson argues that in the context of *furusato zukuri*, *ofukuro-san* "refers connotatively to the notion of females as repositories . . . of 'traditional' values deposited for safekeeping by the (male) engineers of *furusato zukuri* programs" (Robertson 1991, 22).

10. Because a one-vote-per-household voting structure formally governed (and still influences) the workings of Japan's local agricultural co-ops, farm wives have also been called "unseen members" without an independent voice (Miyaki 2001, 35).

11. I discuss strategies to recruit female settlers to Japan's countryside under the auspices of agritourism and "interchange" (*kōryū*) in Love (2007).

12. *Satoyama* is a nostalgic rallying point for national forestry interests dismayed over the abandonment of Japan's forests as sites of industry.

13. See, for example, the collection *Think of Satoyama: 101 Hints* (*Satoyama wo kangaeru: 101 no hinto*) (Nihon ringyōgijutsu kyōkai 2000).

14. Hinting at tensions between locals and novice gatherers, most mountain flora guidebooks elaborate "mountain vegetable gathering manners" to clarify gathering rights and appropriate social behavior (Okuyama 2003, 6); see also Eguchi (2004, 27).

15. Rice reduction policies were implemented in the 1960s to stabilize the farm sector amid falling rice prices. They did not succeed, as intended, in reforming Japan's farm sector. Rather, Jussaume (1991) suggests part-time farming households proliferated as a workable means to sustain rural communities; Mulgan (2000) argues that the lobbying muscle of Japan's agricultural co-op and the power of the rural vote determined the shape and limited success of agricultural reform.

WORKS CITED

Arioka Toshiyuki. 2004. *Satoyama I*. Tokyo: Hōsei Daigaku.

Barham, Elizabeth. 2003. "Translating *terroir*: The global challenge of French AOC labeling." *Journal of Rural Studies* 19:127–38.

Bestor, Theodore. 2004. *Tsukiji: The Fish Market at the Center of the World*. Berkeley: University of California Press.

Chiiki kasseika sentā. 1993. *Machi-zukuri handobukku 2: Shōchō no jigyō, kōsō keikaku*. Tokyo: Toppan.

Eguchi Hiroshi, ed. 2004. *Shun no shokuzai: Haru, natsu no yasai*. Tokyo: Kōdansha.

Figal, Gerald. 1996. "How to *jibunshi*: Making and marketing self-histories of *showa* among the masses in postwar Japan." *Journal of Asian Studies* 55, no. 4: 902–33.

Fukuta Ajio. 1984. "Minzoku no botai toshite no mura." In *Mura to murabito, kyōdōtai no seikatsu to girei*. Ed. H. Tsuboi. Tokyo: Tosho.

Higuchi Keiko and Adachi Yukiko. 1995. *Gambare josei no "shoku" gyō okoshi*. Tokyo: Nōrin Gyōson Bunka Kyōkai.

Hiramatsu Morihito. 1990. *Chiiki kara no hassō*. Tokyo: Iwaizumi Shinso.

Hodges, Matthew. 2001. "Food, time, and heritage tourism in Languedoc, France." *History and Anthropology* 12, no. 2: 179–212.

Ishizaka Satoko. 1996. *Ofukuro no aji, furusato no aji*. Naganoshi: Yanagizawa.

Jussaume, Raymond. 1991. *Japanese Part-time Farming: Evolution and Impacts*. Ames: Iowa State University Press.

Kaneko Katsu. 2005. "'Chisana seifu' wa kuni no seikinin nagesute." *Shinbun akahata*, November 13.

Kawade Tadae. 2007. "Nōson komyunitei bijinesu, jitsugen ni josei no hatasuru yakuwari wa okii." *Shokuryō nōgyō nōson: 21 seki no Nihon wo kangaeru* 244:4–9.

Kelly, William. 1986. "Rationalization and nostalgia: Cultural dynamics of a new middle-class Japan." *American Ethnologist* 13, no. 4: 603–18.

Kirschenblatt-Gimblett, Barbara. 1998. *Destination Culture: Tourism, Museums, Heritage*. Berkeley: University of California Press.

Kobayashi Masato. 2000. "Totoro no satoyama." In *Satoyama wo kangaeru: 101 no hinto, Nihon ringyō gijutsu kyōkai*. Tokyo: Tokyo Shoseki.

Kobori Hiromi and Richard Primack. 2003. "Participatory conservation for *satoyama*, the traditional landscape of Japan." *AMBIO* 32: 307–11.

Kokuritsu shakai hoshō, jinkō mondai kenkyūjo. 2007. *Nihon no todōfukenbetsu shōrai suikei jinkō*. Tokyo: Author.

la Pradelle, Michele de. 2006. *Market Day in Provence*. Trans. A. Jacobs. Chicago: University of Chicago Press.

Love, Bridget. 2007. "Fraught field sites: Studying community decline and heritage food revival in rural Japan." *Critical Asian Studies* 39, no. 4: 541–60.

Mabuchi Masaru. 2001. "Municipal amalgamations." In *Local Government Development in Post-war Japan*, 185–205. Ed. M. Muramatsu, F. Iqbal, and I. Kume. Oxford: Oxford University Press.

Makidaichi Tatsuhiro. 2001. "Chiiki nōgyō shinkō nōson josei kigyō." In *Seikō suru nōson josei kigyō*. Ed. Y. Iwasaki and M. Miyaki. Tokyo: Ie no Hikari Kyōkai.

Martinez, D. P. 2004. *Identity and Ritual in a Japanese Diving Village: The Making and Becoming of Person and Place*. Honolulu: University of Hawaii Press.

Mitsuoka Kōji. 2001. *Nihon nōson no joseitachi*. Tokyo: Nihon Keizai.

Miyaki Michiko. 2001. "Joseitachi no ugoki o 'mieru mono' ni." In *Seikō suru nōson josei kigyō*. Ed. Y. Iwasaki and M. Miyaki. Tokyo: Ie no Hikari Kyōkai.

Mori Iwao. 1992. *Chiiki-okoshi saisenzen*. Tokyo: Ie no Hikari Kyōkai.

Mulgan, Aurelia. 2000. *The Politics of Agriculture in Japan*. New York: Routledge.

Nagaya Matsurō. 1999. "Kyōtsū mokuhyō zukuri to kiryō kūkan no ari katsudō ni yotte chiiki wa genki ni nareru." *21 Seki no Nihon wo kangaeru* 11:12–20.

Nihon ringyō gijutsu kyōkai, ed. 2000. *Satoyama wo kangaeru: 101 no hinto*. Tokyo: Tōkyō Shoseki.

Nōrinsuisanshō, ed. 2005. *Shokuryō nōgyō nōson hakusho.* Tokyo: Author.

Okabe Mamoru. 2000. *Nōson josei ni yoru kigyō to hōjinka.* Tokyo: Tsukuba Shobō.

Okuyama Hisashi. 2003. *Sansai to kinome no zukan.* Tokyo: Popurasha.

Ōsawa Akira. 2003. *Yama no sachi: Riyū hyakka.* Tokyo: Nōbunkyō.

Ōta Takashi. 2000. *Shichōsonmei hensen shitōzusōran.* Tokyo: Tōyōshorin.

Ōyama Zenichirō. 2000. *Gendai chihō jichi ki-wa-do 186.* Tokyo: Kojin no Yusha.

Robertson, Jennifer. 1991. *Native and Newcomer: Making and Remaking a Japanese City.* Berkeley: University of California Press.

Sawauchi bussan. 2001. *Yuki guni no aji.* (Advertising pamphlet).

———. 2005. *Mirakuru Nishiwaga.* (Advertising pamphlet).

Sōma Satoru. 2004. "Shun no yasai no igi." In *Shun no shokuzai: Haru, natsu no yasai.* Ed. Eguchi Hiroshi. Tokyo: Kōdansha.

Takeuchi Kazuhiko, Robert Brown, Izumi Washitani, Atsushi Tsunekawa, and Yoko-hari Makoto. 2003. *Satoyama: The Traditional Rural Landscape of Japan.* Tokyo: Springer-Verlag.

Tanaka Mitsuru. 1999. *Chiiki o ikase mura-okoshi.* Chiba: Nōson Kaihatsu Risa Chi.

Traphagan, John. 2004. *The Practice of Concern: Ritual, Well-being, and Aging in Rural Japan.* Durham, N.C.: Carolina Academic Press.

Wigen, Karen. 1996. "Politics and piety in Japanese native-place studies: The rhetoric of solidarity in Shinano." *Positions* 4, no. 3: 491–517.

Yamaguchi Tomomi. 2005. "Feminism, timelines, and history-making." In *A Companion to the Anthropology of Japan.* Ed. Jennifer Robertson, 50–58. Oxford: Blackwell.

Yasui Manami. 2002. "Mura." In *Atarashii minzokugaku e.* Ed. K. Komatsu. Tokyo: Serikashobō.

Yuda chō. 1971. Shūraku saihensei kihon keikaku: Atarashii nōson komyunitei no sōzō. (Town Hall report for municipal circulation).

———. 1979. *Yuda chō shi.* Kitakami: Monoguramusha.

———. 2002. *Tsukurō "yama no sachi," sansai saibai to tame.* (Town Hall report for municipal circulation).

Yuda chō Sawauchi mura. 2003. *Yuda chō Sawauchi mura atarashii jidai no "yui" ni yoru machi-zukuri.* (Town Hall report for municipal circulation.)

12 Reinventing Culinary Heritage in Northern Japan
Slow Food and Traditional Vegetables

STEPHANIE ASSMANN

CHINESE DUMPLINGS: RECENT FOOD SCANDALS IN JAPAN

AT THE BEGINNING OF THE YEAR 2008, Japan was shaken by a food poisoning scandal over frozen dumplings (*gyōza*) imported from a Chinese company. Ten people in Hyogo and Chiba prefectures were reported to have fallen ill after consuming the tainted dumplings that contained traces of two pesticide organophosphates (MHLW website 2008; Yoshida 2008). The food-poisoning scandal has triggered a call for a return to domestic food production (*kokusan*) in the media. A telephone survey conducted by Kyodo News on February 9 and 10, 2008, revealed that 76 percent of the respondents intended not to use Chinese food products after this incident (Japan Times Online 2008, February 11).

The recent emphasis on domestic food products can be seen as a response to the concern over Japan's low self-sufficiency rate and a series of food-related incidents that have occurred in Japan over the past several years in a relatively short amount of time. In January 2007, the Japanese confectioner Fujiya had to halt production after admitting the repeated use of expired ingredients and the mislabeling of consume-by dates of its products. In the same year, an investigation of the Mie prefectural government revealed that the confectioner Akafuku had falsified production dates of its popular bean-jam sweets (Japan Times Online 2007, March 2 and October 21).

Yet, despite the fact that a number of these food scandals have involved Japanese food companies, consumers tend to equate food safety (*shokuhin anzen*) with the consumption of domestic food products (*kokusan*). A reason for this trust lies in the notion that domestic food products are often associated with greater traceability, transparency of food distribution channels, and reliability of their origins. A food product whose "producer's face is visible" (*seishansha no kao ga mieru*) is considered trustworthy. Furthermore, food laws with an emphasis on quality checks of food products such as the Food Safety Basic Law (*Shokuhin anzen kijun hō*) and the Food Sanitation Law (*Shokuhin eisei hō*) aim to ensure food hygiene and investigations of food products with regards to their safety (Takarajima-sha 2008, 12).[1]

JAPAN'S LOW SELF-SUFFICIENCY RATE

As the above-cited telephone survey by Kyodo News revealed, the recent food-poisoning scandal over frozen Chinese dumplings has reaffirmed the fears of many Japanese consumers of imported food products. Yet the desire to become independent of imported foods may prove to be wishful thinking. Japan remains highly dependent on food imports. The United States of America and China are Japan's major food suppliers, followed by Australia. According to data compiled by the Japan External Trade Organization (JETRO), during the first half of the year 2006, Japan imported 22.9 percent of its food from the United States of America and 16.8 percent from China, followed by 8.1 percent of foods from Australia (JETRO 2008). Japan has a food self-sufficiency rate of around 40 percent, which is the lowest among the major industrialized nations.[2] Japan's food self-sufficiency rate shows a gradual decline from 78 percent in 1961 to 50 percent in 1987 and reached a record low of only 37 percent in 1993 (MAFF 2008).[3]

One reason for the decline of the food self-sufficiency rate is the decrease of farm households in Japan. Farming has become less attractive as a professional occupation over the past forty years. The number of farm households declined from 5.4 million in 1970 to 3.3 million in 1998. Correspondingly, the number of farmers has decreased from 37.7 million in 1950 to 14.8 million in 1998 (Mulgan 2000, 3). Another reason for Japan's low food self-sufficiency rate lies in a gradual shift from the consumption of rice, Japan's major staple food, to an increased consumption of wheat and meat. According to data from the Ministry of Agriculture, Forestry, and Fisheries (MAFF), the consumption of rice has decreased from 48.3 percent of a Japanese person's total diet in 1960 to 30.1 percent in 1980. In the year 2004, the consumption of rice only amounted to 23.4 percent of the diet of a Japanese person. At the same time, the share of oil and fat rose from 4.6 percent in 1960 to 14.2 percent in 2004 (Suematsu 2008, 44–46). The introduction of milk and wheat through the U.S. Food Aid Program marked a major shift in the Japanese diet that occurred after the end of World War II (Cwiertka 2006, 157–58). Milk and wheat products became part of school lunches (*kyūshoku*) that were provided to children and provoked a change of eating habits of an entire generation. A further major shift of eating habits occurred at the beginning of the 1970s when fast food chains such as McDonald's, which was established in Japan in 1971, became popular in Japan (Cwiertka 2006, 164–67).

"BUY LOCAL"—A RESPONSE TO GROWING CONCERNS ABOUT FOOD SAFETY AND FOOD IMPORTS

Increasing concerns over Japan's low food self-sufficiency rate and a number of recent food scandals have triggered a response by a variety of initiatives that proclaim a return to local foods (*furusato no ryōri* or *jimoto no ryōri*) in order to counterbalance a growing diversification of food practices, to maintain regional agricultural products, and to ensure a high quality of food. As an example, in Miyagi prefecture in the northern part of the main island, the prefectural government has made an effort to enhance the attractiveness of the area as a tourist venue by forging connections between local culinary specialties and the natural resources in the region such as hot springs. In order to attract more tourists through the combination of nature and food, the prefectural government also promotes the initiative of "Green Tourism"—a combination of "farm stay and restaurant" and the revival of "traditional" vegetables (*dentō yasai*) (Miyagi Prefectural Government 2008). Interestingly, fast food chains such as Mos Burger have also adapted to demands for regional and seasonal products.

SLOW FOOD JAPAN

Given such various channels of preserving culinary heritage, I examined the question of how accessible local foods are for different economic groups, and how practical the integration of these local foods into daily food practices will prove to be. One initiative that promotes a return to supposedly safer local foodways and has focused on exclusive local food specialties is the NGO Slow Food Japan, which maintains close ties to its mother organization, the Italian Slow Food movement. Slow Food is currently active in a 132 countries around the world and aims to counterbalance the globalization of food and the popularization of fast food. In 2005, Slow Food had 38,000 members in Italy. The United States followed with almost 15,000 members, third was Germany with approximately 7,500 members, followed by Switzerland with 3,800 members (Petrini and Padovani 2006, 132). The basic local unit is the convivium, which "is the basic structural unit of Slow Food, the local chapter that serves as the most immediate point of contact between members, their local food culture and networks, and the wider public" (Parkins and Craig 2006, 21). Members of local convivia coordinate a variety of food-related activities such as wine and food tastings, food fairs, and public lectures to provide information about local foods, cultivation techniques, and special ways of preparation. They highlight food as a way to experience conviviality and pleasure, and advocate a slower pace of life, but they also seek to preserve local agricultural products that are in danger of vanishing. Additionally, members of all Slow Food *convivia* are encouraged to give advice to food producers on how to improve their marketing and distribution strategies and to increase the consciousness of consumers for culinary products in their immediate vicinity. In other words, Slow Food invites people to rethink their conventional eating habits while emphasizing the pleasures of (sharing) food.

As stated earlier, Slow Food Japan maintains close ties with Slow Food Italy, which acts as an advisor on structure and administration to its Japanese counterpart. Slow Food Japan was launched in 1998 and has approximately 2,000 members (Miyagi Slow Food website, February 9, 2010). Approximately 140 members are involved in the activities of the Slow Food convivium in Miyagi prefecture. Members of Slow Food Miyagi occupy a wide range of professions. Some members work in health-related and food-related professions, such as restaurant owners, cooks, and sake brewers whereas other members work in education as teachers, lecturers, professors, or researchers. Slow Food Japan seeks to protect regional cuisines and regional agricultural products, and the branch in Miyagi is active in this goal. The Slow Food organization has created the "Ark of Taste" (in Japanese, *aji no hakobune*) to safeguard various endangered regional foods. Slow Food Japan only accepts products into the Ark of Taste that are at risk of extinction and have a long history. To be included on the list of endangered products, the product in question needs to have an excellent taste and a long history. Moreover, the product needs to be of environmental, economic, and historic relevance in the region of its cultivation. It should be cultivated on a small scale and finally must truly be at risk of dying out (Slow Food Japan Tokyo, 2006). As of February 2010, the following twenty-two products in Japan have been listed on the Ark of Taste as products that are on the verge of vanishing.

Haretsu corn (*Hachiretsu tōmorokoshi*), Hokkaidō
Atsukaji radish (*Atsukaji daikon*), Iwate prefecture

Maibara leafy vegetable (*Maibara yukina*), Yamagata prefecture
Long grilled goby (*Nagatsura no yaki haze*), Miyagi prefecture
Japanese Shorthorn (*Nihon tankaku shu*), Iwate prefecture
Hanazukuri radish (*Hanazukuri daikon*), Yamagata prefecture
Amarume Green Onion (*Amarume negi*), Miyagi prefecture
Katakuchi Iwashi *shiokara*,[4] Nagasaki
Unzen leafy vegetable (*Unzen kobutakana*), Nagasaki
Kosena radish (*Kosena daikon*), Miyagi prefecture
Fish shōyu of sandfish (*Hatahata no shottsuru*),[5] Akita prefecture
Preserved mackerel (*Saba no narezushi*),[6] Fukui prefecture
Dried persimmons (*Dōjō hachiyakaki*), Gifu prefecture
Red turnip (*Kiso akakabu*), Nagano prefecture
Nagasaki cabbage (*Nagasaki hakusai*), Nagasaki
Yatabe green onion (*Yatabe negi*), Fukui prefecture
Noguchi leafy vegetables (*Noguchi sai*), Nikkō
Masakari pumpkin (*Masakari kabocha*), Hokkaidō
Sapporo green onion (*Sapporo kii*), Hokkaidō
Dobsonfly (*Zazamushi*), Shinju
Red onion (*Akanegi*), Ibaraki prefecture
Citrus fruit (*Yūkō*), Nagasaki

Three of these vanishing products are cultivated in Miyagi and named after their location. The Kosena radish (*Kosena daikon*), whose long leaves are edible and especially tender, is one of these agricultural products. The availability of the Kosena radish is confined to its area of cultivation, as is the grilled and dried goby (*Nagatsura no yaki haze*). The Amarume green onion (*Amarume negi*) is known for its delicate taste and has an arched shape due to a special cultivation technique called *yatoi*. This vegetable is cultivated in humid soil and removed once during its growth to be replanted in a bended position. Although the Amarume green onion is rarely obtainable, a different version of the Amarume green onion is widely available in greengrocers and supermarkets in Sendai, the prefectural capital of Miyagi, under the name Sendai twisted leek (*Sendai magari negi*) (personal communication with Satō Keizō on February 9, 2008). Thus, unlike the rest of the products listed in the Ark of Taste that are so rare, expensive, and delicate that it is not feasible to integrate them into daily food practices, the Sendai twisted leek is more affordable. Yet as the following example of a revival of culinary heritage of the Edo period (1600–1868) in Miyagi prefecture shows, attempts to revive local foodways often yield costly results.

COOKING WITH REVIVED PRODUCE

Initiatives to revive local food produce are not unique to Japan, but in Japan they are given a local expression as seen in the example of Slow Food in Miyagi prefecture. Since the summer of 2007, Satō Keizō, a specialist cook of traditional cuisine, has found a way to connect to the culinary heritage of prefectural cooking by offering a classic cuisine lunch box (*koten ryōri bentō*) at the cafeteria of Tohoku University that enables visitors to experience the taste of the sophisticated banquet cuisine of the Edo period. This classic cuisine lunch is limited to twenty lunch boxes and is only available on weekends for the price of 2,000 yen (approximately $22) in a separate corner of the university cafeteria. The content of the lunch box is based on a variety of historical recipe collections such as the *Cookery Collection* (*Ryōrishū*) compiled in 1733 by Kikkawa Fusatsune (n.d.), who served as a cook for the feudal lord Date Yoshimura of the Sendai domain. Thus, the menus served at the Komorebi Café are patterned after those served at feudal banquets and attuned to celebrating seasonal events such as the New Year. The menu changes monthly and consists of four major components: sashimi, grilled foods (*yakimono*), *nishime*,[7] and snacks (*sakana*). The following menu was served to members of Slow Food Miyagi on July 21, 2007:

MENU
Sashimi
    Vinegared fish-salad of flatfish seasoned with salt and *irizake*[8] (*Koita kozukenamasu*)
    Mountain Mallow (*sangi*)
    Herbs (*kōryō*)
    Flavored Sake (*irizake*)[9]
Grilled foods (*yakimono*)
    Tofu made with eel (*seta tōfu*)
    Nori
    Tofu
    Japanese pepper (*sanshō ni*)
Snacks (*sakana yonjū*)
    Eggplant
    A cooked salad with dressing (*chinta ae*)
    Devil's tongue (*kon'yaku*)
    Miso paste made of leeks (*negi* miso)

Dried herring (*mikaki nisshin*)
Japanese pepper
Nishime
  Stewed taro (*satoimo umani*)
  Shiitake mushrooms (*shiitake fukume ni*)
  Mugwort (*yomogi*)
  Foilage of trees (*konoha nakyō umani*)
  Rikyū egg (*Rikyū tamago*)[10]
Cold miso soup (*hiyashiro* or *hiyajiro*) made with *dashi* made of Miyagi
  Nagatsura goby (*haze*) with Sendai miso
Rice (*meshi*)
Mioga (*myōga*), Asakusa nori, eggplant, dried beefsteak plant (*shiso*),
  cucumber
Pickles (*kō no mono*)
  Radish (*daikon*), sake, soy sauce, citron (*yuzu*)
  Japanese green pepper
Sweets (*kanmi*)

Despite serving this meal to members of Slow Food, Satō reported that the ingredients he used for this and his other elaborate historical menus were not included in the Slow Food Movement's Ark of Taste. He explained that the foods on the Ark were too rare, too difficult to obtain, and too expensive (personal interview with Satō on February 9, 2008). However, Satō stated that he was indeed making an effort to purchase domestic ingredients (*kokusan*) exclusively, especially foods from the Tōhoku region in the north of Japan's main island and Hokkaidō, such as scallops (*hotate*) from Hokkaidō (*Hokkaidō san*) and *Sendai miso* (personal communication with Satō on March 1, 2008). The origin, such as "Hokkaidō produce" (*Hokkaidō san*), was marked clearly on the packages he showed me, but Satō admitted that he needed to trust the labels on the packages and could not further clarify the origin of the ingredients (*sore ijō ni kakunin dekinai*). He also stated that he was making an effort to buy foods according to season, such as bamboo shoots (*takenoko*) from Kōchi (Shikoku), whose peak season lasts until the end of April. Therefore, in terms of seasonal foods, Satō purchases as many foods as possible from the northern prefectures while using additional seasonal ingredients from other parts of Japan.

Despite Satō's creative cooking using local products to create historical dishes, access to these remains limited. Satō's cooking has been featured in the news (*Kahoku Shimpō* Online, July 7, 2007), but there have not been any extensive efforts to promote his cooking style. Furthermore, the availability of his classic lunch box is restricted to lunch hours on weekends and reservations are required. In addition, the price of the *bentō* of ¥2,000 (approximately $22) is more than students who eat at the cafeteria would in most cases be willing to spend for a Saturday lunch. Taking these factors into consideration, Satō commented that the classic cuisine lunch boxes are usually served on special occasions such as festive banquets, as opposed to being a typical lunch. The enjoyment of refined regional culinary specialties is connected to special events that are directed at a very limited audience.

SENDAI TRADITIONAL VEGETABLES AND GREEN TOURISM

Another example of a revival of traditional foodways in Miyagi is the Miyagi prefectural government's promotion of "Sendai traditional vegetables" (*Sendai dentō yasai*). The prefectural government lists six agricultural products on its website, including the Amarume green onion. These products are marked as "Sendai traditional vegetables" (*Sendai dentō yasai*) in order to make consumers more aware of the fact that they are buying a regional product. The names of these vegetables are:

Sendai cabbage (*Sendai hakusai*)
Sendai long eggplant (*Sendai naganasu*)
Karatori potato yam (*Karatori imo Sendai*)
Sendai leafy vegetable (*Yukina Sendai*)
Sendai Amarume green onion (*Amarume negi*)
Sendai Japanese banana plant (*Sendai bashōsai*)

The prefectural government of Miyagi started the promotion of Sendai traditional vegetables in 2003 in collaboration with local farmers who sought to revive local agricultural heritage. There have been similar revitalization campaigns of "traditional vegetables" throughout the country, such as Kaga vegetables [*Kaga yasai*], available in Kanazawa in Ishikawa prefecture, and Yamato vegetables [*Yamato yasai*] in Nara prefecture. These efforts have been embarked on in the course of the past years, with Kyoto being one of the first and best well-known example of a revitalization of local vegetable cuisine. The campaign of Sendai traditional vegetables resembles the promotion of Kyoto vegetables that are known under the terms "Kyoto vegetables" (*kyō yasai*), "seasonal Kyoto vegetables" (*kyō shun yasai*), and "traditional Kyoto vegetables" (*kyō dentō yasai*) (Rath, forthcoming).Various kinds of *kyō yasai* are widely available in Kyoto and the surrounding areas as elaborate "Kyoto vegetable cuisine" (*kyō yasai ryōri*) and as exclusive products in specialty stores.

According to my conversation with Kimura Masaji, chief investigator at the Office for the Promotion of Agriculture in the Sendai region in Miyagi prefecture, the aim of offering traditional vegetables is "to provide local food to the population" and "to create a symbol for farmers," meaning a vegetable that represents local agriculture. However, the vegetables grown are rare, their cultivation is limited to a particular region in Sendai, called *Wakabayashi*, and they are seasonally specific. For example, in the case of Sendai, the traditional vegetables named earlier are exclusively grown by seven farmers who specialize in the cultivation of either one or two of these local agricultural products. Equally limited is the distribution of these agricultural products. In most cases, the vegetables are directly delivered to restaurants that serve special dishes based on traditional vegetables. One of these restaurants in Miyagi is Sakunami Onsen, a hot-spring resort in Sakunami in the vicinity of Sendai, which began serving Sendai traditional vegetable cuisine in December 2007 (personal communication with Kimura Masaji, chief investigator at the Office for the Promotion of Agriculture in the Sendai region in Miyagi prefecture, on March 3, 2008).

"Farmers' restaurants" (*nōka resutoran*) located in the suburbs of cities in Miyagi provide another example of places serving traditional produce. One of the farmers involved in cultivating Sendai vegetables, Kayaba Ichiko, runs a farmer's restaurant called Moroya together with her husband, Kayaba Tetsuo, and their two daughters. The Kayaba family grows over a hundred different kinds of vegetables and operates a delivery service for vegetables for people living in Sendai. Customers who visit the place to relax for a day outside the city enjoy a menu that changes monthly and offers "seasonal vegetables" (*shun no yasai*). This farmers' restaurant is one among approximately forty farmers' restaurants in Miyagi prefecture and has been featured in *Fountains*, the magazine of JAL Hotels (Japan Airlines [JAL] 2007, 10–11). However, similar to the box lunches mentioned earlier, the customer base of this farmers' restaurant is limited. Reservations are required, and it is not possible to visit this restaurant alone as the preparation of these vegetable dishes is too time consuming to be done for just one person.

SLOW FOOD AT FAST FOOD RESTAURANTS:
THE CASE OF MOS BURGER IN MIYAGI

The arrival of fast food chains such as McDonald's in 1971 and Starbucks in 1996 has influenced the nutritional habits of Japanese people. However, a very different and accessible way to integrate local food products into food practices has interestingly been made by a fast food chain, supposedly the main enemy of local food initiatives. The Japanese fast food chain Mos Burger, which serves teriyaki burgers and rice burgers, has begun to use local products on their fast food menus (Saijo 2008). As stated earlier, Japanese consumers tend to equate domestic food products whose origins are traceable and transparent with greater food safety. Responding to the increasing desire of customers for food safety, Mos Burger began using organically grown vegetables and started informing customers about the origin of its supply of vegetables. Customers who eat at Mos Burger can trace the origin of the food they consume: "Upon entering a store, customers can view a blackboard that informs them that the lettuce being used today comes from farmer x in y prefecture, the tomatoes from farmer w in z prefecture" (Jussaume, Hisano, and Taniguchi 2000, 221). In 1997, Mos Burger started cooperating with 2,000 farmers to use their agricultural products for their fast food menus under the motto "fresh vegetables of Mos" (*mosu no nama yasai*) and "vegetables that reveal the faces of producers" (*seisansha no kao ga mieru yasai*) (Mos Burger Japan website 2008).

Since June 2002, the company has offered special burgers that are only available in a certain areas (*chiiki gentei*), during a certain season (*kisetsu gentei*), and/or during a specific time period (*kikan gentei*). For example, in January 2008, Mos Burger launched the "Iwate Prefecture Nanbu Dori Burger" (*Iwate ken san nanbu dori bāgā*) in the Tōhoku area and in Hokkaidō (Mos Burger Japan website 2008). This emphasis on local food products points to Mos Burger's marketing strategy that aims to distinguish it from other fast food companies such as McDonald's by positioning Mos as a local business that values national and regional culinary treasures (Ohnuki-Tierney 1997). At the same time, Mos Burger has created local foods that are affordable. A typical local burger costs ¥320 ($3), which is much less than a $20 classic lunch box served in the upscale restaurant mentioned earlier.

A return to local foodways may appear to be one answer to recent food scandals involving foreign foods. However, excepting the fast food chain Mos Burger, the accessibility of "traditional" food products is restricted and confined to a limited number of occasions and a small audience. If only small segments of Japanese consumers can afford more costly and supposedly healthier local foods, these foods will not pose a practical alternative to foods that are perceived to be harmful. Despite the rhetoric of the Slow Food movement and the efforts of chefs and the Miyagi prefectural government in reviving traditional foods and promoting safe foods, it is ironic that a fast food chain has provided the only accessible versions of these foods thus far. Albeit local foods are currently not fully integrated into Japanese daily food practices, the significance of local produce lies in the potential tie-up of food and ecotourism, and in the integration of local food products into conventional eateries or even fast food restaurants.

NOTES

Field research for this chapter was conducted through participant observation, interviews, and online research between February 2007 and May 2008. I am grateful to my informants for the time and the information they shared with me. I would especially like to thank Fukano Setsuko, the representative of Slow Food Japan in Miyagi, for allowing me take part in a number of activities held by the organization. I would also like to express my gratitude to Satō Keizō and Kayaba Ichiko for patiently explaining various ingredients of their gastronomic endeavors to me, and Kimura Masaji for resources on traditional vegetables in Sendai made available to me. An earlier version of this chapter was presented at the annual meeting of the Association for Asian Studies in Boston in March 2007. I am grateful to our discussant, Professor Theodore Bestor, and the participants of this panel for their insightful and encouraging comments. I would also like to thank Eric C. Rath, Paul Vlitos, Satomi Fukutomi, and Sebastian Maslow for many conversations about food and helpful suggestions on earlier drafts of this manuscript.

1. The Food Safety Basic Law (*Shokuhin anzen kijun hō*) can be found at http://www.ron.gr.jp/law/law/shok_anz.htm, last accessed on February 9, 2010, and the Food Sanitation Law (*Shokuhin eisei hō*) can be accessed at http://www.houko.com/00/01/S22/233.htm, last accessed on February 9, 2010. The Food Safety Basic Law contains regulations with regards to the assessment of safety of food products, labeling as part of food safety, and the education of citizens with regards to food safety. The Food Sanitation Law prescribes standards for food additives, labeling and advertising, packaging, and food inspection.

2. I refer to the self-sufficiency rate computed on a caloric scale, which is calculated as follows: The supply of calories based on domestic food products per day for one person is divided by the supply of calories based on all foods (domestic and nondomestic food products) per day for one person (Suematsu 2008, 17).

3. By international comparison, the self-sufficiency rates of other major indus-

trialized countries are much higher: According to data compiled for the year 2003, the United States of America has a self-sufficiency rate of 128 percent, Australia's self-sufficiency rate lies at 237 percent, Canada's at 145 percent, France has a self-sufficiency rate of 122 percent while Germany's self-sufficiency rate lies at 84 percent (MAFF 2008).

4. *Shiokara* consists of different parts of fish such as the flesh, eggs, and inner organs that are pickled in salt (Hosking 1996, 138).

5. Hosking lists this food as fish *shōyu* (*uoshōyu*), "a salty, golden-colored, clear liquid, the product of fermentation with salt" (Hosking 1996, 166). This dish is especially well known in Akita prefecture.

6. *Narezushi* is an ancient technique of sushi, used to preserve fish using salt (Hosking 1996, 105).

7. *Nishime* consists of dry boiled foods such as fresh or dried vegetables, fish, and also meats that are simmered until no liquid remains. These foods are seasoned with ginger, *mirin*, and often soy sauce. *Nishime* is a dish that is often offered for New Year (Hosking 1996, 110).

8. Hosking (1996, 103) and Matsushita (1996, 105–6).

9. The origins of soy sauce (*shōyu*) can be traced to the Muromachi period (1336–1573). At the beginning of the Edo period, the soy sauce industry came into practice, and only in the middle of the Edo period did soy sauce begin to be consumed more widely. Up until that point, *irizake* was used instead of soy sauce.

10. The *Rikyū* egg was named after the tea master Sen Rikyū or Sen Sōeki (1522–91), who was said to like foods made of sesame. This dish consists of a dissolved egg to which ground sesame (*goma*) and a little bit of sake (Japanese rice wine) is added before it is steamed. Alternatively, instead of sesame, walnuts (*kurumi*) can be used for this egg dish (Matsushita 1996, 200).

WORKS CITED

Cwiertka, Katarzyna J. 2006. *Modern Japanese Cuisine: Food, Power and National Identity*. London: Reaktion Books.

Hosking, Richard. 1996. *Dictionary of Japanese Food: Ingredients and Culture*. Boston: Tuttle.

Japan Airlines, ed. 2007. *Fountains: The Magazine of JAL Hotels*. Vol. 46. Brochure, Japan Airlines.

Japan External Trade Organization (JETRO). *Nihon no shokuryō yunyū (jōi 10 kakoku)*. Available at http://www.jetro.go.jp/jpn/stats/trade/pdf/20052006_import_2 .pdf, accessed on February 12, 2008.

Japan Times Editorial. 2006, July 8. "Revitalizing national agriculture."

———. 2008, February 3. "Late response to food poisoning."

———. 2008, February 11. "Avoid hysteria over food."

Japan Times Online. 2007, March 2. "Fujiya restarts sweets production after sour month."

———. 2007, October 21. "Akafuku hit by fresh food safety allegations."

———. 2008, February 11. "Seventy-six percent plan to avoid Chinese food. 'Gyoza' contamination takes toll on products' popularity."

Jussaume, Raymond A. Jr., Hisano Shūji, and Taniguchi Yoshimitsu. 2000. "Food Safety in Modern Japan." In *Japanstudien 12. Essen und Ernährung im modernen Japan*. Ed. Nicola Liscutin and René Haak, 211–28. Munich: Iudicium Verlag.

Kahoku Shimpō (Online). 2007, July 7. "*Date na aji dōzo. Tōhoku daigaku shoku ga Sendai han no kondate saigen,*" accessed on February 5, 2008.

Ministry of Health, Labor, and Welfare (MHLW). 2008, February 11. *Chūgoku san reitō gyōza ni yoru kenkō higai ga kōhyō sareta hi ikō ni todōfuken nado ni atta sōdan /hōkoku sū ni tsuite*. Available at http://www.mhlw.go.jp/houdou/2008/02/h0211–1.html, accessed on February 12, 2008.

Matsushita Sachiko. 1996. *Zusetsu Edo ryōri jiten*. Tokyo: Kashiwa Shobō.

Ministry of Agriculture, Forestry, and Fisheries (MAFF). 2008. *Shuyō senshinkoku no shokuryō-ritsu (1960–2003)*. Available at http://www.maff.go.jp/j/zyukyu/zikyu_ritu/013.html, accessed on February 10, 2009.

Miyagi Prefecture, ed. 2008. *Sendai dentō yasai ni tsuite*. Available at http://www.pref.miyagi.jp/sd-nokai/sendaiyasaihp/index.htm, accessed on February 12, 2008.

Mulgan, Aurelia George. 2000. *The Politics of Agriculture in Japan*. London: Routledge.

Ohnuki-Tierney, Emiko. 1997. "McDonald's in Japan. Changing Manners and Etiquette." In *Golden Arches East: McDonald's in East Asia*. Ed. James L. Watson, 161–82. Stanford, Calif.: Stanford University Press.

Parkins, Wendy, and Geoffrey Craig. 2006. *Slow Living*. Oxford: Berg.

Petrini, Carlo, and Gigi Padovani. 2006. *Slow Food Revolution: A New Culture for Eating and Living*. New York: Rizzoli.

Rath, Eric C. Forthcoming. "New meanings for old vegetables in Kyoto." In *Cuisine, Consumption and Culture*. Ed. Ted Bestor and Victoria Bestor.

Saijo, Eriko. 2008. "Toward a sustainable Japan—Corporations at work." In *Japan for Sustainability* (JFS). Article Series Article No. 35, "Food as a bridge between humans and nature" (Mos Food Services, Inc.). Available at http://www.japanfs.org/en/business/corporations35.html, accessed on February 9, 2010.

Slow Food Japan Tokyo. 2006. *Aji no hakobune (aruka)*. Press information obtained on February 20, 2007 via e-mail.

Takarajima-sha, ed. 2008, June 20. "Shokuhin no karakuri 10. 'Kokusan' 'anshin' no tabemono wa kore da": 10–11.

Suematsu Hiroyuki. 2008. *Shokuryō jikyū-ritsu no "naze." Dōshite hikui to ikenai no ka?* Tokyo: Fusosha Shinsho.

Yoshida Reiji. 2008, January 31. "10 sick after eating tainted 'gyoza' from China." *Japan Times*.

WEBSITES

The Food Safety Basic Law (*Shokuhin anzen kijun hō*). http://www.ron.gr.jp/law/law/shok_anz.htm, accessed on August 11, 2009.

The Food Sanitation Law (*Shokuhin eisei hō*). http://www.houko.com/00/01/S22/233.htm, accessed on August 11, 2009.

Ministry of Health, Labor, and Welfare (MHLW). http://www.mhlw.go.jp/houdou/2008/02/h0211-1.html, accessed on February 9, 2010.

Miyagi Prefecture, ed. (2008). *Sendai dentō yasai ni tsuite*, http://www.pref.miyagi.jp/sd-nokai/sendaiyasaihp/index.htm, accessed on February 9, 2010.

Miyagi Prefectural Government, ed. http://www.pref.miyagi.jp/kankou/EN/Green_Tourism/GT_main.htm, accessed on February 9, 2010.

Mos Burger Japan. (2008). http://www.mos.co.jp/company/pr_pdf/pr_080118_1.pdf, accessed on February 9, 2010.

Slow food. http://www.slowfood.com, accessed on February 5, 2008.

Slow food Japan. http://www.slowfoodjapan.net/new.html, accessed on February 5, 2008.

PARTICIPANT OBSERVATION AND INTERVIEWS

Interview, Fukano Setsuko, representative of Slow Food Miyagi, Sendai, February 5, 2007.

Slow Food Festival Kessenuma, Kesenuma, Miyagi prefecture, February 25, 2007.

Visits to Slow Food Fair, Yokohama, Minato Mirai, April 28 and 29, 2007.

Visits to the Komorebi Café, Sendai, July 21, 2007, February 9, 2008 and March 1, 2008.

Interview with Kimura Masaji, head of the Office for the Promotion of Agriculture in the Sendai region in Miyagi prefecture (*Miyagi ken Sendai shi chihō shinkō jimusho nōgyō shinkō bu*), March 3, 2008.

Visit to the farmers' restaurant Moroya and conversation with Kayaba Ichiko, May 10, 2008.

13 Rāmen Connoisseurs
Class, Gender, and the Internet

SATOMI FUKUTOMI

RĀMEN AND JAPANESE CONSUMERS

ON MARCH 20, 2007, JAPANESE newspapers and television news programs featured images of a long line of consumers waiting patiently outside Taishōken, a small, time-honored rāmen specialty shop.[1] After forty-five years of dedicated service, it was the last day on the job for the founder of the shop, Yamagishi Kazuo,[2] who is said to be the inventor of the *tsuke men*[3] type of rāmen. Customers hoping to taste Yamagishi's rāmen one last time had to wait longer than usual; the first customer in line waited outside the shop for over twelve hours, and the average wait was four to five hours. The dedication displayed by these loyal customers illustrates the degree to which rāmen, a fast and inexpensive food, is being transformed into an object of connoisseurship.

In this chapter, I argue that connoisseurship is a mode of consumption and embedded in everyday life in contemporary Japan. I define connoisseurship[4] as a taste for and an expert knowledge of a subject or an object—for example, wine, which has long been recognized as an object of connoisseurship (oenology). Connoisseurship often connotes aesthetic qualities, high class (exclusiveness of other classes), and a sense of leisure, and is often considered an appurtenance of "high culture." However, Michel de Certeau alludes to the inclusiveness of all classes and says that certain skills of everyday life have their connoisseurs (de Certeau 1984, 18). I argue that certain practices of rāmen consumption challenge the normative association of elite status with connoisseurship. More specifically, I discuss how and why particular everyday commodities become connoisseurial objects in the context of Japanese consumer culture.

Rāmen is an everyday food that has, for a number of complex reasons, come to be considered a national dish (*kokumin shoku*) in contemporary Japan. By "national dish" I mean foods that the majority of a nation's citizens, if not the entire national body, know about and most likely have eaten. Rāmen in its capacity as a national food is embedded in the daily life of many Japanese and conjures a specific set of mnemonic images. Given these conditions, rāmen is not a stereotypical object of connoisseurship—the more established objects of connoisseurship tend to be exceptional and often class-specific objects.

Connoisseurship holds aesthetics and provides an "opportunity to establish 'cult' scenarios and value systems" (Bhattacharya 2006, 11). Nevertheless, these value systems are arbitrary. The values established through connoisseurship are not necessarily directly proportional to economic value but represent knowledge of aesthetic value combined with intrinsic worth that may be increased by uniqueness (Bhattacharya 2006, 35). Certain sets of people—connoisseurs—are able to create and share these values. Anthropologist Susan Terrio (2005) examines the authenticating of French-crafted chocolate and argues that producers arbitrarily facilitate connoisseurship of certain products; in this case, the producers manipulate consumers to choose particular chocolates as indicators of refined taste. She asserts that "taste" is produced and reproduced culturally, politically, and economically, and that producers are able to (re)invent authenticity and connoisseurship by adding prestige. An object that is successfully produced and marketed as an indicator of taste attracts consumers on the basis that taste reaffirms class hierarchy.

This notion of prestige is largely associated with class, which is extensively discussed in Pierre Bourdieu's *Distinction* (1984). Bourdieu argues that economic and cultural divisions dictate tastes for cultural goods such as foods, sports, and the arts. Class, however, rarely conforms to rigid definitions, and Bourdieu states that the complex web of class indices extends beyond occupation, income, and educational levels (Bourdieu 1984, 101–2).

Likewise, I argue that both taste and class conditions in contemporary Japan are fluid, and it is important to consider the ways in which particular commodities come to be ranked in terms of class. In the early stages of its introduction to developing nations, American fast food often bears high-class symbolic value, but this symbolic value diminishes as nations achieve economic or social power. Accordingly, the introduction of a new manner of eating linked to a new food item can blur class distinctions by violating etiquette or through disassociation from the lower classes (Ohnuki-Tierney 1997, 175–80). In this study of rāmen, what was once considered a low-class food for men is now consumed by a wide range of consumers.

Due to its association with class, connoisseurship is critical to the study of consumption and popular culture in contemporary Japan. Many studies of popular culture address issues including fanatics and enthusiasm (Hosokawa and Matsuoka 2004; Kelly 2004; Tobin 2004), identity, gender, or nostalgia

(Yano 2002), but the subject of connoisseurship in Japanese consumption has so far received little attention. The Internet is yet another subject that has been neglected in studies of Japanese consumption, despite the explosion of Internet usage in recent years and the new dimensions that the Internet has added to consumer culture.

The Internet has become an object of consumption rather than an information device. It not only offers an infinite array of goods, but it also "makes every buyer into a seller" (Zukin 2005, 244). Anthropologist Elizabeth Chin suggests a broader understanding of consumption. She argues that consumption is complex and involves more than the simple act of purchasing, and includes engagement with images, idea, and identities (2001, 7). According to Chin's definition, browsing the Internet and communicating through the Internet are acts of consumption that not only provide information about commodities but also create communities in which consumers exchange opinions, products, or share their identities.

In light of these assertions, this study examines the ways in which (1) an ordinary food is transformed into a connoisseurial object, and (2) how the Internet plays a key role in allowing consumers to demonstrate connoisseurship as identity and to illustrate issues existing in rāmen consumption. I analyze rāmen shops in Tokyo, customers in rāmen establishments, and online communities. I focus on interactions between rāmen aficionados as a means of understanding how online communities influence individual decision making and transform rāmen into a connoisseurial object and aficionados into connoisseurs.

This study is based on interviews, an ethnography of a rāmen shop,[5] and discussions/interactions in online communities (limited to the Japanese language) consisting of both men and women. I conducted hour-long face-to-face interviews with rāmen shop owners, employees, and rāmen critics, and online interviews with rāmen aficionados. There is no widely accepted terminology for rāmen aficionados; a small sampling of the names applied includes rāmen nerd (*raota*), rāmen lover (*rāmen zuki*) and rāmen expert/connoisseur (*rāmen tsū*). For the purposes of this article, I refer to them as aficionados.

RĀMEN AS A JAPANESE "NATIONAL DISH"

Rāmen has been consumed in Japan for roughly one hundred years.[6] It was originally consumed by immigrants in the Chinatowns of major Japanese metropolises. Later, it was prepared by Chinatown cooks and sold from moveable street stalls to students and physical laborers. What began as a kind of street food for Chinese immigrants was eventually transformed into a mass food for Japanese people (Okada 2002, 78). Not merely a main dish to be consumed at designated meal times, rāmen is consumed between meals, after drinking alcohol, and as a midnight snack. Over the course of a century, this Chinese import has been adapted to various regional tastes and has undergone a series of metamorphoses, ultimately infiltrating Japanese daily life as a national dish (Okuyama 2003, 114–18).

The anthropologist Katarzyna Cwiertka defines a national cuisine as "an imagined national identity and cultural homogeneity" (Cwiertka 2006, 12). Cultural anthropologist Arjun Appadurai (1988) notes that various milieus, such as class, gender, media, entertainment, and mobility, greatly reflect and reproduce national cuisine. In the case of rāmen, its regionalization and popularity make rāmen a national dish. Today, approximately 80,000 rāmen shops[7] are scattered across Japan. There are an estimated 200,000 sites, including amusement parks, department stores, train stations, and beach vendors, selling rāmen in Japan (Okada 2002, 205). Rāmen varies in flavor according to individual shops, region, or neighborhood.

Cost is a key determinant in classifying types of rāmen in Tokyo; the average cost of a bowl of rāmen in "new-wave shops" is over 800 yen ($8.70).[8] More traditional, older shops and small family-owned businesses offer bowls from 550 yen ($6.00) and up, and even a poor, hungry student can afford a 290-yen ($3.10) bowl offered at some franchised shops. These three types of shops often overlap; for example, some new-wave shops and traditional stores are also family-owned businesses.

Rāmen has become a convenient, effective commodity for attracting people and fostering the development of particular places, especially in remote areas. It is presented as a "local specialty food" (*meibutsu*), which is called *gotōchi rāmen*, in virtually every region of Japan (Okada 2003, 473). Sapporo rāmen in Hokkaidō, the northernmost island of Japan, consists of a miso soup base, lard, and curly noodles (Ōsaki 2002). In the southwestern island Kyūshū, Hakata rāmen is known for its muddy white pork-marrow soup base and tiny noodles. Traditional Tokyo rāmen features a light soy sauce flavor and tiny, curly noodles, although more recently, Tokyo rāmen cooks have begun developing their own individual flavors and products, *gotōnin rāmen*. It is only within the past ten years that myriad types of rāmen shops have come to be recognized.

As a result of this appreciation of varieties, regional rāmen products have become available in a specialized rāmen museum and in parks in Tokyo. The Shin Yokohama Rāmen Museum opened in a newly developed part of Yokohama in March 1994. The museum offers several regional rāmen interpretations and creates a domestic eating tour of Japan with nostalgic features. The manner of presentation might be considered "edutainment" (Creighton 1992), which combines education (the exhibition of the history of rāmen and rāmen shops) and entertainment (visitors come to enjoy a recreated postwar town). In January 2005, a three-year rāmen competition was inaugurated at the Rāmen Kokugikan[9] theme park. In this competition, thirty-six popular rāmen shop owners compete for the championship. To convey exoticism, images of America are attached to rāmen; for example, in April 2005, Tachikawa Rāmen Square—a miniature of Times Square in New York City—opened in a shopping mall in a suburb of Tokyo. In September 2006, Rāmen Sangyō Ten (the Rāmen Industrial Exposition), designed to increase growth in the Japanese rāmen industry, was held at the Pacifico Yokohama convention center. These are just a few examples of the numerous rāmen events held throughout Japan.

Ōsaki Hiroshi, Watanabe Juan, Ishigami Hideyuki, and other individuals known as rāmen critics/consultants[10] promote rāmen production and consumption. Ōsaki founded an information company called Rāmen Data Bank. He commodifies rāmen information in the company-published journal *Torasan*; the name is an abbreviation of *Tokyo no rāmen'ya san* (rāmen shops in Tokyo). The journal *Torasan* also conveys a sense of familiarity and nostalgia because it is the name of the protagonist of the popular Japanese film, *Otoko wa tsurai yo* (Being a Man Is Tough),[11] which was released in 1969. Torasan is nationally known as a generous man and the iconic blue-collar worker of "good old neighborhoods."

The Rāmen Data Bank distributes information on rāmen shops over the Internet and broadcasts monthly online interviews with rāmen aficionados. Ōsaki claims that over the past decade, the rising popularity of the Internet in Japan has dramatically altered rāmen consumerism (Ōsaki 2002, 4–5). Over 34 million Japanese Internet websites offer rāmen-related topics, and this number is constantly growing.[12] Rāmen aficionados post critiques of rāmen and rāmen establishments within hours of new openings. These aficionados also use the Internet to exchange information and establish an emotional dimension to eating at particular rāmen shops.

CROSSING CLASS BOUNDARIES
AND RITUALIZING RĀMEN

Rāmen was formerly almost exclusively associated with the blue-collar sphere and a rough masculinity, since it was an inexpensive, quick food prepared by male producers (street stall cooks) for male consumers (physical laborers and students).[13] However, based on my observation of rāmen shops between 2006 and 2007, connoisseurial elements such as aestheticization, craftsmanship, and the social element of "dining out" have accrued to new-wave rāmen shops. These elements have effectively submerged low-class images in certain rāmen shops, transforming this ordinary comestible into a connoisseurial object.

Since the late 1980s, rāmen has appeared in the mass media as "B-grade gourmet" (B-kyū gurume). The designation "B-grade gourmet" refers to inexpensive or quotidian foods that have been transformed into connoisseurial objects (Sand 2006, 105). Television programs have featured rāmen as well as rāmen aficionados displaying their knowledge of rāmen. Ōsaki claims that the year 1996 witnessed "the rāmen revolution" in Tokyo. In 1996, men who had formerly been white-collar workers (datsu sara)[14] opened three rāmen shops—Men'ya Musashi, Kujira-ken, and Aoba—in Tokyo and its suburbs. Until this time, rāmen shop owners were thought to be less educated, and preparing rāmen was considered to be the province of lower classes. In contrast to these stereotypes, many owners of new-wave rāmen shops have university degrees and have founded their own businesses—several even came from the fashion industry.[15] These émigrés from the fashion industry have added an aesthetic dimension to rāmen culture. Consequently, the opening of new-wave rāmen establishments was significant, as they added new aesthetic elements to rāmen culture.

The aesthetic elements of rāmen include uri (selling point), which refers to distinctiveness, the unique characteristics of a commodity, and involves products, shops, owners, and services. It also includes the genealogy and style that have established rāmen as a separate category or food niche. Both producers and consumers may understand uri as the composite aesthetic elements of rāmen and shops. Sociologist Gary Alan Fine, in his discussion of American restaurant kitchens, claims that "restaurant food, like all food, has an aesthetic, sensory dimension and is evaluated as such by both producers and consumers" (Fine 1996, 13). Uri plays a crucial role in the connoisseurship of rāmen and restaurant food in general. The process of repositioning rāmen as a non-low-class food has required new-wave rāmen shops to present themselves as "restaurants" rather than fast food shops through the manipulation of *uri*. The majority of rāmen shops opened after 1996 strive for the *uri* of traditional Japanese restaurants, Western-style restaurants, or native/foreign hybrids with atmospheres of refinement and originality.

Furthermore, the conscious emphasis on Japaneseness—exemplified through recognizably Japanese décor—reformulates rāmen as a Japanese food. Rāmen shops frequently place a "blue or a white curtain at the entrance," (*noren*) which is a common feature of Japanese eateries (Ashkenazi 2004, 30). The very word *rāmen*, previously written in the Japanese *katakana* syllabic writing system used primarily for words imported from abroad, is increasingly printed on menus and signs with combinations of Chinese characters (*kanji*) to distinguish different varieties such as *chūka soba* (Chinese noodles). This style of calligraphy is also utilized to authenticate rāmen shops in Tokyo with names like Ore no Sora (My Own Sky) and Ikaruga (a historical place in Japan). This sense of authenticity delivers attractive images of "old Japan."

In order to create originality beyond names and recipes,[16] aspects of unique performance and qualified service are employed by shops. The word "cool" (*kakkoii*) is often used in reference to the Men'ya Musashi shop located in Shinjuku, one of the biggest entertainment districts in Tokyo. The name is derived from Miyamoto Musashi (1584?-1645), a famous samurai hero, and his images dominate the shop décor. The shop is designed like a small theater in which the employees deliver more than a bowl of rāmen and craft "the raw objects of space, words, and tastes" (Yan 2005, 81) to generate a cool atmosphere. In the open kitchen,[17] employees from their mid-twenties to early thirties, dressed in red t-shirts, brown aprons, and bandanas, shout (*kakegoe*) when each bowl of noodles is prepared to completion. These shouts are not necessarily semantically significant but rather deliver a ritualistic quality. This kind of utterance is commonly used to generate spiritual or physical rapport among performers at festivals but has an added incentive of entertaining audiences. Audiences also shout to encourage performers such as singers at concerts and Kabuki actors (Yano 2002, 78). These shouts are suggestive of Japanese "traditions" or rituals, and Men'ya Musashi uses these traditional resonances to establish distinction.

The reason for transforming rāmen into a cool food by inviting white-collar people and others with a fashion-oriented sense is to raise the status of rāmen shops. The target clientele of Kogane, a rāmen shop located in Shinjuku, is businessmen between the ages of twenty and forty (personal interview on November 24, 2006). Matoba Yasushi, the manager of the shop, explains that many businessmen are from sales divisions and travel frequently; unlike many students, they can afford to pay 800 yen ($8.90) for lunch.

Women are also being targeted by new-wave rāmen shops. The shop Ryūta, located in Shitamachi (the old town and blue-collar working area of Tokyo) and next to a fashion institute, targets solitary women, including housewives, students, and office clerks. The owner claims that he designed the shop with a fashionable interior that would appeal to women, and provides service items such as paper aprons and hair bands, which allow customers to eat rāmen without getting messy and thereby violating table etiquette (personal interview on November 9, 2006). As a result of the increased attention paid to new aesthetic elements, establishments such as Men'ya Musashi, Kogane, and Ryūta have created a rāmen fad among middle-class people and businesspeople.

Consumers also create rāmen fads, and issues of class and connoisseurship with relation to rāmen appear in the film *Tampopo*[18] (1985). The film is director Itami Jūzō's satire of low-class food (inexpensive fast food) that is transformed into a connoisseurial object through ritualization and aestheticization. Itami initially anthropomorphizes rāmen and subsequently sexualizes it. In doing so, he creates specialized material worlds as a means of expressing personal sentiments or valuations. The sociologist Susan Pearce explains the relationship between the material world and human beings by asserting that "people and ideas can be reified and objects, if not deified, at any rate humanified" (1995, 405). This is not to say that all aficionados place humanized and/or gendered images upon the objects of their desire, but those who do so are able to express their emotionality.

The film starts with a discussion of the appropriate etiquette for consuming rāmen; a "mentor/master" (*sensei*) who has studied noodles for forty years gives a lecture on how to "practice" rāmen in a ritualistic manner:

> First, observe the whole bowl. Appreciate its gestalt. Savor the aromas. Jewels of fat glittering on the surface. Shinachiku roots shining. Seaweed slowly sinking. Spring onions floating. Concentrate on the three pork slices . . . they play the key role, but stay modestly hidden. First caress the surface with the chopstick tips . . . to express affection. Then poke the pork. . . . Caress with the chopstick, gently pick it up, and dip it into the soup on the right of the bowl. What's important here is to apologize to the pork by saying, "See you soon." Finally, start eating, the noodles first . . . while slurping the noodles, look at the pork. Eye it affectionately. (Quote from a translated dialogue of the movie *Tampopo*, released in America in 1987)

This meticulous instruction elevates a predominantly low-class food to a higher level. Through his "sermon," the mentor first humanizes and then sexualizes rāmen. The mentor, dressed in kimono to underscore the dignity and formality of the event, sits at the counter of an ordinary, low-class rāmen shop. His ritualization imitates traditional Japanese cultural practices such as the tea ceremony or flower arrangement. Much like wine tasting, rāmen consumption requires a synthesis of sight, smell, taste, and touch in the film. In his demonstration, the mentor slurps his noodles loudly and quickly—it is important to note that slurping noodles and sipping soup are connoisseurial values in rāmen consumption.

"EATING LOUD" AND GENDER IN RĀMEN

The act of slurping noodles and sipping soup—"eating loud"—is considered to be appropriate etiquette for consuming rāmen. With the exception of other noodles in Japan, eating loud is hardly common protocol, particularly not for middle-class women dining out. Generally speaking, dining out is an act associated with higher social status, although associations differ according to the establishment and circumstances. Dining out is a ritual governed by a complex system of rules that determine what, where, and how to eat. For example, in 1920s and 1930s Japan, middle-class working women displayed their modernity by eating out at cafés (Tipton 2000), and in the 1990s, businesswomen hesitated to eat at rāmen shops, which might be seen as low-class establishments and thus reflect negatively on their class identity.

The notion of eating loud in rāmen consumption includes the speed of eating. Based on online discussions, the majority of rāmen aficionados claim that the average time they spend eating a bowl of rāmen is about ten minutes. For this reason, new-wave rāmen shops can preserve the critical fast food characteristic of speedy service and preparation; while getting consumers inside the shop is important, getting them to leave quickly is equally important. This is especially true during peak hours (11:30 A.M. to 1:30 P.M.), when customers are expected to leave as soon as they finish eating to make space for those waiting, who are often staring hungrily into the backs of those slurping noodles. More popular establishments have customers lined up outside the shop. New-wave rāmen shops, however, do not replace or challenge the more venerable kinds of rāmen shops; rather, an ever-increasing diversity of environments has been achieved.

The Shitamachi shop Rāmen Hideyoshi, where I worked, offers a loud eating atmosphere. I chose this shop for two reasons. First, rāmen aficionados had identified the shop as a survivor from the 1980s, which meant that it predated the "rāmen revolution." Second, it has a markedly blue-collar working-class atmosphere, with old tables, music of bygone days floating in the air, and a wall-calendar featuring women in lingerie. The owner got into the rāmen business in the 1980s as a street vendor. The shop is open from 11:00 A.M. to 5:00 A.M. (eighteen hours every day) seven days a week. Generally, long business hours are associated with easy access and rarely with quality and authenticity, but the *uri* of this shop, which features big portions served with pork fat at a cost of only 650 yen ($7.30), brings in many repeat customers.

Due to the male-oriented interior and the high caloric content of the shop's offerings, the majority of customers, regular and sporadic, are men and some blue-collar women. Customer types vary according to the time of the day. Deliverymen, students, and young punk-rockers share the shop with senior citizens and businesspeople during lunch and dinner hours. Bar hostesses, who have remained a fixture in rāmen shops since the 1960s, often come to the shop late at night, and taxi drivers frequently appear at dawn for a meal before going home. While waiting to be served, solitary customers kill time by playing with their cellular phones; reading newspapers, magazines, or novels; or observing kitchen preparation and watching other customers eating. Once the customers receive their bowls, however, single-minded attention is given to the eating process.

At this type of eatery, fashionable women and businesswomen are a rare sight, but the process of socializing them to low-class-oriented rāmen shops is underway and often of recognizable importance to proprietors. The reasons underlying this development are illustrated by the comment of a male co-worker, who said, "Women have power. They are sensitive to media and consumer culture, and have a powerful influence on the market. That is why we in the rāmen business need to target them" (personal interview on June 14, 2007). Of the small numbers of women who do come, very few eat alone in the shop; most either do takeout or come with male colleagues.

Solitary eating in Japan is gendered—a woman eating alone may be perceived very differently than a man eating alone, depending on the establishment. For women, solitary eating is rare at rāmen shops but not uncommon at other types of eateries. For instance, female office clerks often go to coffee shops by themselves. At the other end of the spectrum, a solitary man eating at a specialty dessert shop may be the object of (perhaps negative) attention. In the 1960s and 1970s, during the early stages of Japan's economic growth, rāmen was popularized by street vendors and Japanese-owned Chinese eateries (*chūka ya*).[19] Consumers ranged from bar hostesses to families with small children but did not yet include businesswomen, who were expected to desire elegant commodities (Anguru 1979). In the late 1980s and early 1990s, with the sudden onset of the Japanese economic recession, rāmen gained in popularity. Innumerable shops have upgraded their images in order to attract an expanding clientele of middle-class women and businesswomen, as may be seen in the presentation of new-wave rāmen shops. Coincident with this meteoric rise, different groups of women have emerged as important figures in the rāmen business.

GENDERED SPACE IN VIRTUAL CONSUMPTION

A wide range of women have entered the sphere of rāmen consumption, and nowhere has this become more evident than on the Internet. Since the mid-1990s, the increase in Internet usage in Japan has dramatically influenced rāmen culture by introducing a new type of solitary, virtual consumption. In virtual consumption, not only rāmen aficionados but also female consumers in general participate in and talk about rāmen culture. Through virtual consumption, rāmen consumers are able to create a social bond over a food that is most often eaten solitarily.

Samuel Wilson and Leighton Peterson argue that the Internet serves to establish community and popular culture and create identity (Wilson and Peterson 2002, 456). With virtual identities, the members "meet" and negotiate or exchange their opinions more comfortably and conveniently than in person, which illustrates the dichotomy of the solitary and the collective. On the same subject, Anne Allison discusses the ways in which the Internet is used by Japanese *otaku* (freaks or geeks), noting that they are often out of touch with the actual world but very much in touch with the cyberworld (Allison 2006, 391). Accordingly, online rāmen communities offer members a site where they can connect together while separate from the actual world. In Japan, cellular phones—whose numbers are immense and growing—are commonly used to access the Internet.[20] In spite of increased usership among large swaths of rāmen consumers, class and age boundaries continue to exist in this sphere of virtual consumption, and much of the blue-collar working class is excluded. Blue-collar workers and the elderly also often use cell phones, but they are not as familiar with Internet usage. In contrast, many white-collar people use this technology daily during their commutes and sometimes even during working hours. Though usership is ever-increasing, the Internet continues to exclude certain pockets of active consumers from virtual consumption.

Among various available Internet sites, blogs and online communities are the most widely used sites by rāmen aficionados to express and practice their connoisseurship. Aficionados articulate their opinions in a sophisticated manner demonstrating knowledge, expertise, and experiences. Rather than exaggerating their feelings for rāmen, aficionados quietly forge and share their identities through more subdued practices of connoisseurship. They share criticism of franchises or luxurious rāmen shops, forming a rāmen cadre. Most of these rāmen shops are not appealing to aficionados who derive more satisfaction from discovering and introducing relatively unknown shops.

Discussions among aficionados are marked by shared enthusiasm and a common understanding of *uri* attached to various rāmen shops and products. These discussions foster fellowship, which is developed by sharing a perceived communal value of rāmen as a food. The aspect of fellowship is examined in We Love Rāmen. With more than 200,000 members, it is one of the largest online rāmen communities and is featured on the popular Japanese website Mixi. According to their profiles, these members range in age from early twenties to early fifties and include both men and women. This community has an administrator whose sole task is to delete redundant questions and inappropriate comments. The community occasionally holds offline gatherings (*ofu kai*) that most often center on trips to rāmen shops, giving members an opportunity to meet in person.

Being a purveyor of information is also an aspect of connoisseurship. Discussions of rāmen and shops are conducted in a holistic manner, and include genealogies of shops, biographies of owners, evaluations of customer service, regional variations of ingredients, and aspects of presentation, along with taste and price. Discussions extend to gendered space in rāmen shops. In August 2005, Ryoko, a female member of We Love Rāmen, posted the question "Do you know any rāmen shops where a woman feels comfortable eating alone?" Her question persisted as a discussion thread until November 2007.

Ryoko's question invoked the issue of gender, highlighting or reconfirming the notion of rāmen shops as a place for men and motivating male members to demonstrate their connoisseurship. She received a wide variety of responses, providing detailed information about eateries where women were believed to eat; conspicuous among the attributes listed were neat and clean décor, spaces reserved for women, the presence of female employees, and dessert offerings on the menu. There was virtually no information on rāmen itself.

The major foci of rāmen shops that women are concerned about are the levels of comfort and privacy. One female member of the community says, "I like Ichiran Rāmen because it is private, with partitions that prevent me from seeing and being seen by other customers and employees—so I can comfortably order extra noodles." Ichiran Rāmen is originally a product of Fukuoka, on the southwestern island Kyūshū; there are now twenty-four shops located throughout Japan. Customers are seated in individual stalls and write their orders on small pieces of paper and hand them to employees through a small slot concealed by a pull-down screen. Through the slot customers and employees see nothing but one another's hands.

According to the discussion in online communities, rāmen shops are not conceived as places for the average woman. However, connoisseurs strive to overcome these stereotypes. One female member writes, "I love rāmen and go to rāmen shops by myself. At first I was not comfortable eating alone, but now I am used to it, and there are only a few particular shops where I still feel uncomfortable." Numerous male contributors responded to this statement in an encouraging fashion. One such commenter wrote, "I don't think it's strange to see a woman eating rāmen alone. In fact, I think it's cool. It's even cooler if she's eating at an old-school, no-frills rāmen shop."

The expression cool[21] (*kakkoii*) is ordinarily used to compliment men. Exceptions to this gendered usage usually occur when a woman performs activities or behavior normatively associated with masculinity, such as engaging in sports. It would be highly unlikely that men would describe a woman eating alone at a sweet shop or an American fast food shop as cool; the evaluation of cool is dependent on the hypothetical woman's challenge of male space. This discussion ultimately reinforces notions of rāmen shops as men's space and consumption of rāmen as a male activity.

Online communities offer women the opportunity to establish fellowship, sometimes to the exclusion of men. Noriko, a female member of We Love Rāmen, started a separate Internet community that holds monthly gatherings, primarily at new-wave rāmen shops. By talking with one another in the online community, these women bonded and established fellowship on the basis of female commonality in both the virtual context and the physical premises of a male-centered food space. Likewise, this fellowship perpetuates the process of gendering rāmen.

The perceptions of men and women of the socially constructed, gendered aspect of rāmen are most visible and talked about in the online community. In face-to-face interviews, most rāmen critics, shop owners, employees, and consumers claim that they believe that more women are coming to rāmen shops than before, in spite of the high proportion of male customers and testimonial evidence to the contrary. The relative anonymity of online communities presents an opportunity for members to share their ideas in an atmosphere conducive to unrestrained expression, and in this space socially constructed, gendered images of food emerge. Women, particularly fashionable women, are still thought to prefer other types of food such as foreign cuisines, desserts, and food served in small portions. Rāmen and other generously portioned, quick, and inexpensive foods are still considered to be the domain of men and the lower classes.

Women are conscious of the issues pertaining to image and identity that are raised by the act of solitary eating at rāmen shops. Perhaps in part because of this sensitivity, men (especially those who claim to be rāmen connoisseurs), admire women eating at "old-school, no-frills" shops. Men also admit, however, that any woman sharing space at a table or counter with men at rāmen shops becomes an object of the men's attention. At first glance the woman may be considered an intruder or stranger who has wandered into the wrong place. Upon consideration, some male customers respect women who show an understanding of rāmen, rather than those who consume the food merely as fashion.

Online discussion seems to indicate that women eating rāmen in the company of other men do not transgress gender boundaries. The presence of company places women in a more normative position. Solitary women, however, occupy a more liminal position in rāmen shops, becoming an object of male observation, analysis, and categorization. On the other hand, Ryoko and other female aficionados regard women eating alone as independent on account of their voluntary entrance into this liminal sphere without the social protection offered by company.

CONCLUSION

Rāmen in Japan is a popular commodity by which shop owners forge their careers, and aficionados create a connoisseurial identity and establish a community. The introduction of new-wave rāmen shops has resulted in "aestheticizing" and "ritualizing" of the industry without eradicating more traditional images of the solitary blue-collar worker, the longtime primary target of rāmen proprietors. Contrary to Bourdieu's (1984) argument for taste as an indication of class, rāmen represents a more diffuse subject of taste and connoisseurship through its appeal across class divides.

The expanding usage of the Internet in the 1990s and 2000s has led to an explosion of blogs and online communities dedicated to rāmen and the establishment of fellowship among aficionados. One potentially divisive aspect of online groups is the tendency to recapitulate socially constructed norms of class and gender (Norris 2004). Rather than alleviate anxiety, male participants' comments often serve to perpetuate notions of rāmen as "men's food" and rāmen shops as male-centered spaces. Hence, gendered boundaries remain.

On Yamagishi's last day at Taishōken,[22] as widely reported in the news, male and female consumers waited hours in line to eat one last bowl of the esteemed owner's rāmen. Regardless of his or her reason for being there, each customer conferred his or her own connoisseurial value on Yamagishi and his rāmen. The high-profile presence of Yamagishi and Taishōken in the Japanese news media attests to the degree to which rāmen, an inexpensive, widely available food, has been transformed into a connoisseurial object.

NOTES

1. This study focuses on rāmen as a food for eating out and excludes instant rāmen.

2. The order of Japanese names places the family name first, followed by the given name.

3. For this type, a bowl of soup and a bowl of noodles are served separately. Noodles are dipped in the soup before being eaten. It was primarily employees' food when Yamagishi first worked for a rāmen shop in the 1950s.

4. Random House Webster's dictionary defines connoisseur as "a person who is especially competent to pass critical judgments in an art, particularly one of the fine arts, or in matters of taste" (*Random House Webster's Unabridged Dictionary* 2001, 432).

5. Some names of rāmen shops, informants, and online communities appearing in this paper are fictitious.

6. In the early 1900s, rāmen was also served at cafés frequented by middle-class Japanese people (Okuyama 2003, 58). However, rāmen as a middle-class food has been willfully ignored, resulting in the designation of rāmen as "low" food in the popular consciousness.

7. Many of these shops are featured in 100-plus different magazines per year (Internet interview with Ōsaki Hiroshi, the president of Rāmen Data Bank).

8. $1 = 92.24 yen (July 12, 2009).

9. This is a parody of the *Kokugi kan*, the site of national sumo competitions.

10. Critics/consultants make a business of reviewing and writing about rāmen.

11. In total, forty-eight episodes were released between 1969 and 1995, and a special version in 1997.

12. *Rāmen Dēta Bēsu* (Rāmen Database), http://ramendb.supleks.jp/, accessed on July 12, 2009; *Gurunabi Rāmen* (Google navigator of Rāmen), http://ramen.gnavi .co.jp/i/, accessed on July 12, 2009.

13. It is important to note that in the Taishō period (1912–26) a Chinese cooking boom emerged and gradually spread into mass culture. Rāmen recipes were introduced in magazines aimed mainly at housewives in the 1950s (Okada 2002, 100).

14. Some businessmen left previous jobs or were laid off during Japan's economic recession, which bankrupted many businesses and sent workers scurrying for employment, sometimes far afield.

15. There is no specific data compiled to indicate the educational backgrounds of rāmen shop owners. My information is based on interviews with owners and aficionados.

16. Healthy ingredients—more specifically, natural ingredients substituted for the more common MSG—are now in high demand, and new combinations of fish and animal stocks are experimented with to reproduce original recipes.

17. Most rāmen shops in Tokyo have open kitchens. Some shops are shaped in the form of an amphitheater, with the open kitchen representing the stage.

18. *Tampopo* has been previously examined, but mainly with regards to social relations and status during the 1980s (Ashkenazi 2004; Iles 2000).

19. *Chūka ya* is a type of family restaurant that stereotypically serves not only rāmen but also foods such as fried rice, dumplings, and big bowls of rice with meat or tempura.

20. According to ICT (Information and Communication Technology) statistics from 2006, in Japan the number of mobile cellular subscribers is 79.32 percent of the population and that of Internet users 68.27 percent (International Telecommunication Union 2007).

21. This applies for a Japanese word *kakkoii* (cool) and not the English word cool (*kūru*).

22. On January 15, 2008, one of Yamagishi's apprentices reopened the shop in a different location. There are approximately 100 Taishōken branch shops, including one in Honolulu, Hawaii.

WORKS CITED

Allison, Anne. 2006. "New-age fetishes, monsters, and friends: Pokémon capitalism." In *Japan after Japan: Social and Cultural Life from the Recessionary 1990s to the Present.* Ed. Tomiko Yoda and Harry Harootunian, 331–57. Durham, N.C.: Duke University Press.

Anguru. 1979. *Ima ya magire mo nai 2 dai kokumin shoku. Hissatsu-no tabearuki 30 pēji ippon shōbu: Rāmen vs. karē.* Tokyo: Shufu to Seikatsusha.

Appadurai, Arjun. 1988. "How to make a national cuisine: Cookbooks in contemporary India." *Comparative Studies in Society and History* 30, no. 1: 3–24.

Ashkenazi, Michel. 2004. "Food, play, business, and the image of Japan in Itami Juzo's *Tampopo*." In *Reel Food: Essays on Food and Film*. Ed. Anne L. Bower, 27–40. New York: Routledge.

Bhattacharya, Nandini. 2006. *Slavery, Colonialism and Connoisseurship: Gender and Eighteenth-Century Literary Transnationalism*. Aldershot, U.K.: Ashgate.

Bourdieu, Pierre. 1984. *Distinction: A Social Critique of the Judgment of Taste*. Trans. Richard Nice. Cambridge, Mass.: Harvard University Press.

Chin, Elizabeth. 2001. *Purchasing Power: Black Kids and American Consumer Culture*. Minneapolis: University of Minnesota Press.

Creighton, Millie. 1992. "Consuming rural Japan: The marketing of tradition and nostalgia in the Japanese travel industry." *Ethnology* 36, no. 3: 239–52.

Cwiertka, Katarzyna. 2006. *Modern Japanese Cuisine: Food, Power and National Identity*. London: Reaktion Books.

de Certeau, Michel. 1984. *The Practice of Everyday Life*. Berkeley: University of California Press.

Fine, Gary Alan. 1996. *Kitchens: The Culture of Restaurant Work*. Berkeley: University of California Press.

Hosokawa, Shuhei, and Hideaki Matsuoka. 2004. "Vinyl record collecting as material practices: The Japanese case." In *Fanning the Flame: Fans and Consumer Culture in Contemporary Japan*. Ed. William W. Kelly, 151–67. Albany: State University of New York Press.

Iles, Timothy. 2000. "*Tampopo*: Food and the postmodern in the work of Itami Jūzō." *Japanstudien* 12:283–97.

International Telecommunication Union. 2007. *ICT Statistics 2006*. Available at http://www.itu.int/ITU-D/icteye/DisplayCountry.aspx?countryId=120, accessed on January 6, 2008.

Kelly, William, ed. 2004. "Introduction: Locating the fans." In *Fanning the Flames: Fans and Consumer Culture in Contemporary Japan*. Ed. William Kelly, 1–16. Albany: State University of New York Press.

Norris, Pippa. 2004. "The bridging and bonding role of online communities." In *Society Online: The Internet Context*. Ed. Phillip N. Howard and Steve Jones, 31–41. Thousand Oaks, Calif.: Sage.

Ohnuki-Tierney, Emiko. 1997. "McDonald's in Japan: Changing manners and etiquette." In *Golden Arches East: McDonald's in East Asia*. Ed. James L. Watson, 161–82. Stanford, Calif.: Stanford University Press.

Okada Tetsu. 2002. *Rāmen no tanjō*. Tokyo: Chikuma Shobō.

———. 2003 *Tabemono kigen jiten*. Tokyo: Tōkyōdō Shuppan.

Okuyama Tadamasa. 2003. *Bunka menruigaku: Rāmen*. Tokyo: Akashi Shoten.

Ōsaki Hiroshi. 2002. *Muteki no rāmen ron*. Tokyo: Kōdansha.

Pearce, Susan M. 1995. *On Collecting: An Investigation into Collecting in the European Tradition*. London: Routledge.

Random House Webster's Unabridged Dictionary. 2001. New York: Random House Reference.

Sand, Jordan. 2006. "The ambivalence of the new breed: Nostalgic consumerisms in 1980s and 1990s Japan." In *The Ambivalent Consumer: Questioning Consumption in East Asia and the West*. Ed. Sheldon Garon and Patricia L. Maclachlan, 85–108. Ithaca, N.Y.: Cornell University Press.

Terrio, Susan J. 2005. "Crafting *grand cru* chocolates in contemporary France." In *The Cultural Politics of Food and Eating: A Reader*. Ed. James Watson and Melissa Caldwell, 144–62. Malden, Mass.: Blackwell.

Tipton, Elise K. 2000. "The café: Contested space of modernity in interwar Japan." In *Being Modern in Japan: Culture and Society from the 1910s to the 1930s*. Ed. K. Tipton and John Clark, 119–36. Honolulu: University of Hawai'i Press.

Tobin, Josef, ed. 2004. "Introduction." *Pikachu's Global Adventure: The Rise and Fall of Pokémon*. Ed. Josef Tobin, 3–11. Durham, N.C.: Duke University Press.

Wilson, Samuel, and Leighton Peterson. 2002. "The anthropology of online communities." *Annual Reviews of Anthropology* 31:449–67.

Yan, Yunxiang. 2005. "Of hamburger and social space: Consuming McDonald's in Beijing." In *The Cultural Politics of Food and Eating: A Reader*. Ed. James Watson and Melissa Caldwell, 81–103. Malden, Mass.: Blackwell.

Yano, Christine. 2002. *Tears of Longing: Nostalgia and the Nation in Japanese Popular Song*. Cambridge, Mass.: Harvard University Asia Center.

Zukin, Sharon. 2004. *Point of Purchase: How Shopping Changed American Culture*. New York: Routledge.

14 Irretrievably in Love with Japanese Cuisine

DAVID E. WELLS

THE FILM *TOKYO STORY* (*Tōkyō monogatari*, 1953) by the great Ozu Yasujiro got me interested in how the Japanese view things.[1] So much so, that in 1980 I found myself in Tokyo on an exchange program at Waseda University. At the end of a one-year program, I was the only one of 150 foreign exchange students to remain in Japan. I enrolled in the Intensive Language Program at Waseda University, where I got a silly notion to do a speech in Japanese in front of 3,000 people about the impact that Japanese cuisine had made upon me. This speech was significant in that it revealed not only how irretrievably in love I was with Japanese cuisine but also that I was unable to prepare the food myself. At the same time, I realized that I would be unable to live in the United States again.

This realization left me with no other choice than to enroll in a Japanese culinary school, which was easier said than done. I found a school and applied, but at first they would not even take me seriously: the language barrier was a real obstacle. I was able to understand the words, but not always what they meant. In addition, the school administration did not want to deal with my visa paperwork. Years later, I found out that the administrators were just plain puzzled and did not know what to make of me. The question for them was: "Why would a non-Japanese want to or even think that they could begin to understand our cuisine?" So, I was flatly turned down and told that if I was really interested in studying to come back the next school year and they would consider my application again. I did the unexpected and returned; they fulfilled their promise, and I was in.

The first year of culinary school starts off with the basics of cleanliness. Before you begin to cook, you clean. While you cook, you clean. And once you finish, you leave your workspace cleaner than it was before you began. Next is prevention: the prevention of contagious diseases along with all the public health factors. Actual cooking makes up about one third of class time. During the first year, all students are required to learn Western, Chinese, and

Japanese cuisines. The following year, each student must choose one cuisine and stick with it.

The curriculum consisted of two parts, lectures and actual cooking. These two were a world apart. When we were lectured on nutrition, hygiene, or economics, the atmosphere in the classroom was like in an elementary school. Half of the class would be sleeping or reading manga while the other half were talking or playing around. There were some students who did not have to listen because they were sons or daughters of famous Japanese restaurant owners. But when the cooking began, everyone would watch the teacher prepare the menu with the greatest awe. Next, we would form groups of five people and go about preparing the same menu with the same precision down to the finest detail. We were judged and graded on our technical abilities, presentation, speed, and cleanliness; in addition, we had to pass a couple of individual tests.

These tests expressed our ability in handling the three basic knives: one test involved taking the long and wide thin-bladed vegetable knife (*usuba*) and cutting a carrot into a plum blossom. Another test was to take a fat, perfectly cylindrical, long white radish (daikon) and peel it lengthwise as long and as thinly as possible with the same *usuba*.

This took lots of practice and many a daikon to master the difficult eye-and-hand coordination. I had all my neighbors eating all thicknesses of daikon for some time. A *deba*, which is an almost triangular bladed knife, was used for a timed fish-filleting test. Hand pressure on the fish and the sharpness of the tip of the *deba* were two important elements, for one does not serve warm raw

The three basic types of Japanese knives (Photograph by Takayuki Osumi)

fish, which brings me to the next test: using a sashimi knife (*yanagiba*). This test involved slicing a block of tuna and moving it across the cutting board, placing each slice at a precise angle with just one movement of the blade.

I had a hard time with this from the very beginning because I am left-handed. When I picked up a sharp-as-a-razor Japanese knife for the first time, I realized it is made with the blade on the left of the handle and is concave on the backside, making it a true right-handed knife. My teacher gave me a long, emphatic story about the flow and movement in the kitchen and how bumping elbows was not ever a part of that scenario, a rule that I was told to follow. So, from the beginning of the following year, I changed hands. Using the right hand is important not just because of the flow in the kitchen but also in presentation. Imagine cutting sashimi. If you use your left hand, the top piece cannot be picked up by someone using a chopstick in his or her right hand.

The second year of cooking school was primarily cooking, and for me this meant all Japanese cuisine. The menu was almost always made up of seasonal ingredients and maybe an inedible leaf or flower presented on the plate to further enhance the seasonal theme. The basic menu could be a rice dish with a vegetable side dish and a grilled or boiled fish dish plus a soup and pickles. You are probably thinking that the fish is the main dish, but that is not the way it is understood. Rice is the main dish. All other foods are seasoned with the main goal of complementing the taste of the rice.

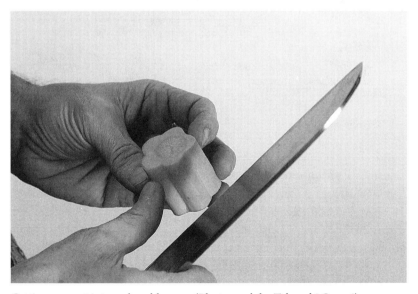

Cutting a carrot into a plum blossom (Photograph by Takayuki Osumi)

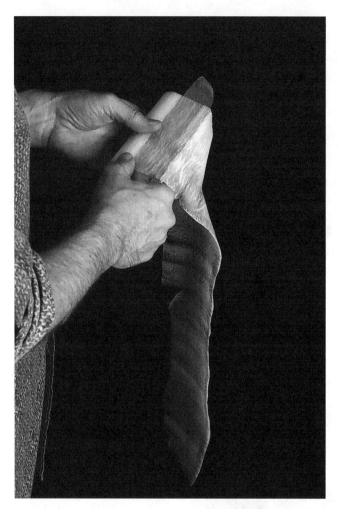

Chef peeling a daikon (Photograph by Takayuki Osumi)

That year, I felt, was the first time in my life I truly experienced the four seasons, each with its own identity. In the spring, we would have to find a nearby blossoming cherry tree and remove a few small branches of flowers. These were placed on a plate with a "cherry blossom sea bream" (*sakura tai*), named to reflect the fact that the fish changes from a light to a darker shade of pink that time of year. The hot and humid summer is expressed in light shades of porcelain dishware and glass, in comparison to fall, where you will find woven bamboo baskets and grasses or maybe even for a final touch a thin sheet of smoldering cedar used to further the mood. And in the winter, the cooking pot is taken from the kitchen and placed on a burner on the table; it is left up to the guests to cook for themselves.

This ultimate seasonal variety of tastes and strong visual presentation was more than enough to push me toward throwing myself into a two-year apprenticeship in a *kaiseki* restaurant. An older teacher in my school went far out of her way to give me an introduction to the *kaiseki* restaurant that accepted me. I was put up in the restaurant dormitory with six other guys who were all my seniors. This has nothing to do with age as most were actually younger than I, with the youngest being a sixteen-year-old dropout and me a twenty-three-year-old Ivy Leaguer, considered to be an "old man" by most of them. We all worked six days a week, twelve hours a day, with a two-hour break from 3 to 5 P.M. Then I chose to join the owner of the restaurant on his once-a-week visits to the main fish market, Tsukiji. I would get up just in time to put on the same old jacket and rubber boots, and stuff a handkerchief in my back pocket for wiping my hands after touching the fish, and be outside by 6 A.M. When we got to the market, we would walk in quickly, maneuvering around whatever or whoever got in our path without missing a step. At each of the specialized booths, we made our routine stop. Our fishmonger would show us what he had. The owner would lift up the gill or press lightly on the belly or look at the fish's eyes for clarity, always taking the time to give me tidbits of information that have become my basis for judging fish. Later, the fish would be delivered on a bed of ice, or if they were alive they would be swimming in a large aquarium attached to the back of a truck. That is, except for the live shrimp; they would come in small boxes completely filled with sawdust instead of water.

After the visit to Tsukiji, I would return to the restaurant just in time to join the other guys who had work to do before and after our shift. Usually, I would get up before everyone else in the morning and shave a whole stick of dried bonito (*katsuo*), a fish that is a member of the tuna family. It is cooked and then smoked. First, I would clean it up by removing the skin completely. Then, sitting on my knees on the floor over a wooden box with a one-blade shaver facing up, I would hold the hard-as-plastic bonito between my hands and press down and pull back as fast as I possibly could for a whole hour— that is, if the blade position did not shift. These bonito flakes plus a big bag of purchased flakes along with dried *konbu* seaweed make up the basic broth (*dashi*) in Japanese cuisine. Another chore, always the worst, came after closing when I had to wash the big metal tempura pot. It was huge and it had to be cleaned outside while it was still hot or else it would take twice as long. The floor also had to be scrubbed every day with a deck brush.

During my first year, I was given special permission to assist the hors d'oeuvres (*zensai*) chef. This put me on cloud nine. Thinking back, I really feel sorry for him. He thought he was getting a competent assistant but I turned out to be just a determined guy with a serious language handicap. But then again, I was not the only one with a handicap. He turned out to be left-handed—can you believe it?—after all that I had gone through to change hands. Needless to say, we spent the next year bumping elbows. The other thing was that he never talked or answered questions in complete sentences or reacted to foreseeable problems even though I had given him information to reheat something or that we were running low on something. He just would not stand up and take control, and I could not say anything without making the serious mistake of stepping on my senior's toes.

No college language training could have prepared me for what I had to do next: decipher the biweekly menu. The head chef wrote what looked at a first glance to be a doctor's prescription on a two-page notebook paper that he stuck on the wall, but it was in reality just a traditionally written (from right to left, top to bottom) menu made up of Chinese characters and the two Japanese syllabaries (*hiragana* and *katakana*). As soon as it was hung on the wall, I would take it down before anyone else could. Here again, I was jumping the gun. Being on the bottom of the totem pole, I was supposed to wait until my seniors had finished going over it before I made my move. But breaking the rule often worked to my advantage. Everyone would gather around me, and I would get them to translate it into legible Japanese. Then I would use a professional Japanese *kaiseki* menu dictionary to look up the terms in Japanese during my afternoon break and at nights, waking up many a time with my face planted in a dictionary. Sometimes I had the hardest time with a character that I could not make heads or tails of, or what I thought was a character that would turn out to be, for example, the crest that belonged to the clan that first started to grow sweet potatoes. Usually, I would use a Japanese-English dictionary to understand the meaning. Even for a simple term like "blanching," placing meat into boiling water until it turns white, the translation process was time consuming. In Japanese, blanching is called *shimofuri*, which literally means "frost." (By the way, the same term is also used to describe the marbleized pattern of the very popular Kobe beef).

During this apprenticeship, I was in charge of all of the side dishes, so knowing where everything was in the refrigerator and what condition it was in required me to keep up a morning tasting routine of twenty or so items.

I would first check the reservation list, add a few extras, count the contents of each container, and then divide each into smaller containers while rearranging the refrigerator.

On every plate of hors d'oeuvres served to a customer, three to five "tastes" are arranged. In a traditional hierarchy, I should have been grating wasabi or carrying prepared dishes to the *nakaisan*, middle-aged or older ladies dressed in kimono who would serve and host. One friend had an even worse duty when he started off in a nearby *kaiseki* restaurant: he was stationed in the storehouse counting big bags of dried beans, never being able to see the food, much less taste it. As my heart went out to him, it made me realize how lucky I was.

I had begged for this hors d'oeuvres position for two reasons. Visually, the hors d'oeuvres use the plate to enhance themselves, allowing both to come alive. The other reason was that this taste-testing gave me the opportunity to memorize a wide variety of tastes in one short year; and a wide variety it was! I came to find out that in a full-course dinner, the five basic tastes—sweet, sour, bitter, salty, and savory (*umami*)—are all presented, as are different textures. Here in Japan, textures are considered to be tastes and there are many adjectives. A few examples are *mochi-mochi* or marshmallow-like; *shaki-shaki*, the crunch of a lettuce or watery leaf; or *pari-pari* the crunch of peanut brittle or a rice cracker (*senbei*).

Apart from the hors d'oeuvres tasks, I also had to make the employees' lunch basically out of a single pot if and only when a burner on the stove was free. This meant becoming friends with the sous-chef by making him a good cup of tea whenever I got the chance, bringing up trivia about his favorite sport, or whatever it took to make the guy like me. This was true with all the other guys above me as well. I probably made many mistakes as the new guy, burning things, adding too much soy sauce or vinegar, but the biggest mistake I ever made was a casserole that I baked in the oven. I must have been trying to be creative that day or something because I added yogurt to the casserole . . . and no one would eat it. They took one bite and made one of those faces like "No way!" I was harassed about that one for a long time.

That was a long but short—or short but long—year. At one point, it was all too much to handle and I got to the end of my rope. But my friends and teachers were there for me, thank goodness. And then my second year began as a tempura assistant.

The owner of the restaurant said that everyone likes tempura and learning how to make it would be to my advantage. So, I began making this traditional Tokyo style of tempura my own. What makes tempura especially unique is the blending of a large percentage of sesame oil into the frying oil, which creates an almost indescribable balance between taste, texture, and aroma—now *that's* tempura. I thought this year would be a lot easier than the previous year, but it turned out that I still had a lot to learn. The oil temperature was one thing. There was no thermometer and when I saw what the chef was doing I thought he was taking me for a ride. What he did was unthinkable: he stuck his finger in the hot oil to test the temperature! Well, what could I do, I stuck my finger into the hot oil myself—and to my disbelief, I was not burned. Actually, this has now also become my way of gauging the temperature. The only thing is that when I do it in front people I have found it to be unnerving and now I try to be discreet.

Another secret that I found cool and not so easy to manage in the beginning was using long metal chopsticks with my right hand. They are long because the tempura pot is wide and deep and they are made of metal because when you use them to pick up something that has cooked through you can feel the "tremble" that says "I am ready." But beyond teaching me the crucial skills of the kitchen, what being at this post really did was to give me a whole new perspective on how the separate stations in the kitchen move in relation to each other. I saw what happens when a group of professionals get together with one specific goal. It is like a dance. Everyone is totally immersed in whatever he or she is doing, as well as watching everyone else and judging the timing of the courses.

This brings me to what it takes to become a professional Japanese chef. When I said I learned each and every taste, it was actually much deeper than that. In a *kaiseki* dinner, anywhere from fifty to eighty ingredients are used, with 85 percent seasonal fish, plants, and animals and the rest a salt, soy, or miso variation of preserved ingredients. This means that for only one seasonal meal a year a chef has to remember each process of the preparation and the taste of each ingredient and be able to reproduce this taste the following year. This is the reason why I think everyone says that it takes at least ten years in order to become a professional *kaiseki* chef.

Almost in the blink of an eye, the year was coming to an end. Four seasons had passed and I was on my way back to the United States, to New York City. My plans were to open a Japanese restaurant, a dream that I never realized in that city. But a bigger dream did come to life after what felt like a never-ending job in a Japanese restaurant there. In this restaurant, I was the only non-Japanese staff and I guess I stuck out when the rich and famous like Brooke Shields, Andy Warhol, or Catherine Deneuve came in. This is where

Tempura (Photograph by Takayuki Osumi)

I met a couple who made me an offer that I could not turn down: to study at their friend's cooking school in Osaka and to become their private chef after returning. Thanks to them, my life was changed.

I ended up spending six months at the Tsuji School of Cooking, arriving there not knowing what to expect. At that point in my studies, I felt as if I had a good idea of what cuisine was about—after all, I had a firsthand experience with the seasons three times over. To my surprise I was seated in the middle of a large room with approximately fifty teachers and the owner, Tsuji Shizuo. His presence in itself was enough to make me realize that I had stepped into a higher academic level of culinary training. And as I came to find out, I had.

It was great to be behind the scenes, assisting the teachers in preparation for their classes, attending these classes, and being given the rank of a fellow colleague. I received a free pass to study whatever classes interested me. Planning and making lunches for the staff was another opportunity for learning. Then, in the evenings, I went with the teachers to well-known Japanese restaurants of chefs who would visit the school and give special workshops. The conversations we had with them while visiting their restaurants were actually a serious part of my training.

The owner of the Tsuji School once told me, "If one is to be a good chef, one must learn by tasting first, then by making." This is very true, but it is also said that one "eats with one's eyes." Which is it? For me, I have chosen both and am aiming to make both of these sayings mine.

What I have done in my own cooking is to choose various themes, as in the practice of traditional *kaiseki*, except that I have also made the plates that coordinate with the food and particular themes. I use my handmade dishware to present the soul of the cuisine. In order to be able to do this, I submerged myself into the study of ceramics under the leadership of Ando Minoru, an old hippie-looking, high-energy guy who was not only a ceramic artist but also a calligrapher, painter, writer, art collector, and a restaurant producer. He stresses design over high-technical skills. Afterwards I went on to refine my technical skills in a ceramic factory, studying three styles: Oribe, Shino, and Kiseto. After that I was off to Arita in Kyūshū, the home of Imari ware, to enroll myself into the government-run porcelain school, where I completed a one-year program on under- and overglaze painting. On Saturdays I worked at a factory in exchange for porcelain pieces to practice my own designs on.

This is not a typical route for a graduate of a culinary school. Japanese cooks usually go from one two-year restaurant apprenticeship to the next, building up experiences, seeing and experiencing the seasons through the eyes of other professionals in an attempt to make the cuisine their own, as well as passing the consummate features of Japanese cuisine down to the next generation. Then maybe in their retirement days they will take on ceramic making as a hobby and only then realize that the ultimate in perfection can only be attained when the same hands that make and present the food are also the same hands that make the plates.

NOTES

1. Editors' note: The film depicts the conflict between traditional and modern Japanese culture in terms of a conflict between generations, the conservative parent versus the modern-thinking child.

FURTHER READING

Tsuji, Shizuo. 2006. *Japanese Cooking: A Simple Art*. Tokyo: Kodansha International.

Tsuji, Shizuo, and Koichiro Hata. 1986. *Practical Japanese Cooking: Easy and Elegant*. Tokyo: Kodansha International.

Tsuji Kaiichi. 1985. *Shoku no bi utsuwa no bi*. Tokyo: Chūō Kōronsha.

Contributors

STEPHANIE ASSMANN is a lecturer at the Center for the Advancement of Higher Education at Tōhoku University in Sendai, Japan. She holds a PhD in Japanese studies from the University of Hamburg, Germany. Her publications include *Value Change and Social Stratification in Japan: Aspects of Women's Consumer Behavior* (Wertewandel und soziale Schichtung in Japan: Veränderungen im Konsumentenverhalten von Frauen, Institute for Asian Affairs Hamburg, Germany) in 2005 and "Between Tradition and Innovation: The Reinvention of Kimono in Japanese Consumer Culture" (*Fashion Theory: The Journal of Dress, Body and Culture*, Berg, Vol. 12, 2008: 359–76).

GARY CHARLES SŌKA CADWALLADER holds an MA (1975) in Japanese language and literature from the University of Texas, Austin. He came to Japan on a Monbusho Fellowship in 1975 to study Japanese art history at Osaka University. He soon found a private tea teacher then later joined Urasenke's program for non-Japanese, the Midorikai. After five years of schooling, he began teaching both Japanese and non-Japanese students as a kyōju (professor) and *chadō kōshi* (tea lecturer). He has more than thirty years of continuing tea training in the Urasenke Grand Tea Master's classes and has held or directed several hundred *chaji*, the full tea functions.

KATARZYNA J. CWIERTKA is associate professor in the Japanese Studies Program at Leiden University and the principal researcher of the project "Sustaining Total War: Militarization, Economic Mobilization and Social Change in Japan and Korea (1931–1953)" funded by the Netherlands Organization for Scientific Research (NWO). Cwiertka is the co-editor of *Asian Food: The Global and the Local* (University of Hawaii Press, 2002) and author of *Modern Japanese Cuisine: Food, Power and National Identity* (Reaktion Books, 2006).

SATOMI FUKUTOMI is a PhD candidate in the Department of Anthropology at University of Hawai'i–Mānoa and currently writing a dissertation on rāmen and the connoisseurship of B-grade gourmet foods.

SHOKO HIGASHIYOTSUYANAGI is a PhD candidate in the Department of Comparative Culture at International Christian University in Tokyo. She is also a lecturer of Japanese life history and dietary culture at Japan Women's University, Kyoritsu Women's University, and Hokuriku University. Her research interest is Japanese dietary culture. Higashiyotsuyanagi is the coauthor of *Kindai ryōrisho no sekai* (*The World of Modern Cookbooks*) (Domes Shuppan, 2008) and *Nihon Shokumotsushi* (*The History of Japanese Food*) (Yoshikawa Kōbunkan, 2009).

JOSEPH R. JUSTICE came to Japan in the late 1970s to study traditional bronze casting in Kyoto. A fondness for making edible art turned into a fascination with Japanese cooking and he began to study *kaiseki* with both professional chefs and housewives. He studied with Tsujitome, the Urasenke *kaiseki* doyen, as well as with Kakiden, the Omotesenke equivalent. He then entered the Mushanokōji cooking school, under the headmistress, Sen Sumiko. Justice taught *kaiseki* at the Mushanokōji Sen Chadō Bunka Gakuen for five years and also worked for one of Kyoto's most famous *nama fu* (wheat gluten) producers, Fu-Ka, where he taught classes for several years. He is one of the very few nonprofessional masters of *cha kaiseki* in the world.

MICHAEL KINSKI, professor of history of Japanese culture and thought at the University of Frankfurt, Germany, holds a PhD degree in Japanese studies from Tübingen University, Germany, and received his professor's qualification (Habilitation) in 2004 from Humboldt University Berlin. His main publications include *Knochen des Weges. Katayama Kenzan als Vertreter des eklektischen Konfuzianismus im Japan des 18. Jahrhunderts* (*The Bones of the Way: Katayama Kenzan as a Representative of Eclectic Confucianism in 18th-Century Japan*) (Otto Harrassowitz Verlag: Wiesbaden, 1996) and "Admonitions Regarding Food Consumption: Takai Ranzan' s Shokuji-kai. Introduction, Transcription, and Translation" (*Japonica Humboldtiana*, vols. 7 [2003] and 9 [2005], Otto Harrassowitz Verlag).

BARAK KUSHNER teaches modern Japanese history in the Faculty of Asian and Middle Eastern Studies at the University of Cambridge and has a PhD in history from Princeton University. He worked in the U.S. Department of State as a political officer in East Asian affairs and taught Chinese and Japanese history in North Carolina. He has written on wartime Japanese and Chinese propaganda in *The Thought War* (Hawaii, 2006), Japanese media, and Asian comedy, and is presently penning a cultural history of cuisine in East Asia. He is also working on a third book that examines the legal adjudication of Japanese war crimes in China and its influence on early cold war Sino–Japanese relations.

BRIDGET LOVE is a lecturer at the University of Oklahoma's Expository Writing Program and Interdisciplinary Perspectives on the Environment Program. She received a PhD in anthropology from the University of Michigan. Her dissertation, based on ethnographic fieldwork in rural Japan, examines place-making and village depopulation in Iwate prefecture.

JOJI NOZAWA is a PhD candidate in early modern history at the University of Paris–Sorbonne (Paris IV). He is currently writing a dissertation on the role of the Dutch East India Company in the global expansion of European wine culture in the seventeenth and eighteenth centuries. His areas of interest include European East India Companies, the globalization of food culture, and the comparative histories of Asian port cities.

TOMOKO ONABE is a historian of science and teaches courses in the history of technology, ecology, and philosophy at Ritsumeikan University and Ryūkoku University in Kyoto. Her book on late-Edo period optics and the adaptation of Western theories of perspective was published as *Zettai tōmei no tankyū* (*The Quest for Absolute Transparency*) by Kyōtō Shibunkaku in 2006. Onabe was trained in the history of science at Harvard University (MA) and at the International Research Center for Japanese Studies (PhD). She has published widely on the Japanese *bentō*, theories of vision, and co-translations of plays by Issey Ogata and Umehara Takeshi.

ERIC C. RATH is associate professor in premodern Japanese history in the Department of History at the University of Kansas and the author of *Food and Fantasy in Early Modern Japan* (University of California Press, 2010), "Banquets against Boredom: Towards Understanding (Samurai) Cuisine in Early Modern Japan," *Early Modern Japan: An Interdisciplinary Journal* 16 (2008): 43–55, and numerous other articles on Japanese foodways and the performing arts, which are his research specialties.

AKIRA SHIMIZU is a PhD candidate in the Department of History at the University of Illinois at Urbana-Champaign. He is currently working on his dissertation, "Eating Edo, Sensing Japan: Food and Foodways in the Tokugawa Period (1603–1686)," which investigates the culture of food during the Tokugawa period.

GEORGE SOLT is an assistant professor in the Department of History and East Asian Studies at New York University. His dissertation, *Food, Labor, and Everyday Life: The Politics of Rāmen*, uses Chinese noodle-soup as a critical vantage point to examine how transformations in labor, agriculture, international politics, trade, and industrial organization concretely manifested themselves in the changing dietary habits of people in modern Japan.

DAVID ELLIS WELLS was born in South Carolina and is a personal chef of *kaiseki* currently based in Tokyo. Inspired by the films of the Japanese film director Ozu and after studying Japanese in college, Wells became fascinated with Japanese cuisine, which led to many years of study in Japanese culinary schools, work in restaurants in Japan, and efforts with the essence of *kaiseki*, the refined form of Japanese cuisine, to create the plates for his food events. Wells is also an accomplished ceramicist.

MIHO YASUHARA is a member of the research team of the project "Sustaining Total War: Militarization, Economic Mobilization and Social Change in Japan and Korea (1931–1953)," funded by the Netherlands Organization for Scientific Research and hosted by Leiden University. She received a PhD from Nara Women's University in 2004 and currently teaches part-time at Kobe Women's Junior College.

Index

beef, 5–6, 19; in early modern period, 93–96, 104; in Meiji-era, 131, 141, 142n4, 202–4; in WWII, 171–72, 178–79. *See also* meat

bentō (lunch box), 174, 201; color use in, 205–10; expressing maternal love, 210–15; Meiji-era, 202–4; regional foods in, 248–50

black market, 166, 172, 176, 181, 186, 192–96

Bourdieu, Pierre, 2, 42, 118, 258, 270

ceramics, 78, 83–84, 86n3, 88n26

cha (tea) *kaiseki*, 23, 69–70; menus for *daimyō cha* (warlord tea), 76–83; menus of Sen Sōshitsu, 70, 72–77; *wabi* (rustic) *kaiseki* compared to *daimyō kaiseki*, 83–85

Chinese cuisine (*Shina ryōri*), 145–46, 149, 155–59, 195–96. *See also* rāmen

cookbooks, 8; Chinese, 145–46; early modern, 23, 129–30; Meiji-era, 131–36; Taishō-period, 138, 140–41

cuisine, 1, 4, 13n2, 145, 260; regional, 224, 246. *See also* Chinese cuisine; *honzen* cuisine; Japanese cuisine; *kaiseki* cuisine; Korean cuisine; Taiwanese cuisine; Western cuisine

culinary schools, 275–78, 283–84

daimyō cha (warlord tea), 70; menus for, 76–83

Dutch East India Company, 108–9, 112

food shortages: during World War II, 166, 169–73, 176, 186, 188; in postwar era, 190–92, 228

food stands (*yatai*), 149, 186, 194–97

foodways, 1, 13n1; Japanese, 145

globalization, 3, 245

honzen (main tray) cuisine, 19; menu for Emperor Gomizuno'o, 31–34; model menus, 24–30; structure, 20–21, 49–50; table manners, 22–23

Japanese cuisine (*Nihon ryōri, washoku*), 7, 13, 145, 152–53, 160, 173, 279

kaiseki cuisine, 5, 68. *See also cha* (tea) *kaiseki*

kitchen, 84; conditions of, 147, 150, 155, 160; in restaurants, 263, 277, 282; women's management of, 132–36, 139

Kōjimachi, 92, 99–100, 104

Korean cuisine: Japanese views of, 146–47

meat: consumption in early modern period, 6, 92–97; laws prohibiting eating, 97–99; native accounts of eating, 99–104. *See also* medicinal eating

medicinal eating (*kusurigui*), 92, 96–97, 99–100, 103

mountain vegetables (*sansai*), 223, 226; as regional products, 227–30, 233–37

MSG, 150–53, 160, 272n16

national food, 145–46, 259–60

nutrition, 154–55, 158, 192; color coordination of, 207–10

poetry: and menu structure, 19–20; poetically named foods, 34–36

rāmen, 186, 257; etiquette for eating, 264–66; as a national dish, 259–61; new wave shops, 262–64; origin of, 156–57; postwar history, 194–99; women as consumers of, 267–70

rationing, 169–73, 187–92

restaurants, 262–63; Chinese, 155–56, 158; early modern era, 19, 96, 99–105, 130; modern, 131, 133, 159–60; rāmen, 257, 260–64; regional, 251–52; working in, 279–82, 284; in World War II, 173, 176–81

rice, 3, 95, 139, 145, 277; agriculture, 235, 240n15; etiquette for eating, 22–23, 46–47, 51–53, 60n29; methods of preparing, 59n17, 60n30, 60n33, 61n38, 89n47, 150; rationing of, 141, 169–71, 173–74; shortages during and after WWII, 187–89,

194; as staple food, 19, 68, 119, 145–49, 159, 186, 244

sansai. See mountain vegetables

seasonality, 25, 223, 228–29, 278, 282

Sen no Rikyū, 68–72, 77, 254n10

school lunches, 158, 193–94, 197, 211, 244

Slow Food Movement, 245–47

sugar, 35, 169–70, 173

sumptuary laws, 21, 25

table manners: categorization of, 50–55; for *honzen* cuisine, 22–23, 46–49; as subcategory of rules of etiquette, 42–43, 45–46, 55–57, 264–66

Taiwanese cuisine: Japanese views of, 147–48

wabicha (rustic tea), 5, 68–69; contrast with *daimyō cha* (warlord tea), 83–85

Western cuisine, 131–32, 203–5

Western foods, 13, 105, 125, 131–33

wine, 108; Japanese market for, 114–19; use in early 1600s, 109–14

women: dining etiquette for, 44–49, 51, 53–54; as housewives (*shufu*), 134–36, 138–42, 154–55; in Meiji era, 129, 132; rural women, 229–31

*The University of Illinois Press
is a founding member of the
Association of American University Presses.*

Composed in 10.25/13.25 Minion Pro
by Celia Shapland
at the University of Illinois Press
Manufactured by Sheridan Books, Inc.

University of Illinois Press
1325 South Oak Street
Champaign, IL 61820-6903
www.press.uillinois.edu